FROMMER'S

EasyGuide

TO

FRANCE

By
**Margie Rynn, Lily Heise,
Tristan Rutherford and
Kathryn Tomasetti**

EasyGuides are ✦ Quick To Read ✦ Light To Carry
✦ For Expert Advice ✦ In All Price Ranges

FrommerMedia LLC

Published by
FROMMER MEDIA LLC

Copyright © 2014 by Frommer Media LLC, New York City, New York. All rights reserved. No part of this publication may be reproduced, stored in a retrieval system, or transmitted in any form or by any means, electronic, mechanical, photocopying, recording, scanning or otherwise, except as permitted under Sections 107 or 108 of the 1976 United States Copyright Act, without the prior written permission of the Publisher. Requests to the Publisher for permission should be addressed to the Permissions Department, Frommer Media LLC at partnerships@frommermedia.com.

Frommer's is a registered trademark of Arthur Frommer. Used under license. All other trademarks are the property of their respective owners. Frommer Media LLC is not associated with any product or vendor mentioned in this book.

ISBN 978-1-62887-002-2 (paper), 978-1-62887-032-9 (e-book)

Editorial Director: Pauline Frommer
Editor: Alexis Lipsitz Flippin
Production Editor: Heather Wilcox
Cartographer: Elizabeth Puhl
Cover Design: Howard Grossman

For information on our other products or services, see www.frommers.com.

Frommer Media LLC also publishes its books in a variety of electronic formats. Some content that appears in print may not be available in electronic formats.

Manufactured in the United States of America

5 4 3 2 1

CONTENTS

ABOUT THE AUTHORS

Margie Rynn has been living and writing in France for more than 13 years, mostly in Paris. The author of *Pauline Frommer's Paris*, she has also written features for such magazines as *Budget Travel*, *Time Out New York*, and *Yoga Journal*.

Lily Heise has been perfecting *la joie de vivre* in Paris since 2000. She contributes to various international and local travel publications and has recently published her first book.

Tristan Rutherford has been a freelance travel writer since 2002. His lucky first assignment took him to Nice, and he has been based there ever since. He has visited more than 60 countries and written about 20 of them for the *Independent* and the *Sunday Times Travel Magazine*. Tristan also lectures in travel journalism at London's Central Saint Martins.

U.S.-born, Italian-raised **Kathryn Tomasetti** writes travel and food stories for the likes of the *Guardian* and the *Times*. Her library of holiday photos—snapped from as far afield as China, Albania, and Chile—has been published by *National Geographic and Time Out*. Kathryn blogs about Provence and the French Riviera at www.ohmyriviera.com.

ABOUT THE FROMMER TRAVEL GUIDES

For most of the past 50 years, Frommer's has been the leading series of travel guides in North America, accounting for as many as 24% of all guidebooks sold. I think I know why.

Though we hope our books are entertaining, we nevertheless deal with travel in a serious fashion. Our guidebooks have never looked on such journeys as a mere recreation, but as a far more important human function, a time of learning and introspection, an essential part of a civilized life. We stress the culture, lifestyle, history and beliefs of the destinations we cover, and urge our readers to seek out people and new ideas as the chief rewards of travel.

We have never shied from controversy. We have, from the beginning, encouraged our authors to be intensely judgmental, critical—both pro and con—in their comments, and wholly independent. Our only clients are our readers, and we have triggered the ire of countless prominent sorts, from a tourist newspaper we called "practically worthless" (it unsuccessfully sued us) to the many rip-offs we've condemned.

And because we believe that travel should be available to everyone regardless of their incomes, we have always been cost-conscious at every level of expenditure. Though we have broadened our recommendations beyond the budget category, we insist that every lodging we include be sensibly priced. We use every form of media to assist our readers, and are particularly proud of our feisty daily website, the award-winning Frommers.com.

I have high hopes for the future of Frommer's. May these guidebooks, in all the years ahead, continue to reflect the joy of travel and the freedom that travel represents. May they always pursue a cost-conscious path, so that people of all incomes can enjoy the rewards of travel. And may they create, for both the traveler and the persons among whom we travel, a community of friends, where all human beings live in harmony and peace.

Arthur Frommer

THE BEST OF FRANCE

France presents visitors with an embarrassment of riches—you may find yourself overwhelmed by all the choices. We've tried to make the task easier by compiling a list of our favorite experiences and discoveries. In the following pages, you'll find the kind of candid travel advice we'd give our closest friends.

FRANCE'S best AUTHENTIC EXPERIENCES

- **Sipping Pastis in Provence:** Pastis is synonymous with Provence. This anise-flavored liquor is sipped at sundown on every town square, from Arles to the Italian border. Beware: The Provençal are seriously brand-conscious. Order a "51" if you want to look like a local, or a "Janot" for the region's latest organic offering. Impress the barman by ordering a *tomate* (pastis with a dash of grenadine) or a *perroquet* (literally a parrot, which is pastis with a splash of green mint syrup). See chapter 7.

- **Breaking the Bank at Monte-Carlo:** The **Casino de Monte-Carlo** has been the most opulent place to have a flutter—for exactly 150 years. Its creation by architect Charles Garnier (of Paris Opera House fame) in 1863 turned the tables for Monaco, transforming a provincial port into a world-class tourist destination. Expect frescoed ceilings and wealthy, well-dressed clientele from as far afield as China, Russia, and the U.S. See p. 237.

- **Ogling the Pomp of the Pope's Medieval Party Pad:** Those medieval popes knew a thing or two about interior design. Avignon's **Palais des Papes,** or Pope's Palace, is a moneyed medley of Gothic architecture, vast banqueting halls, and frescoed suites. The Châteauneuf-du-Pape papal vineyards just north of Avignon still produce some of the most noted wine in France. See p. 162.

- **Buying Your Daily Bread:** That cute little boulangerie just down the street? Depending on where you are, there's likely to be another—or several—a short stroll away. The daily baguette run is a ritual for many French people. Get your coins ready (one euro, give or take 10 centimes) and join the queue. To really fit in, ask for your baguette chewy (*pas trop cuite*), or crusty (*bien cuite*).

- **Donning Your Chapeau and Heading to the Races:** From April through late October, the greater Parisian Region and Deauville (Normandy) host a number of world-famous horse races. You can rub shoulders with the French elite, people-watch, and get caught up in the excitement. Hemingway spent a good deal of his earnings out at the Longchamp track in the Bois de Boulogne. See p. 116.

○ **Shopping on a Market Day:** Market days are one of the best ways to explore French towns like a local. We recommend the open-air market in **Arles,** one of Provence's most authentic destinations. A colorful line of vendors sells olives, fresh bread, cheese, and local ham underneath the city ramparts, a few blocks from the town's Roman amphitheater. See p. 171.

○ **Whiling Away an Afternoon in a Parisian Cafe:** There is something quintessentially Parisian about doing nothing in a public space, especially when that space is a café. You can read a book, look out the window, chat with a friend, sip some wine, or simply ponder the mysteries of life, and no one will bother you, even if you sit there for hours.

○ **Strolling along the Seine:** Flowing through the city and giving it life, the Seine is at the center of Paris's history, which becomes obvious when you stroll along its banks. Just about every major monument can be seen from here, including the Eiffel Tower, Notre-Dame, and the Louvre. And now that many of Seine's embankments have been restored and improved, strolling them is a pedestrian delight.

○ **Chateau-hopping through the Loire Valley:** An excursion to the châteaux dotting the valley's rich fields and forests will familiarize you with the French Renaissance's architectural aesthetics and the intrigues of the kings and their courts. Visit the main castles, such as **Chambord** or **Chenonceau,** and then stop in at some lesser-visited ones, like **Chaumont** or **Valencay.** See chapter 6.

○ **Sampling the Best of Chinon's Cellars:** Vines blanket the whole of the Loire, providing an excellent oenological break from castle touring. The area around Chinon is a treasure trove of welcoming vineyards where you can experience winemaking firsthand—and, of course, taste delicious *vins.* See chapter 6.

FRANCE'S best RESTAURANTS

○ **La Couronne,** Rouen (Normandy): Julia Child enjoyed her first-ever French meal at this traditional Norman restaurant. A bustling *auberge* in business for more than 6 centuries—and pulling in plenty of celebrity diners along the way—La Couronne makes the most of this region's hearty produce, from *côte de boeuf* (rib steak) to aged Camembert cheeses. See p. 109.

○ **Marché aux Poissons,** Trouville (Normandy): This fish market's dozen seafood stalls perch on the banks of the Touques River. Each one will happily plate up your own unique *plateau de fruits de mer* (seafood platter): Take your pick of fresh oysters, lobsters, scallops and more, then dig in at one of the market tables. Be sure to order a glass of Normandy's famous cider (*cidre*), a delicate, fermented version of apple juice that is a refreshing alcoholic tipple. See p. 117.

○ **Oustau de Baumanière,** Les Baux (Provence): The isolated, cinematic setting of the ancient fortress of Les Baux had troubadours singing in its streets during the Middle Ages. Today it is no less romantic. An abundance of picturesque hideaways is tucked into the hills surrounding the village, including this double-Michelin-starred gem housed in a 16th-century farmhouse. See p. 170.

○ **L'Atelier Jean-Luc Rabanel,** Arles (Provence): Fixed-price tasting menus—no à la carte allowed—are becoming increasingly popular. If you're ready to put yourself in the hands of a talented chef, try Jean-Luc Rabanel's sublime creations. This culinary genius cultivates most of his organic ingredients himself. Truly an amazing experience. See p. 172.

- **La Merenda,** Nice (Riviera): Utterly unpretentious, this snug bistro doesn't take reservations or credit cards. But it remains one of the Riviera's top spots for sampling traditional Niçois cuisine. Try slow-cooked beef *daube, petits-farcis* (stuffed vegetables), and *pissaladière,* a pizzalike local flatbread topped with caramelized onions. See p. 223.
- **Le Louis XV,** Monaco (Riviera): Superchef Alain Ducasse oversees this iconic restaurant—regularly rated one of the finest in the world—located in Monte-Carlo's Hôtel de Paris. Dining is extravagant, with fare steeped in lavish ingredients, from white truffles to foie gras, and served in an ornate, golden dining room. Yet many dishes of elegant simplicity are equally magnificent. Best for serious epicureans. See p. 240.
- **Le Grand Véfour** (Paris): There aren't many restaurants where you can both savor an exquisite meal and eat it in a room where Napoléon Bonaparte once dined. Tucked under an arcade at the Palais Royal, Le Grand Véfour has fed everyone from Cocteau to Colette amid magnificent 18th-century decor—now it's your turn. See p. 52.
- **Bistrot Paul Bert** (Paris): When you think bistro, you probably imagine a little place like this: dark wood furniture, cream-colored walls, and vintage lighting fixtures, all evoking a timeless ambience. The menu here is equally classic, and what's more, the kitchen is one of the best in town. See p. 57.
- **Le Domaine des Hauts de Loire,** between Blois and Amboise (Loire): For more than 20 years, Rémy Giraud has been wowing locals and weary chateau-hoppers at his double-Michelin-starred restaurant. The menu showcases seasonal and regional ingredients, such as Aquitaine caviar on pecan shortbread or crispy Gatinais quail with celery cream. See p. 142.
- **La Roche le Roy,** Tours (Loire): The finest in Touraine cuisine is delicately prepared at this award-winning 18th-century manor. Alain Couturier reinvents tradition, with eel simmered in Chinon wine and freshly caught Loire pikeperch on a bed of leeks. See p. 144.

FRANCE'S best HOTELS

- **La Cabro d'Or,** Les Baux (Provence): Spilling out from an original 18th-century farmhouse, La Cabro d'Or makes a luxurious Provençal bolthole. The labyrinthine grounds are undoubtedly some of the loveliest in France. Expect to stumble across walled gardens, bubbling fountains, and flower-strewn courtyards. See p. 170.
- **Hotel Royal Barrière,** Deauville (Normandy): A vision of crushed red velvet, this sumptuous hotel welcomes Hollywood superstars every autumn during the Deauville Festival of American Film. But its glamour endures year-round, with elegant guest rooms, a private beach, and the Michelin-starred Restaurant L'Etrier. See p. 115.
- **Mama Shelter,** Marseille (Provence): The work of legendary designer Philippe Starck, this contemporary hotel is located in the hip cours Julien neighborhood. On the ground floor, there's a courtyard pastis bar, perfect for sampling the city's favorite aperitif. See p. 183.
- **Château Saint-Martin,** Vence (Riviera): Perched on a hilltop just 20 minutes from Nice, Château Saint-Martin is one of the Riviera's most splendid hotels. The gardens are sprinkled with wildflowers. The infinity pool quite literally goes on forever.

And a truly exquisite spa is onsite. Lucky guests can gaze at the Mediterranean from bed. See chapter 8, p. 216.

- **Hôtel Belles-Rives,** Juan-les-Pins (Riviera): Once a vacation villa to Zelda and F. Scott Fitzgerald, the Hôtel Belles-Rives still maintains a flamboyant, 1920s feel. Sip a sundowner on the hotel's sea-facing terrace, or try waterskiing at the hotel's aquatic club, the very spot where the sport was invented almost a century ago. See p. 207.

- **Nice Pebbles** (Riviera): Want to live like a local? Nice Pebbles manages around 100 top-quality vacation apartments dotted throughout Nice and along the Riviera's nearby coast. Accommodation is boutique-hotel standard—but at just a fraction of regular hotel rates. See p. 222.

- **Hôtel Caron de Beaumarchais** (Paris): This adorable inn re-creates the ambience of 18th-century Paris, when the hotel's namesake, the author of "The Barber of Seville," was cavorting in the neighborhood. Rooms are covered in fine reproductions of period fabrics and furnished with authentic antique writing tables, ceiling fixtures, and paintings—a bit of Old France right in the middle of the trendy Marais. See p. 42.

- **Relais St-Germain** (Paris): A luxurious mix of past and present makes this hotel a romantic and modern haven, just steps from the bustle of Boulevard St-Germain. Run by the same management as the famous restaurant Le Comptoir du Relais (downstairs), this beautiful spot makes the perfect gourmet getaway. See p. 47.

- **Château d'Artigny,** south of Tours (Loire): Complete your castle experience by staying at one of the Loire's most regal château-hotels. You really will feel like a king, bedding down in Louis XV–style rooms and relaxing in the hotel's luxurious spa. See p. 145.

- **Le Manoir Les Minimes,** Amboise (Loire): Regional charm and character shine through at this reasonably priced manor, a perfect base for exploring the château country. Tucked behind its high walls, it has many rooms facing the river, while others offer glimpses of the royal château of Amboise. See p. 140.

secret **FRANCE**

- **Cycling in the Countryside:** The country that hosts the Tour de France offers thousands of options for bike trips, all of them ideal for leaving the crowds far behind. You're even welcome to take your bike aboard most trains in France, free of charge. For cycling through Provence's vineyards and past pretty hilltop villages, check out **Vélo Loisir en Luberon**'s downloadable routes. See p. 166.

- **Hunting for Antiques:** The 18th- and 19th-century French aesthetic was gloriously different from that of England and North America, and many objects bear designs with mythological references to the French experience. France has some 13,000-plus antiques shops throughout the country. Stop where you see the sign ANTIQUAIRE or BROCANTE.

- **Hiking the Caps** (Riviera): The Riviera's *sentier du littoral* is an almost continuous coastal footpath that winds its way along the country's seductive southern shores. Leave the coastal hubbub behind and spend a day wandering between the wealthy private mansions and the sparkling sea on Cap Ferrat or Cap d'Antibes. See chapter 8.

- **Exploring the Capital of Culture** (Provence): Marseille reveled in its role as European Capital of Culture 2013. The average tourist may eschew this busy port, but the last year has been nothing short of dynamic, with scores of stellar sights—as well as restaurants, bars, and shops—opening across the city. See chapter 7.

o **Traveling First Class:** France's TGV rail network is the world's fastest. Yet these trains are not just high-speed. When routes are booked in advance, they're wallet-friendly too. Throw in decor by Christian Lacroix and PlayStation Portables available to rent, and you're looking at the classiest public transport in the world. See chapter 9.

o **Cruising France's Rivers:** Floating slowly down one of France's major rivers is a superb way to see hidden corners of the countryside. Most luxury barge cruises offer daily excursions, elegant dinners on deck, and bicycles for solitary exploration. See chapter 9.

o **Reveling in St-Etienne-du-Mont:** One of the prettiest in Paris, this stunning church that sits atop the highest point in the Latin Quarter is often left off the tourist itinerary. A delightful mix of late-Gothic and Renaissance styles, the church has a 16th-century chancel boasting the city's only rood screen, a magnificent work with decorations inspired by the Italian Renaissance. See p. 85.

o **Sipping Tea at the Mosquée de Paris:** A delicious fountain trickles in the patio of this beautiful tearoom, which serves mint-scented tea and Middle Eastern pastries in lovely mosaic-tiled surroundings. An ideal spot for relaxing after a long day of sightseeing.

o **Going Underground at Touraine's Troglodyte Caves:** Admire art, sample regional wine, and even stay the night underground in the Loire's Touraine region, home to France's largest concentration of Troglodyte caves. See p. 149.

o **Returning to the Time of the Crusades:** See the history behind the Crusades at the 12th-century Abbey of Fontevraud, one of the largest medieval monasteries in Europe and the final resting place of most of the Plantagenets. See p. 155.

FRANCE'S best FOR FAMILIES

o **Climbing the Heights of Mont-St-Michel** (Normandy): Straddling the tidal flats between Normandy and Brittany, this Gothic marvel is the most spectacular fortress in northern Europe. Said to be protected by the archangel Michael, much of it stands as it did during the 1200s. As of 2014, however, a brand-new pedestrian path connects the visitor center to Mont-St-Michel itself. You can now stroll, bike, or trot (in a horse-drawn carriage) across the fortress. See chapter 7.

o **Getting Medieval in the Hilltop Town of Les Baux** (Provence): The age-old hill-town of **Les Baux** commands views over hundreds of miles of Provençal countryside. The film-set location, including the hilltop ruins of its "ghost village," plus a volley of great restaurants have made it a retreat for France's rich and famous. Kids will love its car-free medieval streets and awesome views, not to mention the daily display of a siege engine catapult. See chapter 8.

o **Making the Most of Modern Art in Antibes** (French Riviera): The **Musée Picasso** (Picasso Museum) in Antibes highlights some of the most accessible art in France. The Spanish painter set up shop in the atmospheric old quarter of Antibes's Chateau Grimaldi some 70 years ago. In such relaxed surroundings, children can appreciate the color, vibrancy, and playfulness that made Picasso one of the greats of the 20th century. The far-out sculptures and sunny views of the surrounding coastline will please non-art fans, too. See p. 211.

- **Joining the Cowboys in the Camargue** (Provence): Riding a sturdy Camarguais horse and with a local cowboy to guide you, make your way through the marshes of these beautiful, remote wetlands. Spot pink flamingos and watch the *gardians* with their large felt hats rounding up black bulls bred for the bullrings of the south. If the children don't ride, slow boat, bicycle, or Jeep make great alternatives. See chapter 8.

- **Exploring the Calanques** (Provence): In 2013 the Parc National des Calanques became France's newest national park. This stunning series of limestone cliffs and tumbling fjords stretch along the coast for 20km (12 miles) southeast of Marseille. Serious hikers can trek the Calanques' rocky promontories. Families with little ones can take in the coastline from aboard one of the many tour boats that depart from Marseille's port. See p. 184.

- **Learning about History and Fallen Heroes on Normandy's D-Day Beaches:** On June 6, 1944, the largest armada ever assembled departed on rough seas and in dense fog from southern England. For about a week, the future of the civilized world teetered between the Nazi and Allied armies. Today the entire family can immerse itself in the past with superb interactive exhibits, such as the personal tales detailed at the **Normandy American Visitor Center.** Kids can then run wild on the windswept sands below. See p. 126.

- **Playing in the Jardin des Plantes** (Paris): A splendid place for a picnic, this historic botanical garden is a quiet oasis in the Latin Quarter, where families can relax and tiny travelers can enjoy the playground, hothouses, and green spaces. When playtime is over, everyone can wander over to the small zoo or the adjoining natural-history museum. See p. 83.

- **Stargazing at Cité des Sciences et de l'Industrie** (Paris): Set amid the vast Parc de la Villette, this huge museum of science and industry includes a planetarium, an Imax theater, and even an authentic submarine that kids can climb into. But the biggest draw is the Cité des Enfants, a supremely kid-friendly collection of hands-on exhibits and displays.

- **Walking through a Real Fairy Tale** (Loire): The whole region of the Loire offers kids the chance to live out their fairy-tale fantasies. Step right into a storybook at the **Château d'Ussé,** the inspiration for "Sleeping Beauty." See p. 154.

- **Staring Down a Shark** (Loire): Peek at local fish mingling with exotic electric eels or check out the scary piranhas and sharks zooming around their tanks at the **Grand Aquarium de Touraine,** one of France's top aquariums.

FRANCE'S best BEACHES

- **Plage de Deauville** (Normandy): Coco Chanel used the chic resort of Deauville to propel herself to stardom and then added greatly to the town's sense of glamour. Revel in the sun-kissed sense of style and nostalgia with a stroll along the elegant Les Planches boardwalk, which skirts the edge of Deauville's silky, sandy, parasol-dotted *plage* for 2km (1¼ miles). See p. 116.

- **Plage de Pampelonne,** St-Tropez (French Riviera): Any blonde feels like Brigitte Bardot in sunny St-Tropez. And the scantily clad satyrs and nymphs splashing in the summertime surf at Plage de Pampelonne can perk up the most sluggish libido. The real miracle here is that the charm of this 5km (3-mile) crescent of white sand still manages to impress, despite its celebrity hype and hordes of A-list visitors. See p. 194.

o **Hi-Beach,** Nice (French Riviera): A day along the Riviera seaside may be a little different from home: Most beaches here feature private clubs with mattresses, parasols, and chilled Champagne on demand. Nice's Hi-Beach certainly offers all of the above. Yet its contemporary design, organic restaurant, and stellar cocktails set it apart from the crowd. See p. 227.

o **Paloma Plage,** Cap Ferrat (French Riviera): Tucked into one of Cap Ferrat's sheltered bays, petite Paloma Plage is part restaurant/chic beach club and part family-friendly stretch of pebbly shoreline. In the afternoon, fragrant Aleppo pines shade much of the beach. And Brad and Angelina have been known to stop by for dinner. See p. 232.

o **Plage de Arromanches-les-Bains** (Normandy): This immense beach is dotted with the mammoth, otherworldly remains of Winston, a prefabricated port essential during the D-Day landings. At low tide, the sandy expanse is firm (you can push a stroller or cycle along it!) and truly vast, making it popular with families. See p. 126.

o **The beaches of Juan-les-Pins** (French Riviera): In the resort that invented waterskiing, it's little surprise that all the summertime action centers around Juan-les-Pins' golden shores. Spread your towel on central **Plage de Juan-les-Pins.** Or follow the locals to the unnamed sandy suntrap of beach pinched between the Hôtel Belles-Rives and Port Gallice. See p. 208.

o **Calanque d'En Vau** (Provence): Nestled into the heart of Parc National des Calanques, Calanque d'En Vau wouldn't look out of place in the tropics: Imagine an ice-white pairing of pebbly sands and transparent turquoise waters. Sitting at the base of a limestone cliffs, it's accessible only on foot (for experienced hikers) or by boat. See p. 184.

o **Plage des Marinières,** Villefranche-sur-Mer (French Riviera): A perfect, seemingly endless sweep of honey-hued sand, this popular beach sits at the base of a wide bay. It's perfect for families, as the sea shelves slowly and waves are seldom seen. See p. 229.

o **Paris Plage** (Paris): The wildly popular initiative of Paris's mayor, Bertrand Delanoë, has brought tons of sand, activities, and fun to the banks of the Seine. Every year from mid-July to mid-August, you can find a sandy beach with lounge chairs, snack stands, concerts, dances, and so forth along the edge of the Right Bank and on the Bassin de la Villette.

o **Plage de la Garoupe,** Cap d'Antibes (French Riviera): The sun rises at dawn over the Cap d'Antibes' most mythical beach. Views pan out over Antibes to the Alps beyond; beach bars served chilled rosé behind. And a coastal footpath around the secluded peninsula starts to your right. What more could you possibly want? See p. 209.

SUGGESTED ITINERARIES IN FRANCE

2

When the Frommer's guidebooks were first launched, founder Arthur Frommer cautioned his readers, "You can get lost in France." It's still an apt warning—and promise—today.

For those with unlimited time, one of the world's great pleasures is getting "lost" in France, wandering at random, making new discoveries off the beaten path. Few of us have this luxury, however, and so here we present 1- and 2-week itineraries to help you make the most of your time.

France is so treasure-filled that you could barely do more than skim the surface in a week. So relax and savor Paris, Mont-St-Michel, Arles, or Cannes—among other allurements—saving the rest for another day. You might also review chapter 1, "The Best of France," to find out what experiences or sights have special appeal to us and then adjust your itineraries to suit your particular travel plans.

The itineraries that follow take you to some major attractions and some charming off-the-beaten-track towns. The pace may be a bit breathless for some visitors, so skip a town or sight occasionally to give yourself some chill-out time. You're on vacation, after all. Of course, you may also use these itineraries merely as a jumping-off point to develop your own custom-made trip.

THE REGIONS IN BRIEF

Although France's 547,030 sq. km (211,209 sq. miles) make it slightly smaller than the American state of Texas, no other country has such a diversity of sights and scenery in such a compact area. A visitor can travel through the north's flat, fertile lands; the Loire Valley's green hills; or the southeast's Mediterranean coast. Even more noteworthy are the cultural and historical differences that define each region. To help you decide where best to spend your time, this guide is focused on Paris, plus the country's four most popular regions: Normandy, the Loire, Provence, and the Riviera.

Destinations in France are within easy reach from Paris and each other. **French National Railroads (SNCF)** offers fast service to and from Paris. For example, the highlights of Normandy and the Loire Valley (the château country) are just 1 or 2 hours away from Paris by train. You can travel from Paris to Cannes on the Riviera in 5 hours—or fly down to the Riviera in 45 minutes.

You can motor along nearly 71,000km (about 44,020 miles) of French roads, including a good number of well-maintained superhighways. But do your best to drive the secondary roads too: Nearly all of France's scenic splendors are along these routes.

A "grand tour" of France is nearly impossible for the visitor who doesn't have a lifetime to explore. If you want to get to know a province, try to devote at least a week to a specific region. Note that you'll probably have a more rewarding trip if you concentrate on getting to know two or three areas at a leisurely pace rather than racing around trying to see everything!

PARIS   France was born in the temperate basin of the Ile de France, where the attractions include **Paris, Versailles, Fontainebleau, Notre-Dame de Chartres,** and **Giverny.** For more information, see chapter 4.

NORMANDY   This region will forever be linked to the 1944 D-day invasion. Some readers consider a visit to the D-day beaches the most emotionally worthwhile part of their trip. Normandy boasts 599km (371 miles) of coastline and a maritime tradition. It's a popular weekend getaway from Paris, and many hotels and restaurants thrive here, especially around the casino town of **Deauville.** Normandy's great attractions include the **Rouen** cathedral and medieval **Bayeux.** For more information, see chapter 5.

THE LOIRE VALLEY   This area includes two ancient provinces, Touraine (centered on Tours) and Anjou (centered on Angers). It was beloved by royalty and nobility until Henry IV moved his court to Paris. Head here to see the most magnificent castles in France. Irrigated by the Loire River and its many tributaries, the valley produces many superb wines. For more information, see chapter 6.

PROVENCE   One of France's most popular destinations stretches from the southern Rhone River to the Italian border. Long frequented by starving artists, *la bourgeoisie,* and the downright rich and famous, its premier cities are **Aix-en-Provence,** associated with Cézanne; **Arles,** famous for bullfighting and Van Gogh; **Avignon,** the 14th-century capital of Christendom; and **Marseille,** a port city established by the Phoenicians that today is the melting pot of France. Quieter and more romantic are villages such as **St-Rémy-de-Provence, Les Baux,** and **Gordes.** For more information, see chapter 7.

THE FRENCH RIVIERA (CÔTE D'AZUR)   The resorts of the fabled Côte d'Azur (Azure Coast) still evoke glamour: **Cannes, St-Tropez, Cap d'Antibes,** and **Juan-les-Pins.** July and August are the most buzzing months, while spring and fall are still sunny but way more laid-back. **Nice** is the biggest city and most convenient base for exploring the area. The Principality of **Monaco** occupies only about 2 sq. km (¾ sq. mile) but has enough sights, restaurants, and opulence to go around. Along the coast are some sandy beaches, but many are pebbly. Topless bathing is common, especially in St-Tropez, and some of the restaurants are citadels of conspicuous consumption. Dozens of artists and their patrons have littered the landscape with world-class galleries and art museums. For more information, see chapter 8.

1 WEEK IN PARIS & NORMANDY

If you budget your days carefully, 1 week provides enough time to visit the major attractions of Paris, such as the **Musée du Louvre** (the world's greatest art gallery), the **Eiffel Tower,** and **Notre-Dame.** After 2 days in Paris, head for the former royal stamping grounds of **Versailles,** followed by Normandy (an easy commute from Paris), visiting such highlights as the **D-Day beaches,** the cathedral city of **Rouen** (where Joan of Arc was burned at the stake), the tapestry of **Bayeux,** and the incredible monastery of **Mont-St-Michel.**

Days 1 & 2: Arrive in Paris ★★★

Take a flight that arrives in Paris as early as possible on Day 1. Check into your hotel and hit the nearest cafe for a pick-me-up café au lait and a croissant before sightseeing. Take the Métro to the Palais Royal–Musée du Louvre for a visit to the **Musée du Louvre** (p. 69). Spend at least 2 hours here viewing world-class masterpieces such as Leonardo da Vinci's "Mona Lisa." After leaving the Louvre, walk south toward the **Quays of the Seine,** spending an hour taking in the tree-shaded banks and panoramic vistas of Paris. Head for **Ile de la Cité** to explore its attractions, including **Ste-Chapelle** (p. 72) and the monumental **Notre-Dame** (p. 64) and its gargoyles. As the evening fades, head for the **Eiffel Tower** for the greatest cityscape in Europe.

On Day 2, begin at the **place de la Concorde** (p. 80) and its Egyptian obelisk, then stroll up the 1.8km (1-mile) avenue of French grandeur, the **Champs-Elysées,** until you reach the **Arc de Triomphe** (p. 76), which you can scale for another panoramic view of Paris. Afterward, head for the **Ile St-Louis,** Ile de la Cité's petite island neighbor. Lacking monumental attractions, this little isle is a sight in itself, with pretty quays and small side streets dotted with antiques shops and bistros.

After lunch in one of those snug bistros, visit the **Musée d'Orsay** (p. 87), home to the world's greatest collection of Impressionist paintings. As the after-noon fades, head for **Basilique du Sacré-Coeur** (p. 81) for a crowning view of Paris as the sun sets. Have a final dinner in a Montmartre cafe.

Day 3: A Day Trip to Versailles ★★★

Having survived 2 days in the capital of France, bid *adieu* and take the RER Line C to the **Versailles/Rive Gauche station.** You can spend a full day at Versailles—and then some—or else see the highlights in 3 hours, including the Grands and Petits Appartements, the glittering Hall of Mirrors, Gabriel's Opera House, the Royal Chapel, and the Gardens of Versailles.

Day 4: Normandy's Capital of Rouen ★★

Take an early train to Rouen and check in to one of the city's great hotels. Spend at least 2 hours exploring the city's ancient core, especially its **Cathédrale Notre-Dame** (p. 110), immortalized in paintings by Monet. Stand at the **place du Vieux-Marché** (p. 109), where Joan of Arc was executed for heresy in 1431, and visit the **Eglise St-Maclou** (p. 110), a 1432 church in the Flamboyant Gothic style. After lunch, rent a car for the rest of your trip and drive to **Giverny**—it's only 60km (37 miles) southeast of Rouen. At Giverny, visit the **Claude Monet Foundation,** returning to your hotel in Rouen for the night.

Day 5: Bayeux ★★ & Caen ★

Even after a leisurely breakfast, you can easily be in the city of Caen by late morning, with plenty of time to visit **Abbaye aux Hommes** (p. 120), founded by William the Conqueror. After a hearty Norman lunch in Caen, continue west to the city of **Bayeux** to view the celebrated **Musée de la Tapisserie de Bayeux** (p. 124). Stay overnight in Bayeux.

France in 1 Week ①–⑦
Day 1 Arrive in Paris
Day 2 Paris
Day 3 Day Trip to Versailles
Day 4 Rouen: Normandy's Capital
Day 5 Bayeux & Caen
Day 6 The D-Day Beaches
Day 7 Mont-St-Michel

France in 2 Weeks ①–⑭
Day 8 Orléans
Day 9 Amboise & Chenonceau
Day 10 Avignon
Day 11 Avignon to St-Tropez
Day 12 Cannes
Day 13 Nice
Day 14 Nice to Monaco

France for Families ●
Days 1 & 2 Paris
Day 3 Versailles
Days 4 & 5 Disneyland Paris
Day 6 Nice
Day 7 Monaco

An Art Lover's Tour of France ●
Days 1 & 2 Paris
Day 3 Aix-en-Provence
Day 4 St-Tropez
Day 5 Antibes & Vallauris
Days 6 & 7 Nice

Day 6: The D-Day Beaches ★★★

Reserve this day for exploring the D-Day beaches, where Allied forces launched "the Longest Day," the mammoth invasion of Normandy in June 1944 that signaled the beginning of the end of Hitler's Third Reich.

Your voyage of discovery can begin at the seaside resort of Arromanches-les-Bains, where you can visit the **Musée du Débarquement** (p. 126) before heading to **Omaha Beach** (p. 125), the moving **Normandy American Visitor Center** (p. 126), and the brand-new **Overlord Museum** (p. 126), with an easy roadside lunch en route.

That evening, drive to **Mont-St-Michel** (less than 2 hr. away) and overnight in the pedestrianized village on "the Rock," giving you plenty of time for an early-morning—and relatively tourist-free—visit to this popular UNESCO-protected attraction.

Day 7: Mont-St-Michel ★★★

Allow around 3 hours to explore **Mont-St-Michel** (p. 122). Taking an English-language tour is one of the best ways to enjoy its great abbey, founded in 966. After lunch, return your car to Rouen, where you'll find frequent train service back to Paris and your flight home the following day.

A 1-WEEK EXTENSION TO THE LOIRE VALLEY & THE CÔTE D'AZUR

If you have 2 weeks to explore France, you'll have time to visit several regions—not only Paris, but also the best of the Loire Valley châteaux, the most history-rich town of Provence (Avignon), and several resorts on the Riviera, taking in the beaches, art galleries, and even the Principality of Monaco.

For **days 1 through 7,** follow the "1 Week in Paris & Normandy" itinerary, above.

Day 8: Orléans, Gateway to the Loire Valley ★

Leave Paris on an early train to **Orléans** (trip time: 1 hr., 15 min.). Rent a car here and drive west to the **Château de Chambord** (p. 136), the largest château in the Loire Valley, representing the apogee of the French Renaissance architectural style. Allow 2 hours for a visit. Back on the road again, continue southwest to the **Château de Blois** (p. 135), called "the Versailles of the Renaissance" and a virtual illustrated storybook of French architecture. Stay overnight in Blois.

Day 9: Amboise ★★ & Chenonceau ★★★

In the morning, continue southeast from Blois to **Amboise,** where you can check into a hotel for the night. Visit the 15th-century **Château d'Amboise** (p. 140), in the Italian Renaissance style, and also **Clos-Lucé** (p. 140), last residence of Leonardo da Vinci. In the afternoon, drive southeast to the **Château de Chenonceau** (p. 141), famous for the French dames who have occupied its precincts, including Diane de Poitiers (mistress of the king) and Catherine de Médici (the jealous queen). You can spend a couple of hours at the château before driving back to Amboise for the night.

Day 10: Avignon, Gateway to Provence ★★★

From Amboise, get an early start and drive east to Orléans to return your rental car. Then take an early train from Orléans to Paris's Gare d'Austerlitz, then the Métro or a taxi to the Gare de Lyon, and hop on a TGV bound for Avignon (2½ hr.).

Check into a hotel in **Avignon,** one of Europe's most beautiful medieval cities. Before the day fades, you should have time to wander through the old city to get your bearings, shop for Provençal souvenirs, and see one of the smaller sights, such as the **Pont St-Bénézet.** See p. 162.

Day 11: Avignon to St-Tropez ★★★

In the morning, spend 2 hours touring the **Palais des Papes** (p. 162), the capital of Christendom during the 14th century. After lunch in one of Avignon's cozy bistros or cobblestoned outdoor cafes, rent a car and drive to **St-Tropez** (p. 194). Spend a good part of the early evening in one of the cafes along the harbor, indulging in that favorite French pastime of people-watching.

Day 12: Chic Cannes ★★★

Before leaving St-Tropez in the morning, check out the Impressionist paintings at **Musée de l'Annonciade** (p. 194). Drive 50km (31 miles) east along the coast until you reach Cannes.

Assuming it's summer, get in some time at the beach, notably at **Plage de la Croisette** (p. 201), and feel free to wear your most revealing swimwear. In the afternoon, take the ferry to **Ile Ste-Marguerite** (p. 203), where the "Man in the Iron Mask" was imprisoned. You can visit his cell. That evening, you may want to flirt with Lady Luck at one of the plush **casinos** (p. 203).

Day 13: Nice, Capital of the Riviera ★★★

It's only a 32km (20-mile) drive east from Cannes to **Nice,** the Riviera's largest city. After checking in to a hotel (the most affordable along the Riviera), stroll through **Vieille Ville** (p. 224), the Old Town. Enjoy a snack of *socca,* a round crepe made with chickpea flour that vendors sell steaming hot in the cours Saleya market. Then head for the **promenade des Anglais** (p. 224), the wide boulevard along the waterfront. In the afternoon, head for the famed hill town of **St-Paul-de-Vence,** only 20km (12 miles) to the north. You can wander its ramparts in about 30 minutes before descending to the greatest modern-art museum in the Riviera, the **Foundation Maeght** (p. 214).

Continue on to **Vence** (p. 217) for a visit to the great Henri Matisse's artistic masterpiece, **Chapelle du Rosaire** (p. 218). From there, it's just 24km (15 miles) southeast to Nice, where you can enjoy dinner at a typical Niçois bistro.

Day 14: Nice to Menton ★★

While still overnighting in Nice, head east for the most thrilling drive in all of France, a trip along the **Grande Corniche** highway, which stretches 31km (19 miles) east from Nice to the little resort of **Menton** near the Italian border. Allow 3 hours for this trip. Highlights along this road include **Roquebrune-Cap Martin** and **La Turbie.** The greatest view along the Riviera is at the **Eze Belvedere,** at 1,200m (3,936 ft.).

FRANCE FOR FAMILIES

France offers many attractions for kids. Our suggestion is to limit the bustle of **Paris** to 2 days, and then spend a day wandering the spectacular grounds and glittering interiors of **Versailles,** 2 days in **Disneyland Paris,** and 2 days on the **Riviera.**

Days 1 & 2: Paris ★★★

Take the kids for a morning visit to **Notre-Dame** (p. 64). The highlight is climbing the 387 narrow and winding steps to the top of one of the towers for a fabulously Quasimodo view of the gargoyles and Paris. After a visit, head over to the street market along rue Cler to pick up picnic goodies, best enjoyed in the nearby **Champ de Mars,** which also stages great puppet shows.

After lunch, scale the iconic **Eiffel Tower** (p. 90). Then take the children for a stroll through the **Jardin des Tuileries** (p. 68), where there are donkey rides, ice-cream stands, and a marionette show. At the circular pond, you can rent a toy boat.

On Day 2, visit the **Musée du Louvre** (p. 69). Even if your child is not a museum lover or bores easily, he or she will surely be intrigued by the many displays. Over the years, we've observed that kids are particularly fascinated by the Egyptian art and antiquities in the Sully and Denon wings, the largest exhibition of such artifacts outside of Cairo.

After the Louvre, take the Métro to Porte de la Villette, where you can spend 2 or 3 hours at **Cité des Sciences et de l'Industrie.** The mammoth structure is home to a planetarium, a 3-D cinema, and interactive exhibits, as well as the kid-friendly Cité des Enfants.

Space is too tight in this book to document all activities in Paris of interest to children, but you may want to spend a couple of hours in the **Jardin d'Acclimatation,** in the northern part of the Bois de Boulogne, which include rides, a farm, a house of mirrors, a puppet theater, a huge playground, and kiosks selling waffles.

As the afternoon fades, head for **Butte Montmartre,** with its fiesta atmosphere. Take the Métro to Anvers and walk to the funicular, the cable car that carries you to the **Basilique du Sacré-Coeur** (p. 81). From here you can take your brood for a merry-go-round ride at **place des Abbesses** (p. 81).

Day 3: Versailles ★★★

Tear yourself away from the glories of Paris for a day spent at the **Château de Versailles** (p. 101). Take the RER line C to the Versailles/Rive Gauche station. Kids delight in the Hall of Mirrors and in the grand apartments. You can buy the makings of a picnic lunch in Paris and enjoy it on the grounds, or else purchase a sandwich at one of the stalls placed in discreet corners of the garden.

Days 4 & 5: Disneyland Paris ★★

Disneyland Paris is the top family vacation destination in France. Allow a full day to see the highlights of the park, plus another day to absorb some or all of its secondary adventures. Our recommendation is to visit **Main Street, U.S.A., Frontierland,** and **Adventureland** on the first day, saving **Fantasyland, Discoveryland, Walt Disney Studios,** the entertainment center at **Village Disney,** and **Sleeping Beauty Castle** for the second day. You can stay in the Disney hotels onsite, available in various price ranges from very expensive to budget. The RER commuter express train A takes you from Etoile in Paris to Marne-la-Vallée/Chessy in 45 minutes.

Day 6: Nice ★★★

Return to Paris and fly to Nice, capital of the French Riviera. If you flew Air France transatlantic, Nice can often be attached as a low-cost extension of your round-trip fare.

In Nice, you can check into your hotel for 2 nights, as the city has the most affordable hotels on the coast. Set out to explore this old city. There's always a lot of free entertainment in summer along Nice's seafront boardwalk, the **promenade des Anglais** (p. 224), and the people-watching on the Riviera—particularly on the beach—is likely to leave your kids wide-eyed.

In the afternoon, journey to the evocative hill town of **St-Paul-de-Vence** (p. 212). Children delight in touring the ramparts, strolling along the pedestrian-only rue Grande, or exploring the sculpture garden at the **Foundation Maeght** (p. 214), one of France's greatest modern-art museums.

Return to Nice for the evening and take your kids for a stroll through the Old Town, dining as the sun dips over the Mediterranean.

Day 7: Monaco ★★★

While still based in Nice, head for the tiny principality of Monaco, which lies only 18km (11 miles) east of Nice.

Children will enjoy the changing-of-the-guard ceremony at **Les Grands Appartements du Palais** (p. 237), where Prince Albert married South African swimmer Charlene Wittstock in July 2011. But the best part of Monaco for kids is the **Musée Océanographique de Monaco** (p. 237), home to sharks and other exotic sea creatures. Hundreds of cool vintage cars are also on display at the **Collection des Voitures Anciennes de S.A.S. le Prince de Monaco** (p. 236).

Return to Nice that night and prepare for your flight home in the morning.

ART LOVERS' TOUR OF FRANCE

From contemporary art in Paris to modern masters along the southern coast, France is a country infused with art. Art aficionados can experience an unforgettable trip taking in Paris (2 days), Aix-en-Provence (1 day), and then the Riviera between St-Tropez and Nice (4 days). Museum visits can be interspersed with wonderful meals, sunbathing, and stops at the area's architectural and artistic highlights.

Days 1 & 2: Paris ★★★

Start your art tour of Paris with a quick check of what's currently on the city: The **Grand Palais** (p. 76), **Musée de Luxembourg,** and the **Pinacothèque de Paris** all host excellent temporary exhibitions.

You can attend a show at any of these venues, or begin your day at the newly renovated **Musée de Montmartre** (p. 81), formerly home to both Renoir and Utrillo. Then hop onto the Métro and head south to the Jardin du Luxembourg. The offbeat **Musée Zadkine,** dedicated to Russian sculptor Ossip Zadkine, is located here. It's a tiny little museum in a small house with a pretty little garden. Enjoy a leisurely lunch at one of the neighborhood's many bistros. Round out the afternoon by taking in a cutting-edge contemporary exhibition at the iconic **Palais de Tokyo** (p. 79).

On Day 2, spend the morning admiring the contemporary art on display at **La Maison Rouge.** After lunching at the museum's onsite branch of the popular Rose Bakery, head over to the **Marais** (p. 74), the city neighborhood currently boasting the highest concentration of art galleries.

Midafternoon, jump aboard one of the many TGV trains heading south to Aix-en-Provence. The journey takes around 3 hours, leaving you plenty of time to enjoy a typical Provençal dinner upon arrival.

Day 3: Aix-en-Provence ★★

Paul Cézanne is Aix's most celebrated son. Begin your day at his **Atelier** (p. 179), almost perfectly preserved as it was when the great artist worked here more than a century ago. There are regularly scheduled English-language tours of the site. Afterward, a visit to the city's famed **Musée Granet** (p. 179)—one of the region's most superb modern-art museums—is a must.

Aix's plane-tree-shaded **cours Mirabeau** is almost a work of art in itself. Be sure to stop into **Brasserie Les Deux Garçons** (p. 178), where Cézanne used to drink and debate with the famous French writer Émile Zola.

After lunch, rent a car and drive to **St-Tropez** (p. 194). Warm evenings are best enjoyed strolling the port's pretty quays or taking in the million-dollar panoramas from the hilltop **Citadelle** (p. 194).

Day 4: St-Tropez ★★★

Since the 1890s, when Signac and Bonnard discovered St-Tropez, artists and their patrons have been drawn to the French Riviera. Spend the morning appreciating the **Musée de l'Annonciade**'s (p. 194) Impressionist paintings, many of them depicting St-Tropez and the surrounding coast.

After lunch in one of the town's sidewalk cafés, drive around 100km (62 miles) east along the coast until you reach Nice, where you'll base yourself for the next 3 nights. Return your rental car here—traffic-heavy roads, combined with excellent public transportation, make your own vehicle unnecessary here.

Day 5: Antibes & Vallauris ★★

Today you'll spend the day following in the footsteps of one of the 20th-century's modern masters: Pablo Picasso. Take one of the frequent trains from Nice to Antibes (20 min.). On the edge of the picturesque, strollable Old Town sits the 14th-century Grimaldi Château, now home to the **Musée Picasso** (p. 211). The Spanish artist lived and worked in this castle in 1946.

Stroll through Antibes' covered market, then—appetite piqued—stop into a small bistro, such as **Entre 2 Vins** (p. 210), for a light lunch. Next, make your way to Antibes' bus station, where frequent buses depart for Vallauris (35 min.). Picasso moved to this hilltop village during the 1950s, reviving the local ceramic-making industry and personally producing thousands of pieces of pottery. Visit Picasso's mammoth paintings in the **Musée National Picasso La Guerre et La Paix** (p. 205), the artist's tribute to pacifism.

Make your way back to Nice (it's quickest to simply reverse your route). Spend the evening strolling the promenade des Anglais or wandering the city's atmospheric Old Town.

Days 6 & 7: Nice ★★★

Outside of Paris, Nice is home to more museums than any other city in France. Begin your Day 6 citywide explorations in the neighborhood of Cimiez, where both the famed **Musée Matisse** (p. 226) and the **Musée National Message Biblique Marc Chagall** (p. 226) are located. It's possible to walk between the two (around 15 min.), but be sure to hit the Matisse Museum first — then it's downhill all the way to see Chagall's ethereal artworks.

If it's summertime, spend a couple of hours picnicking on the beach or relaxing with a glass of wine in one of the city's many sidewalk cafés. Midafternoon, make your way over the **Musée Masséna** (p. 225), where a combination of local art and history gives visitors a peek at the ritzy French Riviera of the past.

Use your final day to make a day trip to the hilltop village of **St-Paul-de-Vence** (p. 212), 20km (12 miles) to the north. Wander the St-Paul-de-Vence's ramparts for half an hour, before descending to the world-class modern art on display at the **Foundation Maeght** (p. 214). En route back to Nice, stop into the **Musée Renoir** in Cagnes-sur-Mer. The artist's former home and gardens were reopened in mid-2013 after extensive renovations. Note that you can either rent a car for the day or access both St-Paul-de-Vence and Cagnes-sur-Mer via frequent buses from Nice.

Spend your final night in Nice savoring a hearty Niçois dinner, paired with plenty of local wine.

FRANCE IN CONTEXT

The civilization and culture of France—not to mention the French way of life—makes the country easily the most visited in the world. The savoir-faire of its people lures travelers from across the globe to a country that covers an area smaller than Texas. Yet despite France's size, each region is so intriguing and varied that you may immerse yourself in one province so deeply that you'll never have time to see what's on the other side. You'd be surprised how many people do just that. Perhaps more than any other country in the world, France is a land to be savored. Ideally, France is discovered slowly by car or along the country's magnificent rail network, which lets you to stop whenever and wherever you wish.

No European country, not even England, Italy, or Spain, can beat France in its pageantry of personalities. Its colorful characters range from Madame de Pompadour to Charles de Gaulle, from Jean-Luc Godard to Gustave Flaubert, from Catherine de Médici to Joan of Arc, from Emperor Napoleon to footballer Zinedine Zidane. You'll be introduced to some of these figures in the pages ahead. Seeing where they lived, worked, loved, and became legends is part of the experience of visiting France.

This guide is meant to help you decide where to go in France, but ultimately the most gratifying experience will be your own serendipitous discoveries—sunflowers, a picnic in a poppy field, an hour spent chatting with a small winemaker—whatever it is that stays in your memory for years to come.

FRANCE TODAY

France remains one of the world's most hyped and written-about destinations. It can inspire a masterpiece—and has on countless occasions. Even the cantankerous James McNeill Whistler would allow his masterpiece, a portrait of his mother, to hang in no other city save Paris.

Although not large by North American standards (about the size of Britain and Germany combined), France is densely packed with attractions, both cultural and recreational. Even better, it's permeated with cool and known for its *joie de vivre*.

As for style, it has always been foolhardy to try to compete with the French on their terms. The theatrical backdrops of the sometimes-silly Gallic monarchs have been interpreted by latter-day aesthetes as history's crowning achievement when it comes to conspicuous displays of wealth and prestige.

In politics and ideology, France has long been a leader and remains so today. Fueled by Enlightenment writings, whose most articulate voices were French, the 1789 Revolution toppled Europe's most deeply entrenched regime and cracked the foundations of dozens of other governments. In 1968 the revolutionaries were on the streets again: the original political spring.

Newcomers have commented (often adversely) on the cultural arrogance of the French. But despite its linguistic and cultural rigidity, France has received more immigrants and political exiles than any other European country. Part of this derives from France's status as one of Europe's least densely populated nations per square mile, and part of it from the tendency of the French to let others be until their actions become dangerous or obnoxious, not necessarily in that order.

If you're a first-timer, everything in France, of course, is new. But if you've been away for a long time, expect changes. Taxi drivers in Paris may no longer correct your fractured French, but address you in English—and that's tantamount to a revolution. Part of this derives from the county's interest in music, culture, and films from foreign countries, and part from France's growing awareness of its role as a leader of a united Europe.

Yet France has never been more concerned about the loss of its unique identity within a landscape that has attracted an increasing number of immigrants from its former colonies. Many worry that France will continue to lose the battle to keep its language strong, distinct, and unadulterated by foreign slang or catchwords (and good luck with banning such terms as *l'email* and *le week-end*). But as the country moves deeper into the millennium, foreign tourists spending much-needed cash are no longer perceived as foes or antagonists. *Au contraire:* France welcomes the world to its palaces, parks, beaches, and UNESCO World Heritage sites. And if those tens of millions of guests spend a few euros—and soak up a little local culture while they're here—that's all to the good.

THE HISTORY OF FRANCE

EARLY GAUL   When the ancient Romans considered France part of their empire, their boundaries extended deep into the forests of the Paris basin and up to the edges of the Rhine. Part of Julius Caesar's early reputation came from his defeat of King Vercingetorix at Alésia in 52 B.C., a victory he was quick to publicize in one of the ancient world's literary masterpieces, "The Gallic Wars." In that year, the Roman colony of Lutetia (Paris) was established on an island in the Seine (Ile de la Cité).

As the Roman Empire declined, its armies retreated to the flourishing colonies that had been established along a strip of the Mediterranean coast—among others, these included Orange, Arles, Antibes, and Marseille, which today retain some of the best Roman monuments in Europe.

As one of their legacies, the Roman armies left behind the Catholic Church, which, for all its abuses, was the only real guardian of civilization during the anarchy following the Roman decline. A form of low Latin was the common language. This slowly evolved into the archaic French that the more refined language is based upon today.

THE CAROLINGIANS   From the wreckage of the early first millennium emerged a new dynasty: the Carolingians. One of their leaders, Charles Martel, halted a Muslim invasion of northern Europe at Tours in 743 and left a much-expanded kingdom to his son, Pepin. The Carolingian empire eventually stretched from the Pyrénées to a point deep in the German forests, encompassing much of modern France, Germany, and northern Italy. The heir to this vast land was Charlemagne. Crowned emperor in Rome on Christmas Day in 800, he returned to his capital at Aix-la-Chapelle (Aachen) and created the Holy Roman Empire. Charlemagne's rule saw a revived interest in scholarship, art, and classical texts, defined by scholars as the Carolingian Renaissance.

THE MIDDLE AGES   When the Carolingian dynasty died out in 987, the hectic, migratory Middle Ages officially began. Invasion by Hungarians, Vikings, and the English (who ruled half the country) lent France a cosmopolitan, if fractured, air. Politically driven marriages among the ruling families more than doubled the size of the territory controlled from Paris, a city that was increasingly recognized as the country's capital. Philippe II (reigned 1179–1223) infiltrated more prominent families with his genes than anyone else in France, successfully marrying members of his family into the Valois, Artois, and Vermandois. He also managed to win Normandy and Anjou back from the English. Louis IX (St. Louis) emerged as the 13th century's most memorable king, though he ceded most of the hard-earned military conquests of his predecessors back to the English.

The 14th century saw an increase in the wealth and power of the French kings, an increase in general prosperity, and a decrease in the power of the feudal lords. The death of Louis X without an heir in 1316 prompted more than a decade of scheming and plotting before the eventual emergence of the Valois dynasty.

France's burgeoning wealth and power was checked by the Black Death, which began in the summer of 1348. The rat-borne plague killed an estimated 33 percent of Europe's population, decimating the population of Paris and setting the stage for the exodus of the French monarchs to safer climes in such places as the Loire Valley. A financial crisis, coupled with a series of ruinous harvests, almost bankrupted the nation.

During the Hundred Years' War, the English made sweeping inroads into France in an attempt to grab the throne. At their most powerful, they controlled almost all the north (Picardy and Normandy), Champagne, and parts of the Loire Valley. The peasant-born charismatic visionary Joan of Arc rallied the dispirited French troops as well as the timid dauphin (crown prince), whom she managed to have crowned as Charles VII. As threatening to the Catholic Church as she was to the English, she was declared a heretic and burned at the stake in Rouen in 1431. The place of her demise is now sited in the city's marketplace.

THE RISING POWER   By the early 17th century, France was a modern state. Few vestiges of feudalism remained. In 1624, Louis XIII appointed a Catholic cardinal, the duc de Richelieu, as his chief minister. Amassing enormous power, Richelieu virtually ruled the country until his death in 1642. His sole objective was investing the monarchy with total power, and in trying to attain this goal he committed a series of truly horrible acts, paving the way for the eventual absolutism of a dynasty of future despotic rulers.

Although he ascended the throne when he was only 9, Louis XIV was the most powerful monarch Europe had seen since the Roman emperors. The estimated population of France at this time was 20 million, as opposed to 8 million in England and 6 million in Spain. French colonies in Canada, the West Indies, and America (Louisiana) were stronger than ever. The mercantilism that Louis's brilliant finance minister, Colbert, implemented was one of the era's most important fiscal policies, hugely increasing France's power and wealth. The arts flourished, as did a sense of aristocratic style that's remembered with a bittersweet nostalgia today. Louis's palace of Versailles is the perfect monument to the most flamboyantly consumptive era in French history.

Louis's territorial ambitions so deeply threatened the other nations of Europe that they united to hold him in check. France entered a series of expensive and demoralizing wars that, coupled with high taxes and bad harvests, stirred up much civil discontent. England was viewed as a threat both within Europe and in the global rush for lucrative colonies. The rise of Prussia as a militaristic neighbor posed an additional problem. Fresh political ideas from abroad unsteadied the status quo.

THE REVOLUTION & THE RISE OF NAPOLEON   Meanwhile, the Enlightenment was training a new generation of thinkers for the struggle against absolutism, religious fanaticism, and superstition. On August 10, 1792, troops from Marseille, aided by a Parisian mob, threw the dimwitted Louis XVI and his tactless Austrian-born queen, Marie Antoinette, into prison. After months of bloodshed and bickering among violently competing factions, the two thoroughly humiliated monarchs were executed.

France's problems got worse before they got better. In the ensuing bloodbaths, both moderates and radicals were guillotined in full view of a bloodthirsty crowd that included voyeurs like Dickens's Mme. Defarge, who brought her knitting every day to place de la Révolution (later renamed place de la Concorde) to watch the beheadings. Only the militaristic fervor of Napoleon Bonaparte could reunite France and bring an end to the revolutionary chaos. A political and military genius who appeared on the landscape at a time when the French were thoroughly sickened by the anarchy following their revolution, he restored a national pride that had been severely tarnished. He also established a bureaucracy and a code of law that has been emulated in other legal systems around the world. In 1799, at the age of 30, he entered Paris and was crowned first consul and master of France. Soon after, a decisive victory in his northern Italian campaign solidified his power at home.

Alas, Napoleon's victories made him overconfident—and made the rest of Europe clamor for his demise. Just as he was poised on the verge of conquering the entire continent, Napoleon's famous retreat from Moscow during the winter of 1812 reduced his formerly invincible army to tatters. As a plaque in the Lithuanian town of Vilnius once told the tale: "NAPOLEON BONAPARTE PASSED THIS WAY IN 1812 WITH 400,000 MEN"—and on the other side are the words "NAPOLEON BONAPARTE PASSED THIS WAY IN 1812 WITH 9,000 MEN". Napoleon was then decisively beaten at Waterloo by the combined armies of the English, Dutch, and Prussians. Exiled to the British-held island of St. Helena in the South Atlantic, he died in 1821, probably the victim of a prison poisoner.

THE BOURBONS & THE SECOND EMPIRE   In 1814, following the destruction of Napoleon and his dream of Empire, the Congress of Vienna redefined the map of Europe. The Bourbon monarchy was reestablished, with reduced powers for Louis XVIII, an archconservative. After a few stable decades, Napoleon I's nephew, Napoleon III, was elected president in 1848. Appealing to the property-protecting instinct of a nation that hadn't forgotten the violent upheavals of less than a century before, he initiated a repressive right-wing government in which he was awarded the totalitarian status of emperor in 1851. Steel production was begun, and a railway system and Indochinese colonies were established. New technologies fostered new kinds of industry, and the bourgeoisie flourished. The baron Georges-Eugène Haussmann radically altered Paris by laying out the grand boulevards the world knows today.

As ever, intra-European conflict knocked France off its pedestal once again. In 1870, the Prussians—a rising power in the German east—defeated Napoleon III at Sedan and held him prisoner with 100,000 of his soldiers. Paris was besieged and occupied, an inglorious state for the world's greatest city. After the Prussians withdrew, a violent revolt ushered in the Third Republic and its elected president, Marshal Mac-Mahon, in 1873. Peace and prosperity slowly returned, France regained its glamour, a mania of building occurred, the Impressionists made their visual statements, and writers like Flaubert redefined the French novel into what today is regarded as the most evocative in the world. As if as a symbol of this period, the Eiffel Tower was built as part of the 1889 Universal Exposition.

THE WORLD WARS   International rivalries, lost colonial ambitions, and conflicting alliances led to World War I, which, after decisive German victories for 2 years, degenerated into the mud-slogged horror of trench warfare. Mourning between 4 and 5 million casualties, Europe was inflicted with psychological scars that never healed. In 1917, the United States broke the European deadlock by entering the war.

After the Allied victory, grave economic problems, plus the demoralization stemming from years of fighting, encouraged the growth of socialism and communism. The French government demanded every centime of reparations it could wring from a crushed Germany, humiliating the country into a vengeful spiral that would have repercussions 2 decades later.

The worldwide Great Depression from 1929 devastated France. Poverty and widespread bankruptcies weakened the Third Republic to the point where successive coalition governments rose and fell (although a number of expatriate writers, among them Ernest Hemingway and F. Scott Fitzgerald, enjoyed the dollar exchange rate and relative freedoms while they could). The crises reached a crescendo on June 14, 1940, when Hitler's armies arrogantly marched down the Champs-Elysées, and newsreel cameras recorded French people openly weeping. Under the terms of the armistice, the north of France was occupied by the Nazis, and a puppet French government was established at Vichy under the authority of Marshal Pétain. The immediate collapse of the French army is viewed as one of the most significant humiliations in modern French history. In Europe, Britain was left to counter the Nazi threat alone.

Pétain and his regime cooperated with the Nazis in unbearably shameful ways. Not the least of their errors included the deportation of more than 75,000 French Jews to German work camps. Pockets of resistance fighters (*le maquis*) waged small-scale guerrilla attacks against the Nazis throughout the course of the war. Charles de Gaulle, the irascible giant whose personality is forever associated with the politics of his era, established himself as the head of the French government-in-exile.

The scenario was radically altered on June 6, 1944, when the largest armada in history—a combination of American, British, and Canadian troops—successfully established a beachhead on the shores of Normandy. Paris rose in rebellion even before the Allied armies arrived. On August 26, 1944, Charles de Gaulle entered the capital as head of the government. The Fourth Republic was declared even as pockets of Nazi snipers continued to shoot from scattered rooftops throughout the city.

THE POSTWAR YEARS   Plagued by the bitter residue of colonial policies that France had established during the 18th and 19th centuries, the Fourth Republic witnessed the rise and fall of 22 governments and 17 premiers. Many French soldiers died on foreign battlefields as once-profitable colonies in North Africa and Indochina rebelled. After suffering a bitter defeat in 1954, France ended its occupation of

Vietnam and freed its former colony. It also granted internal self-rule to Tunisia and Morocco.

Algeria was to remain a greater problem. The advent of the 1958 Algerian revolution signaled the end of the much-maligned Fourth Republic. De Gaulle was called back from retirement to initiate a new constitution, the Fifth Republic, with a stronger set of executive controls. To nearly everyone's dissatisfaction, de Gaulle ended the Algerian war in 1962 by granting the country full independence. The sun had finally set on most of France's far-flung empire.

In 1968, major social unrest and a violent coalition hastily formed between the nation's students and blue-collar workers eventually led to the collapse of the government. De Gaulle resigned when his attempts to placate some of the marchers were defeated. The reins of power passed to his second-in-command, Georges Pompidou, and his successor, Valérie Giscard d'Estaing, both of whom continued de Gaulle's policies emphasizing economic development and protection of France as a cultural resource to the world.

In 1981, François Mitterrand was elected the first Socialist president of France since World War II (with a close vote of 51 percent). In almost immediate response, many wealthy French decided to transfer their assets out of the country, much to the delight of banks in Geneva, Monaco, and the Cayman Islands. Though reviled by the rich and ridiculed for personal mannerisms that often seemed inspired by Louis XIV, Mitterrand was reelected in 1988. During his two terms, he spent billions of francs on his *grands projets* (like the Louvre pyramid, Opéra Bastille, Cité de la Musique, and Grande Arche de La Défense), although unemployment and endemic corruption remained.

On his third try, on May 7, 1995, Chirac won the presidency with 52 percent of the vote and immediately declared war on unemployment. But his popularity soon faded in the wake of unrest caused by an 11.5 percent unemployment rate and a stressed economy struggling to meet entry requirements for the European Union that France had signed up for 3 years before.

Financial crisis or not, in May 1996 thousands of Parisian workers took to the streets, disrupting passenger train service to demand a workweek shorter than the usual 39 hours. Most French now work a 35-hour week and retire at 60 years old.

In 1999, France joined with other European countries in adopting the euro as its standard of currency. The new currency accelerated the creation of a single economy comprising over 500 million Europeans, although the ability of several fiscally wayward states to borrow at preferential rates has led to a sovereign debt crisis that remains today. Nonetheless, the European Union now boasts a combined gross national product approaching 17€ trillion, a shade larger than that of the United States.

Although Chirac steadied the ship—and most French today think he ran a decent presidency—in 2005 a rotten core was exposed. Decades of pent-up resentment felt by the children of African immigrants exploded into an orgy of violence and vandalism. Riots began in the suburbs of Paris and spread around the country. Throughout France, gangs of youths battled the French police, torching schools, cars, and businesses. Rioting followed in such cities as Dijon, Marseille, and Rouen. Most of the rioters were the sons of Arab and black African immigrants, Muslims living in a mostly Catholic country. The reason for the protests? Leaders of the riots claimed they live "like second-class citizens," even though they are French citizens. Unemployment is 30 percent higher in the ethnic ghettos of France.

Against a backdrop of discontent regarding issues of unemployment, immigration, and healthcare, the charismatic Nicolas Sarkozy swept into the presidential office in May 2007. Sarkozy, the combative son of a Hungarian immigrant, promised to reinvigorate ties with France's traditional ally, the United States. He even made a summer vacation trip to New England directly after his election.

In the ensuing years, Sarkozy found time to divorce a wife and take a beautiful new bride. A glamorous model-turned-singer, Carla Bruni, became first lady of France in 2008. The tabloids had a field day with Bruni, whose former lovers include Mick Jagger, Eric Clapton, and Donald Trump.

Outside of politics, the French looked at Sarkozy's personal life with ridicule. His marriage to Bruni and his holidays with the rich and famous earned him the title of the "bling bling president." In a show of how divided France was over his administration, he lost the 2012 presidential election to socialist challenger François Hollande by a whisker. Alas, although Hollande promised a government of hard-working technocrats, "Monsieur Normal" proved anything but. A series of gaffes—including employing a minister with a secret Swiss bank account to superintend France's endemic tax evasion—made him, in 2013, the least popular president in 30 years, with a disapproval rating of 75 percent. Soaring unemployment hasn't helped either. Politicians and public alike await the 2017 election with bated breath.

ART

France's manifold art treasures range from Rodin's "The Thinker" to Monet's Impressionist "Water Lilies"; its architecture encompasses Roman ruins and Gothic cathedrals as well as Renaissance châteaux and postmodern buildings like the Centre Pompidou. This brief overview is designed to help you make sense of it all.

A fine place to start is Paris's **Louvre.** The world's greatest museum abounds with Renaissance works by Italian, Flemish, and German masters, including **Michelangelo** (1475–1564) and **Leonardo da Vinci** (1452–1519). Da Vinci's **"Mona Lisa"** (1503–05), the most famous painting on the planet, hangs here.

Back in early 19th century, the **romantics** felt that both the ancients and the Renaissance had gotten it wrong and that the Middle Ages was the place to be. They idealized romantic tales of chivalry and the nobility of peasantry. Some great artists and movements of the era, all with examples in the **Louvre,** include **Theodore Géricault** (1791–1824), who painted "The Raft of the Medusa" (1819), which served as a model for the movement; and **Eugène Delacroix** (1798–1863), whose "Liberty Leading the People" (1830) was painted in the romantic style.

Decades later, the **Impressionists** adopted a free, open style, seeking to capture the *impression* light made as it reflected off objects. They painted deceptively loose compositions, using swift, visible brushwork and often light colors. For subject matter, they turned to landscapes and scenes of modern life. You'll find some of the best examples of their works in the **Musée d'Orsay.**

Impressionist greats include **Edouard Manet** (1832–83), whose groundbreaking "Picnic on the Grass" (1863) and "Olympia" (1863) helped inspire the movement with their harsh realism, visible brush strokes, and thick outlines; **Claude Monet** (1840–1926), who launched the movement officially in an 1874 exhibition in which he exhibited his Turner-inspired "Impression, Sunrise" (1874), now in the **Musée Marmottan; Pierre-Auguste Renoir** (1841–1919), known for his figures' ivory skin and chubby pink cheeks; **Edgar Degas** (1834–1917), an accomplished painter, sculptor, and draftsman—his pastels of dancers and bathers are particularly memorable; and **Auguste Rodin** (1840–1917), the greatest Impressionist-era sculptor, who crafted remarkably expressive bronzes. The **Musée Rodin,** Rodin's former Paris studio, contains, among other works, his "Burghers of Calais" (1886), "The Kiss" (1886–98), and "The Thinker" (1880).

The smaller movements or styles of Impressionism are usually lumped together as "post-Impressionism." Again, the best examples of these turn-of-the-20th-century works are exhibited at the **Musée d'Orsay,** though you'll find pieces by Matisse, Chagall, and the cubists, including Picasso, in the **Centre Pompidou** and the key museums of Nice, Rouen, Avignon and Marseille. Important post-Impressionists include **Paul Cézanne** (1839–1906), who adopted the short brush strokes, love of landscape, and light color palette of his Impressionist friends; **Henri de Toulouse-Lautrec** (1864–1901), who created paintings and posters of wispy, fluid lines anticipating Art Nouveau and often depicting the bohemian life of Paris's dance halls and cafes; **Vincent van Gogh** (1853–90), who combined a touch of crazy Japanese influence with thick, short strokes; **Henri Matisse** (1869–1954), who created **fauvism** (a critic described those who used the style as *fauves,* meaning "wild beasts"); and **Pablo Picasso** (1881–1973), a Málaga-born artist who painted objects from all points of view at once, rather than using such optical tricks as perspective to fool viewers into seeing "cubist" three dimensions.

FRANCE IN POPULAR CULTURE
Books

For a taste of French culture before you travel, we recommend you load a half-dozen titles on your iPad or Kindle. Simon Schama's "Citizens" is the pick of the bunch for a history of the French Revolution. Moving into the 20th century, "Paris Was Yesterday, 1925–1939," is a fascinating collection of excerpts from Janet Flanner's "Letters from Paris" column in the "New Yorker," while "On Paris" comprises a newly bound series of essays by Ernest Hemingway, written for the "Toronto Star" between 1920 and 1924. Two unusual approaches to French history are Rudolph Chleminski's "The French at Table," a funny and honest history of why the French know how to eat better than anyone and how they go about it; and "Parisians: An Adventure History of Paris" by Graham Robb, entertaining historical snippets that range from the French Revolution through the 1968 riots.

And travel? Well, since 1323, some 10,000 books have been devoted to exploring Paris. One of the best is "Paris: Capital of the World," by Patrice Higonnet. This book takes a fresh social, cultural, and political look at the City of Light, exploring Paris as "the capital of sex" and, in contrast, the "capital of art." In "The Flâneur: A Stroll Through the Paradoxes of Paris," Edmund White wants the reader to experience Paris as Parisians do. Hard to translate exactly, a *flâneur* is someone who wanders, loafs, or idles. And for the frequent visitor, Jean-Christophe Napais's "Quiet Corners of Paris: Unexpected Hideaways, Secret Courtyards, Hidden Gardens" is sure to turn up plenty of undiscovered gems.

Representing the city's most fabulous era are "A Moveable Feast," Ernest Hemingway's recollections of Paris during the 1920s, and Morley Callaghan's "That Summer in Paris: Memories of Tangled Friendships with Hemingway, Fitzgerald and Some Others," an anecdotal account of the same period. Another great read is "The Autobiography of Alice B. Toklas," by Gertrude Stein.

For a fictional tour of the 19th century, pick up "Madame Bovary," by Gustave Flaubert. The carefully wrought characters, setting, and plot attest to Flaubert's genius in presenting the tragedy of Emma Bovary; Victor Hugo's "Les Misérables," a classic tale of social oppression and human courage set in the era of Napoleon I; and "Selected Stories," by the master of the genre, Guy de Maupassant.

Films

The world's first movie was shown in Paris on December 28, 1895. Its makers were the Lumière brothers, who scared an audience to death with images of a train moving towards the audience seats. Later, Charles Pathé and Léon Gaumont were the first to exploit filmmaking on a grand scale.

The golden age of the French silent screen on both sides of the Atlantic was 1927 to 1929. Actors were directed with more sophistication, and technical abilities reached an all-time high. The film "Hugo" (2011), directed by Martin Scorsese, is a heart-warming tale set against the film industry's transformation during this period. And despite its mind-numbing length, Abel Gance's masterpiece "Napoleon" (1927) is also sweepingly evocative. Its grisly battle scenes are easily as chilling as any war film made today.

In 1936, the Cinémathèque Française was established to find and preserve old (usually silent) French films. By that time, an average of 130 films a year was made in France, by (among others) Jean Renoir, Charles Spaak, and Marcel Carne. This era also brought such French luminaries as Claudette Colbert and Maurice Chevalier to Hollywood.

After the World War II, two strong traditions—*film noir* and French comedy—offered viewers new kinds of genre, like Jacques Tati's sidesplitting "Les Vacances du Monsieur Hulot" ("Mr. Hulot's Holiday"). By the mid-1950s, French filmmaking ushered in the era of enormous budgets and the creation of such frothy potboilers as director Roger Vadim's "And God Created Woman," which helped make Brigitte Bardot a celebrity around the world, contributing greatly to the image in America of France as a kingdom of sexual liberation.

By the late 1950s, counterculture was flourishing on both sides of the Atlantic. François Truffaut, widely publicizing his auteur theories, rebelled with a series of short films (like "The 400 Blows" in 1959). Other contemporary directors included Jean-Luc Godard ("A Bout de Soufflé"), Alain Resnais ("Muriel"), Agnès Varda ("Le Bonheur"), Jacques Demy ("Les Parapluies de Cherbourg"), and Marguerite Duras ("Detruire, Dit-elle").

Many American films were filmed in Paris (or else used sets to simulate Paris). Notable ones have included the classic "An American in Paris," starring Gene Kelly, and "Moulin Rouge," starring Ewan McGregor as a Parisian artist. "Last Tango in Paris," with Marlon Brando, was one of the most controversial films set in Paris. Woody Allen's acclaimed "Midnight in Paris" is the most recent film to celebrate the City of Light. The film features beautiful shots of the city and includes cameos of iconic figures who lived in Paris in the 1920s. Viewers can also look out to Allen's Gatsby-esque follow-up in 2014, which was filmed on the sun-kissed French Riviera.

One French film that continues to enchant is Jean-Pierre Jeunet's "Amélie," with its beautiful scenes shot in Montmartre. More recently, "La Vie en Rose" earned Marion Cotillard an Oscar in 2008 for her performance as "The Little Sparrow," Edith Piaf.

EATING & DRINKING IN FRANCE

As any French person will attest, French food is the best in the world. That's as true today as it was during the 19th-century heyday of the master chef Escoffier. A demanding patriarch who codified the rules of French cooking, he ruled the kitchens of the Ritz in Paris, standardizing the complicated preparation and presentation of *haute cuisine.*

However, at the foundation of virtually every culinary theory ever developed in France is a deep-seated respect for the *cuisine des provinces* (also known as *cuisine campagnarde*). Ingredients usually included only what was produced locally, and the rich and hearty result was gradually developed over several generations of *mères cuisinières.* Springing from an agrarian society with a vivid sense of nature's cycles, the cuisine provided appropriate nourishment for bodies that had toiled through a day in the open air. The movement is alive and well today with a tradition for eating locally produced—or *zero km*—foods.

Despite the availability of top-quality ingredients across the country, regional cuisine is more sought after than ever before. Try salmon, lark pâté, goat's milk cheese, partridge, rillettes, herb-flavored black pudding, and fine white wines from the Loire Valley. Not forgetting sole, brill, mackerel, turbot, mussels, and big fat lobsters from the Normandy coast, often bathed in the region's rich butter sauce. Just don't forget the Camembert for dessert.

Gourmets, not just beach lovers, should go to the Riviera. Bouillabaisse, an exquisite fish soup said to have been invented by Venus, is Marseille's best-known dish. Riviera specialties include *daube* (slow-cooked beef stew), *soupe au pistou* (vegetable soup with basil), and *salade Niçoise* (traditionally made with tomatoes, olives, radishes, scallions, peppers, and tuna or anchovies). All are best served with a glass of ice-cold *rosé* in the afternoon sun.

And Paris? At the center of the country's gastronomic crossroads, it tops the lot. The city literally has thousands of restaurants to choose from. The best of them are listed in this book, or discussed on websites likes **Chowhound** (www.chow.com) and **Time Out** (www.timeout.fr). Beef from Lyon, lamb from the Auvergne, crêpes from Brittany, and *cassoulet* from southwest France are served up in abundance. This city of 10 million gastronomes has also become a mecca for creative foreign fare. Until you've eaten sashimi, bimimbap, ceviche, and gourmet burgers in Paris, you haven't lived.

To accompany such cuisine, let your own good taste—and your wallet—determine your choice of wine. Most wine stewards, called *sommeliers*, are there to help you in your choice, and only in the most dishonest of restaurants will they push you toward the most expensive selections. Of course, if you prefer only bottled water, or perhaps a beer, or even a cider in Normandy, then be firm and order your choice without embarrassment. Some restaurants include a beverage in their menu rates *(boisson compris)*, either as part of a set tasting menu in ritzy restaurants or as part of a fixed-price formula in cheaper establishments. Some of the most satisfying wines we've drunk in France came from unlabeled house

Impressions

The French will only be united under the threat of danger. Nobody can simply bring together a country that has 265 kinds of cheese.
—Charles de Gaulle

bottles or carafes, called a *vin de la maison*. In general, unless you're a real connoisseur, don't worry about labels and vintages. When in doubt, you can rarely go wrong with a good burgundy or bordeaux. As a rule of thumb, expect to spend about one-third of the restaurant tab on wine.

WHEN TO GO

The best time to visit France is in the spring (Apr–June) or fall (Sept–Nov), when things are easier to come by, from Métro seats to good-tempered waiters. The weather is temperate year-round. July and August are the worst for crowds but best for beaches. That's when Parisians desert their city, leaving it to the tourists.

France's weather varies from region to region. Despite its latitude, Paris never gets very cold. Normandy is a little fresher—and foggier—but the Mediterranean boasts one long summer, with the French Riviera soaking up 300 days of sun per year. Provence dreads *le mistral* (an unrelenting wind), which most often blows in the winter for bouts of a few days at a time, but can also last up to 2 weeks.

Paris's Average Daytime Temperature & Rainfall

	JAN	FEB	MAR	APR	MAY	JUNE	JULY	AUG	SEPT	OCT	NOV	DEC
Temp. °F	38	39	46	51	58	64	66	66	61	53	45	40
Temp. °C	3	4	8	11	14	18	19	19	16	12	7	4
Rainfall (in.)	3.2	2.9	2.4	2.7	3.2	3.5	3.3	3.7	3.3	3.0	3.5	3.1

France Calendar of Events

JANUARY

Monte Carlo Motor Rally (Le Rallye de Monte Carlo). The world's most venerable car race. Mid-January. www.acm.mc

FEBRUARY

Carnival of Nice. Parades, music, fireworks and "Les Batailles des Fleurs" (Battles of the Flowers) are all part of this celebration. The climax is the burning the Carnival king effigy. Late February to early March. www.nice carnaval.com

MARCH

Paris Fashion Week. Jardin des Tuileries, Terrace des Feuillants, 1er, Paris. See what you'll be wearing next season. Early March; also held at end of September. www.whos next.com

Foire du Trône, on the Reuilly Lawn of the Bois de Vincennes, 12e, Paris. This mammoth fun fair operates daily from noon to midnight. Late March to end of May. www. foiredutrone.com.

APRIL

International Garden Festival, Château de Chaumont, Amboise (Loire). An international competition showcasing the best in garden design. Mid-April to mid-October. www. domaine-chaumont.fr

International Marathon of Paris. Runners from around the world compete along the Champs-Elysées. Mid-April. www.paris marathon.com

MAY

Cannes Film Festival (Festival International du Film). Movie madness transforms this Mediterranean town into a media circus. Admission to films and parties is by invitation. Other films play 24 hours a day. Mid-May. www.festival-cannes.com

Normandy Impressionist Festival. New region-wide event that showcases the area's favorite painters (Monet, Manet, Signac) in museums across Normandy, held every 2 to 3 years. May to September. www.normandie-impressionniste.eu

Monaco Formula 1 Grand Prix. The world's most high-tech cars race through Monaco's narrow streets in a blizzard of hot metal and ritzy architecture. Mid-May. www.formula1. com

Festival de St-Denis. A celebration of music in the burial place of the French kings, a grim early Gothic monument in Paris's northern suburb of St-Denis. Late May to late June. www.festival-saint-denis.com

French Open Tennis Championship, Stade Roland-Garros, 16e, Paris. The French Open features 2 weeks of men's, women's, and doubles tennis on hot, red, dusty clay courts. Late May to early June. www.rolandgarros. com

JUNE

Prix du Jockey Club and **Prix Diane-Hermès,** Hippodrome de Chantilly. Thoroughbreds from as far away as Kentucky and Dubai compete in this race. On race days, dozens of trains depart from Paris's Gare du Nord for Chantilly, where racegoers take free shuttle buses to the track. Early to mid-June. www.france-galop.com

Paris Air Show. France's military-industrial complex shows off its high-tech hardware. Fans, competitors, and industrial spies mob Le Bourget Airport. Next event mid-June 2015. www.paris-air-show.com

Les 24 Heures du Mans Voitures. Racing cars blast around the clock at this venerable circuit. Also hosts the huge September motorcycle rally. Mid-June. www.24h-lemans.com

Festival Chopin, Paris. Everything you've ever wanted to hear by the Polish exile, who lived most of his life in Paris. Piano recitals take place in the Orangerie du Parc de Bagatelle, 16e. Mid-June to mid-July. www.frederic-chopin.com

Gay Pride Parade, place du 18 Juin 1940 to place de la Bastille, Paris. A week of expositions and parties climaxes in a parade patterned after those in New York and San Francisco. Late June. www.gaypride.fr

JULY

Les Chorégies d'Orange, Orange. One of southern France's most important lyric festivals presents oratorios, operas, and choral works in France's best-preserved Roman amphitheater. Early July to early August. www.choregies.fr

Les Nocturnes du Mont-St-Michel. This sound-and-light tour meanders through the stairways and corridors of one of Europe's most impressive medieval monuments. Early July to late August. www.ot-montsaint michel.com

Tour de France. The world's most hotly contested bicycle race sends crews of wind-tunnel-tested athletes along an itinerary that detours deep into the Pyrenees, Alps, Provence, and Normandy. The finish line is on the Champs-Elysées. First 3 weeks of July. www.letour.fr

Festival d'Avignon. This world-class festival has a reputation for exposing new talent to critical scrutiny and acclaim. The focus is usually on avant-garde works in theater, dance, and music. Many of the performances take place in the 14th-century courtyard of the Palais des Pâpes. Last 3 weeks of July. www.festival-avignon.com

Bastille Day. Celebrating the birth of modern-day France, the nation's festivities reach their peak with country-wide street fairs, fireworks, and feasts. In Paris, the day begins with a parade down the Champs-Elysées and ends with fireworks at Montmartre. July 14.

Paris Quartier d'Eté. For 4 weeks, music rules sounds around the city. Two-dozen French and international performances take place at a variety of locales, including the church of St-Eustache, the Place de la République, and the Parc de Belleville. Mid-July to mid-August. www.quartierdete.com

Nice Jazz Festival. The most prestigious jazz festival in Europe. Concerts begin in the afternoon and go on until late at night (sometimes all night) in place Masséna and the Jardin Albert 1er, overlooking Nice's promenade des Anglais. Mid-July. www.nicejazzfestival.fr

Festival d'Aix-en-Provence. A musical event *par excellence,* with everything from Gregorian chants to operas composed on synthesizers. Recitals are in the medieval cloister of the Cathédrale St-Sauveur. Expect heat, crowds, and loud sounds. July. Visit www.festival-aix.com

Visitors can purchase tickets for almost every music festival, soccer game, or cultural event in France online. Try the official website first, or log onto **FNAC** (www.fnactickets.com), France's largest music chain, which offers both a digital reservation service as well as in-store ticket booths.

Réncontre d'Arles. The prettiest town in Provence hosts a city-wide photography festival. Prepare to be wowed. July to September. www.rencontres-arles.com.

SEPTEMBER

Deauville American Film Festival. The likes of Clooney, Pitt, and Travolta jet in for a yearly celebration of movies, glitz, and glamour. First week September. www.festival-deauville.com

La Villette Jazz Festival. Some 50 concerts are held in churches, auditoriums, and concert halls in the Paris suburb of La Villette. Past festivals have included Kenny Garrett, Jamie Callum, and other international artists. Early to mid-September. www.jazzalavillette.com

Festival d'Automne, Paris. One of France's most famous festivals is also one of its most eclectic, focusing mainly on modern music, ballet, theater, and art. Mid-September to mid-January. www.festival-automne.com

Festival de la Loire, Orléans (Loire) The Loire River and its banks come alive with sails, music, and food during the largest boat festival in Europe. Late September, every other year; next in 2015. www.orleans.fr

OCTOBER

Paris Auto Show, Parc des Expositions, Porte de Versailles, 15e, Paris. This showcase for European car design comes complete with glitzy attendees, lots of hype, and the latest models. Usually first 2 weeks of October (dates vary). www.mondial-automobile.com

Prix de l'Arc de Triomphe, Hippodrome de Longchamp, 16e, Paris. France's answer to England's Ascot is the country's most prestigious horse race, culminating the equine season in Europe. Early October. www.prixarcdetriomphe.com

NOVEMBER

Armistice Day, nationwide. In Paris, the signing of the document that ended World War I is celebrated with a military parade from the Arc de Triomphe to the Hôtel des Invalides. November 11.

DECEMBER

Boat Fair (Le Salon Nautique de Paris). Europe's major exposition of what's afloat, at the Parc des Expositions, Porte de Versailles. One week in early December. www.salonnautiqueparis.com

Fête de St-Sylvestre (New Year's Eve), nationwide. In Paris, this holiday is most boisterously celebrated in the Quartier Latin. At midnight, the city explodes. Strangers kiss, and boulevard St-Michel and the Champs-Elysées become virtual pedestrian malls. December 31.

RESPONSIBLE TRAVEL

From pioneering eco-friendly *autopartage* (car-sharing) programs to an unabashed enthusiasm for *biodynamique* wines, the French have embraced sustainability. In an age when environmental, ethical, and social concerns are becoming ever more important, France's focus on green principles—whether through traditional markets, carbon-neutral public transport, or all-natural outdoor adventure—offers visitors and residents alike plenty in the way of sustainable tourism.

In 2007, Paris mayor **Bertrand Delanoë** introduced the **Vélib'** scheme (www.velib.paris.fr), a public bicycle "sharing" program. With tens of thousands of bicycles and bike rental stations spread throughout the city, it is a fast and inexpensive way to get around. Similar schemes are in place in many other major French cities, including Nice, Avignon, Aix-en-Provence, Rouen, and Marseille.

Also under Delanoë's guidance, a similar car-sharing program called the **Autolib'** (www.autolib.fr) was launched in Paris in 2011. More than 5,000 eco-friendly and exhaust-free public cars now slip silently around the Parisian streets; passes for their use can be purchased by the hour, day, month, or year.

In order to criss-cross France's vast countryside, many French ditch their cars and opt instead for travel on a **TGV** (www.tgv-europe.com). This network of high-speed trains is powered by SNCF, France's government-owned rail company, which is dedicated to becoming completely carbon-neutral. TGVs run from Paris's hub to cities throughout the country, including Nantes, Rouen, Avignon, Aix-en-Provence, Nice, and Marseille.

Many hotels in France have undertaken measures to preserve the environment, and those that have are awarded with a green label. Look for hotels with the title of *La Clef Verte* (Green Key; www.laclefverte.org) or the **EU Ecolabel** (http://ecolabel.defra.gov.uk). Both labels reward hotels that take a more environmental approach to water, energy and waste, and help raise the awareness of their guests. Even if you don't stay at a green hotel, you can still do your bit: Turn off the air-conditioning when you leave the room, request that your sheets aren't changed every day, and use your towels more than once. Laundry makes up around 40 percent of an average hotel's energy use.

When planning your travels, it's equally important to consider the impact your visit will have on the environment. France's rippling vineyards, **Grande Randonée (GR)** hiking trails, and pristine coastline all make for enchanting (and eco-friendly) escapes.

Responsible tourism also means leaving a place in the same condition you found it. You can do this by not dropping litter and respecting the color-coded garbage bin system. Support the local economy and culture by shopping in small neighborhood stores and at open-air markets that showcase the seasonal harvest of local, often organic *(bio)* producers. Look out for organic and *biodynamique* (biodynamic) wines, frequently sold at wine shops and farmers' markets too. And given the myriad of tiny, family-run restaurants scattered throughout France's cities, towns, and countryside, it's all too easy to dig into a home-cooked meal.

PARIS

by Margie Rynn

The word "Paris" conjures up such a potent brew of images and ideas that it's sometimes hard to find the meeting point between myth and reality. But the city's graceful streets, soaked in history, really are as elegant as they say, its monuments and museums as extraordinary; and a slightly world-weary, *fin-de-siècle* grandeur really is part of day-to-day existence. Paris is much more than a beautiful assemblage of buildings, however; it is the pulsing heart of the French nation.

Where to begin? With so many wonderful things to see, it's easy to get overwhelmed in the City of Light. If you are here for only a few days, you'll probably be spending most of your time in the city center, the nucleus of which is the Île de la Cité. The **top neighborhoods** on most short-term visitors' hit parade are the 1st through 8th arrondissements (see "City Layout," below), which includes the Île de la Cité, the Louvre area, the Champs Elysées, the Eiffel Tower, the Latin Quarter, the Marais, and St-Germain. **If you have a bit more time,** you should explore some of the outlying neighborhoods, like the funky and dynamic eastern areas of Mesnilmontant, Belleville, Canal St-Martin, and Bastille, or the elegant, museum-rich depths of the 16th arrondissement. Whether you're here for a few days or longer, this chapter is designed to give you the essential information you need to create a Paris itinerary that's just right for you.

ESSENTIALS & ORIENTATION

Arriving
BY PLANE
Paris has two international airports: **Aéroport d'Orly,** 18km (11 miles) south of the city (www.aeroportsdeparis.fr; ℂ **00-33-1-70-36-39-50** from abroad, or **39-50** from France), and **Aéroport Roissy-Charles-de-Gaulle** (also known as CDG; ℂ **01-48-62-12-12,** or 39-50 in France), 30km (19 miles) northeast. If you are taking Ryanair or another discount airline that arrives at **Beauvais** (www.aeroportbeauvais.com; ℂ **08-92-68-20-66**), be advised that that airport is located about 70km (40 miles) from Paris.

Getting to the City Center from the Airport
CHARLES DE GAULLE AIRPORT (ROISSY) **By commuter train:** The quickest way into central Paris is the **RER B** (www.ratp.fr), suburban trains that leave every 10 to 15 minutes between 5am and 10pm (midnight

on weekends). It takes about 40 minutes to get to Paris, and RER B ⬚⬚⬚
Métro stations including Châtelet-Les-Halles, Saint-Michel-Notre-D⬚⬚
bourg. A single ticket costs 9.50€ and you can buy it from the mach⬚⬚
stations at both terminals.

By bus: Air France operates two bus routes (**Les Cars Air Fran⬚⬚**
airfrance.com; ✆ **08-92-35-08-20**) from the airport to Port Maillot/Charles d⬚
Etoile and Gare de Lyon/Gare Montparnasse. Depending on the route, a one-way ⬚⬚
costs 15€ to 16€ adults and 7.50€ to 8€ children 2 to 11; both trips take about an hour,
depending on traffic. Buses leave every 30 minutes between 6am and 9:30pm. The
Roissybus (www.ratp.fr; ✆ **32-46** from France only) departs from the airport daily
from 6am to 11pm and costs 10€ for the 60-minute ride. The bus leaves you in the
center of Paris, at the corner of rue Scribe and rue Auber, near the Opera House.

By taxi: A taxi from Roissy into the city will cost at least 50€, not including 1€ per
item of luggage, and the fare is 15 percent higher from 5pm to 10am, as well as on
Sundays and Bank Holidays.

ORLY AIRPORT   By commuter train: Take the 8-minute monorail **OrlyVal** to the
station in the town of Anthony, and take the **RER B** into the center. Combined travel
time is about 45 to 55 minutes. Trains run between 6am and 11pm, and the one-way
fare for the OrlyVal plus the RER B is 11€ adults and 5.65€ children under 10. Alternatively, you can take the **Paris par le Train bus** to the "Pont de Rungis" station and
then get **RER C** to Paris. Buses leave every 15 minutes between 4:40am and 1am.
Combined travel time is about 30 minutes, and the one-way fare for the Paris par le
Train bus and the RER C is 6.40€.

By bus: **Les Cars Air France** (www.cars-airfrance.com; ✆ **08-92-35-08-20**) leaves
every 20 minutes between 6am and 11:40pm, stopping at Gare Montparnasse,
Invalides, and Charles de Gaulle-Etoile. The fare is 12€ one-way, 19€ round-trip, and
5.50€ children ages 2 to 11. Depending on the traffic, the journey takes about an hour.

By taxi: A taxi from Orly to central Paris will cost at least 50€, not including 1€ per
item of luggage, and the fare is 15 percent higher from 5pm to 10am, as well as on
Sundays and Bank Holidays.

BEAUVAIS AIRPORT   Buses leave about 20 minutes after each flight has landed,
and, depending on the traffic, take about 1 hour and 15 minutes to get to Paris. The bus
drops you at Porte Maillot (Métro: Porte Maillot). To return to Beauvais, you need to
be at the bus station at least 3 hours before the departure of your flight. A one-way
ticket costs 16€.

BY TRAIN

Paris has six major train stations: **Gare d'Austerlitz** (13th arrond.), **Gare de Lyon**
(12th arrond.), **Gare Montparnasse** (14th arrond.), **Gare St-Lazare** (8th arrond.),
Gare de l'Est (10th arrond.), and **Gare du Nord** (10th arrond.). Each station can be
reached by bus or Métro; details on each station can be found on the **SNCF** station site
(www.gares-connexions.com/en). **Warning:** As in most major cities, the stations and
surrounding areas are rather seedy and frequented by pickpockets. Be alert, especially
at night.

BY BUS

Most long-haul buses arrive at the **Eurolines France** station on the eastern edge of the
city, 28 av. du Général-de-Gaulle, Bagnolet (www.eurolines.fr; ✆ **08-92-89-90-91;**
Métro: Gallieni).

⌐ris Neighborhoods

RIGHT BANK

1 Louvre & Île de la Cité (1st)
2 Opéra & Grands Boulevards (2nd & 9th)
3 The Marais (3rd & 4th)
4 Champs-Elysées, Trocadéro & Western Paris (8th, 16th & 17th)
5 Montmartre (18th)
6 République, Bastille & Eastern Paris (11th & 12th)
7 Belleville, Canal St-Martin & La Villette (10th, 19th & 20th)

LEFT BANK

8 Latin Quarter (5th and 13th)
9 St-Germain-des-Prés & Luxembourg (6th)
10 Eiffel Tower & Les Invalides (7th)
11 Montparnasse (14th & 15th)

ouldn't recommend driving in Paris to my worst enemy, renting a car and
ound France before or after your Paris trip can be a lovely way to see the
ll of the major car-rental companies have offices here (see below), but you'll
often get better deals if you reserve before you leave home. **AutoEurope** (www.
autoeurope.com) is an excellent source for discounted rentals. Check its prices against
Avis (www.avis.com; ℗ **08-21-23-07-60/**.12€ per min); **Budget** (www.budget.com;
℗ **08-25-00-35-64**); **Europcar** (www.europcar.com; ℗ **08-25-358-358**); **Hertz** (www.
hertz.com; ℗ **08-25-861-861**); **Rent-a-Car** (www.rentacar.fr; ℗ **08-91-700-200**);
Thrifty (www.thrifty.com; ℗ **01-82-88-16-77**).

Before you step on the gas, at the very least, try to get a hold of a list of international
road signs; your rental agency should have one.

Getting Around Town

For everything you ever wanted to know about the city's public transport, visit the
RATP (www.ratp.fr; ℗ **08-92-69-32-46,** or 32-46 in France). Paris and its suburbs are
divided into six travel zones, but you'll probably only be concerned with zones 1 and
2, which cover the city itself.

RATP tickets are valid on the Métro, bus, and RER. You can buy tickets over the
counter (if you are lucky—ticket booths are an endangered species) or from machines
at most Métro entrances. A **single ticket** costs 1.70€ and a *carnet* of 10 tickets costs
13€. Children 4 to 10 years old pay half price; kids under 4 ride free. Tourists can
benefit from a **Paris Visite** pass, which offers unlimited travel in zones on bus, Métro,
and RER, and discounts on some attractions. A 1-day adult pass for zones 1 to 3 costs
11€, a 2-day pass 17€, a 3-day pass 23€, and a 5-day pass 34€. Each day begins at
5:30am and finishes at 5:30am the following day. It is also possible to buy more
expensive passes for zones 1 to 5. Slightly cheaper is the 1-day **Mobilis** ticket, which
offers unlimited travel in zones 1 and 2 and costs 6.60€. For travelers under 26, look
for the **Ticket Jeunes,** a 1-day ticket that can be used on a Saturday, Sunday, or bank
holiday and provides unlimited travel in zones 1 to 3 for 3.65€. The day begins at
5:30am and finishes at 2:30am the following day.

BY MÉTRO OR RER (SUBWAY)

The city's first Métro, or subway, was at the apex of high tech when it was inaugurated on July 19, 1900. Today, more than a century later, it still functions very well.
Aside from the occasional strike or work slowdown, the Métro is usually efficient and
civilized, especially if you avoid rush hour (7:30–9:30am and 6–8pm). It's generally
safe at night (although you might want to think twice about using it to get to more
isolated parts of the city); the service shuts down between midnight and 1am weekdays, and at 2am on Friday, Saturday, and pre-holiday evenings. The suburban trains
(the RER; see below) close down around the same time (without the weekend bonus
hour). The **RER** (pronounced "ehr-euh-ehr") is the suburban train network that
dashes through the city making limited stops. The downsides are: (a) They don't run
as often as the Métro, and (b) they're hard to figure out since they run on a different
track system and the same lines can have multiple final destinations. **Important:**
Make sure to hold on to your ticket; you'll need it to get *out* of the turnstile on the
way out.

Velib': A Great Way to Cycle Around Paris

Since July 2007, when the mayor's office inaugurated the **Velib'** (vel-LEEB) system of low-cost bike rentals, Parisians have been pedaling up a storm. Traffic be dammed: It's fun to ride around town, drop off your bike near your destination, and not have to worry about locking it up. The way it works is this: You buy a 1- or 7-day subscription (1.70€ or 8€, respectively) from the machine at one of hundreds of bike stands, which gives you the right to as many half-hour rides as you'd like for 1 or 7 days. If you want to go over a half-hour, you pay 1€ for your extra half-hour, 2€ for the half-hour after that one and 4€ for the third half-hour on. Everything is meticulously explained, in English, on the website, www.velib.fr. There's one big catch, however—to use the machines you must have a credit or debit card with a chip in it. This can be a problem for North American tourists, so I advise either getting a TravelEx "cash passport" with money on it (www.travelex.com), or, even easier, just buy your subscription online (make sure you have your secret code to punch in on the stand). Helmets are not provided, so if you're feeling queasy about launching into traffic, bring one along. There are few bike lanes so far, but success has been such that new ones are being added, and cyclists have the right to ride in the bus lanes. **One more tip:** Before you ride, get a map of the city that shows where the bike stands are so you don't waste precious time looking for a place to check in or check out.

BY BUS

Thanks to a rash of new dedicated bus lanes, the buses can be an efficient way to get around town, and you'll get a scenic tour to boot. The majority run from 6:30am to 9:30pm (a few operate until 12:30am), and service is reduced on Sundays and holidays. You can use Métro tickets on the buses or you can buy tickets directly from the driver (1.90€). Tickets need to be validated in the machine next to the driver's cabin. Your ticket gives you a free transfer, to be used within 1½ hours.

BY TRAM

Over the past few years, Paris has added three new tramway lines, with extensions and new lines in progress. They connect Paris with its suburbs; within Paris they run along the outer circle of boulevards that trace the city limits. Tickets are the same price as the Métro.

BY BICYCLE

Cycling in Paris has been revolutionized by the hugely successful **Vélib'** bike rental scheme (the name comes from *vélo* meaning bicycle and *liberté* meaning freedom) launched in 2007. It takes a little effort for a tourist to sign up, but it's worth it to see Paris from two wheels (see box, below).

Alternatively, you can rent a bike from **Paris à vélo, c'est sympa!,** 22 rue Alphonse Baudin (www.parisvelosympa.com; ✆ **01-48-87-60-01;** Métro: St-Sébastien-Froissart or Richard Lenoir). Rentals cost 12€ for half a day and 15€ for a full day, but they do require 250€ or a passport as a deposit.

BY CAR

Driving is *not* recommended in Paris, but the auto-adventurous may want to try tooling around in a small electric car through **Autolib'** (www.autolib.eu; *©* **08-00-94-20-00**), the recent outgrowth of the popular Velib' bicycle rental program (see above). A similar concept to its cycling cousin, the scheme involves short-term electric car rental. To register you can go to one of the Autolib' parking spaces or to the Autolib' information center (5 rue Edouard, 5th arrond.) with your driving license, a valid form of I.D., and a credit card, or you can simply register online. A 1-day subscription is free, but you pay 9€ per half-hour. A 7-day subscription is 10€ plus 7€ per half-hour, a month is 25€ plus 6.50€ per half-hour, and a year is 120€ plus 5.5€ per half-hour. You are given a badge that you then pass over a sensor at a rental station to unlock the car. Unplug it from the charger and drive away. To return it, you must find a spot at an Autolib' station and plug in your car.

Visitor Information

A good place to start any information quest is at the Paris Tourist Office (25 rue des Pyramides, 1st arrond.; www.parisinfo.com; *©* 08-92-68-30-00/34€ per minute; Métro: Pyramides). There's always a multilingual person on the other end of the line when you call (if you'd prefer not to spring for an international call, surf to their comprehensive website). The Tourist Office has several branches sprinkled around the city; check the website for addresses and hours.

City Layout

One of the nice things about Paris is that it's relatively small. It's not a sprawling megalopolis like Tokyo or London; in fact, Paris *intramuros,* or inside the long-gone city walls, numbers a mere 2.2 million habitants, and, excluding the large exterior parks of Bois de Vincinnes and the Bois de Boulogne, measures about 87 sq. km (34 sq. miles). (The suburbs, on the other hand, are sprawling, but chances are you won't be spending much, if any, time there.) So getting around is not difficult, provided you have a general sense of where things are.

The city is vaguely egg shaped, with the Seine cutting a wide upside-down "U"-shaped arc through the middle. The northern half is known as the **Right Bank,** and the southern, the **Left Bank.** To the uninitiated, the only way to remember is to face west, or downstream, so that the Right Bank will be to your right, and the Left to your left.

If you can't get your banks straight, don't worry, because most Parisians don't talk in terms of Right or Left Bank, but in terms of *arrondissements,* or districts. The city is neatly split up into 20 official arrondissements, which spiral out from the center of the city. So the lower the number, the closer you'll be to the center, and as the numbers go up, you'll head toward the outer limits. Though their borders don't always correspond to historical neighborhoods, they do chop up the city into easily digestible chunks, so if you know what arrondissement your destination is in, your chances of finding it easily go way up. Your chances will be even better if you have a good map. Even if you're only in the city for a week, it's worthwhile to invest in a purse-size map book (ask for a "Paris par Arrondissement" at bookstores or larger newsstands), which costs around 8€. The book should include a street index and a detailed set of maps by arrondissement—one of the best is called "Le Petit Parisien," which includes separate Métro, bus, and street maps for each district. To get a general sense of where the arrondissements are, see the map on p. 34.

WHERE TO STAY

Paris has more than 1,500 hotels, from palaces fit for a pasha... tions whose best features are their warm welcome and person... should be able to find something in line with your budget, your... personal tastes. But even if you can't find the hotel of your dreams... don't despair—at the end of this section I list a few alternative lodging... ing bed-and-breakfasts and short-term apartment rentals.

The Right Bank
LOUVRE & ÎLE DE LA CITÉ (1ST ARRONDISSEMENT)

The area surrounding the Louvre is littered with hotels, most of which are dreadfully overpriced. Yes, if you only are in town for 1 or 2 days, a central locale is key, since time is of the essence. But if you have a little more time, you'll find much more comfortable lodgings, at the same or lower prices, a 10-minute walk away.

Expensive

Hotel Brighton ★★   Did someone say "view"? How about a panorama of the Louvre and the Tuileries gardens from your bed? While not every room in this gracious hotel has the jackpot view, those in the "deluxe" and "executive" categories do, and all have a subdued, classic look with elegant fabrics draping windows and tasteful decorative touches. This classy establishment under the arcades of the rue de Rivoli may not be not quite as grand as the Meurice, just down the block, but it is also about one-third the price. Understandably, rooms with views book up early, so plan ahead.

218 rue de Rivoli, 1st arrond. ℂ **01-47-03-61-61.** www.hotel-britannique.com. 61 units. 239€–450€ double; 339€–420€ suite. Métro: Tuileries. **Amenities:** Bar, concierge, room service, Wi-Fi (free).

Moderate

Hôtel Thérèse ★★   Just a few steps from the Palais Royal and the Louvre, these recently overhauled lodgings combine old-fashioned Parisian charm with modern Parisian chic. Soft grey/teal blues highlight a creative decor that complements the building's age instead of fighting it. Comfy sofas invite you to relax in the lobby, whose stylish look includes mirrors, bookcases, and unique lighting fixtures. The comfort factor extends to the rooms, many of which have very high ceilings, interesting drapery fabrics, and upholstered headboards.

5–7 rue Thérèse, 1st arrond. ℂ **01-42-96-10-01.** www.hoteltherese.com. 40 units. 180€–350€ double. Métro: Palais-Royal or Pyramides. **Amenities:** Library/bar, Wi-Fi (free).

Le Relais du Louvre ★   This friendly hotel is right around the corner from the Louvre; some rooms even have great views of both the museum's neoclassical colonnade and the flying buttresses of the church of Saint-Germain l'Auxerrois. While not particularly stylish, rooms are very nicely outfitted with top-grade mattresses and Directoire-style furniture. Most are average size, but some are remarkably large for Paris; families will be particularly happy with the spacious triples, suites, and connecting rooms.

19 rue des Prêtres-St-Germain-l'Auxerrois, 1st arrond. ℂ **01-40-41-96-42.** http://relais-du-louvre-paris.com/fr/. 22 units. 175€–250€ double; 250€–290€ triple; 290€–330€ suite. Métro: Louvre-Rivoli or Pont Neuf. **Amenities:** Computer and printer for guests, concierge service, room service, Wi-Fi (free).

...ank Hotels & Restaurants

HOTELS ■

Cosmos Hotel **41**
Ermitage
  Sacré-Coeur **20**
Hôtel Alison **6**
Hôtel Arvor
  Saint Georges **15**
Hôtel Balzac **3**
Hotel Brighton **8**

Hôtel Caron de
  Beaumarchais **30**
Hôtel Chopin **23**
Hôtel du Cygne **25**
Hôtel Jeanne d'Arc
  le Marais **33**
Hôtel Résidence
  Alhambra **40**
Hôtel Thérèse **12**

Le Citizen **43**
Le Relais du Louvre **27**
Le Relais Montmartre **18**
New Orient Hôtel **5**
Pavillon de la Reine **34**

RESTAURANTS ◆

Aki **13**
Bar Le Passage **7**
Benoit **28**
Bob's Juice Bar **42**
Boulangerie
  Joséphine **2**
Café des
  Musées **32**

Caïus **1**
Casa Olympe **14**
Chartier **24**
Chéri Bibi **21**
Chez Grenouille **17**
Chez Michel **22**
L'As du Fallafel **31**
L'Ebauchoir **36**

La Gazzetta **35**
Lasserre **4**
Le Bistrot du
  Peintre **39**
Le Bistrot
  Paul Bert **37**
Le Felteu **29**
Le Grand
  Véfour **11**

Le Nemours **10**
Le Pantruche **16**
Mansouria **38**
Nansouty **19**
Pinxo **9**
Rosa Bonheur **44**
Spring **26**

Inexpensive

Hôtel du Cygne ★ Chock-full of exposed beams and stone walls, this 17th-century building has been carefully restored, and the simple lodgings receive ongoing tender loving care. Most rooms are predictably small but cheerfully decorated, with fresh white walls, floral bedspreads, and the owner's personal touch. If you can handle the climb to the top floor, you'll be rewarded with a roomy suite that sleeps three. The hotel is located near Les Halles (a little seedy at night) and the Montorgueil neighborhood (very hip at night). There is no elevator.

3–5 rue du Cygne, 75001 Paris. ✆ **01-42-60-14-16.** www.cygne-hotel-paris.com. 18 units. 122€–132€ double; 147€ suite. Métro: Etienne Marcel. RER: Les Halles. **Amenities:** Wi-Fi (free).

LE MARAIS (3RD & 4TH ARRONDISSEMENTS)

Centuries ago, this neighborhood was a swamp *(marais)*, but now it's merely swamped with stylish boutiques, restaurants, and people who seem to have just stepped out of a hair salon. Stunning 16th- and 17th-century mansions house terrific museums; the narrow streets harbor clothing stores, cool bars, clubs, and the remnants of the city's historic Jewish quarter.

Expensive

Pavillon de la Reine ★★★ Just off the place des Vosges, the "Queen's Pavilion" harkens back to the days when the magnificent square was home to royalty. Set back from the hustle and bustle of the Marais, this heavenly hideaway feels intimate, like a lord's private hunting lodge in the country. The decor is a suave combination of subtle modern and antique: The dark period furniture blends with rich colors on the walls and beds; choice objects and historic details abound. Several deluxe duplexes have staircases leading to cozy sleeping lofts.

28 place des Vosges, 3rd arrond. ✆ **01-40-29-19-19.** www.pavillon-de-la-reine.com. 54 units. 400€–550€ double; 600€–1,200€ suite. Métro: Bastille. **Amenities:** Bar; concierge; fitness room, room service, spa, Wi-Fi (free).

Moderate

Hôtel Caron de Beaumarchais ★★★ In the 18th century, Pierre Auguste Caron de Beaumarchais—author of "The Barber of Seville"—lived near here, and this small hotel celebrates both the playwright and the magnificent century he lived in. Delightful details give you a taste of what life was like back in the day: Walls are covered in high-quality reproductions of period fabrics; rooms are furnished with authentic antique writing tables; and period paintings and first-edition pages of "The Barber of Seville" hang on the walls. A pianoforte that dates from 1792 stands in the lobby, next to an antique card table set up for a game. You half expect Pierre Auguste himself to come prancing through the door.

12 rue Vieille-du-Temple, 4th arrond. ✆ **01-42-72-34-12.** www.carondebeaumarchais.com. 19 units. 165€–195€ double. Métro: St-Paul or Hôtel de Ville. **Amenities:** Wi-Fi (free).

Inexpensive

Hôtel Jeanne d'Arc le Marais ★★ With a prime location, comfortable rooms, and great prices, it's no wonder this hotel books up months in advance. It's located in the lower Marais, right next to the leafy place du Marché St-Catherine. Most of the rooms here sport an old-fashioned look, with warm colors and wooden furniture; several others have recently been given a makeover, with a fresh decor and new bathrooms. The management is art-inclined: The mosaic mirror in the lobby and the painted walls in the breakfast room are creations of local artists. Note: There is another hotel with the same name in the 13th arrondissement—make sure you are contact the right when you reserve, or you'll be in for an unpleasant surprise.

3 rue de Jarente, 4th arrond. ℰ **01-48-87-62-11.** www.hoteljeannedarc.com. 35 units. 81€–119€ double; 149€ triple; 164€ quad. Métro: St-Paul. **Amenities:** Wi-Fi (free).

CHAMPS-ÉLYSÉES, TROCADÉRO & WESTERN PARIS (8TH, 16TH & 17TH ARRONDISSEMENTS)

Affordable lodgings are scarce in this opulent environment, especially near the Champs and the Arc de Triomphe, where high prices often have more to do with location than the quality of the lodging. Ironically, the location is not particularly central; it's a good hike from here to Notre-Dame.

Expensive

Hôtel Balzac ★★★   Built for the director of the Paris Opéra in 1853, this classy townhouse occupies the site of Balzac's last residence, which he bought when he finally married his great love, Ewelina Hanska. Just a few steps away from the Champs-Élysées, these luxurious lodgings feature refined bedrooms in soothing shades of gray and beige, warmed up with upholstery and window dressings in vibrant colors such as plum and copper. The delightful decor remains faithful to the building's 19th-century origins, while integrating a dash of modern edge. Some rooms have views of the Eiffel Tower; all have marble bathrooms.

6 rue Balzac, 8th arrond. ℰ **01-44-35-18-00.** www.hotelbalzac.com. 69 units. 340€–600€ double; 650€–1,200€ suite. Métro: George V. **Amenites:** Restaurant, bar, room service, concierge, private parking (23€), Wi-Fi (free).

Moderate

Hôtel Alison ★★   While the lobby decor at this comfortable, family-run hotel hasn't changed since at least 1982 (think Almodóvar movies), it's impeccably clean and shiny, as are the relatively spacious rooms. However you feel about beige walls and chocolate carpets, you should be pleased with the generally high level of comfort here, and the location is excellent: around the corner from the Madeleine and a short stroll to the Champs Elysées and the Place de la Concorde.

21 rue de Surène, 8th arrond. ℰ **01-42-65-54-00.** www.hotel-alison.com. 34 units. 162€–189€ double. Métro: Charles-de-Gaulle–Etoile or George V. **Amenities:** Bar, Wi-Fi (free).

Inexpensive

New Orient Hôtel ★★   This lovely hotel, which offers comfortable rooms with high ceilings, 19th-century moldings, and antique headboards and armoires, may not be on top of the Champs Elysées, but it's not far, and it is close to stately Parc Monceau and a quick trot to the Saint Lazare train station. The friendly owners, inveterate flea market browsers, have refinished and restored the antique furniture themselves. Rooms (many of which have small balconies) are in tip-top shape, and bathrooms sparkle. Though there's an elevator, you'll have to negotiate stairs to get to it.

16 rue de Constantinople, 8th arrond. ℰ **01-45-22-21-64.** www.hotelneworient.com. 30 units. 140€–175€ double, 185€ suite for 4. Métro: Villiers, Europe, or St-Lazare. **Amenities:** Computer in lobby, Wi-Fi (free).

OPÉRA & GRANDS BOULEVARDS (2ND & 9TH ARRONDISSEMENTS)

This area offers a lovely mix of hip bars and restaurants and old-time Paris, with a sprinkling of small museums for a dose of culture. While the area has few big monuments, its up sides include lower room rates and a more neighborhood-y feel.

4

Moderate

Hôtel Arvor Saint Georges ★★   Located in the charming "New Athens" neighborhood, where 19th-century Romantics like George Sand and Frédéric Chopin lived and worked, these spiffy lodgings offer an arty yet relaxed atmosphere, where fresh white walls show off modern photography and Daniel Buren graphics. Rooms are a little small, but simple and chic, with white walls, a splash of color, and a distinctive table or armchair. The airy lobby area, with large windows and bookshelves (natch) is an invitation to kick back and read or sip a cup of tea. The tasty breakfast is served here or outside in the flower-filled patio when the weather is nice. The friendly staff will give you a map of their favorite nearby restaurants.

8 rue Laferrière, 75009 Paris. ✆ **01-48-78-60-92.** http://hotelarvor.com. 30 units. 100€–220€ double. Métro: St-Georges. **Amenities:** Bar; Wi-Fi (free).

Inexpensive

Hôtel Chopin ★   Nestled at the back of the delightful Passage Jouffroy, this budget hotel has remarkably quiet rooms considering its location in the middle of the rush and bustle of the Grands Boulevards. The staircase is a little creaky (you have to climb a flight to get to the elevator), and the decor is nothing to write home about, but the rooms are clean and colorful and the bathrooms are spotless. Rooms on the upper floors get more light; many have nice views of Parisian rooftops.

10 bd. Montmartre or 46 passage Jouffroy, 9th arrond. ✆ **01-47-70-58-10.** www.hotel-chopin.com. 36 units. 98€–118€ double; 140€ triple. Métro: Grands Boulevards or Richelieu-Drouot. **Amenities:** Wi-Fi (free).

MONTMARTRE (18TH ARRONDISSEMENT)

Once you leave behind the tourist hordes that invade the Sacré-Coeur and Place du Tertre, you'll find a neighborhood of lovely little lanes and small houses, harkening back to the days when Picasso and the boys were at the Bateau Lavoir. Unfortunately, the pickings are slim if you want to actually sleep here. Another consideration: Although Montmartre is charming, it's on the northern edge of the city, so you'll need to budget extra time to get back down the hill to the center of town.

Moderate

Le Relais Montmartre ★★   Run by the same management as Le Relais Louvre, these comfortable lodgings include small but impeccable rooms decked out in light, warm colors and a classic decor. Nothing particularly hip or stylish here, just quality accommodations in tasteful floral prints, plus reliable service. The one decorative quirk: exposed beams on the ceilings in shades of lavender and blue. The hotel is located on a peaceful little side street, right around the corner from a delicious stretch of food shops on Rue Lepic. There are connecting rooms for families, and a lovely little patio for breakfasting in good weather.

6 rue Constance, 18th arrond. ✆ **01-70-64-25-25.** www.hotel-relais-montmartre.com. 26 units. 176€–259€ double, 218€–259€ triple. Métro: Blanche. **Amenities:** Concierge service, laundry service, iPad for guests, Wi-Fi (free).

Inexpensive

Ermitage Sacré-Coeur ★★★   Built in 1890 by a rich gentleman for his mistress, this beautifully preserved townhouse has been lovingly converted into an intimate hotel. It may not offer room service (although a complimentary breakfast is served in your room) or much by way of amenities, but the ambience is unique. Tucked behind the Sacre-Coeur, this small mansion still feels like a private home. In fact, it virtually is: The Canipel family has run these unconventional lodgings for more than 40 years. Each of the five rooms is decorated in period prints and draperies, with beautiful antique bedsteads and armoires. The hallways and entry are done up in deep blues and gold leaf; the wall murals and paintings are the works of a local artist. The hotel has no elevator.

24 rue Lamarck, 18th arrond. ℰ **01-42-64-79-22.** www.ermitagesacrecoeur.fr. 5 units. 115€–120€ double; 150€ triple; 170€ quad. Rates include breakfast. No credit cards. Métro: Lamarck-Caulaincourt. Parking 20€. **Amenities:** Wi-Fi (free).

RÉPUBLIQUE, BASTILLE & EASTERN PARIS (11TH & 12TH ARRONDISSEMENTS)

Encompassing the recently overhauled place de la République, as well as the historic place de la Bastille, this area is a good choice for both budget travelers and creatures of the night—it includes the bars and clubs of the Oberkampf and Charonne neighborhoods, and is close to the Marais.

Inexpensive

Cosmos Hotel ★   Just around the corner from the animated Oberkampf neighborhood, this budget option is one of the best deals in town. The modern rooms are generally spotless; aside from a few nicks on the walls, everything from the bed linens to the floor covering looks spanking new. And such a deal: only 65€ to 72€ a double. Furthermore, the staff is friendly and helpful. The only downside: Weekend nights can be noisy as people spill out of the busy bars and cafes nearby.

35 rue Jean-Pierre Timbaud, 75011 Paris. www.cosmos-hotel-paris.com. ℰ **01-43-57-25-88.** Fax 01-43-57-25-88. 36 units. 62€–70€ double; 78€ triple. AE, MC, V. Métro: Parmentier. **Amenities:** TV, hair dryer, Wi-Fi (free).

Hôtel Résidence Alhambra ★   Recently reopened after a complete overhaul, this budget classic now sports a lobby in chic shades of gray and lots of polished concrete. Rooms are polished as well, with splashes of bright color. Tucked in the crook of this L-shaped hotel is a large, leafy garden with tables for alfresco breakfasts. You can even bring your own eats and picnic here after 10am. Eight of the guest rooms on the bottom floor open directly onto a balcony over the garden; about half of the others face onto it. Requests for garden views are taken, but no guarantee you'll get it.

13 rue de Malte, 11th arrond. ℰ **01-47-00-35-52.** www.hotelalhambra.fr. 53 units. 124€–149€ double; 189€–209€ triple; 229€ quad; 249€–299€ family suite. Métro: Oberkampf. **Amenities:** Computer and printer in lobby, Wi-Fi (free).

BELLEVILLE, CANAL ST-MARTIN & LA VILLETTE (10TH, 19TH & 20TH ARRONDISSEMENTS)

When historic arty neighborhoods like Saint-Germain and Montmartre became too expensive for up-and-coming artists, many immigrated to these more proletarian neighborhoods, giving the area a funky, bohemian feel. Even though it's gentrifying, Belleville is still known for artists' studios, while dozens of hip cafes and restaurants have popped up along the Canal St-Martin and the Bassin de la Villette. The young and adventurous will appreciate this part of town, but others may find it too much of a commute to the city center.

Moderate

Le Citizen ★★   Maybe it's the smiling young staff in jeans, or the ecological ethos, but there's something alternative in the air at this adorable boutique hotel on the Canal St-Martin. While the rooms are on the small side, they are light and airy, with lots of blonde wood and clean lines; all look out on the tree-lined canal. When you check in, you'll be handed an iPad loaded with information and apps on Paris. A delicious buffet breakfast is included in your room rate.

96 quai de Jemmapes, 10th arrond. ℭ **01-83-62-55-50.** www.lecitizenhotel.com. 12 units. 199€– 249€ double, 289€ suite, 470€ apartment. Rates include breakfast. AE, MC, V. Métro: Jacques Bonsergent. **Amenities:** Room service; smoke-free rooms; A/C, TV, minibar (free), hairdryer iPad, Wi-Fi (free).

The Left Bank
LATIN QUARTER (5TH & 13TH ARRONDISSEMENTS)
Central and reasonably priced, the Latin Quarter is a long-time favorite for travelers in search of affordable accommodations. As a consequence, a few corners of this famously academic neighborhood are overrun with tourists and trinket shops. The streets immediately surrounding the place St-Michel (especially around rue de la Huchette) are where you'll find the worst tourist traps, both hotel and restaurant-wise; better prices and quality are to be had in the quieter and more authentic areas around the universities, a little farther from Notre-Dame but still within easy walking distance.

Moderate
Hôtel des Jardins du Luxembourg ★★   Just around the corner from its glorious namesake, these intimate lodgings are tucked away on a quiet impasse, an excellent hideaway for a romantic honeymoon or cozy retreat. The building's claim to fame is that Sigmund Freud stayed here on his first visit to Paris; perhaps this has something to do with the 1930s and 1940s touches to the decor. The Art Deco ambience of the lobby and lounge invites deep reflection or at least a nice rest in one of the plush armchairs; for full relaxation, indulge in a visit to the sauna. While the standard rooms are quite pretty, with curly wrought-iron headboards and puffy comforters (cotton or feather), the superior rooms, which cost only 10€ more, have nicer views, small balconies, snazzy bathrooms, and designer-fabric-covered walls.

5 impasse Royer-Collard, 5th arrond. ℭ **01-40-46-08-88.** www.les-jardins-du-luxembourg.com. 26 units. 142€–188€ double. Métro: Cluny–La Sorbonne. RER: Luxembourg. **Amenities:** Bar; Wi-Fi (free).

Hôtel Saint-Jacques ★★   The spacious rooms in this delightful hotel retain lots of architectural details from its Belle Epoque past. Most of the ceilings are adorned with masses of curlicues, and some have restored 18th-century murals to gaze at while you laze in bed. Modern reproductions of famous French paintings hang on the walls; Second Empire–themed murals decorate the lobby and breakfast room. The romantic decor has a light, feminine feel, all shades of light blue, cream, and gray—considerably more inviting than when the hotel served as a set for the Audrey Hepburn/Cary Grant classic "Charade." Service is especially friendly here.

35 rue des Ecoles, 5th arrond. ℭ **01-44-07-45-45.** www.paris-hotel-stjacques.com. 26 units. 135€–260€ double; 180€–292€ triple. Métro: Maubert-Mutualité. **Amenities:** Babysitting, bar, Wi-Fi (free).

Inexpensive
Hôtel des Grandes Ecoles ★★★   Tucked into a private garden on the slope of the Montagne St-Genviève, this hotel makes you feel as if you have just walked out of Paris and into the countryside. A path leads to a flower-bedecked interior

courtyard, where birds chirp in the trees; the reception area adjoins an inviting breakfast room with potted plants and an upright piano. The spotless rooms are filled with country-style furniture and papered in old-fashioned prints; crocheted bedspreads and framed etchings of flowers complete the look. The calm is such that the hotel has nixed TVs. Incredibly, this unique ambience comes at an extremely reasonable price. Families will appreciate the six large suites that can sleep four.

75 rue de Cardinal-Lemoine, 5th arrond. ℭ **01-43-26-79-23.** www.hotel-grandes-ecoles.com. 51 units. 120€–140€ double; 145€–150€ family room. Parking 30€. Métro: Cardinal Lemoine or Place Monge. **Amenities:** Wi-Fi (free).

ST-GERMAIN-DES-PRÉS & LUXEMBOURG (6TH ARRONDISSEMENT)

Sleek boutiques and restaurants abound in this legendary neighborhood; historic cafes and monuments lend plenty of atmosphere. Unlike some other Parisian neighborhoods, this one is lively even late at night; it is also centrally located and within walking distance of many top sights.

Expensive

Relais St-Germain ★★★ Fashioned from three adjoining 17th-century townhouses, this intimate hotel mixes old-world charm and jazzy modernity. Exposed beams abound in the spacious rooms, even the smallest of which are equipped with a comfortable sitting area. The decor artfully blends period furniture with modern prints, like the Louis XV armchair covered in zigzagged leather, or the 18th-century painting hung in the middle of a wall of mirrors. The effect is both stylish and deeply comforting. There are some extra stairs between floors, so if you have mobility issues, be sure to make that clear when you reserve. Guests have priority at the hotel restaurant, **Le Comptoir** (p. 60), where you might otherwise have a 6-month wait for a reservation. Book your room at least a month in advance.

9 carrefour de l'Odéon, 6th arrond. ℭ **01-44-27-07-97.** www.hotelrsg.com. 22 units. 285€–370€ double; 395€ suite. Rates include breakfast. **Amenities:** Restaurant; free Wi-Fi. Métro: Odéon.

Inexpensive

Hotel Mayet ★★ You would never know it, but the owner of this young-at-heart hotel was once a gerontologist. There is certainly nothing elderly about the lobby, which sports two murals, one by American graffiti artist JohnOne and the other by his French counterpart André. Rooms are snug but colorful, with white walls and touches of bright orange. The hotel has a lighthearted North African theme, with paintings of camels in the desert and vintage photos of beautiful Moroccan movie stars. This family-run enterprise also has an apartment for rent next door that sleeps four with a kitchen and washer-dryer.

3 rue Mayet, 75006 Paris. ℭ **01-47-83-21-35.** www.mayet.com. 23 units. 130€–175€ double; 170€–190€ triple. Métro: Duroc. **Amenities:** Bar, free Wi-Fi.

EIFFEL TOWER & NEARBY (7TH ARRONDISSEMENT)

For some reason, many visitors to Paris clamor for hotels that are right near the Eiffel Tower, perhaps under the mistaken impression that this is a central location. It isn't. Still, there's no denying that this extremely posh area is beautiful, and there is something magical about wandering out of your hotel in the morning and seeing the Eiffel Tower looming in the background.

Left Bank Hotels & Restaurants

HOTELS ■

Hôtel des Bains **11**
Hôtel des Grandes
  Ecoles **27**
Hôtel des Jardins
  du Luxembourg **26**
Hôtel du Champ
  de Mars **4**
Hôtel Eber Mars **5**
Hôtel Londres Eiffel **3**
Hôtel Mayet **9**
Hôtel Muget **6**
Hôtel Saint-Jacques **24**
L'Apostrophe **14**
Relais St-Germain **21**

RESTAURANTS ◆

Café Constant **2**
Café de Flore **15**
Café de la Mairie **17**
Cobéa **12**
Crêperie Josselin **10**
Dans les Landes **29**
Foyer Vietnam **28**
Itinéraires **25**
La Régalade **13**

L'Arpège **8**
Le Casse Noix **1**
Le Comptoir
  du Relais **20**
Le P'tit Fernand **18**
Le Pré Verre **23**
Le Relais Louis XIII **19**
Les Deux Magots **16**
Restaurant Auguste **7**
Restaurant Polidor **22**

Expensive

Hôtel Londres Eiffel ★★   From the moment you enter, you feel like you are in a private home. In fact, you may very well be welcomed by Samba, the lovely golden retriever, before you meet the Prigents, the friendly owners. Polished wood banisters lead up spiral staircases to narrow hallways and cozy rooms decorated with a personal touch. The hotel has an old-fashioned, if modern, feel; walls are covered with fabrics printed with tasteful 19th-century kitsch motifs, furniture is 1940s style, and the comfort level is terrific. A few rooms have views of the Eiffel Tower (just steps away). It books up early. Connecting rooms are available for families.

1 rue Augereau, 7th arrond. 🕐 **01-45-51-63-02.** www.londres-eiffel.com. 30 units. 240€–280€ double; 300€ triple. Métro: Ecole Militaire. **Amenities:** Wi-Fi (free).

Moderate

Hôtel Eber Mars ★★   When you walk in the door, chances are you will be greeted by none other than Monsieur Eber himself, who has spent the last 10 years lovingly renovating his hotel. The 1930s-era decor is low-key and specifically Parisian. Walls in the spacious rooms are papered in period patterns in neutral colors, lit by authentic Art Deco hanging fixtures found at antiques fairs. Old-fashioned radiators have been scraped and lacquered; prints dating from the Universal Exposition of 1889 (which unveiled the Eiffel Tower—another decor theme) are hung on the walls. Rooms in this hotel are unusually large for Paris; the triples and connecting suites are ideal for families.

117 av. de la Bourdonnais, 7th arrond. 🕐 **01-47-05-42-30.** www.hotelebermars.com. 25 units. 120€–280€ doubles, 200€–300€ triples. Métro: Ecole Militaire. **Amenities:** Free Wi-Fi and computer access in common areas, in-room Wi-Fi (2€/day).

Hôtel Muget ★   Comfort is key at this personable hotel, where the conscientious staff has considered the smallest details of your stay. The lovely rooms are fitted with faux-antique furniture, big wood headboards hand-painted with a lily-of-the-valley *(muguet)* motif, and pretty new bathrooms with old-fashioned wooden washstands and mirror frames. Rooms are relatively large for Paris, and the triples are downright spacious. Five doubles have a great view of the Eiffel Tower, three others of Les Invalides; needless to say these book up months in advance. The others, which are equally comfy and less expensive, look out on either the quiet street or the airy courtyard. Three rooms on the ground floor look onto a small but lush garden.

11 rue Chevert 7th arrond. 🕐 **01-47-05-05-93.** www.hotelmuguet.com. 43 units. 175€–280€ double, 250€–300€ triple. Métro: Varenne or La Tour Maubourg. **Amenities:** Computer and printer in lobby; Wi-Fi (free).

Inexpensive

Hôtel du Champ de Mars ★★   An adorable and affordable little inn right around the corner from the food shops of rue Cler—what more could you ask for? Owners Françoise and Stéphane Gourdal offer all of their comfortable doubles at one great price: 120€. The impeccably maintained rooms are decorated with the kind of care people generally reserve for their own homes: thick cotton bedspreads, framed etchings, and printed fabrics in warm colors on the walls and windows. The friendly staff includes a delightful cocker spaniel named Cannelle.

7 rue du Champ de Mars, 7th arrond. 🕐 **01-45-51-52-30.** www.hotelduchampdemars.com. 25 units. 120€ double. Métro: Ecole Militaire. **Amenities:** Laptop loan for guests; Wi-Fi (free).

MONTPARNASSE & NEARBY (14TH & 15TH ARRONDISSEMENTS)

Montparnasse is more centrally located than it might seem—it's right on the border of St-Germain and close to the Luxembourg gardens. Also, the train station is a major transit hub for a bundle of Métro lines and bus routes. Though the utterly unaesthetic Tour Montparnasse now casts a shadow over this ancient artists' haunt (Henry Miller, Man Ray, Chagall, Picasso . . .), the little streets in the surrounding area are still full of personality.

Moderate

L'Apostrophe ★   Honoring the neighborhood's literary history (nearby writers' haunts include La Coupole and the Closerie des Lilas), this "poem hotel" is dedicated to the beauty and mystery of writing. The decor is a little off the wall, but very tastefully so, starting with an impressive silhouette of a tree on the hotel's façade. Inside, rooms are themed: "Caligraphy" has Chinese characters splashed on royal blue walls, "Musique" features stenciled sheet music, instruments, and giant piano keys. The larger rooms include a Jacuzzi bathtub right in the room.

3 rue de Chevreuse, 6th arrond. ℂ **01-56-54-31-31.** www.apostrophe-hotel.com. 16 units. 149€–310€ standard double; 199€–353€ double with a Jacuzzi. Métro: Vavin. **Amenities:** Bar; free Wi-Fi.

Inexpensive

Hôtel des Bains ★★   With cute, comfortable rooms and excellent rates, this friendly hotel is one of the best deals on the Left Bank, especially for families. In a city where large rooms are rare, it offers several good-size, two-room suites for up to four people. Doubles are amply sized as well, with high ceilings; the largest ones face the pretty courtyard. The decor is simple but nicely accessorized with objects and artwork from the art market that takes place on the nearby square every Sunday. The elevator stops at a landing between floors, which have a few stairs.

33 rue Delambre, 14th arrond. ℂ **01-43-20-85-27.** www.hotel-des-bains-montparnasse.com. 42 units. 98€ double; 130€–165€ suites for 2–4 people. Métro: Vavin, Edgar Quinet or Montparnasse. **Amenities:** Wi-Fi (free).

WHERE TO EAT

Everywhere you look in Paris, someone is doing their best to ruin your waistline. *Boulangeries* (bakeries) with buttery croissants and decadent pastries lurk on every street corner; open-air markets tempt the senses; and restaurants with intriguing menus sprout up on every block.

Fortunately, you don't have to have a king-size budget to dine like royalty. As ever, there are those world-famous, multistarred restaurants that everyone has heard about. But recently, a whole new crop of "neo-bistros" has emerged, offering high-quality eats for a fraction of what you would pay in a gourmet palace. One outgrowth of this movement is the obsession with "noble" ingredients—that is, high-quality, regional produce or products, often from a specific small-scale farm or artisan, sometimes organic, but always in keeping with the oldest and best traditions.

Note: Restaurants tend to be small in Paris, and when it comes to reservations, size matters. To be sure to get a table, reserve ahead for most of the restaurants listed below under the "Expensive" or "Moderate" categories.

The Right Bank

LOUVRE & ÎLE DE LA CITÉ (1ST ARRONDISSEMENT)

Dining near the Louvre can be an expensive and frustrating affair; it's rife with over-priced, mediocre tourist restaurants boasting menus in at least five languages. If you poke around some of the smaller streets however, you'll discover plenty of little restaurants where you can eat well and affordably. That said, if you are ready to spend, gourmet opportunities abound.

Expensive

Le Grand Véfour ★★★ CLASSIC FRENCH   Channel centuries of history at this illustrious restaurant, where Napoléon, Danton, Hugo, Colette, and Cocteau all once dined. Thanks to Guy Martin, chef and owner for the past decade, the food is as memorable as the magnificently preserved 18th-century salon: Signature dishes like Prince Rainier III pigeon and truffled oxtail parmentier share the menu with new creations with contemporary flavors like sumac and star anise. The desserts are incredible, especially the *palet* (a thick biscuit) with milk chocolate and hazelnuts, served with caramel and sea-salt ice cream. Reserve at least 2 weeks in advance, and note that the lunch fixed-price menu is a third of the price of the dinner prix fixe.

17 rue de Beaujolais, 1st arrond. ⓒ **01-42-96-56-27.** www.grand-vefour.com. Main courses 84€–105€; fixed-price lunch 98€, fixed-price dinner 298€. Mon–Fri 12:30–1:45pm and 8–9:45pm. Closed August. Métro: Louvre–Palais-Royal or Pyramides.

Spring ★★★ MODERN FRENCH   One of the city's most talked-about restaurants has a chef who is—gasp—American! Try not to think about that and just enjoy the amazing dishes that come out of the kitchen. Chef Daniel Rose, native of Chicago, pays utmost respect to all things French while adding a dash of Yankee derring-do to his superb creations. The menu changes all the time, but it might start with quail eggs with lemony eggplant caviar, followed by filet of sole with mussels, smoked ham, and green tomatoes. It's a four-course fixed-price menu only, which doesn't seem to be a problem for diners, who fight for a seat here. The buzz is so strong and the capacity so small (40 diners max) that you should reserve around 3 months in advance.

6 rue Bailleul, 1st arrond. ⓒ**01-45-96-05-72.** www.springparis.fr. Fixed-price lunch 49€, fixed-price dinner 79€. Wed–Fri noon–2pm; Tues–Sat 7–10pm. Closed 2nd week in Aug. Métro: Louvre-Rivoli.

Moderate

Pinxo ★★ MODERN FRENCH/TAPAS   Sample renowned chef Alain Dutournier's exquisite cooking in a relaxed atmosphere at this modern tapas restaurant where food is made to be shared. Everyone grazes on small plates with magnificent mouthfuls (each dish is priced per person on the menu) such as lobster ravioli with artichoke emulsion; nuggets of lamb with cépes (wild mushrooms); or organic marinated salmon with herring and fennel. The best way to wash it all down is with a glass of wine (of course)—choose from 120 bottles, many of which are available by the glass. A second location is at 82 rue Mazarine in the St-Germain neighborhood.

9 rue d'Alger, 1st arrond. ⓒ **01-40-20-72-00.** www.alaindutournier.com. Portions per person 5€–9€, meal per person 35€–40€. Mon–Fri 12:15–2:15pm and 7–10:30pm, Sat 7–10:30pm. Closed Aug. Métro: Tuileries.

Inexpensive

Aki ★ JAPANESE   Of the dozens of Japanese restaurants on rue Ste-Anne, this one, which specializes in *okonomiyaki,* stands out. This delicious dish is a sort of grilled

It's 3pm. All of the restaurants are closed and you are dreaming of something light and healthy to eat. Fear not: Look for one of the following healthy gourmet chains that are multiplying around offices and shopping areas.

Cojean (21 locations; www.cojean.fr): A creation of an ex-MacDonald's executive with an almost religious fervor for fresh, healthy food, these airy, modern boutiques serve innovative salads, as well as quiches, sandwiches, and fresh-squeezed juices. Many veggie options. Open until 4 or 5pm in most locations.

Exki (8 locations; www.exki.com): This Belgian chain (pronounced "ex-KEY," like the Fren___ "exquisite") offers a te___ tasty, healthy sandwich___ desserts (vegetarian ch___ or 10pm. It uses lots of ___ trade, seasonal ingredie___ ___ ___ a low ecological footprint.

Boco (3 locations; www.boco.fr): This place is almost too good to be true. Organic takeout from Michelin-starred chefs for under 15€? Be still, my beating heart. Hot food, cold food, light meals, and desserts are served daily until 8 or 10pm (Mon–Fri 11am–4pm at Saint-Lazare location). Main dishes run around 10€, and, gasp, a three-course meal costs 15€.

omelet topped with meat or seafood and a yummy sauce. Watch the cooks create yours on a griddle in the open kitchen. It also serves udon and soba noodles. Arrive early or be prepared to wait in line.

11bis rue Sainte Anne, 1st arrond. ℂ **01-42-97-54-27.** Main courses 10€–15€. Mon–Sat 11am–10:45pm. Métro: Pyramides.

OPÉRA & GRANDS BOULEVARDS (2ND & 9TH ARRONDISSEMENTS)

Buzzing with cafes and theaters back in the 19th century, the long-overlooked Grand Boulevards have come back to life, especially near the Opéra and the hip part of the 9th arrondissement that borders Montmartre. Less trendy, but also less expensive, the little streets around the Bourse (the French stock exchange) have a wide range of restaurant options, especially at lunchtime.

Expensive

Casa Olympe ★★ MEDITERRANEAN/MODERN FRENCH   Olympe Versini earned a Michelin star in her 20s and has been writing cookbooks and dazzling discerning palates ever since. One of the pioneers of "nouvelle cuisine" in the 1970s, she has since moved on to warmer climes, as reflected in the menu. There is a distinctly Mediterranean flair to dishes like marinated sardines, sautéed swordfish with almonds, sweetbreads with Pantelleria capers, and roast shoulder of lamb with thyme. Finish off with whipped lemon sherbet with Prosecco.

48 rue St-Georges, 9th arrond. ℂ **01-42-85-26-01.** www.casaolympe.com. Main courses 24€–30€; fixed-price menu lunch 25€, fixed-price menu dinner 42€. Mon–Wed noon–2pm and 7:30–10:30pm; Thurs–Fri noon–2pm and 7:30–11pm; Sat 7:30–11pm. Closed 2nd and 3rd week of Aug. Métro: St-Georges.

Moderate

Chez Grenouille ★ TRADITIONAL FRENCH   Chef Alexis Blanchard has won prizes for his pâtés and *boudins* (blood sausage), so you'll find all manner of on the menu here, plus updated classics such as suckling pig with foie gras, ...mentier, sweetbreads, oxtail, and pigs' feet, plus a fish dish or two for lighter ...s. The cooking may not be "heart smart," but it is delicious. Finish with a boozy baba au rhum.

52 rue Blanche, 9th arrond. ⓒ **01-42-81-34-07.** www.restaurant-chezgrenouille-paris.com. Main courses 20€–35€; fixed-price lunch 25€, fixed-price dinner 35€. Mon–Fri noon–3pm and 7–11pm; Sat 7–11pm Métro: Trinité.

Le Pantruche ★★ TRADITIONAL FRENCH/BISTRO   The name is old-fashioned slang for Paris, but this little bistro has a decidedly modern feel to it. Another case of a runaway chef from Michelin-starred restaurants, Le Pantruche offers flavorful updated bistro fare like braised sweetbreads with carrots in a licorice glaze, or suckling pig with pears, celery root, and chestnuts. The atmosphere is relaxed, and the fixed-price menus at lunch and dinner are a terrific value.

3 rue Victor Massé, 9th arrond. ⓒ **01-48-78-55-60.** www.lepantruche.com. Lunch main courses 14€; dinner main courses 19€–25€, fixed-price dinner 34€; fixed-price lunch 18€. Mon–Fri noon–2:30pm and 7:30–10:30pm. Closed 1st 3 weeks of Aug. Métro: Pigalle.

Inexpensive

Chartier ★★ TRADITIONAL FRENCH   With a dining room that can seat over 300, this gargantuan establishment is one of the last of the *bouillons,* or workers' restaurants, found all over Paris back in the 19th century. The idea was to offer good food at modest prices, a concept that still speaks to working Parisians some 100 years later, if the line out the door is any indication. You come here for the experience more than for the food, which is tasty but certainly won't win any Michelin stars. The menu covers a wide variety of traditional dishes like roast free-range chicken with fries, or rump steak with pepper sauce. Service is fast and furious (how could it not be with this many tables?), but it's all part of the atmosphere, which is something that belongs to another time and place. It takes no reservations, so be prepared to wait.

7 rue du Faubourg Montmartre, 9th arrond. ⓒ **01-47-70-86-29.** www.restaurant-chartier.com. Main courses 8.60€–12€. Daily 11:30am–10pm. Métro: Grands-Boulevards.

LE MARAIS (3RD & 4TH ARRONDISSEMENTS)

You should have no trouble finding good things to eat in the Marais. Between its working-class roots and its more recent makeover, it offers s a wide range of choices, from humble falafel joints to trendy brasseries.

Expensive

Benoit ★★ TRADITIONAL FRENCH   This historic bistro had already hosted a century's worth of Parisian notables when Alain Ducasse took the helm in 2005. The dining room is still lined with mirrors, zinc, and tiles, while the classic menu has been given an extra dash of pizzazz. Escargots in garlic butter and brill braised with Jura wine share the stage with roasted milk-fed lamb from the Pyrenées and sautéed scallops *grenobloise.* The sommelier will help you navigate the huge wine list.

20 rue St-Martin, 4th arrond. ⓒ **01-42-72-25-76.** www.benoit-paris.com. Main courses 24€–52€; fixed-price lunch 38€. Daily noon–2pm and 7:30–10pm. Closed first 3 wks of Aug. Métro: Hôtel-de-Ville.

Moderate

Café des Musées ★★ TRADITIONAL FRENCH/BISTRO   Weary culture vultures who've tried to do both the Picasso museum and the Musée Carnavalet on the same day will appreciate this bustling corner cafe with its appealing sidewalk tables. This is not just any old corner cafe, mind you, but one where the inventive chef works wonders with bistro classics like steak frîtes and *andouillette* (tripe sausage) as well as lighter fare like fresh vegetable casserole with basil oil, or shrimp with Thai curry. The lunch fixed-price menu is particularly good value.

49 rue de Turenne, 3rd arrond. ℂ **01-42-72-96-17.** www.cafedesmusees.fr. Main courses 12€–21€; fixed-price lunch 15€, fixed-price dinner 25€. Daily noon–3pm and 7–11pm. Closed mid-Aug to early Sept. Métro: St. Paul or Chemin Vert.

Inexpensive

L'As du Fallafel ★ FALAFEL/ISRAELI   This Marais institution offers, without a doubt, the best falafel in Paris. True, falafel joints are scarce in this city, but that doesn't take away from the excellence of these overstuffed beauties, brimming with cucumbers, pickled turnips, shredded cabbage, tahini, fried eggplant, and those crispy balls of fried chickpeas and spices. Wash it down with an Israeli beer. Service is fast and furious, but basically friendly—be prepared to deal with hordes of tourists and locals at lunch. Closed Friday afternoon and all day Saturday.

34 rue des Rosiers, 4th arrond. ℂ **01-48-87-63-60.** Main courses 6€–16€. Sun–Thurs 11am–11:30pm; Fri 11am–5pm. Métro: St. Paul.

Le Felteu ★ TRADITIONAL BISTRO   It's easy to walk right by this unassuming restaurant, where locals crowd in to the clean but shabby dining room for copious portions of excellent food. You'll usually find either Brigitte or her husband, Jerry, the longtime owners, behind the bar chatting with the regulars. Meanwhile, the kitchen is sending out grilled lamb, blood sausage *(boudin)* and sautéed apples, or some other delicious bistro fare. Each dish is garnished with the vegetable du jour and/or a hearty portion of potato gratin.

15 rue Pequay, 4rd arrond. ℂ **01-42-72-14-51.** Main courses 14€–22€. No credit cards. Mon–Fri 12:30–2:15pm and 8–10:30pm, Sat 8–10:30pm. Closed Aug. Métro: Rambuteau or Hôtel de Ville.

CHAMPS-ÉLYSÉES & WESTERN PARIS (8TH, 16TH & 17TH ARRONDISSEMENTS)

Mobbed with tourists, oozing with opulence, the Champs-Elysées is a difficult place to find a good meal, unless you are willing to spend a lot of money. Mediocre chain restaurants abound on the grand avenue itself, and kebob joints mingle with frighteningly expensive gourmet palaces on the surrounding side streets.

Expensive

Caïus ★★ MODERN FRENCH   While the chef at this elegant dinning room is a fan of spices and herbs from faraway lands, Jean-Marc Notelet's subtle cuisine also makes use of top-quality French ingredients, like mussels from Brittany, veal from Corrèze, and free-range pork raised on apples and acorns. Menu must-haves include cod with lemongrass and combava, grilled duck with sumac, and beef confit with tonka beans and niora. Be sure to reserve: Tables fill quickly with a devoted local clientele.

6 rue d'Armaillé, 17th arrond. www.caius-restaurant.fr. ℂ **01-42-27-19-20.** Main courses 26€; fixed-price dinner 42€. Mon–Fri noon–2pm and 7:30–10:30pm. Closed 3 wks in Aug. and last wk in Dec. Métro: Argentine.

Lasserre ★★★ GOURMET FRENCH   André Malraux, Salvador Dali, Audrey Hepburn, Marlene Dietrich—the list of celebrities who have dined at this legendary restaurant is understandably long. What famous person wouldn't want to eat in this superb dining room, where the ceiling opens when the weather is willing? A silk-draped, arch-windowed affair, the room glistens with fine porcelain, silver knick-knacks, and crystal candelabras. The young chefs have recently brought new life to the classic menu, adding their own subtle creations, such as sea bass with vegetables in chardonnay, or roasted lamb confit with artichokes and apples. Reserve at least 2 weeks ahead. Dinner jackets required for men.

17 av. Franklin D. Roosevelt, 8th arrond. ℂ **01-43-59-02-13.** www.restaurant-lasserre.com. Main courses 70€–115€; fixed-price lunch 80€, fixed-price dinner 195€. Thurs–Fri noon–2pm; Mon–Sat 7–10pm. Closed Aug. Métro: Franklin Roosevelt.

Moderate

Bar Le Passage ★★ MODERN FRENCH   So you want to experience the cuisine of Alain Senderens but don't want to empty your bank account? This bar/restaurant located on the first floor of the gourmet palace serves the same quality food at an incredible price: just 36€ for a three-course lunch and 41€ for a four-course dinner. You might sample an asparagus velouté with quail eggs, a vanilla-infused lobster, or a yuzu dacquoise for dessert. Anything's possible. If you don't trust the chef, you can also order à la carte. The room is small and fills up quickly; reserve at least a week in advance for a table on the weekend.

9 place de la Madeleine (entrance passage de la Madeleine), ℂ **01-42-65-56-66.** www.senderens. fr. Main courses 20€–30€; fixed-price lunch 36€, fixed-price dinner 41€. Daily noon–2:45pm and 7:30–11pm. Closed 1st 3 weeks of Aug. Métro: Madeleine.

Inexpensive

Boulangerie Joséphine BAKERY/SANDWICHES/FRENCH   This terrific bakery near the Arc de Triomphe has a nice outdoor terrace and a pretty upstairs dining room that fills quickly with local office workers and businesspeople at lunchtime. You can buy sandwiches and salads (and desserts, of course) to go, or sit down for table service and sample one of the excellent daily specials, like stuffed vegetables, roast chicken, or osso bucco. Also open for continental breakfast from 7am.

69 av. Marceau, 8th arrond. ℂ **01-47-20-49-62.** www.josephine-boulangerie.com. Main courses 5€–15€. Mon–Fri 7am–7pm. Closed for 1 wk in mid-Aug. Métro: Charles de Gaulle–Etoile.

MONTMARTRE (18TH ARRONDISSEMENT)

When you get away from the tourist traps of Place du Tertre, you start to understand why this neighborhood is a favorite with the arty-hipster set. And where there's art, you are bound to find an artist in the kitchen.

Moderate

Chéri Bibi ★ TRADITIONAL FRENCH   Sitting pretty on the eastern side of the Sacré-Coeur, Cheri Bibi has become the unofficial canteen for the young and artsy Montmartre crowd. The affordable menu features classic French fare with modern touches, like a tender flank steak with homemade chutney or beef stew with coriander. The decor is understated hip, with flea-market chairs and exposed stone walls. The crowd gathered around the restaurant's zinc bar sipping wine sometimes spills out onto the sidewalk on a warm night. Open only in the evenings.

15 rue André del Sarte, 18th arrond. ℂ **01-42-54-88-96.** Main courses 16€–35€; fixed-price dinner 23€–26€. Mon–Sat 8–11pm (until 2am for the bar). Métro: Barbes-Rochechouart or Chateau Rouge.

Nansouty ★★ MODERN FRENCH   Just north of the Butte de Montmartre, this popular wine bar will appeal to both gourmets and wine enthusiasts. Choose from than

100 bottles on the massive blackboard, and supplement with top-quality nibbles. Can't make up your mind? Just ask the waitstaff, who are wise in the ways of Bacchus. The changing seasonal menu features tasty, hearty offerings. Open only in the evenings.

35 rue Ramey, 18th arrond. ℰ **01-42-52-58-87.** Main courses 17€–26€. Mon–Sat 7:30–11:30pm. Métro: Lamarck-Caulincourt or Château Rouge.

RÉPUBLIQUE, BASTILLE & EASTERN PARIS (11TH & 12TH ARRONDISSEMENTS)

Home to a mix of working-class families, hipsters, and *bobos* (bourgeois bohemians), the area between République and Nation is diverse, young, and fun. This might be why there are so many good restaurants around here. It's also a good neighborhood for discovering the flavors of Africa in restaurants featuring dishes from France's former colonies.

Expensive

La Gazzetta ★★ MODERN FRENCH   Just down the street from the bustling outdoor food market at Aligre, this beautiful, old-fashioned-looking bistro is helmed by a chef whose cooking is anything but traditional. How about spelt risotto with nettles, or mackerel with burnt spring onions—topped off with goat-cheese ice cream with roasted apricots for dessert? It may sound strange, but it tastes fantastic. Fans of experimental cooking can savor the seven-course tasting menu for 65€; at lunch the less adventurous can order a fixed-price menu with three tiny appetizers and a main dish for 17€, an excellent price for this level of quality.

29 rue de Cotte, 12th arrond. tel] **01-43-47-47-05.** www.lagazzetta.fr. Fixed-price dinner 39€–65€; fixed-price lunch 17€. Tues–Sat noon–3pm and 7–11pm. Métro: Ledru-Rollin.

Moderate

Le Bistrot Paul Bert ★★ BISTRO/TRADITIONAL FRENCH   Ask any local food writer to name his or her favorite classic bistro, and there's a good chance you'll be directed here. The chalkboard menu changes with the seasons, but you can usually count on one of the city's best steak frîtes (here crowned with a glistening morsel of marrow), followed by a generous slice of *tarte tatin* (apple tart) served with thick crème fraîche. The decor is a jumble of wooden tables, cracked tile floors, flea-market finds, and polished zinc bar—exactly how you imagine a neighborhood bistro should be.

18 rue Paul Bert, 11e. ℰ **01-43-72-24-01.** Reservations required. Main courses 17€–25€; fixed-price dinner 34€. MC, V. Tues–Sat noon–2pm and 7:30–11pm. Métro: Faidherbe-Chaligny.

Mansouria ★★ MOROCCAN   Generally accepted as the queen of Moroccan cooking (she's published half a dozen cookbooks), Fatéma Hal rules supreme in the kitchen of this elegant restaurant. Naturally, it offers wide variety of delicious couscous dishes, garnished with fragrant broths and grilled meats, but the real treat here are the *tagines,* or stews, like the one with chicken and walnut-stuffed figs, or another with lamb, eggplant, and preserved lemons. Hal goes to the roots of this illustrious cuisine: One dish, La Mourouzia, is prepared from a 12th-century recipe featuring lamb seared in real *ras al hanout*—an intense mixture of 27 spices—and stewed in honey, raisins, and almonds.

11 rue Faidherbe, 11th arrond. ℰ **01-43-71-00-16.** www.mansouria.fr. Main courses 18€–20€; fixed-price dinner 28€–36€. Mon 7:30–11pm; Tues–Sat noon–2pm and 7:30–11pm. Métro: Faidherbe-Chaligny.

Inexpensive

L'Ebauchoir ★ Located in an unlikely corner of the 12th arrondissement, this neighborhood hangout offers a great selection of modern bistro cooking at reasonable prices. The high ceilings, sunny yellow walls, and wooden fixtures create a friendly atmosphere for Mediterranean-inspired dishes like roast lamb with sweet garlic, polenta and olives, or grilled bonito with a peach and preserved lemon salad. Vegetarian options include eggplant and feta with olives and fresh capers. Serving one of the last surviving reasonable three-course lunches (15€), this place gets jammed at noontime, so try to reserve.

43 rue des Citeaux, 12th arrond. ℂ **01-43-42-49-31.** www.lebauchoir.com. Main courses dinner 18€–25€; fixed-price lunch 13€–15€. Mon 8–11pm, Tues–Fri noon–2:30pm and 8–11pm, Fri–Sat noon–2:30pm and 7:30–11pm. Métro: Faidherbe Chaligny or Reuilly Diderot.

BELLEVILLE, CANAL ST-MARTIN & NORTHEAST PARIS (10TH, 19TH & 20TH ARRONDISSEMENTS)

One of the last strongholds of Paris's bohemian set, here you can find both gourmet bistros and funky cheap eats, as well as a good number of wine bars that serve both nibbles and the fruit of the vine.

Moderate

Chez Michel ★★ BRETON/SEAFOOD Prices haven't budged in a decade at this popular restaurant, where chef Thierry Breton improvises on recipes from back home (Brittany), including, naturally, lots of seafood dishes, like *cotriade*, a Breton fish stew, or fresh crab salad. A massive oven has been installed in the dining room itself, cooking up slow-cooked specialties like braised lamb. For dessert, try the copious rice pudding or the awe-inspiring Paris-Brest (a choux pastry filled with praline cream).

10 rue de Belzunce, 10th arrond. ℂ **01-44-53-06-20.** Fixed-price lunch 28€–34€, fixed-price dinner 34€. Tues–Fri noon–3pm and Mon–Fri 7pm–midnight. Closed Aug. Métro: Gare du Nord.

Rosa Bonheur ★ TAPAS This unconventional space is named after an unconventional 19th-century painter/sculptress. Yes, it's a restaurant and tapas bar, but it's also a sort of off-the-wall community center, hosting various expositions and events—it even has its own chorus and soccer team. Located in an old *buvette* (refreshment pavilion) inside the Parc des Buttes Chaumont, dating from the Universal Exposition of 1900, the restaurant boasts a sprawling terrace and one of the best panoramic views in town. A huge crowd gathers to drink and nibble tapas outside or sample dishes from the creative menu. An indoor play area and kids' menu make this a good family option.

2 av. de la Cascade, 19th ℂ **01-42-00-00-45.** www.rosabonheur.fr. Tapas 6€–9€; main courses 16€–22€. Wed–Sun noon–midnight. Métro Botzaris.

Inexpensive

Bob's Juice Bar ★ VEGETARIAN Hip Parisians are tripping all over themselves to try "smoossies" (that is, smoothies) these days, and some of the best can be found at this terrific vegetarian restaurant, which has muffins, bagels, soups and other delicious goodies. The brainchild of Marc Grossman (alias "Bob"), an erstwhile New Yorker, this may not be the most authentically French experience, but it certainly is a tasty one. Sit down or take out here, or try the larger **Bob's Kitchen** in the Marais (74 rue des Gravilliers), which is open on weekends.

15 rue Lucien Sampaix, 10th arrond. ℂ **09-50-06-36-18.** Smoothies 4€; main courses 7€–8€. Mon–Fri 8am–3pm. Métro: Jacques Bonsergent.

The Left Bank

LATIN QUARTER (5TH & 13TH ARRONDISSEMENTS)

Steer clear of the unbearably touristy area around rue de la Huchette and the often mediocre restaurants on rue Moufftard. Venture farther afield, where innovative restaurateurs have been cultivating a knowledgeable clientele of professors, professionals, and savvy tourists like yourself.

Expensive

Itinéraires ★★ FRENCH FUSION After earning acclaim at 24 years old with his tiny tapas bistro in the 11th arrondissement, gifted chef Sylvain Sendra has opened this elegant enterprise devoted to finding the meeting point between French and more farflung cuisines. The seasonal menu features lots of organic ingredients and might include a lamb confit with sweet spices and cauliflower couscous or poached cod in sage broth with mushrooms and aioli. Finish your meal with a Vahlrona chocolate soufflé tart with coffee ice cream.

5 rue de Pontoise, 5th arrond. ℂ **01-46-33-60-11.** www.restaurantitineraires.com. Main dishes 25€–28€; fixed-price lunch 29€ and 35€, fixed-price dinner 59€ and 79€. Tues–Sat noon–2pm and 7pm–10:30pm. Closed Aug. Métro: Maubert-Mutualité.

Moderate

Dans les Landes ★★ SOUTHWESTERN FRENCH/TAPAS Chef Julien Duboué takes inspiration from his native homeland and neighboring Basque country to create luscious tapas to be sampled with (many) glasses of great regional wines. Fried *chipirions* (small squid that are crisp, golden, and dusted with smoky pepper), polenta with smoked duck breast, Basque-style mussels—the list is long and tempting. During the winter months the restaurant offers a regular-sized *plat du jour* (daily special) for those who want a "real" meal. It's packed at night, so get there early or reserve a table.

119 bis rue Monge, 5th arrond. ℂ **01-45-87-06-00.** Tapas 5€–23€; plat du jour 16€. Daily noon–11pm. Closed Aug. Métro: Censier-Daubenton.

Le Pré Verre ★★ MODERN FRENCH/ASIAN FUSION This crowded and convivial gourmet wine bar offers dishes that are a scrumptious blend of traditional French and exotic ingredients—not particularly flashy or trendy or even spicy, just deliciously unexpected. One of the signature dishes is a meltingly tender *cochon de lait* (milk-fed pork) served with a smooth cinnamon-infused sauce and a delectably crunchy mass that turns out to be cabbage. The weekday lunch menu is a particularly great deal: You get an appetizer, a main dish, a glass of wine, and coffee for 14€.

8 rue Thenard, 5th arrond. ℂ **01-43-54-59-47.** www.lepreverre.com. Main courses 20€; fixed-price lunch 14€–31€, fixed-price dinner 31€. Tues–Sat noon–2pm and 7:30–10:30pm. Métro: Maubert-Mutualité or Cluny-La Sorbonne.

Inexpensive

Foyer Vietnam ★★ VIETNAMESE A local institution, this humble restaurant is usually crammed with students, professors, and working stiffs who come for the generous portions of Vietnamese classics. The Foyer has recently become an official nonprofit dedicated to all things Vietnam, so you can enjoy art and seminars after you slurp your steaming bowl of *pho* (meat broth with vermicelli and vegetables). Another yummy meal in a bowl, *bò bún* (6€), is a heap of rice vermicelli with sliced beef and a delicious tangy sauce. Finish with a Vietnamese *cà phê*, a drip coffee—the beans are roasted with butter and rum, giving it an exquisite flavor.

80 rue Monge, 5th arrond. ⓒ **01-45-35-32-54.** www.foyer-vietnam.org. Main courses 7€–9.50€; fixed-price lunch 10€. No credit cards. Mon–Sat noon–2pm and 7–10pm. Métro: Place Monge.

ST-GERMAIN-DES-PRÉS (6TH ARRONDISSEMENT)

Saint Germain is a mix of expensive eateries that only the lucky few can afford and stalwart holdouts from the days when poverty-stricken intellectuals and artists frequented the Café de Flore. Though the Marché St-Germain has been transformed into a type of mall, the restaurants hugging its perimeter offer a wide range of possibilities.

Expensive

Le Comptoir du Relais ★★ TRADITIONAL FRENCH/BISTRO   The brainchild of super-chef Yves de Camdeborde, this small and scrumptious bistro is still bringing in the crowds almost a decade after it opened. During the day, it's a bistro serving relatively traditional fare, say, a slice of lamb with thyme sauce or maybe the *panier de cochonaille,* a basket of the Camdeborde family's own brand of smoked meats. On weeknights, it's a temple to haute cuisine, with a five-course tasting menu. You'll need to reserve several weeks (at least) in advance for this meal, which changes every night and is nonnegotiable—the chef decides what you are going to eat. There are no reservations at lunch or on the weekends, when the bistro menu is served from noon to 11pm, so arrive early or be prepared to wait.

9 carrefour de l'Odéon, 6th arrond. ⓒ **01-44-27-07-50.** www.hotel-paris-relais-saint-germain.com. Main courses weekends and weekdays 15€–29€; fixed-price dinner weeknights 60€. Daily noon–11pm. Métro: Odéon.

Le Relais Louis XIII ★★★ CLASSIC FRENCH   This acclaimed restaurant pays homage to traditional French cuisine at its most illustrious. No tonka beans or reduced licorice sauce here—Chef Manuel Martinez trains his formidable skills on classic sauces and time-honored dishes like sea-bass *quenelles* and roast duck, though he's not opposed to topping off the meal with a little lemon-basil sherbet. Signature dishes include lobster and foie gras ravioli, or braised sweetbreads with wild mushrooms. The atmospheric dining room, crisscrossed with exposed beams and ancient stonework, makes you wonder if the Three Musketeers might tumble through the doorway bearing your millefeuille with bourbon vanilla cream.

8 rue des Grands-Augustins, 6th arrond. ⓒ **01-43-26-75-96.** www.relaislouis13.fr. Main courses 55€; fixed-price lunch 50€, fixed price dinner 80€–130€. Tues–Sat noon–2:30pm, 7:30–10:30pm. Closed Aug. Métro: Odéon or St-Michel.

Moderate

Le P'tit Fernand ★★ TRADITIONAL FRENCH/BISTRO   This tiny slice of a restaurant packs a flavorful punch. Red-checked tablecloths provide a homey background for excellent bistro dishes like thick steak with a confit of shallots and creamy mashed potatoes, or duck *magret* (breast) served with morello-cherry sauce. You could start with a nice light beet and rhubarb gazpacho or go nuts and order the homemade terrine of foie gras. Whatever it is, it will be executed with loving care and quality ingredients, which is why this restaurant has a devoted clientele.

7 rue Lobineau, 6th arrond. ⓒ **01-40-46-06-88.** www.lepetitfernand.fr. Main courses 18€–26€. Daily noon–2pm and 7–11:30pm. Métro: Mabillon.

Inexpensive

Restaurant Polidor ★ TRADITIONAL FRENCH/BISTRO   An unofficial historic monument, Polidor is not so much a restaurant as a snapshot of a bygone era.

The decor has not changed substantially for at least 1[...] Rimbaud, the bad boys of poetry, would come here for [...] would continue to be a literary lunch room for decades: In [...] "the College of Pataphysics" by a rowdy group of young ups[...] Ernst, Boris Vian, and Eugene Ionesco; André Gide and Erne[...] reputed regulars. The menu features hefty bistro standbys like boe[...] *blanquette de veau* (veal stew with white sauce), but you'll also fin[...] salmon with basil and chicken breast with morel sauce. These days, [...] moved elsewhere; you'll probably be sharing the long wooden tables w[...]ur-ists, along with a dose of locals. Though the food is not particularly me[...]ble, the ambience is unique.

41 rue Monsieur-le-Prince, 6th arrond. ℂ **01-43-26-95-34.** www.polidor.com. Main courses 12€–25€; fixed-price menu 24€–35€. No credit cards. Daily noon–2:30pm; Mon–Sat 7pm–12:30am; Sun 7–11pm. Métro: Odéon.

EIFFEL TOWER & NEARBY (7TH ARRONDISSEMENT)

Crowded with ministries and important people, this neighborhood is so grand, you half expect to hear trumpets blowing each time you turn a corner. Though it's a rather staid neighborhood, a few streets are fairly lively, namely rue Cler, a pretty market street, and rue St-Dominique, home to some of the best restaurants on this side of the Seine.

Expensive

L'Arpège ★★★ MODERN FRENCH   This is probably the only Michelin-three-star restaurant where vegetables are the stars of the show. You can still find meat on the menu, but it takes a back seat to carrots, turnips, sweet peas, or whatever other lovely plant life is in season. This pristine produce, which comes from Chef Alain Passard's farm, is often picked in the morning and ends up on diners' plates the same evening. The menu comes in two sections: the "grand crus" of the vegetable garden, and the "memory" dishes: milk-fed lamb from the Aveyron with wild celery, or fresh fish from Brittany with lovage and sweet peas. Don't miss the *tarte aux pommes bouquet de roses* (tart composed of apple ribbons rolled into tiny rosettes). Reservations are required at least 2 weeks in advance.

84 rue de Varenne, 7th arrond. ℂ **01-47-05-09-06.** www.alain-passard.com. Main courses 67€–180€; fixed-price lunch 135€, fixed-price tasting menu (lunch and dinner) 365€. Mon–Fri noon–2pm and 7–10:30pm. Métro: Varenne.

Restaurant Auguste ★★ MODERN FRENCH/SEAFOOD   It's not every famous chef that can call himself "Mr. Goodfish." Gael Orieux's love of the sea and everything in it has led him to become spokesperson for an association dedicated to protecting the oceans. Naturally, that means what you see in your plate is not only delicious, but also ecologically correct. Let's hope he makes an impact on his clientele, many of whom are politicians taking a break from the nearby Assemblée Nationale. Your dish might look like artwork, but it's actually something like red mullet with sweet and sour cherries, turnips in coconut sauces, and wild elderberries, or turbot with tomatoes, green peppers, and quail eggs. Meat eaters may appreciate the veal with juniper berries served with sweet peas and rhubarb.

54 rue de Bourgogne, 7th arrond. ℂ **01-45-51-61-09.** www.restaurantauguste.fr. Main courses 38€–49€; fixed-price lunch 35€, fixed-price dinner 85€. Mon–Fri noon–2:30pm and 7–10:30pm. Closed 3 wks in Aug. Métro: Varenne.

Eating alfresco in a park can be a delightful pause during an action-packed day of sightseeing. It's also a great way to eat on the cheap in expensive Pairs. You can find picnic fixings in *charcuteries* or *traiteurs* (take-outs), which both sell prepared foods, but the easiest thing to do is to pop into a *boulangerie* (bakery) at lunchtime and buy a sandwich made on a freshly baked baguette. Many offer a *formule*, or fixed menu, that includes a sandwich, drink, and dessert for a mere 7€–8€, which must be **the city's best lunch bargain.** The best bakeries have a line out the door at lunchtime. Good chains include **Eric Kayser** (www.maison-kayser.com), and the ubiquitous **Paul** (www.paul.fr) is not bad either.

Moderate

Le Casse Noix ★★ TRADITIONAL FRENCH/BISTRO The result of yet another great chef realizing his bistro dreams, this relaxed restaurant offers high-caliber food in a casual, affordable setting. The decor is nostalgic (note the nutcracker collection and vintage advertisements), and the traditional French cooking is sincere and generous, featuring dishes like roast pork shoulder Ibaïona with olive puree, or a classic *petit salé* (lentils with smoky ham). About a 10-minute walk from the Eiffel Tower, this is a good bet for those looking for a bit of authenticity in an otherwise very touristy neighborhood. At dinnertime, the fixed-price menu is *obligatoire,* so no à la carte ordering. Lunch is more flexible.

56 rue de la Fédération, 15th arrond. ✆ **01-45-66-09-01.** www.le-cassenoix.fr. Main courses at lunch 18€–22€; fixed-price lunch 20€–25€, fixed-price dinner 32€. Mon–Fri noon–2:30pm and 7–10:30pm. Closed Aug and between Christmas and New Year. Métro: Dupleix.

Inexpensive

Café Constant ★★ TRADITIONAL FRENCH/BISTRO Of the three Christian Constant restaurants on this street, this one is the most relaxed; you may find the master himself at the bar smoking a cigar here during his off-hours. The menu features modern versions of French comfort food like tangy poached cod with aioli, melt-in-your-mouth beef *daube* (stew) with carrots, or steak with shallots and creamy potato puree. The weekday lunch *formule* is a two-course meal (chef's choice) for 16€, a terrific deal for this level of quality. No reservations.

139 rue Saint-Dominique, 7th arrond. ✆ **01-47-53-73-34.** www.maisonconstant.com. Main courses 16€–26€; lunch fixed-price menu 16€–23€. Daily noon–3pm and 7–11pm. Métro: Ecole Militaire.

MONTPARNASSE & NEARBY (14TH & 15TH ARRONDISSEMENTS)

The famous cafes where struggling writers and artists like Picasso, Hemingway, and Chagall once hung out are now much too expensive for most ordinary mortals, so having a drink is probably the best way to enjoy them. But there are plenty of other good options, from Breton crêperies near the train station to a bundle of new gourmet bistros farther south.

Expensive

Cobéa ★★ MODERN FRENCH Chef Philippe Bélissent invents concoctions that are as delicate and refined as the dining room in this pretty little house: Perfectly

CAFE SOCIETY: PARIS'S top cafes

Cafe life is an integral part of the Parisian scene, and it simply won't do to visit the capital without joining in. Here are a few ideas for your own personal cafe tour. **Tip:** Coffee or other drinks at the bar often cost half of what they do at a table.

Café de Flore Every great French intellectual and artist seems to had their moment here: Apollinaire, André Breton, Picasso, Giacometti and of course, Simone de Beauvoir and Jean-Paul Sartre, who virtually lived here during WWII. The atmosphere today is less thoughtful and more showbiz, but it's still worth an overpriced cup of coffee just to come in and soak it up.

172 bd. St-Germain, 6th arrond. ☏ **01-45-48-55-26.** www.cafedeflore.fr. Daily 7am–2am. Métro: St-Germain-des-Prés.

Les Deux Magots The literary pedigree here is impressive: Poets Verlaine and Rimbaud camped out here, as did André Gide and Albert Camus. Sartre and de Beauvoir moved in postwar and stayed for decades. The outdoor terrace is pleasant early in the morning before the crowds awake.

6 place St-Germain-des-Prés, 6th arrond. ☏ **01-45-48-55-25.** www.lesdeuxmagots.fr.

Daily 7:30am–1am. Métro: St-Germain-des-Prés.

Le Bistrot du Peintre Artists, hipsters, and other fauna from the bustling rue de Charonne area flock to this popular spot, which sports an authentic Art Nouveau interior with the original peeling paint.

116 av. Ledru-Rollin, 11th arrond. ☏ **01-47-00-34-39.** www.bistrotdupeintre.com. Daily 7am–2am; Métro: Ledru-Rollin;

Café de la Mairie What could be nicer than sitting outdoors at a sidewalk cafe on the place St-Sulpice? Indoors, it's a 1970s archetype: Formica bar, boxy chairs, and an odd assortment of pensioners, fashion victims, students, and would-be novelists.

8 place St-Sulpice, 6th arrond. ☏ **01-43-26-67-82.** Mon–Fri 7am–2am. Sat 8am–2am, Sun 9am–2am. Métro: Mabillon or St-Sulpice.

Le Nemours Cuddled up in a corner next to the Comedie Française, this beautiful café has a great terrace stretching out onto the Place Colette. The ideal spot for taking a load off after a day at the nearby Louvre.

2 place Colette, ☏ **01-42-61-34-14.** Mon–Fri 7am–1am, Sat 8am–1am,

cooked veal with fava beans and polenta; freshly caught John Dory; or pigeon with artichokes and olives might show up on the mix-and-match menu. The concept at dinner is as follows: There is one menu, from which you decide whether you'd like to try four (70€), six (85€), or eight (105€) courses. Service is impeccable.

11 rue Raymond Losserand, 14th arrond. ☏ **01-43-20-21-39.** www.cobea.fr. Fixed-price lunch 44€–68€, fixed-price dinner 70€–105€. Tues–Sat noon–1:30pm, 7–9:30pm. Closed Aug. Métro: Gaïté or Pernety.

Moderate

La Régalade ★★ TRADITIONAL FRENCH/BISTRO With its cracked tile floors, polished wood, and burgundy banquettes, chef Bruno Doucet's neo-bistro is an homage to the good things in life, like foie gras in asparagus bouillon or marinated sea scallops with basil and Parmesan. Main dishes are generally variations on French comfort food, such as a succulent pork breast with sweet peas, or lively innovations like a creamy squid risotto with sautéed prawns. Dessert could be a stinky Reblochon cheese, a molten Guanaja chocolate cake, or the house specialty, rice pudding. Reserve a week in advance.

14 av. Jean-Moulin, 14th arrond. (© **01-45-45-68-58.** Fixed-price menu 35€. Tues–Fri noon–2:30pm; Mon–Fri 7–11:30pm. Closed first 2 wks of Aug. Métro: Alésia.

Inexpensive
Crêperie Josselin ★★ CREPERIE This is one of the best of the dozens of crêperies concentrated near the Montparnasse train station. The cooks working the griddle know exactly how to achieve the lacy, golden edges of a perfect galette, and they are not shy with the butter. Josselin's specialty is the "couple," a double crêpe that uses two of these lacy confections in one dish. It's delicious but filling; if you are not starving ask the waiter to make it a "simple." Tradition demands that this meal be accompanied by a bowl of hard cider (low alcohol content; for adults only). The easy prices, continuous service, and wide range of flavor combinations make this a great option for children as well.

67 rue du Montparnasse, 14th arrond. (© **01-43-20-93-50.** Main courses 7€–9.80€; fixed-price menu 11€. No credit cards. Tues–Fri 11:30am–3pm and 6–11:30pm, Sat noon–midnight, Sun noon–11pm. Métro: Montparnasse-Bienvenüe.

EXPLORING PARIS

With more than 130 world-class museums to visit, scores of attractions to discover, extraordinary architecture to gape at, and wonderful neighborhoods to wander, Paris is an endless series of delights. Fortunately, you can have a terrific time in Paris even if you don't see everything. In fact, some of your best moments may be simply roaming around the city without a plan. Lolling on a park bench, dreaming over a drink at a sidewalk cafe, or noodling around an unknown neighborhood can be the stuff of some of your best travel memories.

The following pages highlight the best that Paris has to offer, from iconic sights known the world over to quirky museums and hidden gardens, from medieval castles to galleries celebrating the most challenging contemporary art.

The Right Bank
LOUVRE & ÎLE DE LA CITÉ (1ST ARRONDISSEMENT)
This is where it all started. Back in the city's misty and uncertain beginnings, the Parisii tribe set up camp on the right bank of the Seine and started hunting on the **Île de la Cité.** Many centuries later, the **Louvre** popped up, first as a fortress and now one of the world's mightiest museums. The city's epicenter packs in a high density of must-see monuments and museums, but don't miss the opportunity for aimless strolling, in the magnificent **Tuileries Gardens,** say, or over the **Pont Neuf. Note:** For simplicity's sake, the entire Île de la Cité has been included in this section, though technically half of it lies in the 4th arrondissement.

Cathédrale de Notre-Dame ★★★ CATHEDRAL This remarkably harmonious ensemble of carved portals, huge towers, and flying buttresses has survived close to a millennium's worth of French history and served as a setting for some of the country's most solemn moments. Napoléon crowned himself Emperor here, Napoléon III was married here, and the funerals of some of France's greatest generals (Foch, Joffre, Leclerc) were held here. In August 1944, the liberation of Paris from the Nazis was commemorated in the cathedral, as was the death of General de Gaulle in 1970.

The lines are long and the climb is longer, but the view from the **rooftop balcony** at the base of the cathedral's towers is possibly the most Parisian of all views. After trudging up some 255 steps (in a narrow winding staircase—not for small children or anyone with mobility concerns) you'll be rewarded with a panorama that not only encompasses the Île de la Cité, the Eiffel Tower, and Sacré-Coeur, but is also framed by a collection of photogenic **gargoyles.** One of the most famous is the **Stryga,** a horned and winged beasty holding his head in hi... pensively sticking his tongue o... city below. Another 147 steps up... narrow stairway lead to the summit... the **south tower,** from which you get an endless view of Paris. Come in the morning before the crowds get thick, and avoid weekends (www.monuments-nationaux.fr; *℘* **01-53-40-60-80;** 8.50€ adults, 5.50€ under 26, free under 18; Apr–June and Sept 10am–6pm; July–Aug Mon–Fri 10am–6pm, Sat–Sun 10am–11pm; Oct–Mar 10am–5:30pm).

Construction on the cathedral began in 1163 and lasted more than 200 years. The building was relatively untouched up until the end of the 17th century, when monarchs started meddling with its windows and architecture. By the time the Revolutionaries decided to convert it into a "Temple of Reason," the cathedral was already in sorry condition—and the pillaging that ensued didn't help. The interior was ravaged, statues were smashed, and the cathedral became a shadow of its former glorious self.

We can thank the famous "Hunchback" himself for saving Notre Dame. Victor Hugo's novel "The Hunchback of Notre Dame" drew attention to the state of disrepair, and other artists and writers began to call for the restoration of the edifice. In 1844 Louis-Phillipe hired Jean-Baptiste Lassus and Viollet-le-Duc to restore the cathedral, which they finished in 1864.

Begin your visit at **Point Zéro,** just in front of the building on the parvis (the esplanade). This is the official center of Paris and the point from which all distances relative to other French cities are calculated. Before you are three enormous **carved portals** depicting (from left to right) the Coronation of the Virgin, the Last Judgment, and scenes from the lives of the Virgin and St-Anne. Above is the **Gallery of the Kings of Judah and Israel**—thought to be portraits of the kings of France, the original statues were chopped out of the facade during the Revolution; some of the heads were eventually found in the 1970s and now are in the Musée National du Moyen Age/Thermes de Cluny.

Upon entering the cathedral, you'll be immediately struck by two things: the throngs of tourists clogging the aisles, and, when you look up, the heavenly dimensions of the pillars holding up the ceiling. Soaring upward, these delicate archways give the impression that the entire edifice is about to take off into the sky. Up there in the upper atmosphere are three remarkable stained-glass **rose windows.** The north window retains almost all of its 13th-century stained glass; the other two have been heavily restored. An impressive **treasury** is filled with relics of various saints including the elaborate cases for the **Crown of Thorns,** brought back from Constantinople by Saint Louis in the 13th century. The crown itself is not on display; however, it can be viewed, along with a nail and some pieces of the Holy Cross, on the first Friday of

0 1/4 mi
0 0.25 km

17e

Monceau Courcelles
Parc Monceau
6

Courcelles
de
Monceau
av. des Ternes
Ternes
place des
Ternes
r. du Hoche
r. de Constantinople
place de
Dublin
Liège

square
M. Pagnol

**Gare
St-Lazare**

Charles de Gaulle–
RER Étoile
av. de la
Grande Armée
av. de Friedland
Haussmann
7
8e
St-Augustin
Haussmann
square
Louis XVI
St-Lazare
RER

1 Arc de Triomphe
place Charles
de Gaulle

av. Foch
av. Victor
Hugo
av. Kléber
Kléber
George V
des
Champs
St-Philippe-
du-Roule
Boétie
St-Honoré

Havre-
Caumar

pl. de la
Madeleine

16e
av. d'Iéna
av. Marceau
r. Pierre Charron
François
Franklin D. rond-point
Roosevelt
Champs-Elysées

La Madeleine
8
Madeleine
bd. de la
Madeleine
Capuci

place des
États Unis
Boissière

av. Pierre Premier de Serbie
George
V
pl.
François
Premier
place de
l'Alma
Champs Elysées-
Clemenceau
Champs
Élysées
Concorde
place
Vendô

place
Vendô
Saint-
Honoré
r. de Rivoli

2
3
av.
du
President
Wilson
léna
4 5
cours
voie G. Pompidou
Albert Premier
**Grand
Palais**
**Petit
Palais**
cours
voie G. Pompidou
La Reine
place de la
Concorde
10

Tuileries

**Palais de
Chaillot**
Pont de
l'Alma
Alma-
Marceau
Seine
place de la
Résistance
quai d'Orsay
q. d'Orsay
Seine
11 Jardin des Tuiler
quai des Tuileries
12

*Jardins du
Trocadero*

34
**Musée du
Quai Branly**
quai Branly
de l'Université
Rapp
RER
Invalides
**Palais Bourbon/
Assemblée
Nationale**
Assemblée
Nationale
37 **Musée
d'Orsay**
l'Université
Solférino

**Tour
Eiffel**
33
RER
*Champ de Mars–
Tour Eiffel*
quai Branly
parc du Champ de Mars
St-Dominique
Grenelle
Bourdonnais
7e
La Tour
Maubourg
place des
Invalides
35 **Hôtel des
Invalides**
Varenne
Grenelle
Rue du Bac

15e
av. de la
Motte-Picquet
bd. de la Tour-Maubourg
Saint-Dominique
36 **Musée
Rodin**
Varenne
Bac
Raspail

Dupleix
Grenelle
**École
Militaire**
Joffre
av. de Suffren
av. de Lowendal
av. de Tourville
place
Vauban
de Sèvres
St-François
Xavier
Babylone
*Jardin
Catherine
Labouré*
Sèvres
Sèvres-
Babylon

UNESCO
Breteuil
bd. des Invalides
Vaneau
Cherche
Rennes

place de
Breteuil
Sèvres-
Lécourbe
Duroc
Vaugirard
St-Placide
Notre-Dame-
des-Champs

**HÔPITAL NECKER–
ENFANTS MALADES**
du
de Falguière
place du
18 Juin 1940
Montparnasse-
Bienvenüe
Vavin

Pasteur
bd. Pasteur
MONTPARNASSE
**Tour
Montparnasse**

LEFT BANK

Eiffel Tower **33**	Musée National d'Histoire Naturelle **46**
Hôtel des Invalides/ Napoleon's Tomb **35**	Musée National du Moyen Age/ Thermes de Cluny **41**
Institut du Monde Arabe **44**	Musée Rodin **36**
Jardin des Plantes **45**	Panthéon **42**
Jardin du Luxembourg **40**	St-Etienne-du-Mont **43**
Musée d'Orsay **37**	St-Germain-des-Prés **38**
Musée du Quai Branly **34**	St-Sulpice **39**

PARIS | Exploring Paris

4

the month (3pm), every Friday during Lent (3pm) and Good Friday (10am–5pm). For a detailed look at the cathedral, take advantage of the **free guided tours in English** (Wed–Thurs 2pm, Sat 2:30pm) or rent an **audioguide** for 5€.

When you leave, be sure to take a stroll around the outside of the cathedral to admire the other portals and the famous flying buttresses.

Place du Parvis Notre-Dame, 4th arrond. www.notredamedeparis.fr. ℂ **01-53-10-07-02.** Admission free to cathedral. Treasury 3€ adults, 2€ students and seniors, 1€ ages 6–12, free children 5 and younger. Cathedral Mon–Fri 8am–6:45pm, Sat–Sun 8am–7:15pm. Treasury Mon–Fri 9:30am–6pm; Sat 9:30am–6:30pm; Sun 1:30–6:30pm. Métro: Cité or St-Michel. RER: St-Michel.

Conciergerie ★ HISTORIC SITE   A relic of the darker side of the Revolution, this famous prison commemorates The Terror, when murderous infighting between the various revolutionary factions engendered panic and paranoia that led to tens of thousands of people throughout the country being arrested and executed. Many of the Revolution's most pivotal characters spent their final days here before making their way to the guillotine, including the queen, Marie Antoinette.

Though it's been a prison since the 15th century, the building itself is actually what remains of a 14th-century royal palace built by Philippe le Bel. The enormous **Salle des Gens d'Arms,** with its 8.4m-high (28-ft.) vaulted ceiling, is an impressive reminder of the building's palatial past. As for the prison, though the cells have been outfitted with displays and re-creations of daily life (including wax figures), it's a little difficult to imagine what it was like in the bad old days. However, the **Cours des Femmes** (the women's courtyard) virtually hasn't changed since the days when female prisoners did their washing in the fountain. In a curious attempt to spice up its offerings, the site has recently been hosting contemporary art exhibits, so don't be surprised to see conceptual art as you wander around the prison cells.

2 bd. du Palais, 1st arrond. ℂ **01-53-40-60-80.** www.monuments-nationaux.fr. Admission 8.50€ adults, 5.50€ ages 18–25, free for 17 and younger. Daily 9:30–6pm. Métro: Cité, Châtelet, or St-Michel. RER: St-Michel.

Jardin des Tuileries ★★★ GARDENS   This exquisite park spreads from the Louvre to the place de la Concorde. What you see today is based on the design by 17th-century master landscape artist André Le Nôtre—the man behind the gardens of Versailles. Le Nôtre's elegant geometry of flowerbeds, parterres, and groves of trees made the Tuileries Gardens the ultimate stroll for the era's well-to-do Parisians. It continues to delight both tourists and locals in the 21st century.

During World War II, furious fighting went on here, and many statues were damaged. Little by little in the postwar years the garden put itself back together. Seventeenth- and 18th-century representations of various gods and goddesses were repaired, and the city added new works by modern masters such as Alberto Giocometti, Jean Dubuffet, and Henry Moore. Rodin's "The Kiss" and "Eve" are here, as well as a series of 18 of Maillol's curvaceous women, peeking out of the green **labyrinth** of hedges in the Carousel Gardens near the museum.

Pulling up a metal chair and sunning yourself on the edge of the large **fountain** in the center of the gardens (the **Grande Carrée**) is a delightful respite for tired tourists after a day in the Louvre; tots will enjoy playing with one of the wooden **toy sailboats** that you can rent from a stand (2.50€/half-hour).

Near place de la Concorde, 1st arrond. ℂ **01-40-20-90-43.** Free admission. Daily Apr–May 7am–9pm; June–Aug 7am–11pm; Sept 7am–9pm; Oct–Mar 7:30am–7:30pm. Métro: Tuileries or Concorde.

Musée de l'Orangerie ★★ MUSEUM   Since 1927, this former royal green-house has been the home of Monet's stunning "Nymphéas," or **water lilies,** which he conceived as a "haven of peaceful meditation." Two large oval rooms are dedicated to these masterpieces, in which Monet tried to replicate the feeling and atmosphere of his garden at Giverny. He worked on these enormous canvases for 12 years, with the idea of creating an environment that would soothe the "overworked nerves" of modern men and women—in what could be called one of the world's first art installations.

The other highlight here is the Guillaume collection, an impressive assortment of late-19th- and early-20th-century paintings. The first, light-filled gallery displays works by Renoir and Cezanne. Mostly portraits and still lifes, they include Renoir's glowing, idyllic "Femme Nu dans un Paysage" and Cézanne's rather dour-looking "Madame Cézanne." The rest of the collection includes slightly sinister landscapes by Rousseau, enigmatic portraits by Modigliani, distorted figures by Soutine, as well as some kinder, gentler Picassos ("Les Adolescents" bathed in pink and rust tones).

Jardin des Tuileries, 1st arrond. ℂ **01-44-77-80-07.** www.musee-orangerie.fr. Admission 7.50€ adults, 5€ students 25 and younger. Wed–Mon 9am–6pm. Métro: Concorde.

Musée des Arts Décoratifs ★★ MUSEUM   Possessing some 150,000 items in its rich collection, this fascinating museum offers a glimpse of history through the prism of decorative objects, with a spectrum that ranges from medieval traveling trunks to Philippe Starck stools. The collection is organized in more or less chronological order, so on your journey you will pass by paintings from the First Italian Renaissance, through a room filled with exquisite 15th-century intarsia ("paintings" made out of intricately inlaid wood), before gaping at huge, intricately carved 17th-century German armoires. Other highlights include a tiny room covered in gilded woodwork from an 18th-century mansion in Avignon, a 19th-century courtesan's bedroom, and a stunning Art Nouveau dining room.

The collection weakens after 1930; it's hard to tell if this is due to a lack of imagination on the part of the museum or on the part of 20th-century designers. The chronological sequence can be hard to follow; note that the visit starts on the third floor. There are two other museums in the building (which is actually one of the extremities of the Louvre): the **Musée de la Publicité,** which takes on the history of advertising, and the **Musée de la Mode et du Textile,** which hosts exhibits on the many facets of clothing, including the works of famous couture houses like Jean-Paul Gaultier and Dior (both have the same hours as the main museum and are included in the ticket price to Arts Décoratifs).

Palais du Louvre, 107 rue de Rivoli, 1st arrond. ℂ **01-44-55-57-50.** www.lesartsdecoratifs.fr. Admission 9.50€ adults, 8€ ages 18–25, free children 17 and younger. Tues–Sun 11am–6pm. Métro: Louvre-Palais-Royal or Tuileries.

Musée du Louvre ★★★ MUSEUM   The best way to thoroughly visit the Louvre would be to move in for a month. Not only is it one of the largest museums in the world, with more than 35,000 works of art displayed over 60,000 sq. m (645,835 sq. ft.), but it's packed with enough artistic masterpieces to make the Mona Lisa weep. Rembrandt, Reubens, Botticelli, Ingres, and Michelangelo are all represented here; subjects range from the grandiose (Antoine-Jean Gros's gigantic "Napoleon Bonaparte Visiting the Plague-Stricken in Jaffa") to the mundane (Vermeer's tiny, exquisite "Lacemaker"). You can gape at a diamond the size of a golf ball in the royal treasury, or marvel over exquisite bronze figurines in the vast Egyptian section.

Today, the building is divided into three wings, Sully, Denon, and Richelieu, each one with its own clearly marked entrance, found under I.M. Pei's glass pyramid. Get your hands on a museum map (there's an excellent interactive map on the museum's website), choose your personal "must-sees," and plan ahead. There's no way to see it all, and you'll be an instant candidate for early retirement if you try. Mercifully, the museum is well organized and has been very reasonably arranged into color-coded sections. If you're really in a rush or you just want to get an overall sense of the place, you can take the introductory guided tour in English (1½ hr.; 11:15am, 2pm Wed–Mon; 9€).

The museum's three biggest stars are all located in the Denon wing. La Joconde, otherwise known as the **"Mona Lisa,"** now has an entire wall to herself, making it easier to contemplate her enigmatic smile. Another inscrutable female in this wing is the **"Venus de Milo,"** who was found on a Greek island in 1820. Possibly the most photographed woman in the world, this armless marble goddess gives no hint of the original position of her limbs or her exact identity. The **"Winged Victory of Samothrace,"** another magnificent Greek sculpture, stands at the top of a majestic flight of stairs, her powerful body pushing forward as if about to take flight. This headless deity originally overlooked the Sanctuary of the Great Gods on the island of Samothrace. Note that the "Winged Victory" is undergoing a cleaning and will not be back on view until summer 2014.

Because a complete listing of the Louvre's highlights would fill a book, below is a decidedly biased selection of my favorite areas:

13TH- TO 18TH-CENTURY ITALIAN PAINTING A few standouts in the immense Italian collection include the delicate fresco by Botticelli called "Venus and the Three Graces Presenting Gifts to a Young Woman," Veronese's enormous "Wedding Feast at Cana," and of course, the "Mona Lisa." The Divine Miss M is in a room packed with wonders, including several Titians and Tintorettos. Once you've digested this rich meal, stroll down the endless Grande Galerie, past more da Vincis ("Saint John the Baptist," "The Virgin of the Rock"), as well as works by Raphael, Caravaggio, and Gentileschi.

GREEK & ROMAN SCULPTURE While the "Venus de Milo" is not to be missed (ditto the "Winged Victory of Samothrace," if it's back on exhibit in 2014), the Salle des Caryatides (the room itself is a work of art) boasts marble masterworks like "Artemis" hunting with her stag and the troubling "Sleeping Hermaphrodite," an alluring female figure from behind—and something entirely different from the front.

THE GALERIE D'APOLLON The gold-encrusted room is an excellent example of the excesses of 17th-century French royalty. Commissioned by Louis XIV, aka "The Sun King," every inch of this gallery is covered with gilt stucco sculptures and flamboyant murals invoking the journey of the Roman sun god Apollo (ceiling paintings are by Charles Le Brun). The main draw here is the collection of crown jewels. Among necklaces bedecked with quarter-sized sapphires and tiaras dripping with diamonds and rubies is the jewel-studded crown of Louis XV and the pearl-and-diamond diadem of Empress Eugenie.

THE EGYPTIANS The largest collection outside of Cairo, thanks in large part to Jean-François Champollion, the 19th-century French scientist and scholar who first decoded Egyptian hieroglyphs. Sculptures, figurines, papyrus documents, steles, musical instruments, and of course, mummies, fill numerous rooms in the Sully Wing, including the colossal statue of Ramses II and the strangely moving Seated Scribe. He gazes intently out of intricately crafted inlaid eyes: A combination of copper, magnesite, and polished rock crystal create a startlingly lifelike stare.

LARGE-FORMAT FRENCH PAINTINGS   Enormous floor-to-ceiling (and these are high ceilings!) paintings of monumental moments in history cover the walls in these three rooms. The "Coronation of Napoléon" by Jacques-Louis David depicts the newly minted Emperor crowning Josephine, while the disconcerted pope and a host of notables look on. On the facing wall, "Madame Récamier" (also by David), one of Napoléon's loudest critics, reclines fetchingly on a divan. Farther on are several tumultuous canvases by Eugène Delacroix, including "Liberty Guiding the People," which might just be the ultimate expression of French patriotism. In the painting, which evokes the events of the revolution of 1830, Liberty—breast exposed, a rifle in one hand, the French flag in the other—leads the crowd over a sea of dead bodies. High ideals and gore—sort of sums up the French revolutionary spirit.

Note: When visiting the museum, **watch your wallets and purses**—there has been an unfortunate increase in pickpockets; organized groups even use children to prey on unsuspecting art lovers.

quai du Louvre, 1st arrond. Main entrance in the glass pyramid, cour Napoléon. ℂ **01-40-20-53-17.** www.louvre.fr. Admission 12€, children 17 and younger free. Sat–Mon and Thurs 9am–6pm; Wed and Fri 9am–9:30pm. Métro: Palais-Royal–Musée du Louvre.

Palais Royal ★★ HISTORIC SITE/GARDEN   The gardens and long arcades of the Palais Royal are not only a delight to stroll through, they were also witness to one of the most important moments in French history. Built by Cardinal Richelieu, the lavish palace eventually came into the hands of a certain Duke Louis Phillippe d'Orleans at the end of the 18th century. An inveterate spendthrift, the young lord soon found himself up to his ears in debt. To earn enough money to pay off his creditors, he came up with the shockingly modern idea of opening the palace gardens to development, building apartments on the grounds. The bottom floor of the galleries, which make up three sides of the enclosure you see today, were let out as shops, cafes, and boutiques. Gambling houses and bordellos sprang up between the shops and cafes, and the gardens became the central meeting place for revolutionaries. Things came to a head on July 12, 1789, when Camille Desmoulins stood up on a table in front of the Café de Foy and called the people to arms—2 days later, the mob would storm the Bastille, igniting the French Revolution. In more recent times, the palace was taken over by various government ministries, and the apartments were rented to artists and writers, including Colette and Jean Cocteau.

Today the shops in the arcades are very subdued, and very expensive—mostly antique toy and stamp dealers, a smattering of high-end designer clothes, and a couple of pricey restaurants, including the legendary Grand Véfour (p. 52). The *cour d'honneur* on the south end is filled with black-and-white-striped columns by Daniel Buren; though most Parisians have now gotten used to this unusual installation, when it was unveiled in 1987 it caused almost as much of a stir as Camille Desmoulins did on that fateful day.

Rue St-Honoré, 1st arrond. Free admission. Gardens daily 7:30am–dusk. Métro: Palais Royal–Musée du Louvre.

Place Vendôme ★★ SQUARE In 1686, Louis XIV decided the time had come to design a magnificent square, at the center of which would stand a statue of His Royal Highness. Though the statue is long gone, this is still one of the classiest squares in the city. The work of Jules Hardouin-Mansart, this über-elegant octagonal ensemble of 17th-century buildings today is the home of the original Ritz Hôtel, as well as the world's most glitzy jewelry makers, including Cartier, Van Cleef & Arpels, and Boucheron. The statue reigned over the square up until the Revolution, when it was melted down for scrap. When Napoléon took over, he erected a huge Roman-style column honoring his glorious army (yes, once again), this time documenting its victory at Austerlitz. A long spiral of bas-reliefs recounting the campaign of 1805 march up the Colonne de la Grande Armée, which is crowned by a statue of the Emperor himself.

Enter by rue de Castiglione, 1st arrond. Métro: Tuileries or Concorde.

Sainte-Chapelle ★★★ CHURCH A wall of color greets visitors who enter this magnificent chapel. Stained-glass windows make up a large part of the upper level of the church, giving worshippers the impression of standing inside a jewel-encrusted crystal goblet. What isn't glass is elaborately carved and painted in gold leaf and rich colors: vaulting arches, delicate window casings, and an almost Oriental wainscoting of arches and medallions. The 15 windows recount the story of the Bible, from Genesis to the Apocalypse, as well as the story of St-Louis, who was responsible for the chapel's construction. During the Crusades, Louis IX (who was later canonized) brought home some of the holiest relics in Christendom from Constantinople: the crown of thorns and a piece of the Holy Cross. Such a treasure required an appropriately splendid chapel in the royal palace, and thus the chapel was built (the relics are now in the treasury of Notre-Dame). The record is not clear, but the architect may have been the illustrious Pierre de Montreuil, who worked on the cathedrals of St-Dennis and Notre-Dame. What is sure is that the mysterious architect was brilliant: He managed to support the structure with arches and buttresses in such a way that the walls of the upper chapel are almost entirely glass.

The **lower chapel,** which was meant for the servants, has a low, vaulted ceiling painted in blue and red and gold and covered with fleur-de-lys motifs. Up a small staircase is the **upper chapel,** clearly meant for the royals. This masterpiece suffered both fire and floods in the 17th century and was pillaged by zealous Revolutionaries in the 18th. By the mid–19th century, the chapel was being used to store archives—2m

(6½ ft.) of the bottom of each window was removed to install shelves. Fortunately, renewed interest in medieval art eventually led to a conscientious restoration by a team that was advised by master restorer Viollet-le-Duc. The quality of the work on the windows is such that it is almost impossible to detect the difference between the original and the reconstructed stained glass (which makes up about one-third of what you see).

Palais de Justice, 4 bd. du Palais, 1st arrond. © **01-53-40-60-80.** www.monuments-nationaux.fr. 8.50€ adults, 5.50€ ages 18–25, free 17 and younger. Audioguide 4.50€. Mar–Oct daily 9:30am–6pm; Nov–Feb daily 9am–5pm. Métro: Cité, St-Michel, or Châtelet–Les Halles. RER: St-Michel.

OPÉRA & GRANDS BOULEVARDS (2ND & 9TH ARRONDISSEMENTS)

The grandiose **Opéra Garnier** reigns over this bustling neighborhood, which teems with office workers, tourists, and shoppers scuttling in and around the Grands Magasins (the big department stores) on Boulevard Haussmann. Which may account for why there are perhaps more opportunities for outstanding retail experiences here than for cultural ones.

Opéra Garnier ★★ OPERA HOUSE   Flamboyant, extravagant, and baroque, this opulent opera house is a splendid example of Second Empire architectural excess. Corinthian columns, loggias, busts, and friezes cover the **facade** of the building, which is topped by a gold dome. The interior of the building is no less dramatic. The vast **lobby,** built in a spectrum of different colored marble, holds a spectacular double staircase that sweeps up to the different levels of the auditorium, as well as an array of glamorous antechambers, galleries, and ballrooms that make you wonder how the opera scenery could possibly compete. Mosaics, mirrors, gilt, and marble line these grand spaces, whose painted ceilings dance with fauns, gods, and nymphs. The main event, of course, is the **auditorium,** which might seem a bit small, considering the size of the building. In fact, it holds not even 2,000 seats. The beautiful **ceiling** was painted with colorful images from various operas and ballets by Marc Chagall in 1964.

All of this (with the exception of the Chagall ceiling) sprang from the mind of a young, unknown architect named Charles Garnier, who won a competition launched by Napoléon III. Though the first stone was laid in 1862, work was held up by war, civil unrest, and a change in regime; the Palais Garnier was not inaugurated until 1875. Some contemporary critics found it a bit much (one called it "an overloaded sideboard"), but today it is generally acknowledged as a masterpiece of the architecture of the epoch.

And what about that phantom? Gaston Leroux's 1911 novel, "The Phantom of the Opera," clearly was inspired by the building's **underground lake,** which was constructed to help stabilize the building.

You can visit the building on your own (for a fee; see ticket prices below), but you might want to take advantage of the **guided visits in English** (12€ adults, 9.50€ students, 6.50€ under 10; Sept–June Wed, Sat–Sun 11:30am and 2:30pm; July–Aug daily 11:30am and 2:30pm). Either way, your visit will be limited to the lobby, the surrounding foyers, the museum, and the auditorium—sorry, you won't get to see the lake. Or simply **buy tickets to a show;** consult the Opéra website to see what's on at the Palais Garnier.

8 rue Scribe, 9th arrond. © **08-92-89-90-90** (.34€ per min). www.operadeparis.fr. Admission 10€ adults, 6€ students, children under 10 enter for free. Oct to mid-July daily 10am–5pm, mid-July to Sept 10am–6pm. Métro: Opéra.

LE MARAIS (3RD & 4TH ARRONDISSEMENTS)

Home to royalty and aristocracy between the 14th and 17th centuries, the Marais still boasts remarkable architecture, some of it dating back to the Middle Ages. One of the few neighborhoods that was not knocked down during Baron Haussmann's urban overhaul, Marais has narrow streets still lined with magnificent *hôtels particuliers* (that is, mansions) as well as humbler homes from centuries past. The **Pompidou Center** is probably the biggest and most well-known attraction, but the Marais also harbors a wealth of terrific smaller museums, as well as the delightful **Place des Vosges.** The remnants of the city's **historic Jewish quarter** are found on rue des Rosiers, which has been invaded by chic clothing shops in recent years. These days, the real Jewish neighborhood is in the 19th arrondissement.

Centre Pompidou ★★ MUSEUM   The bizarre architecture of this odd building provokes such strong emotions, it's easy to forget that there is something inside. It was designed in 1971 by Italo-British architects Renzo Piano and Richard Rogers, whose concept was to put the support structure on the outside of the building, thereby liberating space on the inside for a museum and cultural center. The result was a gridlike exoskeleton with a tubular escalator inching up one side and huge multicolored pipes and shafts covering the other. To some, it's a milestone in contemporary architecture; to others, it's simply a horror. Either way, it's one of the most visited structures in France. For the Pompidou is much more than an art museum. Its some 100,000 sq. m (1,076,390 sq. ft.) of floor space includes a vast **reference library,** a **cinema archive,** bookshops, and a **music institute,** as well as a performance hall, a **children's gallery** and areas for educational activities. The actual museum, the **Musée National d'Art Moderne,** is on the fourth and fifth floors.

Because the museum collection is in constant rotation, it's impossible to say what you're likely to see on your visit, but the emphasis is generally on works from the second half of the 20th century, with a good dose of surrealism, Dada, and other modern movements from the first half. It includes relatively tame abstracts by **Picasso** and **Kandinsky** to **Andy Warhol'**s multiheaded portrait of Elizabeth Taylor to a felt-wrapped piano by **Joseph Beuys.** Just outside of the front of the center is the **Atelier Brancusi,** where the sculptor's workshop has been reconstituted in its entirety.

Take note of the monumental sculpture/mobile by Alexander Calder on the vast esplanade that slopes down towards the building, and don't miss the delightful **Stravinsky Fountain** around the side; kids are mesmerized by its colorful mobile sculptures by Niki de Saint Phalle and Jean Tinguely.

Place Georges-Pompidou, 4th arrond. ℂ **01-44-78-12-33.** www.centrepompidou.fr. Admission 11€–13€ adults, students 9€–10€ students, free children 17 and younger; admission varies depending on exhibits. Wed–Mon 11am–10pm. Métro: Rambuteau, Hôtel de Ville, or Châtelet–Les Halles.

The Pont Neuf

Since it's recently had a makeover, it does indeed look brand-spanking *neuf* (new), even though it is, in fact, the oldest bridge in Paris. The bridge was an instant hit when it was inaugurated by Henri IV in 1607: Ample sidewalks, and the fact that it was the first bridge sans houses, made it a delight for pedestrians. It still is, especially if you ignore the cars and just take in the lovely views. Christo wrapped the bridge in 1985.

Gaîté Lyrique ★ CULTURAL INSTITUTION   One of the newer additions to city's cultural scene, this gallery space/concert hall/educational center is devoted to exploring mixed-media and digital art forms. Set in a abandoned 19th-century theatre (hence the name), the building has been transformed to host rotating exhibits that range from music and multimedia performances to design, fashion, and architecture to new media—there's even an interactive room dedicated to video games.

3 bis rue Papin, 3rd arrond. ℂ **01-53-01-52-00.** www.gaite-lyrique.net. Tues–Sun 2–8pm. Métro: Réaumur Sébastopol. Opening hours and admission prices vary according to the exhibitions and events. ,

Hôtel de Ville ★ HISTORIC SITE   No, it's not a hotel. This enormous Neo-Renaissance wedding cake is Paris's city hall, and you can't go inside. But even if you can't get in to see the sumptuous halls and chandeliers, you will be able to feast on the lavish exterior, which includes 136 statues representing historic VIPs of Parisian history. Since the 14th century, this spot has been an administrative seat for the municipality; the building you see before you dates from 1873, but it is a copy of an earlier Renaissance version that stood in its place up until 1870, when it was burned down during the Paris Commune. The vast square in front of the building, which used to be called the place du Grève, was used for municipal festivals and executions, and it was also the stage for several important moments in the city's history, particularly during the Revolution: Louis XVI was forced to kiss the new French flag here, and Robespierre was shot in the jaw and arrested here during an attempted coup. Today the square is host to more peaceful activities: There's usually a merry-go-round or two to captivate the little ones, and in winter an **ice-skating rink** is set up.

29 rue de Rivoli, 4th arrond. ℂ **01-42-76-43-43.** www.paris.fr. Free admission. Métro: Hôtel-de-Ville.

Musée Carnavalet ★★ MUSEUM   Starting with a prehistoric canoe from 4600 BC and continuing into the 20th century, the history of Paris is recounted at this fascinating museum, through items as diverse as Gallo-Roman figurines, Napoléon's toiletry kit, and an 18th-century portrait of Benjamin Franklin when he was the U.S. ambassador to France.

The museum is housed in two magnificent 17th-century mansions, one of which was the home of prodigious letter-writer and woman of the world Madame de Sévigné from 1677 until her death in 1696. Little of the original interior decoration remains in either building, but this is made up for by the importation of entire rooms, including wall paneling and furniture, from various private mansions of different epochs. Highlights include the Louis XV–style **Salon des Philosophes,** with its beautiful *boiseries* (carved wood paneling) and historical objects like the inkwell of Jean-Jacques Rousseau; and the 18th-century **Café Militaire,** a room from an officer's café with gilded and sculpted wood paneling representing military motifs like shields, standards, and crowns of laurels.

The section on the French Revolution includes several fascinating mementos, such as the keys to the Bastille prison and a copy of the Declaration of the Rights of Man that once hung behind the president of the Convention. Particularly moving are the personal objects of the royal family from their last days in prison—a lock of Marie Antoinette's hair, Louis XVI's razor and water glass, the young Dauphin's writing exercises—reminders that these iconic figures were in fact made of flesh and blood.

rt et Histoire du Judaïsme ★★ MUSEUM   Housed in the mag-
el de Saint Aignan, this museum chronicles the art and history of the Jew-
in France and in Europe. It features a superb collection of objects of both
artistic and cultural significance (a splendid Italian Renaissance torah ark, a German
gold and silver Hanukkah menorah, a 17th-c. Dutch illustrated torah scroll, documents
from the Dreyfus trial), which is interspersed with texts, drawings, and photos telling
the story of the Jews and explaining the basics of both Ashkenazi and Sephardic traditions. The final rooms include a collection of works by Jewish artists, including Modigliani, Soutine, Lipchitz, and Chagall. In recent years, this museum has hosted some
terrific temporary exhibits on offbeat subjects like the (Jewish) origins of Superman,
Radical Jewish Culture, and the Walter Benjamin archives. Be prepared for airportlike
security at the entrance.

71 rue du Temple, 3rd arrond. ℂ **01-53-01-86-60.** www.mahj.org. Admission 6.80€ adults, free 25
and younger. Mon–Fri 11am–6pm; Sun 10am–6pm. Métro: Rambuteau or Hôtel de Ville.

Place des Vosges ★★★ PLAZA   Possibly the prettiest square in the city, this
beautiful spot combines elegance, greenery, and quiet. Nowhere in Paris will you find
such a unity of Renaissance-style architecture; the entire square is bordered by 17th-
century brick townhouses, each conforming to rules set down by Henri IV himself,
under which runs arched arcades. The square's history dates back to a royal mishap in
1559, when the site was occupied by a royal palace. During a tournament, feisty king
Henri II decided to fight Montgomery, the captain of his guard. A badly aimed lance
resulted in Henri's untimely death; his wife, Catherine de Medicis, was so distraught
she decided to have the palace demolished. His descendant, Henri IV, took advantage
of the free space to construct a royal square. Over the centuries, a number of celebrities
lived in the 36 houses, including Mme de Sévigny and Victor Hugo. Today the homes
are for the rich, as are many of the chic boutiques under the arcades, but the lush lawns,
trees, fountains, and the children's playground are for everyone.

4th arrond. Métro: St-Paul.

CHAMPS-ÉLYSÉES, TROCADÉRO & WESTERN PARIS
(8TH, 16TH & 17TH ARRONDISSEMENTS)

Decidedly posh, this is one of the wealthiest parts of the city in both per-capita earnings and cultural institutions. While the **Champs-Elysées** is more glitz than glory, the
surrounding neighborhoods offer high-end shops and restaurants as well as some terrific museums and concert halls. This is also where you will find grandiose architectural gestures, like the **Arc de Triomphe** and the **Place de la Concorde,** which
book-end the Champs, and the **Grand Palais** and **Petit Palais,** leftovers from the
legendary 1900 Universal Exposition.

Arc de Triomphe ★★★ MONUMENT   If there is one monument that symbol-
izes "La Gloire," or the glory of France, it is this giant triumphal arch. Crowning the
Champs-Elysées, this mighty archway both celebrates the military victories of the
French army and memorializes the sacrifices of its soldiers. Over time, it has become
an icon of the Republic and a setting for some if its most emotional moments: the laying in state of the coffin of Victor Hugo in 1885, the burial in 1921 of the ashes of an
unknown soldier who fought in World War I, and General de Gaulle's pregnant pause

under the arch before striding down the Champs-Elysées before the cheering crowds after the Liberation in 1944.

It took a certain amount of chutzpah to come up with the idea to build such a shrine, and sure enough, it was Napoléon who instigated it. In 1806, still glowing after his stunning victory at Austerlitz, the Emperor decided to erect a monument to the Imperial Army along the lines of a Roman triumphal arch. Construction soon began on the largest triumphal arch on the planet. Unfortunately, the Empire came to an end before the arch was finished, and construction dragged on until 1836 when it was completed by Louis-Philippe.

The arch is covered with bas-reliefs and sculptures, the most famous of which is the enormous "Depart of the Volunteers" of 1792, better known as the Marseillaise, by François Rude. Just above is one of the many smaller panels detailing Napoleonic battles—in this case, Aboukir—wherein the Emperor trods victoriously over the Ottomans. At the base of the arch is the Tomb of the Unknown Soldier, over which a flame is relit every evening. The inscription reads ICI REPOSE UN SOLDAT FRANÇAIS MORT POUR LA PATRIE, 1914–1918 ("Here lies a French soldier who died for his country").

Don't even think about crossing the vast traffic circle to get to the arch; instead take the underpass near the Métro entrances. The panorama from the rooftop terrace is quite impressive; directly below you will see the 12 boulevards that radiate from the star-shaped intersection (hence the moniker "Etoile"), most of which are named after Napoleonic battles. Out front is the long sweep of the Champs-Elysées, ending at the obelisk of the place de la Concorde, behind which lurks the pyramid of the Louvre. In the other direction you will get a good gander at the modern Grande Arche de la Défense, a huge, hollow cubelike building that could fit Notre-Dame under its arch.

Place Charles de Gaulle–Etoile, 8th arrond. ✆ **01-55-37-73-77.** www.monum.fr. Admission 9.50€ adults, 6€ ages 18–24, free 17 and under. Apr–Sept daily 10am–11pm; Oct–Mar daily 10am–10:30pm. Métro: Charles-de-Gaulle–Etoile.

La Madeleine ★ CHURCH   As you peer up the rue Royale from the place de la Concorde, you'll see something that very closely resembles a Roman temple. Whe the first stone was laid in 1763, it was destined to be a church with a neoclassical façade. But then the architect died, and then the Revolution broke out, and construction ground to a halt. No one knew what to do with the site until Napoléon finally strode onto the scene and declared that it would become the Temple de La Gloire, to honor the glorious victories of his army. He wanted something "solid" because he was sure that the monument would last "thousands of years." Unfortunately for him, military defeats and mounting debt would again delay construction until Napoléon decided that maybe it wouldn't be such a bad idea to make it a church after all—that way Rome would foot the bill. Once Napoléon was out of the picture for good, inertia sunk in again. It wasn't until 1842, under the Restoration, that La Madeleine was finally consecrated.

The inside of the church is pretty dark, due to a lack of windows, but there are some interesting works of art here, if you can make them out in the gloom. On the left as you enter is François Rude's "Baptism of Christ"; farther on is James Pradier's sculpture "La Marriage de la Vierge."

Place de la Madeleine, 8th arrond. ✆ **01-42-65-52-17.** www.eglise-lamadeleine.com. Free admission. Daily 9:30am–7pm. Métro: Madeleine.

Musée d'Art Moderne de la Ville de Paris ★ MUSEUM Housed in a wing of the massive Palais de Tokyo, this municipal modern-art museum covers ground similar to that of the Pompidou Center but on a smaller scale. Though several big names are represented (Picasso, Rouault, and Picaba, to name a few), in general these are not their best-known works; highlights include a room dedicated to surrealism (the personal collection of André Breton) and a series of paintings by Delaunay and Léger. The contemporary section, from 1960 on, covers seriously abstract movements like Fluxus and Figuration. In recent years, the collection has acquired several new works from the 1980s on, but for the most recent cutting edge ideas, you are probably better off at the Palais de Tokyo museum (see below) in the wing next door. There's also a huge room entirely covered with brilliant wall murals by Raoul Dufy ("La Fée Electricité"), as well as another huge room with two enormous versions of "La Danse" by Matisse.

11 av. du Président-Wilson, 16th arrond. ℂ **01-53-67-40-00.** www.mam.paris.fr. Free admission to permanent collections. Tues–Sun 10am–6pm. Métro: Iéna or Alma-Marceau.

Musée Jacquemart-André ★★★ MUSEUM The love-child of a couple of passionate art collectors, this terrific museum takes the form of a 19th-century mansion filled with fine art and decorative objects. Not only is the collection superb, but it is also of a blissfully reasonable size—you can see a wide range of beautiful things here without wearing yourself to a frazzle.

The house itself is a work of art: At its inauguration in 1875, the marble Winter Garden with its spectacular double staircase was the talk of the town. Nélie Jacquemart and Edouard André devoted their lives to filling this splendid dwelling with primarily 18th-century French art and furniture. The paintings of Fragonard, Boucher, and Chardin are in evidence, as is an impressive assortment of Louis XV– and Louis XVI–era decorative objects. There are many superb portraits, including that of an officious-looking "Comte Français de Nantes" by David. To honor the artists that influenced these French painters, the couple also amassed a number of 17th-century Dutch paintings, including a jaunty "Portrait of a Man" by Frans Hals, and Rembrandt's evocative "Pilgrims at Emmaus."

The peripatetic couple, who traveled frequently in search of new items for their collection, also took an interest in Renaissance Italian art; though at the time considered "primitive" by most art fans, that didn't stop Jacquemart and André from snapping up Quattrocento masterpieces like Botticelli's "Virgin and Child." For me, the Italian collection (on the second floor) is the most awe-inspiring part of the museum—not only are there works by masters like Bellini, Uccello, and Mantegna, but they are presented in an intimate space with excellent lighting. You feel like you are walking into a felt-lined jewel box. Leave time to eat a light lunch or have tea in the Jacquemart-André's lovely dining room.

158 bd. Haussmann, 8th arrond. ℂ **01-45-62-11-59.** www.musee-jacquemart-andre.com. Admission 11€ adults, 9.50€ students and children 7–17, free children 6 and younger. Daily 10am–6pm. Métro: Miromesnil or St-Philippe-du-Roule.

Musée Marmottan Monet ★★ MUSEUM Boasting the world's largest collection of Monets, this museum offers an in-depth look at this prolific genius and some of his talented contemporaries. Among the dozens of Monet canvases is the one that provided the name of an entire artistic movement. Pressed to give a name to this misty play of light on the water for the catalog for an 1874 exposition that included Cézanne,

Pissarro, Renoir, and Degas, Monet apparently said, "put 'impression.'" The painting, "Impression, Sunrise," certainly made one, as did the show—thereafter the group was referred to as the Impressionists. Monet never stopped being fascinated with the interaction of light and water, be it in a relatively traditional portrait of his wife and daughter against the stormy sea in "On the Beach at Trouville," or in an almost abstract blend of blues and grays in "Charring Cross Bridge." Monet often painted the same subject at different times of the day, as in his famous series on the Cathedral of Rouen, one of which is here: "Effect of the Sun at the End of the Day." Fans of the artist's endless water lily series will not be disappointed; the collection includes dozens of paintings of his beloved garden in Giverny.

Paintings by Renoir, Sisley, Degas, Gauguin and other contemporaries can be seen in the light-filled rooms on the upper floor, as are works by one of the only female members of the group, Berthe Morisot, who gets an entire room devoted to her intimate portraits and interiors.

2 rue Louis-Boilly, 16th arrond. ℂ **01-44-96-50-33.** www.marmottan.com. Admission 10€ adults, 5€ ages 8–24, free children 7 and younger. Tues–Wed and Fri–Sun 10am–6pm; Thurs 10am–8pm. Métro: La Muette. RER: Bouilainvilliers.

Musée National des Arts Asiatiques Guimet ★★ MUSEUM

Founded in 1889 by collector and industrialist Emile Guimet, today this vast collection of Asian art is one of the largest and most complete in Europe. Here you'll find room after room of exquisite works from Afghanistan, India, Tibet, Nepal, China, Vietnam, Korea, Japan, and other Asian nations. You could spend an entire day here, or you could pick and choose regions of interest (displays are arranged geographically); the free audioguide is a good bet for finding standouts and providing cultural context. Highlights include a Tibetan bronze sculpture ("Hevajra and Nairâtmya") of a multiheaded god embracing a ferocious goddess with eight faces and 16 arms; a blissfully serene stone figure of a 12th-century Cambodian king ("Jayavarman VII") who presided over a short-lived Khmer renaissance; and superb Chinese scroll paintings, including a magnificent 17th-century view of the Jingting mountains in autumn. A few minutes' walk from the museum is the Panthéon Bouddhique (19 av. d'Iéna; ℂ 01-40-73-88-00; free admission; Wed–Mon 10am–5:30pm), an old mansion where Guimet's collection of Buddhist art from Japan is displayed. Digest this artistic cornucopia in the adjoining Japanese garden, a peaceful haven for weary tourists and other serenity-seekers.

6 place d'Iéna, 16th arrond. ℂ **01-56-52-53-00.** www.guimet.fr. Admission to permanent collection 7.50€ adults, 5.50€ ages 18–25, free for ages 17 and younger. Wed–Mon 10am–6pm. Métro: Iéna.

Palais de Tokyo ★★ MUSEUM/PERFORMANCE SPACE

If you're traveling with cranky teenagers who've had enough of La Vieille France, or if you're also sick of endless rendezvous with history, this is the place to come for a blast of contemporary madness. This vast art space not only offers a rotating bundle of expositions, events, and other happenings, but it's also one of the only museums in Paris that stays open until midnight. While some might quibble over whether or not the works on display are really art, there's no denying that this place is a lot more fun than its stodgy neighbor across the terrace (see above). There's no permanent collection, just continuous temporary exhibits, installations, and events, which include live performances and film screenings. The center underwent a major expansion in 2012 that almost tripled its size—it is now one of the largest sites devoted to contemporary creativity in Europe.

In warm weather, you can eat on the splendid terrace or repair to its arty-cool restaurant, **Tokyo Eat.**

13 av. du Président-Wilson, 16th arrond. ℂ **01-71-97-35-88.** www.palaisdetokyo.com. Admission 10€ adults, 8€ ages 18–25, free for ages 17 and younger. Tues–Sun noon–midnight. Métro: Iéna.

Parc Monceau ★★ PARK/GARDENS Marcel Proust used to laze under the trees in this beautiful park, and who could blame him? The lush lawns and leafy trees of this verdant haven would brighten the spirits of even the most melancholy writer. Located in a posh residential neighborhood and ringed by stately mansions, this small park, commissioned by the duke of Chartres in 1769, is filled with *folies,* faux romantic ruins, temples, and antiquities inspired by exotic faraway places. Don't be surprised to stumble upon a minaret, a windmill, or a mini-Egyptian pyramid here. The most famous *folie* is the **Naumachie,** a large oval pond surrounded in part by Corinthian columns. You'll find a sizeable **playground** in the southwest corner, as well as a **merry-go-round** near the north entrance.

35 bd. de Courcelles, 8th arrond. Free admission. 8am–sundown. Métro: Monceau or Villiers.

Place de la Concorde ★★★ PLAZA Like an exclamation point at the end of the Champs-Elysées, the place de la Concorde is a magnificent arrangement of fountains and statues, held together in the center by a 3,000-year-old Egyptian obelisk (a gift to France from Egypt in 1829). Looking at it today, it is hard to believe that this magnificent square was once bathed in blood, but during the Revolution, it was a grisly stage for public executions. King Louis XVI and his wife, Marie-Antoinette, both bowed down to the guillotine here, as did many prominent figures of the Revolution, including Danton, Camille Desmoulins, and Robespierre. Once the monarchy was back in place, the plaza hosted less lethal public events like festivals and trade expositions.

In 1835 the *place* was given its current look: Two immense fountains, copies of those in St. Peter's Square in Rome, play on either side of the obelisk; 18 sumptuous columns decorated with shells, mermaids, and sea creatures each hold two lamps; and eight statues representing the country's largest cities survey the scene from the edges of the action. On the west side are the famous **Marly Horses,** actually copies of the originals, which were suffering from erosion and have since been restored and housed in the Louvre. On the north side of the square are two palatial buildings that date from the square's 18th-century origins: On the east side is the **Hôtel de la Marine,** and on the west side is the **Hôtel Crillon,** where on February 6, 1778, a treaty was signed by Louis XVI and Benjamin Franklin, among others, wherein France officially recognized the United States as an independent country and became its ally.

Note: Cars tend to hurtle around the obelisk like racers in the Grand Prix; if you feel compelled to cross to the obelisk and you value your life, find the stoplight and cross there.

8th arrond. Métro: Concorde.

MONTMARTRE (18TH ARRONDISSEMENT)

Few places in this city fill you with the urge to belt out sappy show tunes like the *butte* (hill) of Montmartre. Admiring the view from the esplanade in front of the oddly Byzantine **Basilique du Sacré-Coeur,** you'll feel as if you've finally arrived in Paris, and that you now understand what all the fuss is about. Ignore the tour buses and crowds mobbing the church and the hideously touristy **place du Tertre** behind you and wander off into the warren of streets towards the **place des Abbesses** or up **rue Lepic,** where you'll eventually stumble across the **Moulin de la Galette** and **Moulin du Radet,** the two surviving windmills (there were once 30 on this hill).

Basilique du Sacré-Coeur ★★ CHURCH   Poised at the apex of the hill like a *grande dame* in crinolines, this odd-looking 19th-century basilica has become one of the city's most famous landmarks. After France's defeat in the Franco-Prussian War, prominent Catholics vowed to build a church consecrated to the Sacred Heart of Christ as a way of making up for whatever sins the French may have committed that had made God so angry at them. Since 1885, prayers for humanity have been continually chanted here (the church is a pilgrimage site, so dress and behave accordingly). Inspired by the Byzantine churches of Turkey and Italy, this multidomed confection was begun in 1875 and completed in 1914, though it wasn't consecrated until 1919 because of World War I. The white stone was chosen for its self-cleaning capabilities: When it rains, it secretes a chalky substance that acts as a fresh coat of paint. Most visitors climb the 237 stairs to the **dome,** where the splendid city views extend over 48km (30 miles).

35 rue Chevalier de la Barre, 18th arrond. ✆ **01-53-41-89-00.** www.sacre-coeur-montmartre.com. Free admission to basilica, joint ticket to dome and crypt 8€ adults, 5€ ages 4–16, free under 4. Basilica daily 6am–11pm; dome and crypt daily 9am–6pm. Métro: Abbesses; take elevator to surface and follow signs to funicular.

Musée de Montmartre ★★ MUSEUM   This newly revamped museum documents the history of this famous butte (hill) from the days when its importance was mainly religious, to the growth of village life, to the gory days of the Paris Commune, and finally to the artistic boom in the 19th and 20th centuries. Highlights include posters by Toulouse-Lautrec, signage from the Chat Noir cabaret, and a collection of photos, lithographs, and etchings that illustrates daily life back in the day. The house once served as a studio for Renoir, who painted "Le Bal du Moulin de la Galette" here, among other legendary canvases. The newly replanted "Renoir Gardens" are filled with fruit trees, rose bushes, and climbing hydrangeas.

12 rue Cortot, 18th arrond. ✆ **01-49-25-89-37.** www.museedemontmartre.fr. Admission 9€ adults, 7€ ages 18–25, 5€ ages 10–17, free under 10. Daily 10am–6pm. Métro: Lamarck-Caulaincourt.

RÉPUBLIQUE, BASTILLE & EASTERN PARIS (11TH & 12TH ARRONDISSEMENTS)

While you can't really point to any major tourist attractions in this area, this is a nice part of town for aimless wandering, especially if you are a) in search of youth-oriented nightlife, b) in search of youth-oriented clothing shops, or c) a history buff. The French Revolution was brewed in the workshops of the **Faubourg St-Antoine** and ignited at the **place de la Bastille.**

Plaza de la Bastille ★   The most notable thing about this giant plaza is the building that's no longer here: the Bastille prison. Now an enormous traffic circle where cars careen around at warp speed, this was once the site of an ancient stone fortress that became a symbol for all that was wrong with the French monarchy. Over the centuries, kings and queens condemned rebellious citizens to stay inside these cold walls, sometimes with good reason, other times on a mere whim. By the time the Revolution started to boil, though, the prison was barely in use; when the angry mobs stormed the walls on July 14, 1789, there were only seven prisoners left to set free. Be that as it may, the destruction of the Bastille came to be seen as the ultimate revolutionary moment; July 14 is still celebrated as the birth of the Republic. Surprisingly, the giant bronze column in the center honors the victims of a different revolution, that of 1830.

12th arrond. Métro: Bastille.

BELLEVILLE, CANAL ST-MARTIN & LA VILLETTE (10TH, 19TH & 20TH ARRONDISSEMENTS)

One of the most picturesque attractions in this area is the **Canal St-Martin** itself, which crosses a formerly working-class neighborhood that is now peopled by an arty mix of regular folk and *bobos* (bourgeois bohemians). The Belleville neighborhood is home to one of the city's bustling **Chinatowns,** as well as many artists' studios.

Cimetière du Père-Lachaise ★★★ CEMETERY   It's hard to believe that a cemetery could be a top tourist attraction, but this is no ordinary cemetery. As romantic and rambling as a 19th-century English garden, this hillside resting place is wonderfully green, with huge leafy trees and narrow paths winding around the graves, which include just about every French literary or artistic giant you can imagine, plus several international stars. Proust, Molière, La Fontaine, Colette, Delacroix, Seurat, Modigliani, Bizet, Rossini are all here, as well as Sarah Bernhardt, Isadora Duncan, Simone Signoret, and Yves Montand (buried side by side, of course), not to mention Oscar Wilde, whose huge stone monument is usually covered with lipstick kisses. Even the Lizard King, Jim Morrison, is here. Though the grave itself is unexceptional, the tomb of the '60s rock star is possibly the most visited in the cemetery. In 1971, battling drug, alcohol, and legal problems, the singer/musician came to Paris; 4 months later, he was found dead in a Parisian bathtub, at age 27.

Celebrity graves can be hard to find, so a map is essential. You can find one at the newsstand across from the main entrance; on the website; or on the Paris municipal site (www.paris.fr; search for "Père Lachaise").

16 rue de Repos, 20th arrond. www.pere-lachaise.com. No telephone number. Admission free. Mon–Fri 8am–6pm; Sat–Sun 8:30am–6pm (closes at 5pm Nov to early Mar). Métro: Père-Lachaise or Philippe Auguste.

Parc des Buttes Chaumont ★ PARK   Up until 1860, this area was home to a deep limestone quarry, but thanks to Napoléon III, the gaping hole was turned into an unusual park, full of hills and dales, rocky bluffs and cliffs. It took 3 years to make this romantic garden; more than a thousand workers and a hundred horses dug, heaped, and blasted through the walls of the quarry to create green lawns, a cool grotto, cascades, streams, and even a small lake. By the opening of the 1867 World's Fair, the garden was ready for visitors. The surrounding area was, and still is, working-class; the Emperor built it to give this industrious neighborhood a green haven and a bit of fresh air. There are **pony rides** for the kids on weekends and Wednesdays, plus a **puppet theater,** a **carousel,** and **two playgrounds.**

Rue Botzaris, 19th arrond. Open 7am–11pm May 1–Sept 30; 7am–9pm Sept 30–Apr 30. Métro: Botzaris or Buttes Chaumont.

The Left Bank

LATIN QUARTER (5TH & 13TH ARRONDISSEMENTS)

What's so Latin about this quarter? Well, for several hundred years, the students that flocked here spoke Latin in their classes at the **Sorbonne** (founded in the 13th c.) and other nearby schools. The students still flock and the Sorbonne is still in business, and though classes are now taught in French, the name stuck. Intellectual pursuits aside, this youth-filled neighborhood is a lively one, packed with cinemas and cafés. History is readily visible here, dating back to the Roman occupation: The **rue St-Jacques** and **boulevard Saint-Michel** mark the former Roman cardo, and you can explore the remains of the **Roman baths** at the **Cluny Museum.**

Jardin des Plantes ★★ GARDENS   This delightful botanical garden, tucked between the Muséum National d'Histoire Naturelle (see below) and the Seine, is one of my favorite picnic spots. Created in 1626 as a medicinal plant garden for King Louis XIII, in the 18th century it became an internationally famed scientific institution thanks to naturalist, mathematician, and biologist Georges-Louis Leclerc, Count of Buffon, with the help of fellow-naturalist Louis-Jean-Marie Daubenton. Today the museums are still part academic institutions, but you certainly don't need to be a student to appreciate the lush grounds.

The garden also harbors a small, but well-kempt zoo, the **Ménagerie du Jardin des Plants** (© **01-40-79-37-94;** 11€ adults, 9€ students 18–26 and children 4–16, free under 4; daily 9am–6pm). Created in 1794, this is the oldest zoo in the world. Because of its size, the zoo showcases mostly smaller species, in particular birds and reptiles, but it also has a healthy selection of mammals, including rare species like red pandas, Przewalski horses, and even Florida pumas.

rue Geoffroy-St-Hilaire, 5th arrond. © **01-40-79-56-01.** www.jardindesplantes.net. Free admission to gardens; 8am–dusk; Métro: Gare d'Austerlitz.

Institut du Monde Arabe ★★ MUSEUM   In an age when Arab culture is all over the headlines, this is a good place to come to find out what the phrase actually means. The building alone is worth the price of admission, designed by architect Jean Nouvel in 1987. The south facade, which has a metallic latticework echoing traditional Arab designs, includes 30,000 light-sensitive diaphragms that regulate the penetration of light by opening and closing according to how bright it is outside. After a major overhaul, this museum, which used to be devoted solely to Islamic art, has now expanded its mission to include the many facets of the Arab world, specifically the 22 countries that helped create this institution in 1987. The collection includes beautiful examples of traditional calligraphy, miniatures, ceramics, woodwork, and carpets, as well as scientific objects, textiles, and illuminated manuscripts.

1 rue des Fossés St-Bernard, 5th arrond. © **01-40-51-38-38.** www.imarabe.org. Admission to permanent collections 8€, 4€ under 26. Tues–Thurs 10am–6pm, Fri 10am–9:30pm, Sat–Sun 10am–7pm. Métro: Jussieu, Cardinal Lemoine, Sully-Morland.

Musée National d'Histoire Naturelle ★★ MUSEUM   This natural-history museum was established in 1793 under the supervision of two celebrated naturalists, the Count of Buffon and Louis Jean-Marie Daubenton. Originally (and still) an academic research institution, this temple to the natural sciences contains a series of separate museums, each with a different specialty. The biggest draw is no doubt the **Grande Galerie de l'Evolution,** where a sort of Noah's ark of animals snakes its way around a huge hall filled with displays that trace the evolution of life and man's relationship to nature. Another interesting hall, the **Galerie de Minérologie et de Géologie,** includes a room full of giant crystals. For dinosaurs, saber-toothed tigers, ancient humans, and thousands of fossilized skeletons, repair to the **Galeries**

de Paléontologie et d'Anatomie Comparée. A new **Galerie des Enfants** has hands-on interactive displays for the little tykes. Except for the Grande Galerie, which has a joint ticket deal with the Galerie des Enfants, you'll have to pay for each Galerie separately.

36 rue Geoffroy, 5th arrond. ℭ **01-40-79-54-79.** www.mnhn.fr. Admission to each gallerie 7€–9€ adults; 5€–7€ students, seniors 60 and older, and children 4–13. Wed–Mon 10am–6pm. Métro: Jussieu or Gare d'Austerlitz.

Musée National du Moyen Age/Thermes de Cluny (Musée de Cluny)

★★ MUSEUM   Ancient Roman baths and a 15th-century mansion set the stage for a terrific collection of Medieval art and objects at this museum. Built somewhere between the 1st and 3rd centuries, the baths (visible from bd. St-Michel) are some of the best existing examples of Gallo-Roman architecture. They are attached to what was once the palatial home of a 15th-century abbot, whose last owner, a certain Alexandre du Sommerard, amassed a vast array of Medieval masterworks. When he died in 1842, his home was turned into a museum and his collection put on display. Sculptures, textiles, furniture, and ceramics are shown, as well as gold, ivory, and enamel work. There are several magnificent tapestries, but the biggest draw is the late-15th-century **"Lady and the Unicorn"** series, one of only two sets of complete unicorn tapestries in the world (the other is in New York City).

Among the many sculptures displayed are the famous severed heads from the facade of Notre-Dame. Knocked off of their bodies during the furor of the Revolution, 21 of the heads of the Kings of Judah were found by chance in 1977 during repair work in the basement of a bank. Other treasures include Flemish retables, Visigoth crowns, bejeweled chalices, wood carvings, stained-glass windows, and beautiful objects from daily life, like hair combs and game boards.

6 place Paul Painlevé, 5th arrond. ℭ **01-53-73-78-00.** www.musee-moyenage.fr. Admission 8€ adults, Free under 26 years old. Wed–Mon 9:15am–5:45pm. Métro/RER: Cluny–La Sorbonne or St-Michel.

Panthéon ★ MAUSOLEUM   High atop the "montagne" (actually a medium-sized hill) of St-Geneviève, the dome of the Panthéon is one of the city's most visible landmarks. This erstwhile royal church has been transformed into a sort of national mausoleum—the final resting place of luminaries such as Voltaire, Rousseau, Hugo, and Zola. Initially dedicated to St-Geneviève, the church was commissioned by a grateful Louis XV, who attributed his recovery from a serious illness to the saint. The work of architect Jacques-Germain Soufflot, who took his inspiration from the Pantheon in Rome, the original must have been magnificent. However, during the Revolution, its sacred mission was diverted towards a new god—the Nation—and it was converted into a memorial and burial ground for Great Men of the Republic. This meant taking down the bells, walling up most of the windows, doing away with religious statuary, and replacing it with works promoting patriotic virtues. The desired effect was achieved—the enormous empty space, lined with huge paintings of great moments in French history, resembles a cavernous tomb. Though the building is of architectural interest, unless you're a fan of one of the men (or women) who are buried under the building (a staircase leads down to the actual crypt), it's probably best admired from the outside.

Place du Panthéon, 5th arrond. ℭ **01-44-32-18-00.** www.monuments-nationaux.fr. Admission 8.50€ adults, 5.50€ ages 18–25, free children 17 and younger. Apr–Sept daily 10am–6:30pm; Oct–Mar daily 10am–6pm. Métro: Cardinal Lemoine, RER: Luxembourg.

St-Etienne-du-Mont ★★ CHURCH   One of the city's prettiest churches, this ecclesiastical gem is a joyous mix of late Gothic and Renaissance styles. The 17th-century facade combines Gothic tradition with a dash of classical Rome; inside, the 16th-century chancel sports a magnificent **rood screen** (an intricately carved partition separating the nave from the chancel) with decorations inspired by the Italian Renaissance. Book-ended by twin spiraling marble staircases, this rood screen is the only one left in the city. Among the church's riches are sumptuous 16th- and 17th-century stained glass. A pilgrimage site, this church was once part of an abbey dedicated to St-Genviève (the city's patron saint), and stones from her original sarcophagus lie in an ornate shrine here. That's about all that is left of her—the saint's bones were burned during the Revolution and their ashes thrown in the Seine. The remains of two other great minds, Racine and Pascal, are buried here.

1 place St-Geneviève, 5th arrond. ✆ **01-43-54-11-79.** www.saintetiennedumont.fr. Free admission. Tues–Sat 8:30am–7:30pm, Sat–Sun 8:30am–noon and 2–7:30pm. Métro: Cardinal Lemoine or Luxembourg.

ST-GERMAIN-DES-PRÉS & LUXEMBOURG (6TH ARRONDISSEMENT)

In the 20th century, the St-Germain-des-Prés neighborhood became associated with writers like Jean-Paul Sartre, Simone de Beauvoir, Albert Camus, and the rest of the intellectual bohemian crowd that gathered at **Café de Flore** or **Les Deux Magots** (p. 63). But back in the 6th century, a mighty abbey founded here ruled over a big chunk of the Left Bank for 1,000 years. The French Revolution put a stop to that, and most of the original buildings were pulled down. Remains of both epochs can still be found in this now-tony neighborhood, notably at the 10th-century church **St-Germain-des-Prés** and the surviving bookstores and publishing houses that surround it.

Jardin du Luxembourg ★★★ GARDENS   Rolling out like an exotic Oriental carpet before the Italianate Palais du Luxembourg (the seat of the French Senate since 1958, not open to the public), this vast expanse of fountains, flowers, lush lawns, and shaded glens is the perfect setting for a leisurely stroll, a relaxed picnic, or a serious make-out session, depending on who you're with. At the center of everything is a fountain with a huge basin, where kids can sail toy wooden sailboats (2€ for a half-hour) and adults can sun themselves in the green metal chairs at the pond's edge. Sculptures abound: At every turn there is a god, goddess, artist, or monarch peering down at you from their pedestal. The most splendid waterworks is probably the Medici Fountain (reached via the entrance at place Paul Claudel behind the Odéon), draped

---

Attention Bored Kids & Tired Parents

Frazzled parents take note: There are lots of activities in the Jardin de Luxembourg for kids who need to blow off steam. First off, there is the extra-large **playground** (1.80€ adults, 2.60€ under 12) filled with all kinds of things to climb on and play in. Then there are the wonderful wooden **sailboats** (2.50€ per half-hour) to float in the main fountain, as well as an ancient **carousel** (1.80€, next to the playground). At the **marionette theater** (4.70€ each for parents and children; Wed, Sat, Sun, and school vacation days; shows usually start after 3pm, Sat–Sun additional shows at 11am), you can see Guignol himself (the French version of Punch) in a variety of puppet shows.

with lithe Roman gods sculptured by Auguste Ottin, and topped with the Medici coat of arms, in honor of the palace's first resident, Marie de Medicis.

In 1621, the Italian-born French queen, homesick for the Pitti Palace of her youth, bought up the grounds and existing buildings and had a Pitti-inspired palace built for herself as well as a smaller version of the sumptuous gardens. During the Revolution, it was turned into a prison. American writer Thomas Paine was incarcerated there in 1793 after he fell out of favor with Robespierre; he narrowly escaped execution. On the plus side, the Revolutionaries increased the size of the garden and made it a public institution. In the southwest corner, visitors can visit a horticulture school where pear trees have been trained into formal, geometric shapes, as well as beehives (yes, beehives) that are maintained by a local apiculture association.

Entry at Place Edmond Rostand, place André Honnorat, rue Guynemer, or rue de Vaugirard, 6th arrond. www.senat.fr/visite/jardin/ 8am–dusk. Métro: Odéon; RER: Luxembourg.

St-Germain-des-Prés ★★ CHURCH   The origins of this church stretch back over a millennium. First established by King Childebert in 543, who constructed a basilica and monastery on the site, it was built, destroyed, and rebuilt several times over the centuries. Nothing remains of the original buildings, but the bell tower dates from the 10th century and is one of the oldest in France. The church and its abbey became a major center of learning and power during the Middle Ages, remaining a force to be reckoned with up until the eve of the French Revolution. Once the monarchy toppled, however, all hell broke loose: The abbey was destroyed, the famous library burned, and the church vandalized. Restored in the 19th century, the buildings have regained some of their former glory, though the complex is a fraction of its original size.

Much of the interior is painted in a range of greens, and golds—one of the few Parisian churches to retain a sense of its original decor. The heart of King Jean Casimir of Poland is buried here, as are the ashes of the body of René Descartes (his skull is in the collections of the Musée de l'Homme). On the left as you exit you can peek inside the **chapel of St-Symphorien,** where during the Revolution over 100 clergymen were imprisoned before being executed on the square in front of the church. The chapel was restored in the 1970s and decorated by contemporary artist Pierre Buraglio in 1992.

3 place St-Germain-des-Prés, 6th arrond. (𝒞 **01-55-42-81-10.** www.eglise-sgp.org. Free admission. Mon–Sat 8am–7:45pm; Sun 9am–8pm. Métro: St-Germain-des-Prés.

St-Sulpice ★★ CHURCH   After years of renovations, the scaffoldings have finally come off the majestic façade of this enormous edifice. Construction started in the 17th century over the remains of a medieval church; it took over a hundred years to build, and one of the towers was never finished. Inside, the cavernous interior seems to command you to be silent; several important works of art are tucked into the chapels that line the church. The most famous of them are **three masterpieces by Eugène Delacroix,** "Jacob Wrestling with the Angel," "Heliodorus Driven from the Temple," and "St-Michael Vanquishing the Devil" (on the right just after you enter the church). Jean-Baptiste Pigalle's statue of the "Virgin and Child" lights up the Chapelle de la Vierge at the farthest most point from the entrance. A bronze line runs north–south along the floor; this is part of a **gnomon,** an astronomical device set up in the 17th century to calculate the position of the sun in the sky. A small hole in one of the stain glass windows creates a spot of light on the floor; every day at noon it hits the line in a different spot, climbing up to the top of an obelisk and lighting a gold disk at the winter equinox.

Place St-Sulpice, 6th arrond. ℰ **01-42-34-59-98.** www.paroisse-saint-sulpice-paris.org. Free admission. Daily 7:30am–7:30pmpm. Métro: St-Sulpice.

EIFFEL TOWER & LES INVALIDES (7TH ARRONDISSEMENT)

Hôtel des Invalides/Napoléon's Tomb ★★ MUSEUM   This grandiose complex houses a military museum, church, tomb, hospital, and military ministries, among other things. Commissioned by Louis XIV, who was determined to create a home for soldiers wounded in the line of duty, it was built on what was then the outskirts of the city. The first war veterans arrived in 1674—between 4,000 and 5,000 soldiers would eventually move in, creating a minicity with its own governor. An on-site hospital was constructed for the severely wounded, which is still in service today.

As you cross the main gate, you'll find yourself in a huge courtyard (102×207m, 335×207 ft.), the *cour d'honneur,* once the site of military parades. The surrounding buildings house military administration offices and the recently renovated **Musée de l'Armée,** one of the world's largest military museums, with a vast collection of objects testifying to man's capacity for self-destruction. The most impressive section is **Arms and Armor,** a panoply of 13th- to 17th-century weaponry. Viking swords, Burgundian battle axes, 14th-century blunderbusses, Balkan *khandjars,* Browning machine guns, engraved Renaissance serpentines, musketoons, grenadiers—if it can kill, it's enshrined here. There is also a huge wing covering the exploits of everyone from **Louis XIV** to **Napoléon III,** another on the two **World Wars,** and a shrine to **Charles de Gaulle.** Also onsite is the **Musée des Plans et Reliefs,** a somewhat dusty collection of scale models of fortresses and battlefields.

The **Eglise du Dôme** is split in two, the front half being the light-filled "Soldier's Church," decorated with magnificent chandeliers and a collection of flags of defeated enemies. On the other side of the glass partition the **Tomb of Napoléon** lies under one of the most splendid domes in France. Designed by Hardouin-Mansart, it took over 2 decades to build. The interior soars 107m (351 ft.) up to a skylight, which illuminates a brilliantly colored cupola. Ethereal light filters down to an opening where you can look down on the huge porphyry sarcophagus, which holds the emperor's remains, encased in five successive coffins (one tin, one mahogany, two lead, and one ebony). Surrounding the sarcophagus are the tombs of two of Napoléon's brothers, his son, and several French military heroes. Don't blame the over-the-top setting on Napoléon; the decision to transfer his remains to Paris was made in 1840, almost 20 years after his death. Tens of thousands crowded the streets to pay their respects as the coffin was carried under the Arc de Triomphe and down the Champs-Elysées to Les Invalides, where it waited another 20 years until the tomb was finished.

Place des Invalides, 7th arrond. ℰ **01-44-42-37-72.** www.invalides.org. Admission to all the museums, the church, and Napoléon's Tomb: 9.50€ adults, free 17 and younger. Apr–Oct 10am–6pm, Nov–Mar 10am–5pm. Métro: Latour-Maubourg, Varenne, Invalides; RER: Invalides.

Musée d'Orsay ★★★ MUSEUM   What better setting for a world-class museum of 19th-century art than a beautiful example of Belle Époque architecture? In 1986, the magnificent Gare d'Orsay train station, built to coincide with the 1900 World's Fair, was brilliantly transformed into an exposition space. The huge, airy central hall lets in lots of natural light, which is artfully combined with artificial lighting to illuminate a collection of treasures. In 2011 the "New Orsay" reopened with even more space, more colors on the walls, and a more coherent arrangement of the works.

The collection spans the years 1848 to 1914, a period that saw the birth of many artistic movements, such as the Barbizon School and Symbolism, but today it is best known for the emergence of Impressionism. All the superstars of the epoch are here, including Monet, Manet, Degas, and Renoir, not to mention Cézanne, and Van Gogh.

The top floor is now the home of the most famous Impressionist paintings, like Edouard Manet's masterpiece, "Le Déjeuner sur l'Herbe." Though Manet's composition of bathers and friends picnicking on the grass draws freely from those of Italian Renaissance masters, the painting shocked its 19th-century audience, which was horrified to see a naked lady lunching with two fully clothed men. Manet got into trouble again with his magnificent "Olympia," a seductive odalisque stretched out on a divan. There was nothing new about the subject; viewers were rattled by the unapologetic look in her eye—this is not an idealized nude, but a real woman, and a tough cookie to boot.

The middle level is devoted to the post-Impressionists, with works by artists like Gauguin, Seurat, Rousseau, and Van Gogh, like the latter's "Church at Auvers-sur-Oise," an ominous version of the church in a small town north of Paris where he moved after spending time in an asylum in Provence. This was 1 of some 70 paintings he produced in the 2 months leading up to his suicide.

A few other standouts:

RENOIR'S "DANCE AT LE MOULIN DE LA GALETTE, MONTMARTRE": The dappled light and the movement of the crowd in this joyous painting are such that you wonder if it's not going to suddenly waltz out of its frame. The blurred brushstrokes that created this effect rankled contemporary critics.

MONET'S "LA GARE ST-LAZARE": Here is another train station when steam engines were still pulling in on a regular basis. The metallic roof of the station frames an almost abstract mix of clouds and smoke; rather than a description of machines and mechanics, this painting is a modern study of light and color.

GAUGUIN'S "THE WHITE HORSE": The horse isn't even really white, but you don't care when you gaze at Gauguin's Tahitian version of paradise. Not everyone was charmed by the artist's vibrant colors: The pharmacist who commissioned the painting refused it because the horse was too green.

1 rue de la Légion d'Honneur, 7th arrond. (℃ **01-40-49-48-14.** www.musee-orsay.fr. Admission 9€ adults, 6.50€ ages 18–25, free ages 17 and younger. Tues–Wed and Fri–Sun 9:30am–6pm; Thurs 9:30am–9:45pm. Métro: Solférino. RER: Musée d'Orsay.

Musée du quai Branly ★★★ MUSEUM   It's just a few blocks from the Eiffel Tower, but this museum's wildly contemporary design has forever changed the architectural landscape of this rigidly elegant neighborhood. Its enormous central structure floats on a series of pillars, under which lies a lush garden, separated from the noisy boulevard out front by a huge glass wall. However you feel about the outside, you cannot help but be impressed by the inside: The vast space is filled with exquisite examples of the traditional arts of Africa, the Pacific Islands, Asia, and the Americas. Designed by veteran museum-maker Jean Nouvel, this intriguing space makes an ideal showcase for a category of artwork that too often has been relegated to the sidelines of the museum world.

This magnificent collection is displayed in a way that invites you to admire the skill and artistry that went into the creation of these diverse objects. Delicately carved headrests from Papua New Guinea in the form of birds and crocodiles and intricately painted masks from Indonesia vie for your attention. Look at and listen to giant wooden flutes from Papua New Guinea, displayed with an on-going recording. A selection of "magic stones" from the island nation of Vanuatu includes smooth abstract busts reminiscent of Brancusi sculptures. A fascinating collection of Australian aboriginal paintings segues into the Asian art section, and the journey continues into Africa, starting with embroidered silks from Morocco and heading south through magnificent geometric marriage cloths from Mali and wooden masks from the Ivory Coast. The Americas collection includes rare Nazca pottery and Inca textiles, as well as an intriguing assortment of North American works, like Haitian voodoo objects and Sioux beaded tunics.

37 quai Branly and 206 and 218 rue de Université, 7th arrond. ℰ **01-56-61-70-00.** www.quaibranly. fr Admission to permanent exhibitions 8.50€ adults, free children 17 and younger. Tues–Wed and Sun 11am–7pm; Thurs–Sat 11am–9pm. Métro: Alma-Marceau. RER: Pont d'Alma.

Musée Rodin ★★★ MUSEUM   There aren't many museums that can draw thousands of visitors who never even go inside. But the grounds of this splendid place are so lovely that many are willing to pay 1€ just to stroll around. Behind the Hôtel Biron, the mansion that houses the museum, is a formal garden with benches, fountains, and even a little cafe. Of course, it would be foolish *not* to go inside and drink in the some of the 6,600 sculptures in this excellent collection (don't worry, not all are on display), but it would be equally silly not to take the time to admire the large bronzes in the garden, which include some of Rodin's most famous works. Take, for example, "The Thinker." Erected in front of the Panthéon in 1906 during a political crisis, Rodin's first public sculpture soon became a Socialist symbol and was quickly transferred here by the authorities, under the pretense that it blocked pedestrian traffic. Other important outdoor sculptures include the "Burghers of Calais," "Balzac," and the "Gates of Hell," a monumental composition that the sculptor worked on throughout his career.

Indoors, marble compositions prevail, although there are also works in terra-cotta, plaster, and bronze, as well as sketches and paintings on display. The most famous of the marble works is "The Kiss," which was originally meant to appear in the "Gates of Hell." In time, Rodin decided that the lovers were too happy for this grim composition, and he explored it as an independent work. As usual with Rodin's works, the critics were shocked by the couple's overt sensuality, but not as shocked as they were by the large, impressionistic rendition of "Balzac," exhibited at the same salon, which critic Georges Rodenbach described as "less a statue than a strange monolith, a thousand-year-old menhir." The museum holds hundreds of works, many of them legendary, so don't be surprised if after a while your vision starts to blur. That'll be your cue to head outside and enjoy the garden. Note: The Hôtel Biron was undergoing much-needed renovations until deep into 2014, so don't be surprised if parts of the building are closed during your visit. The most famous pieces will still be on display (including those mentioned above), and the statues in the garden will all be present and accounted for.

79 rue de Varenne, 7th arrond. ℰ **01-44-18-61-10.** www.musee-rodin.fr. Admission 9€ adults, 5€ ages 18–25, free children 17 and younger. Tues and Thurs–Sun 9:30am–5:45pm, Wed 9:30am–8:45pm; Oct–Mar gardens close at 5pm. Métro: Varenne or St-Francois-Xavier.

Eiffel Tower ★★★ MONUMENT   In his wildest dreams, Gustave Eiffel probably never imagined that the tower he built for the 1889 World's Fair would become the ultimate symbol of Paris and, for many, of France. Originally slated for demolition after its first 20 years, the Eiffel Tower has survived more than a century and is one of the most visited sites in the nation. No less than 50 engineers and designers worked on the plans, which resulted in a remarkably solid structure that despite its height (324m/1,063 ft., including the antenna) does not sway in the wind.

But while the engineers rejoiced, others howled. When the project for the tower was announced, a group of artists and writers, including Guy de Maupassant and Alexandre Dumas fils, published a manifesto that referred to it as an "odious column of bolted metal." Others were less diplomatic: Novelist Joris-Karl Huysmans called it a "hole-riddled suppository." Despite the objections, the tower was built—over 18,000 pieces of iron, held together with some 2.5 million rivets. In this low-tech era, building techniques involved a lot of elbow grease: The foundations, for example, were dug entirely by shovel, and the debris was hauled away in horse-drawn carts. Construction dragged on for 2 years, but finally, on March 31, 1889, Gustave Eiffel proudly led a group of dignitaries up the 1,710 steps to the top, where he unfurled the French flag for the inauguration.

Over 100 years later, the tower has become such an integral piece of the Parisian landscape that it's impossible to think of the city without it. Over time, even the artists came around—the tower's silhouette can be found in the paintings of Seurat, Bonnard, Duffy, Chagall, and especially those of Robert Delaunay, who devoted an entire series of canvases to the subject. It has also inspired a whole range of stunts, from Pierre Labric riding a bicycle down the stairs from the first level in 1923 to Philippe Petit walking a 700m-long (2,296-ft.) tightrope from the Palais de Chaillot to the tower during the centennial celebration in 1989. Eiffel performed his own "stunts" towards the end of his career, using the tower as a laboratory for scientific experiments. By convincing the authorities of the tower's usefulness in studying meteorology, aerodynamics, and other subjects, Eiffel saved it from being torn down.

The most dramatic view of the tower itself is from the wide esplanade at the Palais de Chaillot (Métro: Trocadéro) across the Seine. From there it's a short walk down through the gardens and across the Pont d'Iena to the base of the tower. Though several tower elevators whisk visitors skyward, they do take time to come back down, so be prepared for a wait. The first floor is currently undergoing a major overhaul and is closed until at least mid-2014, so chances are you won't be stopping there. Personally, I think the view from the second level is the best; you're far enough up to see the entire city, yet close enough to clearly pick out the various monuments. But if you are aching to get to the top (and unlike me, don't have vertigo), an airplanelike view awaits. The third level is, mercifully, enclosed, but thrill-seekers can climb up a few more stairs to

the outside balcony (entirely protected by a grill). When the firs̶
will feature chic new pavilions and displays, and part of the fl
over—so you can virtually walk on air.

Champ de Mars, 7th arrond. ℗ **01-44-11-23-23.** www.tour-eiffel.fr. Lift to 2n
7€ ages 12–24, 4€ ages 4–11; Lift to 2nd and 3rd floors 15€ adults, 13€ ages 12⸱
stairs to 2nd floor 5€ adults, 3.50€ ages 12–24, 3€ ages 4–11. Free admission⸱
under. Sept–May daily 9:30am–11pm; June–Aug daily 9am–midnight. Sept–June
to 6pm. Métro: Trocadéro or Bir Hakeim. RER: Champ de Mars–Tour Eiffel.

MONTPARNASSE (14TH & 15TH ARRONDISSEMENTS)

Even though it had its heart ripped out in the early 1970s when the original 19th-cen-
tury train station was torn down and the Tour Montparnasse, an ugly skyscraper, was
erected, this neighborhood still retains a redolent whiff of its artistic past. Back in the
day, artists like Picasso, Modigliani, and Man Ray hung out in cafes like **Le Dôme, La
Coupole, La Rotonde,** and **Le Sélect,** as did a "Lost Generation" of English-speaking
writers like Hemingway, Fitzgerald, Faulkner, and Joyce. Today the cafes are mostly
filled with rich tourists, but you can still find quiet corners. Amazingly, **La Ruche,** the
legendary artists' studio from the Golden Years, is still standing and still has resident
artists (www.la-ruche.fr).

SHOPPING IN PARIS

Like us, most Parisians can't actually afford to buy the French luxury brands so revered
around the world—and yet they manage to look terrifically put together. What's their
secret? Read on as I attempt to shed some light on this puzzling mystery; the shops and
services listed below will give you a good point of departure for your Parisian shopping adventure.

Business Hours

In general, shops are open from 9 or 10am to 7pm; many are closed on Monday, and
most are closed on Sunday. Unfortunately, that means that the stores are jam-packed
on Saturday, so don't say I didn't warn you.

Some smaller, family-run operations sometimes still close between noon and 2pm
for lunch, but most stores stay open all day. Many larger stores and most department
stores stay open late (that is, until 9pm) 1 night a week (called a nocturne). For food
and toiletry emergencies, tiny minimarkets (called *alimentations*) stay open late into
the night 7 days a week. **Note:** Many shops close down for 2 or 3 weeks in July or
August, when the vacation exodus empties out major portions of the city.

Great Shopping Areas
STREETS FOR BARGAIN HUNTING

You can find clothes and knickknacks at significantly reduced prices at discount shops,
which tend to conglomerate on certain streets. **Rue d'Alésia** (14th, Métro: Alésia) is
lined with outlet stores *(déstock)* selling discounted wares, including designer labels
like Sonia Rykiel; and **Rue St-Placide** (6th, Métro: Sèvres-Babylone) has both outlet
stores and discount shops like Mouton à Cinq Pattes (p. 95).

MIDRANGE SHOPPING HUBS

Several areas have high concentrations of chain and other midrange stores where you
can get a lot of shopping done in a small geographic area. They are: **Rue de Rennes**

.; especially near the Tour Montparnasse); **Les Halles** (1st arrond.; the ⬛ des Halles underground mall is still open during the reconstruction of Les ⬛lles above; don't ignore the many nearby shops above); **Rue de Rivoli** (1st arrond., btw. rue du Pont Neuf and Hotel de Ville); and **Grands Magasins** (9th arrond.)—be sure look in the little streets that weave around the Printemps and Galeries Lafayette department stores (see below).

CHIC BOUTIQUE-ING

Paris has an endless number of darling boutiques, ranging from funky to fantastic. A few of the best streets for boutique shopping or simply *lèche-vitrine* (window shopping) are: **Rue des Abbesses** (18th arrond.; Métro: Abbesses), for affordable chic and the shops of hip, young startup designers; **Rue de Charonne** (11th arrond.; Métro: Bastille), a youth-oriented street that has recently taken a turn upscale with a dose of tony boutiques; **Rue des Francs Bourgeois** (4th arrond.; Métro: St-Paul), for a cornucopia of fashionable/cool/hip stores, most of which are open on Sunday; and **Rue Etienne Marcel** (2nd arrond.; Métro: Etienne Marcel), next to the hip Montorgueil pedestrian zone, with stylish boutiques galore.

THE SKY'S THE LIMIT

If you don't look at price tags and are always searching for the ultimate everything, Paris does not disappoint. For centuries, Paris has been the capital of luxury goods, many of them for sale on **Avenue Montaigne** (8th arrond.; Métro: Franklin D. Roosevelt), with breathtakingly expensive designer flagships like Dior and Chanel; the **Place Vendôme** (1st arrond.; Métro: Concorde or Tuileries), with eye-popping jewelry shops (Cartier, Boucheron, and so on); and **Rue du Faubourg St-Honoré** (8th arrond.; Métro: St-Philippe du Roule), where deeply elegant boutiques are filled with choice morsels of designer goods.

Markets: Food & Flea

Marchés (open-air or covered markets) are small universes unto themselves where nothing substantial has really changed for centuries. These markets are great local spots to hunt for fresh food or browse flea-market finds.

FOOD MARKETS

Paris's food markets are noisy, bustling, joyous places where you can buy fresh, honest food. Following is a short list of food *marchés;* you can find more on the municipal website (www.paris.fr; click on the little green basket labeled "Marchés" in the upper righthand corner). **Note:** Unless you see evidence to the contrary, don't pick up your own fruits and vegetables with your hands. Wait until the vendor serves you.

MARCHÉ D'ALIGRE ★★★ (also called Marché Beauveau, place d'Aligre, 12th arrond.; outdoor market Tues–Sun 9am–1pm, covered market Tues–Sat 9am–1pm and 4–7:30pm, Sun 9am–1:30pm; Métro: Ledru Rollin or Gare de Lyon): One of the city's largest markets, this sprawling affair invades a whole neighborhood, with both outdoor stalls and a covered.

MARCHÉ BATIGNOLLES ★★ (bd. Batignolles, btw. rue de Rome and Place Clichy, 17th arrond.; Sat 9am–3pm; Métro: Rome): A terrific, all-organic Saturday market market with fresh regional produce and close proximity to pretty sidewalk cafes for an after-marché coffe.

MARCHÉ RASPAIL ★★ (bd. Raspail, btw. rue de Cherche-Midi and rue de Rennes, 6th arrond.; Tues and Fri 7am–2:30pm; organic Sun 9am–3pm; Métro: Rennes): Stretching several blocks down the center divider of a wide avenue, this outdoor market makes a delicious gourmet stroll.

FLEA MARKETS

MARCHÉ AUX PUCES DE LA PORTE DE VANVES ★★ (Av. Georges-Lafenestre, 14th arrond.; www.pucesdevanves.typepad.com; Sat and Sun 7am–7:30pm; Métro: Porte de Vanves): This weekend event sprawls along two streets and is the best flea market in Paris—dealers swear by it. Look for old linens, vintage Hermès scarves, toys, ephemera, costume jewelry, perfume bottles, and bad art. Get there early—the best stuff goes fast.

MARCHÉ AUX PUCES DE PARIS ST-OUEN–CLIGNANCOURT ★ (Porte de Clignancourt, 18th arrond.; www.marcheauxpuces-saintouen.com; Sat 9am–6pm, Sun 10am–6pm, Mon 11am–5pm; Métro: Porte de Clignancourt): At the northern edge of the city, this claims to be the largest antiques market in the world. It was once a bargain-hunter's dream, but prices now often rival those of regular antiques dealers. Still, hard-core browsers will get a kick out of wandering the serpentine alleyways of this Parisian medina. **Note:** Beware of pickpockets.

Shopping A to Z

ANTIQUES & COLLECTIBLES

L'Objet qui Parle ★★ This delightful and quirky shop sells a jumble of vintage finds, including framed butterflies, teapots, furniture, chandeliers, crockery, hunting trophies, religious paraphernalia, and old lace. Great for souvenir shopping. 86 rue des Martyrs, 18th arrond. ✆ **06-09-67-05-30.** Métro: Abbesses.

Village St-Paul ★★ When you pass through an archway on rue St-Paul, you come upon a lovely villagelike enclosure, the remnant of a centuries-old hamlet that was swallowed up by the city. Today, it's a village of antiques dealers and design shops, selling everything from old bistro chairs and vintage lingerie to Brazilian eco-furniture and Iranian kilim rugs. www.levillagesaintpaul.com. No phone. Métro: St-Paul.

BEAUTY & PERFUME

The Different Company ★★ This independent perfume house makes its own unique fragrances with mostly natural materials. Signature scents include Osmanthus, Sel de Vétiver, and Rose Poivrée, but let your nose lead the way when you visit the store. 10 rue Ferdinand Duval, 4th arrond. www.thedifferentcompany.com. ✆ **01-42-78-19-34.** Métro: St-Paul.

Make Up Forever ★ This French cosmetics company, which trains professional makeup artists, also runs this boutique where you can buy products and get a **makeup lesson** (25 min. for 25€, 60 min. for 60€; call to reserve). A second location is at 5 rue de la Boétie in the 8th arrondissement. 5 rue des Francs Bourgeois, 4th arrond. ✆ **01-42-71-23-19.** www.makeupforever.fr. Métro: St-Paul.

BOOKS

San Francisco Book Company ★★ Since new books in English are very expensive in Paris, there's a steady traffic in used ones in the expatriate community,

Despite recent changes to the laws that restricted sales to certain times of the year, stores still follow the traditional sale (soldes) seasons. Two times a year, around the second week in January and the second week in July (specific dates are plastered all over the city), retailers go hog-wild and slash prices; the rest of the year sale prices don't dip down much below 30 percent. When opening day finally arrives, chaos ensues. There are good deals to be had, but try to avoid the first days of havoc and especially the weekends.

with a couple of bookstores devoted to the task. This centrally located shop has a good stock of both hardback classics and paperback airplane reading, as well as rare and out-of-print editions. 17 rue Monsieur Le Prince, 6th arrond. © **01-43-29-15-70.** www.sanfrancisco booksparis.com. Métro: Odéon.

Shakespeare & Company ★★★ This venerable shrine is a must on any Parisian literary tour. Run by George Whitman for some 60 years before he passed away in 2011 at 98, today it is helmed by his daughter, Sylvia, who was named for Sylvia Beach (who founded the original bookshop in 1919). Many a legendary writer has stopped in over the decades for tea; many an aspiring author has camped out in one of the back rooms (Whitman liked to think of his store as a "writer's sanctuary"). Today, Whitman's presence is still felt at this historic bookshop, which sells used and new books. Check the website for ongoing readings and other events. 37 rue de la Bûcherie, 5th arrond. www.shakespeareandcompany.com. © **01-43-25-40-93.** Métro/RER: St-Michel–Notre-Dame.

CLOTHING & ACCESSORIES

Antoine & Lili ★ Hot pink is the signature color at this wacky store, where the gaily painted walls are hung with oodles of colorful objects from around the world. The women's clothes are innovative and fresh yet wearable, and come in a range of bright colors. It has six other branches in town; check the website for addresses. 95 quai de Valmy, 10th arrond. © **01-40-37-41-55.** www.antoineetlili.com. Métro: Jacques-Bonsergent.

Des Filles à la Vanille ★★ Marrying "parfum et couture," this store smells as good as it looks.It has a great selection of big, fuzzy, funky sweaters, unusual long slit skirts, and gauzy dresses, as well as its own line of perfumes, including a vanilla-scented number, *bien sûr.* Another branch is at 150 bd. St-Germain in the 6th. 56 rue St-Antoine, 4th arrond.; © **01-48-87-90-02.** www.desfillesalavanille.com. Métro: St-Paul.

Children

Lilli Bulle ★★ If you are looking for something a little different and original, this is a good place to start. These cool and colorful clothes will make your kids look like they live in this fun and funky neighborhood. 3 rue de la Forge Royale, 11th arrond. © **01-43-73-71-63.** www.lillibulle.com. Métro: Faidherbe-Chaligny.

Marie Puce ★★ A little softer and gentler than Lilli, Marie offers easy elegance for tots who need to dress up (at least a little) but can't stand frills. Most of the clothing here is 100 percent Made in France. 60 rue du Cherche Midi, 6th arrond. © **01-45-48-30-09.** www.mariepuce.com. Métro: Sèvres-Babylone or St-Placide.

Discount

Mouton à Cinq Pattes ★★   Sift through the packed racks of designer markdowns and you just might find Moschino slacks or a Gaultier dress at a fabulous price. If you do, grab it fast—it might not be there tomorrow. The store at No. 8 is women's apparel only; No. 18 serves both sexes. 8 and 18 rue St-Placide, 6th arrond. ℂ **01-45-48-86-26.** www.moutonacinqpattesparis.com. Métro: Sèvres-Babylone.

Lingerie

Orcanta ★★   This chain has a great selection of name brands (such as Lise Charmel, Chantal Thomas, and Huit) and usually at least a rack or two of discounted items. More locations on the website. 60 rue St-Placide, 6th arrond. ℂ **01-45-44-94-44.** www. orcanta.fr. Métro: St-Placide.

CONCEPT STORES

Over the last few years, these hard-to-categorize stores with eclectic collections have popped up in several parts of the city. These are good places to hunt for that atypical gift you've been seeking.

Bü   A cross between Colette (see below), Ikea, and an upscale hardware store, this new and enigmatically named store (it's French, not Scandinavian) has reasonably priced housewares, stationary, leather handbags, luggage, and toys, as well as regional edibles. 45 rue Jussieu, 5th arrond. www.bu-store.com. ℂ **01-40-56-33-22.** Métro: Jussieu or Cardinal-Lemoine.

Colette ★★   What can you say about a store that sells both Hermès scarves and knitted hot dogs? This shopping phenom offers both high style and high concept—basically, if it's utterly cool and happening, they sell it. Karl Lagerfeld jeans, heart-shaped sunglasses, psychedelic nail polish, designer toilet brushes, and so forth. 213 rue St-Honoré, 1st arrond. ℂ **01-55-35-33-90.** www.colette.fr. Métro: Tuileries.

DEPARTMENT STORES

Galeries Lafayette ★★   The biggest of the *grand magasins* (department stores) sports an over-the-top Art Nouveau dome under which oodles of fashionable goodies are displayed for style-conscious shoppers. A bit less expensive than its more glamorous rival next door (see Printemps, below), it's also so huge that you can usually find just what you are looking for. It has everything from luxury labels to kids' stuff, not to mention books, stationary, wine, and a gourmet shop. 40 bd. Haussmann, 9th arrond. ℂ **01-42-82-34-56.** www.galerieslafayette.com. Métro: Chaussée d'Antin-Lafayette.

Le Bon Marché ★★★   Founded in the mid-1800s, this was the one of the world's first department stores. Despite its name (*bon marché* means affordable), this is the most expensive of Paris' *grand magasins*. It is also the most stylish, with beautiful displays and fabulous clothes of every imaginable designer label, both upscale and midrange. Right next door is its humongous designer supermarket, **La Grande Epicerie** (see "Specialty Groceries," below). 24 rue de Sèvres, 7th arrond. ℂ **01-44-39-80-00.** www.lebonmarche.com. Métro: Sèvres–Babylone.

Printemps ★★   The glistening domes of this 19th-century building bring to mind a grand hotel on the French Riviera. High fashion gets priority here; four of the seven floors of women's wear are devoted to designer labels. If you can't handle the crowds inside, you can always enjoy the famed *vitrines,* or **window displays,** outside. Better yet, ride to the top of Printemps Beauté/Maison and enjoy the splendid **panoramic view;** it even has a café at the top where you can lunch. 64 bd. Haussmann, 9th arrond. ℂ **01-42-82-50-00.** www.printemps.com. Métro: Havre-Caumartin or St-Lazare.

FOOD & DRINK
Chocolate

Michel Chaudun ★★★ If you are looking for a chocolate cellphone, look no further. Or how about chocolate pliers or ping-pong paddles? Known for his sculpting skills, Chaudun is also renowned for the exquisite taste of his masterworks. Be sure to try the pavés—melt-in-your-mouth little squares of chocolate ganache made to resemble cobblestones. 149 rue de l'Université, 7th arrond. ℂ **01-47-53-74-40.** Métro: Invalides.

Patrick Roger ★★ This cutting-edge chocolate boutique could easily be mistaken for a jewelry shop. Here you can sample chocolates with names like "Mellowness" (pistachio and almond) and "Zanzibar" (thyme and lemon), as well as candied fruits, nougat, and other delicacies. Four other stores in the city. 108 bd. St-Germain, 6th arrond. ℂ **01-43-29-38-42.** www.patrickroger.com. Métro: Cluny-La Sorbonne.

Specialty Groceries

Fauchon ★ Some (like me) find it overhyped and overpriced; others think it's heaven on Earth. Founded in 1886, this tea-room-cum-luxury-food-emporium has been wowing the crowds for over a century, and the crowds are certainly still coming. In 2004, the establishment received a shocking pink makeover and expanded exponentially—now you can find Fauchon from Hamburg to Ho Chi Min City. 26 and 30 place de la Madeleine, 8th arrond. ℂ **01-70-39-38-00.** www.fauchon.com. Métro: Madeleine.

La Grande Epicerie Paris ★★ This humongous gourmet grocery mecca, an outgrowth of Le Bon Marché department store (see above) stocks every imaginable gourmet substance you could possibly imagine, and many that you couldn't. Sculpted sugar cubes, designer mineral waters, truffled basalmic vinegar, pink salt from the Himalayas—need I go on? It also has an excellent (if expensive) takeout department for picnic items. 38 rue de Sèvres, 7th arrond, ℂ **01-44-39-81-00.** www.lagrandeepicerie.fr. Métro: Sèvres-Babylone.

Wines

Before you start planning to stock your wine cellar back home, consider this sad truth: Most non–EU countries won't let you bring back much more than a bottle or two. Your best bet is to drink up while you're here.

Legrand Filles et Fils ★★ More than just a wine store, this is a place where you can learn everything there is to know about the sacred grape. 1 rue de la Banque, 2nd arrond. ℂ **01-42-60-07-12.** www.caves-legrand.com. Métro: Bourse.

Les Domaines Qui Montent ★ This association of some 150 wine producers offers a vast selection of wines that come from small, independent vineyards where the emphasis is on quality and *terroir*, not quantity. An on-site wine bar also serves meals. A second location is at 136 bd. Voltaire in the 11th arrondissement. 22 rue Cardinet, 17th arrond. ℂ **01-42-27-63-96.** www.lesdomainesquimontent.com. Métro: Courcelles or Wagram.

JEWELRY

Bijoux Blues ★★ Hand-crafted, unique jewelry at reasonable prices made in an atelier in the Marais—who could ask for more? Designs are fun and funky, yet elegant. Pieces can be custom-designed. 30 rue St-Paul, 4th arrond. ℂ **01-48-04-00-64.** www.bijoux blues.com. Métro: St-Paul.

White Bird ★ If you are looking for a unique engagement ring or present for your sweetheart, this is a good bet. It has a terrific selection of jewelry made by talented, independent craftspeople/designers. 38 rue du Mont Thabor, 1st arrond. www.whitebird jewellery.com. ℂ **01-58-62-25-86.** Métro: Concorde.

STATIONERY

L'Art du Papier ★★   This delightful stationery store has a fabulous selection of colored papers and envelopes, as well as ink-stamps, sealing wax, and the essentials for hobbies like calligraphy and "le scrapbooking." It has three other locations: 16 rue Daunou in the 2nd, 197 bd. Voltaire in the 11th, and 17 ave. de Villiers in the 17th. 48 rue Vavin, 6th arrond.; ℭ **01-43-26-10-12.** www.art-du-papier.fr; Métro: Vavin.

ENTERTAINMENT & NIGHTLIFE

Paris blooms at night; its magnificent monuments and buildings become even more beautiful when they're cloaked in their evening illuminations. The already glowing Eiffel Tower bursts out in twinkling lights for the first 10 minutes of every hour. While simply walking around town can be an excellent night out, the city is also a treasure trove of rich evening offerings: bars and clubs from chic to shaggy, sublime theater and dance performances, top-class orchestras, and scores of cinemas and art-film houses.

With few exceptions, the city's major concert halls and theaters are in action between September and June, taking off during the summer months during the annual vacation exodus. On the upside, summer is the time for several wonderful music festivals, including the **Festival Chopin** and **Jazz à La Villette** (p. 98), many of which take place in Paris's lovely parks and gardens.

GETTING TICKETS   You can get tickets in person at **Fnac,** the giant bookstore/music chain that has one of the most comprehensive box offices in the city (follow the signs to the "Billeterie"). You can also **order your tickets online** at www.fnac spectacles.com or by phone at ℭ **08-92-68-36-22** (.34e per min.). **Ticketnet.fr** offers a similar service where you can buy tickets either online (www.ticketnet.fr) or by phone (ℭ **08-92-39-01-00;** .34e per min.).

Discount hunters can stand in line at one of the city's three **half-price ticket booths,** both run by **Le Kiosque Théâtre** (www.kiosquetheatre.com; Tues–Sat 12:30–8pm, Sun 12:30–4pm). There's one in front of the Montparnasse train station; a second is on the west side of the Madeleine; and a third in the center of Place des Ternes (17th arrond.). Half-price tickets for same-day performances go on sale here at 12:30pm. You can also find plenty of ticket discounts online at **BilletRéduc** (www. billetreduc.com, in French).

THEATER

Paris has hundreds of theaters, many of which have nightly offerings. Although most of it is in French, you can find a few English-language shows (see "Belly Laughs in

Finding Out What's On

For up-to-the-minute dates and schedules for what's happening in music, theater, dance, and film, pick up the **weekly listing magazines "Pariscope"** or **"l'Officiel des Spectacles"** (both .50€) the Parisian bibles for weekly events. Both come out on Wednesdays and are available at any newsstand.

Online, **Télérama's website** has good listings (www.telerama.fr; click on "sortir") as does **Evene** (www.evene.fr). For reviews, try the **"Paris Voice"** (www. parisvoice.com) an English-language online magazine that regularly reviews shows around town.

English," below). Of course, avant-garde shows combining dance, theater, and images really need no translation.

Comédie-Française ★★ Established by Louis XVI in 1680, this legendary theater is the temple of classic French theater (Corneille, Racine, Molière), though in recent decades, the troupe has branched out into more modern territory. In addition to the just-restored main theater **(Salle Richelieu),** the company presents its offerings in its two other theaters: the medium-size **Théâtre du Vieux Colombier** (21 rue du Vieux Colombier, 6th arrond.; ℭ **01-44-39-87-00;** Métro: St-Sulpice or Sèvres–Babylone) and the smaller **Studio-Théâtre** (Galerie du Carrousel du Louvre, under the Pyramid, 99 rue de Rivoli, 1st arrond.; ℭ **01-44-58-98-58;** Métro: Palais Royal–Musée du Louvre). Place Colette, 1st arrond. ℭ 08-25-10-16-80 (.15€ per min). www.comedie-francaise. fr. Métro: Palais-Royal–Musée du Louvre.

Théâtre National de Chaillot ★★ Dance and theater are on equal footing at this beautiful Art Deco theater in the Palais de Chaillot, where contemporary choreographers and theater directors share a jam-packed program. There is a lot of blurring of lines here between the two disciplines; dance programs often include video and text, and theater productions often incorporate the abstract. 1 place du Trocadéro, 16th arrond; ℭ **01-53-65-30-00;** www.theatre-chaillot.fr. Métro: Trocadéro

OPERA, DANCE & CLASSICAL CONCERTS

Cité de la Musique ★★ This modern complex offers a wide range of music options, from classical to contemporary to jazz. Young musicians and rising stars are highlighted; small orchestras and chamber musicians also show up on the program. The Jazz à La Villette festival in August/September is not to be missed. Ticket prices are very democratic, running from 15€ to around 40€. 221 av. Jean-Jaurès, 19th arrond. ℭ **01-44-84-44-84.** www.cite-musique.fr. Tickets 8€–39€. Métro: Porte de Pantin.

Opéra de Paris ★★★ This mighty operation includes both the **Palais Garnier** (place de l'Opéra, 9th arrond.; see p. 73), an attraction in itself, and the **Opéra Bastille** (2 place de la Bastille, 12th arrond.) a slate-colored behemoth that has loomed over the place de la Bastille since 1989. The company has since split its energies between the two venues. In theory, more operas are performed at the Bastille, which has more space and top-notch acoustics, and the Garnier, home of the **Ballet de l'Opèra de Paris,** focuses more on dance, but the reality is you can see either at both. www.operadeparis.fr. ℭ 08-92-89-90-90 (.34€ per minute).

Salle Pleyel ★★★ The Paris equivalent of Carnegie Hall, this mythic concert hall has hosted stars from Otto Klemperer to Louis Armstrong. The **Orchestre de Paris** makes its home here, and the **Radio France Philharmonic** also makes numerous appearances. Jazz and highbrow also pop up on the agenda. 252 rue du Faubourg-St-Honoré, 8th arrond. ℭ **01-42-56-13-13.** www.sallepleyel.fr. Métro: Ternes or Charle de Gaulle–Etoile.

CABARET

Some visitors feel they simply haven't had the true Paris experience without seeing a show at the Moulin Rouge or the Lido, even though there is nothing particularly Parisian, or even French, about them these days. Today's audiences are more likely to arrive in tour buses than touring cars, and the shows are more Vegas than Paris. What you will see here is a lot of scenic razzmatazz and many sublime female bodies, mostly *torse nue* (topless).

The Crazy Horse ★ This temple to "The Art of the Nude" presents an erotic dance show with artistic aspirations. Be advised that unlike the other shows, this

English-language shows are rare, and comics even more so, but a long-standing gig in town is worth a detour. At press time, the best place to go for a good giggle was **How to Become a**

Parisian in One Hour (playing at Théâtre des Nouvautés; details at www.olivier giraud.com), a terrific one-person show written by Olivier Giraud, a Frenchman who spent several years in the U.S.

one is known for what the girls *aren't* wearing. The performers, who slither, swagger, and lip-synch with panache, have names like Zula Zazou and Nooka Karamel. Note that while it has no dining onsite, it has dinner-show packages with nearby restaurants. 12 av. George V, 8th arrond. ℂ **01-47-23-32-32.** www.lecrazyhorseparis.com. 65€ show only with seats at the bar; from 105€ for the show and champagne; show plus dinner packages 184€–215€. Métro: George V or Alma Marceau.

Moulin Rouge ★ When it opened in 1889, the Moulin Rouge was the talk of the town, and its huge dance floor, multiple mirrors, and floral garden inspired painters like Toulouse-Lautrec. Times have changed—today's Moulin Rouge relies heavily on lip-synching and pre-recorded music, backed up by dozens of befeathered Doriss Girls, long-legged ladies who prance about the stage. Be prepared for lots of glitz and not much else. 82 bd. Clichy, place Blanche, 18th arrond. www.moulinrouge.fr. ℂ **01-53-09-82-82.** 99€ show alone; 109€ show with half-bottle of champagne; 180€–210€ show with dinner. Métro: Blanche.

JAZZ CLUBS

Paris has been a fan of jazz from its beginnings, and many legendary performers like Sidney Bechet and Kenny Clark made the city their home. Still a haven for jazz musicians and fans of all stripes, Paris offers dozens of places to duck in and listen to a good set or two. Here are a few of the best:

Caveau des Oubliettes ★ There are not too many jazz clubs in the world where you can both listen to music and admire an authentic, French Revolution–era guillotine. Located in the Latin Quarter, just across the river from Notre-Dame, this underground nightspot was once a medieval prison. Today patrons laugh, drink, talk, and flirt in the narrow passageways and listen to jazz in the lounge. 52 rue Galande, 5th arrond. ℂ **01-46-34-23-09.** www.caveaudesoubliettes.fr. Métro: St-Michel.

Le Sunset/Le Sunside ★★ One of several famous jazz clubs on the rue des Lombards (and it's a short street!), this one has a split personality. Le Sunset Jazz, is dedicated to electric jazz and international music, whereas tle Sunside is devoted to acoustic jazz for the most part. Some of the hottest names in French jazz appear here regularly (Jacky Terrasson, Didier Lockwood) along with a new crop of international stars. 60 rue des Lombards, 1st arrond. ℂ **01-40-26-46-60.** www.sunset-sunside.com. Tickets 20€–30€. Métro: Châtelet.

New Morning ★★★ If you are looking for big names and hot acts, look no further. This place has incredible lineups, including jazz giants, pop legends, and international superstars, as well as top-grade local talent. This relatively large club (the room holds 300) fills up quick, and no wonder: This truly is one of the best jazz venues in town, and the top ticket price is only around 30€. 7 rue des Petites-Ecuries, 10th arrond. ℂ **01-45-23-51-41.** www.newmorning.com. Cover 18€–26€. Métro: Château-d'Eau.

The Bar Scene

Paris may not be the 24-hour party city some other international capitals claim to be, but it has plenty of places to sip, flirt, and be merry. In general, bars stay open until around 2am.

Andy Wahloo ★★   A play on the name of the famous pop artist, this is a tiny temple to 1970s North African culture and kitsch. Sip your drink beneath a silk-screened Moroccan coffee ad and listen to some of the best Algerian raï around. 69 rue des Gravilliers, 3rd arrond. ℰ **01-42-71-20-38.** www.andywahloo-bar.com. Métro: Arts et Métiers.

Experimental Cocktail Club ★   If you're looking for a sophisticated spot to spot stars, you've come to the right place. Known, not surprisingly, for its gourmet cocktails, this cosmopolitan lounge has the feel of a retro speakeasy. 37 rue St-Sauveur, 2nd arrond. ℰ **01-45-08-88-09.** www.experimentalcocktailclub.com. Métro: Sentier.

Le Bar du Plaza Athénée ★★   Knock yourself out and order a shockingly expensive drink at this classy, historic joint, which simply drips with glamour and fabulousness. The bar itself literally glows (it's lit from inside), fashioning an even more luminous aura around the sleek patrons. Scan the iPad menu and order an iced Bellini (26€), then sit back and enjoy the show. Hotel Plaza-Athénée, 25 av. Montaigne, 8th arrond. ℰ **01-53-67-66-00.** www.plaza-athenee-paris.fr. Métro: Alma-Marceau.

WINE BARS

Le Baron Rouge ★★   This neighborhood institution spills out onto a corner that it shares with the sprawling Marché d'Aligre, a giant outdoor and covered market. It only has a few tables, but most people stand at the counter or outside, glass in hand, especially during market hours. It's a little rough-and-tumble getting your drink order in at the bar. 1 rue Théophile Roussel, 12th arrond. ℰ **01-43-43-14-32.** Metro: Ledru-Rollin.

Les Caves Populaires ★★   This is a neighborhood wine bar (yes, they have those in Paris), where locals come to shoot the breeze. The waiters are friendly, the decor low-key, and the wine and cheese-and-sausage platters cheap. 22 rue des Dames, 17th arrond. ℰ **01-53-04-08-32.** Metro: Place de Clichy.

The Club Scene

If you want to go out to a *boîte de nuit* (nightclub), you'll have plenty to choose from in Paris. Keep in mind that the French love their fashion, so dressing to impress is obligatory—sneakers will rarely get you past the line outside. Most clubs don't really get going until at least 11pm, if not later.

NIGHTCLUBS

Batofar ★★   For more than 15 years, this bright red boat has been the site of music and dancing and general good times. Docked on the quai François Mauriac, this multifunctional floating venue includes a dance club, a bar, a restaurant, and a terrace for cocktails hour and low-key soirees. On good nights, hundreds of gyrating dancers move in rhythm to house, garage, techno, and live jazz music. Facing 11 quai François Mauriac, 13th arrond. ℰ **01-53-60-17-00.** www.batofar.org. Métro: Quai de la Gare.

Nouveau Casino ★★   This former movie theater is now a giant dance club with live music, a huge bar that vaguely resembles an iceberg, hanging chandeliers, and a terrific program that includes all sorts of avant-garde dance music and bands with names like Flatbush Zombies and Moon Safari Club. 109 rue Oberkampf, 9th arrond. ℰ **01-43-57-57-40.** www.nouveaucasino.net. Métro: St-Maur, Parmentier, or Ménilmontant.

GAY & LESBIAN BARS & CLUBS

Paris has a vibrant gay nightlife scene, primarily centered around the **Marais.** Pick up one of the magazines devoted to the subject—like **"2x"**—for free in gay bars and bookstores. For lesbians, there is **"Muse & Out."** Also look for **"Têtu"** magazine at newsstands—it has special nightlife sections.

Le Cox ★   You'll know it when you get here; it's where the crowd is spilling out onto the sidewalk. This place still gets big crowds, even thought it's been here for years; people come for the bar as well as the great DJs. The clientele is a pleasant mix, everything from hunky American tourists to sexy Parisians. 15 rue des Archives, 4th arrond. www.cox.fr. ✆ **01-42-72-08-00.** Métro: Hôtel de Ville.

Le 3w Kafe ★   The most popular lesbian bar in the Marais, this is a good place to come to find company. Downstairs, a DJ spins on weekends, when there's dancing. Men can only enter the premises if accompanied by a woman. 8 rue des Ecouffes, 4th arrond. ✆ **01-48-87-39-26.** Métro: St. Paul.

Open Café ★   More relaxed and more diverse than neighboring Le Cox, this cafe-bar has a busy sidewalk terrace that's usually full both day and night. Everyone from humble tourists to sharp-looking businessmen to TV stars hangs out here. 17 rue des Archives, 4th arrond. ✆ **01-42-72-26-18.** www.opencafe.fr. Métro: Hôtel-de-Ville.

DAY TRIPS FROM PARIS

Many visitors (and Parisians, for that matter) make the mistake of thinking that Paris is France, but the minute you disentangle yourself from the city and its suburbs, another country appears: a gentle rural landscape dotted with small towns, not-so-small castles, and other fascinating sites, some of the best of which you can reach without a car.

Versailles ★★★

21km (13 miles) SW of Paris, 71km (44 miles) NE of Chartres

The grandeur of the Château of Versailles is hard to imagine until you are standing before it. Immediately, you start to get an idea of the power (and ego) of the man behind it, King Louis XIV. One of the largest castles in Europe, it is also forever associated with another, less fortunate king, Louis XVI and his wife, Queen Marie Antoinette, who were forced to flee when the French Revolution arrived at their sumptuous doorstep. The palace's extraordinary gardens, designed by the legendary landscape architect André Le Nôtre, are worth a visit all on their own.

ESSENTIALS

GETTING THERE   Take the **RER C** (www.transilien.fr; 30 min. from the Champs de Mars station) to **Versailles Rive Gauche–Château de Versailles. Important:** Make sure the final destination for your train is Versailles Rive Gauche–Château de Versailles, *not* Versailles Chantier, which is a long walk from the château. It's about a 5-minute walk from the Versailles Rive Gauche train station to the château—don't worry, you can't miss it. For the same price, you can also take the **SNCF** Transilien suburban train (www.transilien.fr; 45 min;) from the Gare St-Lazare station to **Versailles-Rive Droite,** and then walk 10 minutes to the château (around 45 min. total).

Unless you have a **Paris Visite** or other pass that includes zones 1–4, you will need to buy a special ticket (one-way fare 4.10€ adults, 2.05€ 4–10, free under 4); a regular Métro ticket will not suffice. Another option is to buy a 1-day **Mobilis** pass for zones 1–4 (11€), which gives you unlimited travel in those zones for the day. You can buy a ticket from any Métro or RER station; the fare includes a free transfer to the Métro.

TICKETS   The all-inclusive **Château Passeport** grants you access to the main chateau, the gardens, the Trianon Palaces, and the Marie Antoinette Estate (Nov–Mar 18€ adults; Apr–Oct 25€ includes Les Grandes Eaux; free 17 and under). You can also buy a **ticket to just the Palace** (15€; free 17 and under) or **just the Trianons and Marie Antoinette's Estate** (10€). The under-18 crowd (who get in free) may have to buy a ticket to get into the gardens (7.50€) from April to October. You can avoid some of the long lines at the entrance by purchasing you tickets online. A **Paris Museum Pass** will get you into everything except Les Grandes Eaux musicales (Apr–Oct).

VISITOR INFORMATION   **Château de Versailles:** www.chateauversailles.fr; ℂ **01-30-83-78-00;** Apr–Oct Tues–Sun 9am–6:30pm, Nov–Mar 9am–5:30pm. **Versailles Tourist Office**: 2 bis av. de Paris; www.versailles-tourisme.com; ℂ **01-39-24-88-88.**

THE CHATEAU OF VERSAILLES: THE BACKSTORY

Back in the 17th century, after having been badly burned by a nasty uprising called Le Fronde, Louis XIV decided to move his court from Paris to Versailles, a safe distance from the intrigues of the capital. He also decided to have the court move in with him, where he could keep a close eye on them and nip any new plots or conspiracies in the bud. This required a new abode that was not only big enough to house his court (anywhere from 3,000–10,000 people would be palace guests on any given day), but also one that would be grand enough to let the world know who was in charge.

Louis, otherwise known as the "Sun King," brought in a flotilla of architects, artists, and gardeners to enlarge the existing castle and give it a new look. Meanwhile, legendary garden designer André Le Notre was carving formal gardens and a huge park out of what had been marshy countryside. Harmonious geometric designs were achieved with flower beds, hedges, canals, and pathways dotted with sculptures and fountains.

Construction, involving as many as 36,000 workers, ground on for years; in 1682 the King and his court moved in, but work continued well into the reign of Louis XV. Louis XVI and his wife, Marie Antoinette, made few changes, but history made a gigantic one for them: On October 6, 1789, an angry mob of hungry Parisians marched on the palace, forcing the royal couple to return to Paris. Versailles would never again be a royal residence. The palace was ransacked during the Revolution, and in the years after it fell far from its original state of grace. Napoléon and Louis XVIII did what they could to bring the sleeping giant back to life, but by the early 1800s, during the reign of Louis-Philippe, the castle was slated for demolition. Fortunately, this forward-thinking king decided to invest his own money to save Versailles for future generations, and in 1837 the vast structure became a national museum.

TOURING THE PALACE

Designed to impress, the main bulk of the tour includes the **Grand Apartments,** used primarily for ceremonial events (a daily occurrence), the **Queen's Apartments,** and the **Hall of Mirrors.** These, along with the **King's Apartments** and the **Chapel,** are must-sees. If you have time and fortitude, you can take a **guided tour** of the royal family's **private apartments** (16€; some in English) for a more intimate look at castle life.

Each room in the **Grand Apartments** ★★★ is dedicated to a different planet (circling the sun, as in Sun King), and each has a fabulous painting on the ceiling depicting the god or goddess associated with said heavenly sphere. The first and most staggering, painting-wise, is in the **Salon d'Hercule** ★★, holding an enormous canvas by Paolo Veronese, "Christ at Supper with Simon," as well as a splendid, divinity-bedecked ceiling portraying Hercules being welcomed by the gods of Olympus by Antoine Lemoyne. At 480 sq. m (5,166 sq. ft), it's one of the largest paintings in France. The **Salon d'Apollon ★**, not surprisingly, was the throne room, where the Sun King received ambassadors and heads of state.

The ornate **Salon de Guerre ★** and **Salon de Paix ★** bookend the most famous room in the place, the **Hall of Mirrors ★★★**, which reopened in 2007 following a 3-year restoration. Louis XIV commanded his painter-in-chief, Charles Le Brun, to paint the 12m-high (40-ft.) ceiling of this 73m-long (240-ft.) gallery with representations of his accomplishments. This masterwork is illuminated by light from the 17 windows that overlook the garden, which are matched on the opposite wall by 17 mirrored panels. Add to that a few enormous crystal chandeliers, and the effect is dazzling. This splendid setting was the scene of a historic event in a more recent century: In 1919, World War I officially ended when the Treaty of Versailles was signed here.

A gorgeous bedroom with silk hangings printed with lilacs and peacock feathers in the **Queen's Apartments ★★** looks exactly as it did in 1789, when Marie Antoinette was forced to flee revolutionary mobs through a secret door (barely visible in the wall near her bed). The **King's Apartments ★★★** are even more splendiferous, though in a very different style: Here the ceilings have been left blank white, which brings out the elaborate white and gold decoration on the walls. The **King's Bedroom ★★★**, hung from top to bottom with gold brocade, is fitted with a sort of banister that separated the King from the 100 or so people who would come to watch him wake up in the morning.

The **Chapel ★★★**, where the kings attended Mass, is a masterpiece of light and harmony by Jules Hardouin Mansart. This lofty space (the ceiling is more than 25m/82 ft. high) reflects both Gothic and Baroque styles, with a vaulted roof, stained glass, and gargoyles with columns and balustrades typical of the early 18th century.

TOURING THE DOMAINE DE MARIE ANTOINETTE

Northwest of the fountain lies the **Domaine de Marie Antoinette ★★★**. (If you don't have a château passport or museum pass, you'll need a separate ticket to get in.) It was here that the young queen sought refuge from the strict protocol and infighting at the castle. She transformed the **Petit Trianon ★★**, a gift from her husband and the small manor that Louis XV used for his trysts, into a stylish haven. When the queen had finished decorating the manor in the latest fashions, she set to work creating an entire world around it, including a splendid **English garden ★**, several lovely pavilions, a jewel-like **theater ★★**, and even a small **hamlet ★**, complete with a working farm and a dairy, where she and her friends would play cards and gossip or just go for a stroll in the "country." The **Grand Trianon ★** is also worth a brief visit. Built by Louis XIV as a family retreat, this small marble palace consists of two large wings connected by an open columned terrace from which there is a delightful **view ★** of the gardens.

TOURING THE GARDENS & PARK

The entire 800-hectare (2,000-acre) park is laid out according to a precise symmetrical plan. From the terrace behind the castle, there is an astounding **view ★★★** that runs past two parterres, down a central lawn (the Tapis Vert), down the **Grand Canal ★★**, and seemingly into infinity. Le Nôtre's masterpiece is the ultimate example of the French-style garden: geometric, logical, and all in perfect harmony, a reflection of the divine order of the cosmos. Given that the Sun King was the star of this particular cosmos, a solar theme is reflected in the statues and fountains along the main axis of the perspective; the most magnificent of these is the **Apollo Fountain ★★★** where the sun god emerges from the waves at dawn on his chariot. Today, you can **picnic, bike ride** (bikes can be rented next to the restaurant), or even **row a boat** in the canal west of the Apollo Fountain on a sunny day.

Place d'Armes. www.chateauversailles.fr. ℭ **01-30-83-78-00.** Palace 15€ adults; free children 18 and under. Marie Antoinette's Domaine 10€ adults; everything free children 17 and younger. Palace Apr–Oct Tues–Sun 9am–6:30pm; Nov–Mar Tues–Sun 9am–5:30pm. Marie Antoinette's Domaine Apr—Oct Tues–Sun noon–6:30pm; Nov–Mar Tues–Sun noon–5:30. Park daily dawn–dusk.

Chartres ★★★

97km (60 miles) SW of Paris, 76km (47 miles) NW of Orléans

You'll spy it long before you see the actual town: the spire of the cathedral of Chartres rising above a sea of wheat fields. You can easily visit this stunning church and its inspiring stain-glassed windows and still have time to wander the narrow streets of the ancient (and beautiful) town.

ESSENTIALS

GETTING THERE From Paris's Gare Montparnasse, **trains** run directly to Chartres, taking about an hour. Tickets cost 30€ round-trip; for more information and reservations, see www.voyages-sncf.com or call ℭ 3635. If **driving,** take A10/A11 southwest from the *périphérique* and follow signs to Le Mans and Chartres. (The Chartres exit is clearly marked.)

VISITOR INFORMATION The **Office de Tourisme** in the Maison du Saumon, 8 rue de la Poissonerie (www.chartres-tourisme.com; ℭ **02-37-18-26-26**).

EXPLORING THE CATHEDRAL

With its carved portals and three-tiered flying buttresses, this would be a stunning sight even without its legendary **stained-glass windows**—though the world would be a far drearier place. For these ancient glass panels are truly glorious, a kaleidoscope of colors so deep, so rich, and so bright, it's hard to believe they are some 700 years old.

Meant as teaching devices more than artwork, the windows functioned as a sort of enormous cartoon, telling the story of Christ through pictures to a mostly illiterate populace. From its beginnings, this was a place of pilgrimage, which accounts at least in part for the superhuman dimensions of the church. Pilgrims came from far and near to see a piece of cloth that believers say was worn by the Virgin Mary during Christ's birth. These days it's a different sort of pilgrim that is drawn to Chartres: More than 1.5 million tourists come from around the globe annually to admire the artistry that went into this magnificent edifice.

A Romanesque church stood on this spot until 1194, when a fire burned it virtually to the ground. All that remained were the towers, the Royal Portal, and a few remnants of stained glass. The locals were so horrified that they sprung to action; in only 3 decades a new cathedral was erected, which accounts for its remarkably unified Gothic architecture. The new cathedral was dedicated in 1260 and has miraculously survived the centuries with relatively little damage. The cathedral was somehow spared during the French Revolution; during World War I and World War II, the precious windows were carefully dismounted piece by piece and stored in a safe place in the countryside.

Before you enter the church, take in the **facade ★★**, a remarkable assemblage of religious art and architecture. The base of the two towers dates from the early 12th century (before the fire). The tower to your right (the **Old Tower,** or South Tower) is topped by its original sober Romanesque spire; that on your left (**New Tower,** or North

Tower) was blessed with an elaborate Gothic spire by Jehan de Beauce in the early 1500s, when the original burned down. Below is the **Royal Portal ★★★**, a masterpiece of Romanesque art. Swarming with kings, queens, prophets, and priests, this sculpted entryway tells the story of the life of Christ. The rigid bodies of the figures contrast with their lifelike faces; it is said that Rodin spent hours here contemplating this stonework spectacle. You can **climb to the top of the New Tower** to take in the **view ★**; just remember to wear rubber-soled shoes—the 300 steps are a little slippery after all these centuries.

Once inside the cathedral, you'll really understand what all the fuss is about. The dimness is pierced by the radiant colors of the **stained-glass windows ★★★**, which shine down from all sides. Three windows on the west side of the building, as well as the beautiful rose window to the south called **Notre Dame de la Belle Verière ★**, date from the earlier 12th-century structure; the rest, with the exception of a few modern panels, are of 13th-century origins.

Another indoor marvel is the **chancel enclosure ★★★**, which separates the chancel (the area behind the altar) from the ambulatory (the walkway that runs around the outer chapels). Started in 1514 by Jehan de Beauce, this intricately sculpted wall depicts dozens of saints and other religious superstars. Back in the ambulatory is the Chapel of the Martyrs, where the cathedral's cherished **relic** resides: a piece of cloth that the Virgin Mary apparently wore at the birth of Christ, which was a gift of Charles the Bald in 876.

Note: The cathedral asks that visitors not talk or wander around during Mass, generally held in the late morning and early evening. You are welcome to sit in on services, of course.

16 Cloître Notre-Dame. www.cathedrale-chartres.monuments-nationaux.fr. © **02-37-21-22-07.** General admission to the cathedral is free; admission to the towers 7€ adults; 4.50€ adults 18–25; free children 17 and under. Cathedral open daily 8:30am–7:30pm.

EXPLORING THE OLD TOWN

Give yourself time to explore the medieval cobbled streets of the **Vieux Quartier (Old Town) ★**. There are several gabled houses in the narrow lanes near the cathedral, including the colorful facades of **rue Chantault,** one of which is 8 centuries old. Seek out rue du Bourg, where you'll find the famous **Salmon House** (which houses the tourist office) and some lovely sculptures (including a certain fish). In the lower town, you can stroll along the picturesque **Eure River** with its stone bridges and ancient wash-houses. On Saturday or Wednesday morning a covered farmer's market is held in **place Billard** (until 1pm), the perfect place to grab supplies for a casual lunch in the park behind the cathedral or along the river.

NORMANDY

by Kathryn Tomasetti

On June 6, 1944, the largest armada ever assembled took the beaches at Normandy and was responsible for regaining control of Europe from the Nazis. Many visitors come to this region exclusively to see the invasion beachheads, D-Day museums, and touching coastal cemeteries.

But although those sights are the area's most famous, they do not exclusively define the region. Normandy's wide beaches attract families from across France. All summer, the Deauville and Trouville sands draw the chicest of the chic from Europe and North America: Not for nothing are these resorts known as the 21st arrondissement of Paris.

Along the coast, Bayeux attracts lovers of history and art, many to see the famed tapestries named for the town. Honfleur, too, is a place of arty pilgrimage; and Rouen pulls in foodies by the score. Exquisite Mont-St-Michel has guarded the western border of Normandy for a millennium. A new pedestrian walkway—opening in 2014—will link the coastline with this castle in the sand for the first time.

So come to see the World War II sights, but don't be shy about exploring further. This is an area that rewards those who linger.

5

ROUEN ★★

135km (84 miles) NW of Paris; 89km (55 miles) E of Le Havre

Thanks to a huge port and a vibrant university, the capital of Normandy buzzes from dawn 'til dusk. Former occupants of Rouen include writer Gustave Flaubert (who grew up along the city's enchanting cobbled streets), Claude Monet (who endlessly painted Rouen's Cathédrale de Notre-Dame), and Joan of Arc ("Oh, Rouen, art thou then my final resting place?"). Today it's the bustling home to half a million people.

Victor Hugo called Rouen "the city of a hundred spires." Half of the city was destroyed during World War II, mostly by Allied bombers. During the reconstruction of the old quarters, some of the almost-forgotten crafts of the Middle Ages were revived. The city on the Seine is rich in historical associations: William the Conqueror died here in 1087, and Joan of Arc was burned at the stake by the Brits on place du Vieux-Marché in 1431.

Essentials

ARRIVING From Paris's Gare St-Lazare, **trains** leave for Rouen about once an hour (trip time: 1½ hr.). The one-way fare is 23€. For rail information and schedules, visit www.voyages-sncf.com or call ℂ **36-35.** To **drive** from Paris, take A13 northwest to Rouen (trip time: 1½ hr.).

VISITOR INFORMATION   The **Office de Tourisme** is at 25 place de la Cathédrale (www.rouentourisme.com; ℭ **02-32-08-32-40**).

CITY LAYOUT   As in Paris, the Seine splits Rouen into a **Rive Gauche** (Left Bank) and **Rive Droite** (Right Bank). The old city is on the Rive Droite.

Getting Around

ON FOOT   Rouen's Old Town is compact, with many of its winding medieval streets entirely pedestrianized. It's best navigated on foot: The Tourist Office offers free maps marked with two easy-to-follow walking tours around the city.

BY BICYCLE Like many French cities, Rouen has its own bike-sharing scheme, **Cy'clic** (http://cyclic.rouen.fr). You can register online or directly at 1 of Rouen's 21 bike stands; fees range from 1€ for 1 day to 5€ for a week.

BY CAR **Rouen Park** (www.rouenpark.com) details the city's five central public parking lots, with information on exact location, number of parking places, and hourly prices.

BY TAXI **Les Taxi Blancs** (℃ **02-35-61-20-50**).

BY PUBLIC TRANSPORT Rouen's **Métro** (www.crea-astuce.fr) has one line, running north-south through the city both above and underground. The most central stations in Old Rouen are Théâtre des Arts, Palais de Justice, and the train station, Gare-Rue Verte. Tickets cost 1.50€ and are on sale at automatic kiosks at each station.

[Fast FACTS] ROUEN

ATMs/Banks Dozens of banks are dotted around the city center, with six along rue Jeanne d'Arc.

Doctors & Hospitals **Centre Hospitalier Universitaire de Rouen** (www.chu-rouen.fr; ℃ **02-32-88-89-90**).

Emergencies The Tourist Office lists a full range of emergency contacts—from a poison center to an emergency cardiology unit—on its website (www.rouentourisme.com). Click on "General Information," then "Emergency Numbers."

Internet Access **The Web Café,** 16 rue du Général Leclerc (℃ **02-32-08-04-25**).

Mail & Postage **La Poste,** 112 rue Jeanne d'Arc (℃ **36-31**).

Pharmacies **Grande Pharmacie du Centre,** 29 place Cathédrale (℃ **02-35-71-33-17**).

Where to Stay

Hotel de Bourgtheroulde ★★★ Just steps from place du Vieux-Marche and rue de l'Horologe, this five-star boutique hotel is Rouen's prettiest hideaway. Each elegant room is a one-off, with interesting features like exposed stone walls, wood paneling, and mosaic-tiled bathrooms. At the **Spa du Drap d'Or,** a hammam, sauna, and Normandy's largest indoor pool are the ideal antidote to an exhausting day of sightseeing. Utterly unique is the hotel's interior courtyard, where ornate 15th-century bas-reliefs depict the meeting of French King Francis I and English King Henry VIII in 1515.

15 place de la Pucelle, Rouen 76000. www.hotelsparouen.com. ℃ **02-35-14-50-50**. 78 units. 150€–250€ double; 380€–550€ suite. Parking 18€. **Amenities:** 2 bars; indoor swimming pool; 2 restaurants; spa; free Wi-Fi.

Hôtel de la Cathédrale ★ For visitors on a budget, Hôtel de la Cathédrale is one of the town's loveliest options. The location—just off a pedestrian street midway between the cathedral and the Eglise St-Maclou, and opposite the Archbishop's Palace where Joan of Arc was tried—is unbeatable. Guestrooms are simple, but each has its own character, with quirky wallpaper or wooden beamed ceilings. In summertime, a buffet breakfast is served in the cobble-covered courtyard.

12 rue St-Romain, Rouen 76000. www.hotel-de-la-cathedrale.fr. ℃ **02-35-71-57-95**. 26 units. 90€–120€ double; 14€ triple; 140€ quadruple. Public parking 11€ nearby. **Amenities:** Tea lounge; babysitting; room service; free Wi-Fi.

Where to Eat

A historical city with a bustling, modern edge, Rouen is an ideal place to sample Norman cuisine. Key local ingredients include fresh fish, rich cream, butter, and apples. For a quick overview of the best seasonal produce, pop into the Old Town's **daily market,** place du Vieux Marché (Tues–Sun 6:30am–1:30pm). Visitors with a sweet tooth will delight in apple *tarte tatin,* chocolate fondant, or plum cake, best tasted in the courtyard garden of **Dame Cakes,** 70 rue St-Romain (www.damecakes.fr; ℰ 02-35-07-49-31).

Auberge Saint Maclou ★ TRADITIONAL FRENCH In a picturesque half-timbered building on the edge of Rouen's antiques district, this lively neighborhood restaurant dishes up hearty French classics. Try the rabbit with rosemary *jus,* rump steak with béarnaise sauce, or a country-style terrine made from the chef's grandfather's recipe. On summer evenings, sidewalk tables spill out into the shadow of Eglise St-Maclou.

222 rue Martainville. ℰ **02-35-71-06-67.** Reservations recommended. Main courses 16€–26€. Tues–Sat noon–2pm and 7–10pm, Sun noon–2pm.

Gill ★★★ MODERN FRENCH This double-Michelin-starred extravaganza teams sophisticated Norman cuisine with zingy Asian flavors, such as ginger and yuzu. The restaurant decor is understated, allowing Chef Gilles Tournadre's creations to shine: Sample citrus-infused lobster maki with crispy seaweed *tuile;* or the ever-popular pigeon *à la Rouennaise,* drizzled in concentrated consommé. Members of the restaurant's Japanese kitchen staff are often in town on apprenticeships from La Maison de Gill, another of Chef Tournadre's eateries, located outside Osaka, Japan.

8-9 quai de la Bourse. www.gill.fr. ℰ **02-35-71-16-14.** Reservations required far in advance. Main courses 31€–60€; business lunch 37€; fixed-price dinner 68€–95€. Tues–Sat noon–1:45pm and 7:30–9:45pm. Closed Aug and 2 weeks in Apr.

La Couronne ★★★ NORMAN Going strong since 1345, La Couronne is the oldest *auberge* in France. Foodies can plump for Julia Child's Menu (65€), which replicates the dishes—including oysters and *sole meunière*—that the great chef savored here during her first-ever French lunch in 1948. The cozy restaurant has continued to attract renowned chefs (Gilles Tournadre, of Gill fame, apprenticed here for 3 years) and celebrities alike: Dozens of autographed photographs of the famous decorate La Couronne's interior, from Josephine Baker to Queen Elizabeth II.

31 place de Vieux Marché. www.lacouronne.com.fr. ℰ **02-35-71-40-90.** Reservations recommended. Main courses 25€–46€; fixed-price lunch menu 25€–39€; fixed-price dinner menu 35€–75€. Daily noon–2:30pm and 7–10:30pm.

Exploring Rouen

Joan of Arc was executed for heresy in place du Vieux-Marché, Rouen's Old Marketplace. Tied to a stake, she was burned on May 30, 1431. Her ashes were gathered and tossed into the Seine. A modern church with stained-glass windows from St-Vincent sits in the center of a monumental complex in the square; beside it, a bronze cross marks the position of St. Joan's stake. This square was also the former home of Rouen's Joan of Arc Museum, which closed in 2012. A new Joan of Arc Visitors' Center is currently under construction and slated to open in early 2015.

The "Street of the Great Clock"—rue de l'Horologe—runs between the cathedral and place du Vieux-Marché. Now pedestrianized, it's named for an ornate gilt Renaissance clock mounted on an arch, Rouen's most popular monument. The arch bridges the street and connects to a Louis XV fountain with a bevy of cherubs and a bell tower. At night the bells still toll a curfew.

Cathédrale Notre-Dame de Rouen ★★★ CATHEDRAL   Monet immortalized Rouen's cathedral (particularly the facade, with its galaxy of statues) in his paintings. Consecrated in 1063, the cathedral, a symphony of lacy stonework, was reconstructed after suffering damage in World War II. Two towers distinguish it: **Tour de Beurre** was financed by the faithful who were willing to pay for the privilege of eating butter during Lent. Containing a carillon of 56 bells, the **Tour Lanterne (Lantern Tower)**—built in 1877 and using 740 tons of iron and bronze—rises to almost 150m (492 ft.), making its spire the tallest in France.

Inside, the cathedral's choir is a masterpiece, with 14 soaring pillars. Particularly interesting is the **Chapelle de la Vierge,** adorned with Renaissance tombs of the cardinals d'Amboise. Also entombed here is the heart of Richard the Lion-Hearted, a token of his affection for the people of Rouen.

Behind the cathedral is the **Palais de l'Archevêché (Archbishop's Palace).** The broken arches and rosette windows witnessed the trial of Joan of Arc in 1431, and her rehabilitation was proclaimed here in 1456.

For a bird's-eye view over the cathedral and square, visit **Le Balcon** (admission 2€; accessed via the Tourist Office), a top-floor viewing platform that opened in 2013.

Place de la Cathédrale. www.cathedrale-rouen.net. *©* **02-35-71-51-23.** Free admission. Apr–Oct Mon 2–7pm, Tues–Sat 9am–7pm; Nov–Mar Mon 2–6pm, Tues–Sat 9am–noon and 2–6pm; Sun and holidays year round 8am–6pm. Closed during Mass and some holidays.

Eglise St-Maclou ★★ CHURCH   St-Maclou was built in the Flamboyant Gothic style with a step-gabled porch and cloisters. It's known for the 16th-century panels on its doors. Our favorite (to the left) is the Portail des Fontaines (Portal of the Fonts). The church was built in 1200, rebuilt in 1432 and consecrated in 1521. Its lantern tower is from the 19th century, and its exterior was completely renovated in 2013.

Well worth a peek is the nearby **Aître Saint-Maclou,** 184 rue Martainville (*©* **02-35-71-71-72**). Half-timbered buildings, decorated with creepy skull motifs, mark the site of a cemetery dedicated to victims of the 1348 Great Plague. It now houses the regional Ecole des Beaux-Arts. It's open Monday to Friday 8am to 6pm, Saturday and Sunday 9am until 6 or 7pm. Admission is free.

3 place Barthélémy. *©* **02-35-08-69-00.** Free admission. Apr–Oct Sat–Sun 10am–noon and 2–6pm; Nov–Mar Sat–Sun 10am–noon and 2–5:30pm.

Musée de la Céramique ★ MUSEUM   Rouen has been an important center for ceramics and pottery production since the 16th century. This small museum highlights local treasures, from reddish-hued 17th- and 18th-century Rouen *faïence* (opaquely glazed earthenware) to two new rooms dedicated to 19th- and 20th-century Sèvres porcelain.

1 rue Faucon. www.rouen-musees.com. *©* **02-35-07-31-74.** Admission 3€ adults, 2€ students, free for children 17 and under. Wed–Mon 2–6pm.

Musée des Beaux-Arts ★★ MUSEUM   One of Normandy's most prestigious collections—more than 8,000 artworks ranging from medieval primitives to contemporary paintings—is housed in this late-19th-century edifice. You'll find paintings by Ingres (seek out his "La Belle Zélie") and a salon devoted to Géricault, including his portrait of Delacroix. Other works are by Veronese, Velázquez, Caravaggio, Rubens, Poussin, Fragonard, and Corot, and by Impressionists such as Renoir, Sisley, and Monet, including several of the latter's paintings of the Rouen cathedral. Blockbuster summer exhibitions take place here during the **Normandie Impressionniste Festival** (www.normandie-impressionniste.fr; next edition 2016).

Esplanade Marcel Duchamp. www.rouen-musees.com. ✆ **02-35-71-28-40.** Admission 5€ adults, 3€ students, free for children 17 and under. Wed–Mon 10am–6pm.

Shopping

Rouen was once one of France's major producers of the fine decorative ceramic ware known as *faïence de Rouen.* For contemporary faïence, your best bet is **Faïencerie Carpentier Augy,** 26 rue St-Romain (✆ 02-35-88-77-47). The well-known studio sells reproductions of historical styles in an array of colors.

Rouen is also an antiques capital, with more than 80 vendors in the Old Town. The best hunting ground is along **rue Eau-de-Robec** (with its lovely mini-canal), **rue Damiette,** and **rue St-Romain.** The city also has a very good **flea market** the first Friday of the month along allée Eugène Boudin.

Other antiques shops worth visiting are **Michel Bertran,** 108 rue Molière (✆ 02-35-98-24-06), with a good selection of 18th- and 19th-century paintings, especially by School of Rouen Impressionists; and **Etienne Bertran,** 110 rue Molière (✆ 02-35-70-79-96), with its collection of antique books dating to the 16th century.

Chocolate lovers will discover a veritable paradise at **Le Cacaotier,** 5 rue Guillaume le Conquérant (www.lecacaotier.com; ✆ 02-35-62-71-06). For 2 years' running, master chocolatier Hubert Masse has been voted 1 of the 12 best chocolate makers in France.

Nightlife

For upscale entertainment, **Opéra de Rouen,** 7 rue du Docteur Rambert (www.operaderouen.fr; ✆ 02-35-98-74-78), schedules year-round ballet, opera, and classical music. A variety of concerts takes place at **Abbatiale Saint-Ouen,** place du Général-de-Gaulle. And at the former hangar **Le 106,** quai Jean de Béthancourt (www.le106.com; ✆ 02-32-10-88-60), there's a jam-packed lineup of French and international pop and rock shows. The Tourist Office website offers a current calendar of events.

Much of the nightlife, especially pubs, centers around place du Vieux-Marché. **La Bohème,** place St-Amand (www.laboheme-discotheque.com; ✆ 02-35-71-53-99), is a small disco with a cozy, publike ambience. **Le P'tit Zinc,** 20 place du Vieux-Marché (www.restaurant-76.fr; ✆ 02-35-89-39-69), is a bistro-style wine bar with early-1900s decor and one of the best wine selections in town. Tired of wine? It's also got an excellent selection of Norman cider.

Finding Old Normandy in Calvados Country

For a taste of old Normandy, motorists heading from Rouen to Deauville should stop in Pont-Audemer, 50km (31 miles) west of Rouen. On the banks of the River Risle, Pont-Audemer is in the heart of Calvados country. In spite of war damage, Pont-Audemer retains much of its old look, especially if you wander its historic streets, rue de la Licorne (unicorn) and rue de la République. Along rue de la République, look for Eglise St-Ouen, dating from the 11th century.

HONFLEUR ★★

201km (125 miles) NW of Paris; 63km (39 miles) NE of Caen

Dating from the 11th century, oh-so-pretty Honfleur is one of Normandy's most perfectly preserved fishing ports. Homes with pastel façades peek out over the town's picturesque harbor, which sits at the mouth of the Seine.

Artists, including Dubourg, Boudin, and Monet, flocked here during the 19th century to capture the town's beguiling local scenes.

To the east, the cable-stayed Pont de Normandie bridge links Honfleur to Le Havre. And the Côte de Grace—the start of the enchanting Côte Fleurie—meanders westwards from here, passing half-timbered Norman homes and ancient chapels en route to Trouville.

Essentials

ARRIVING There's no direct **train** service into Honfleur. From Paris, take one of the half-dozen or so daily trains from Gare St-Lazare to Trouville-Deauville (from 25€ one-way). From there, **Bus Verts du Calvados'** (www.busverts.fr; ✆ **08-10-21-42-14**) no. 20 makes the 25-minute ride to Honfleur; the one-way fare is 2.40€. From Rouen, take the train to Le Havre (15€ one-way; journey time around an hour) and transfer to bus no. 50 (4.65€ one-way), for the 30-minute ride to Honfleur. Several buses (no. 20) run daily between Caen and Honfleur (trip time: 2 hr.); the one-way fare is 8.20€.

To **drive** from Paris (trip time: 2–2½ hr.), take A13 west, then the A29 north in the direction of Le Havre. From Pont l'Evêque or other points southwest, D579 leads to Honfleur's major boulevard, rue de la République.

VISITOR INFORMATION The **Office de Tourisme** is on quai Lepaulmier (www.ot-honfleur.fr; ✆ **02-31-89-23-30**).

[FastFACTS] HONFLEUR

ATMs/Banks Half a dozen banks cluster along rue de la Foulerie, place Pierre Berthelot and rue des Longettes.

Mail & Postage **La Poste,** 7 cours Albert Manuel (✆ **36-31**).

Pharmacies **Pharmacie du Dauphin,** 5 rue Dauphin (✆ **02-31-89-10-80**).

Where to Stay

Absinthe Hôtel ★★ Constructed during the 16th century, the centrally located Absinthe Hôtel occupies a charming brick building—historically a church presbytery—and its sea-facing annex. The decor is a handsome blend of the traditional (wooden beams and exposed stone walls) and the contemporary. Each room has its own whirlpool bath; one suite features a private sauna. The elegant **Absinthe Restaurant,** on the ground floor, peeks out over the town's port.

1 rue de la Ville, Honfleur 14600. www.absinthe.fr. ✆ **02-31-89-23-23.** 11 units. 130€–210€ double; 255€–265€ suite. **Amenities:** Restaurant; free cabled Internet access.

La Maison de Lucie ★★★ This superb hotel is set in a mid-19th-century villa just a short stroll from the town's picturesque port. Guestrooms, clustered around the idyllic walled courtyard, are decorated in printed wallpaper and unique antiques. Some overlook the estuary; others possess their own private patio. Too much sightseeing? Unwind in the hotel's Jacuzzi, tucked into the spacious vaulted cellar under the house.

44 rue des Capucins, Honfleur 14600. www.lamaisondelucie.com. ✆ **02-31-14-40-40.** 12 units. 180€–200€ double; 250€–315€ suite. **Amenities:** Spa; free Wi-Fi.

Where to Eat

Le Bistro des Artistes ★★ NORMAN Overlooking Honfleur's incredibly picturesque harbor, this friendly portside restaurant offers tasty Norman flavors at honest prices. Chef and owner Anne Marie Carneiro dishes up regional classics, such as veal chops *à la normande,* skate in mustard sauce, and *teurgole,* a rich Norman rice pudding. Bread, served with delectable Norman butter, is homemade. Although service can be slow, Le Bistro is real find among the town's many mediocre eateries.

30, place Pierre-Berthelot. ℂ **02-31-89-95-90.** Reservations recommended. Main courses 15€–27€. July–Sept Thurs–Tues noon–2:30pm and 7–10pm, Wed 7–10pm; Oct–June Fri–Tues noon–2:30pm and 7–10pm.

Restaurant Sa.Qua.Na ★★★ CONTEMPORARY FRENCH This double-Michelin-starred eatery is Honfleur's gourmet gem. Chef Alexandre Bourdas trained in Japan, and this Asian influence is reflected both in the streamlined cuisine and the restaurant's minimalist decor. Diners have the choice of two fixed-price menus only (no ordering à la carte). Dishes may include clams sautéed in pork, cabbage, garlic and ginger; wild salmon with peas, candied lemon and purslane; and frozen Moroccan mint cream.

22 place Hamelin. www.alexandre-bourdas.com. ℂ **02-31-89-40-80.** Reservations required. Fixed-price menu 68€–108€. Thurs–Sun 12:30–2:30pm and 7:30–9:30pm.

Exploring Honfleur

Begin your tour of Honfleur by picking up a map from the Tourist Office: Each one is printed with three handy walking routes, all detailing points of interest around town. Stroll the scenic quays, fishing boats, and narrow, slate-roofed houses that line the **Vieux Bassin,** or old harbor. On the north side of the basin, the former governor's house, **Lieutenance,** dates from the 16th century. Nearby is the **Eglise Ste-Catherine,** place Ste-Catherine (ℂ **02-31-89-11-83**), constructed of timber by 15th-century shipbuilders. The church's wooden belfry is on the other side of the street. The church is open July and August daily from 8am to 8pm, September through June daily 8:30am to noon and 2 to 6pm.

For a different perspective on the town and its surrounds, short **boat trips** (www.promenade-en-bateau-honfleur.fr; 45–90 min.; 6€–9.50€) depart from jetties east of the Vieux Bassin.

Les Maisons Satie ★★ MUSEUM Since its opening in 1998, Les Maisons Satie has been Normandy's most unconventional museum. Composer and painter Erik Satie—muse to Picasso and Braque, inspiration to Stravinsky—was born here in 1866. The museum's interactive exhibits are purposefully surreal and require visitors to wear headphones that pipe in a mix of Satie's music, odd sounds, and factual commentary. It's a love-it-or-hate-it experience.

67 bd. Charles V. www.musees-honfleur.fr. ℂ **02-31-89-11-11.** Admission 6€ adults, 4.50€ ages 10–17, free for children 9 and under. May–Sept Wed–Mon 10am–7pm; Oct–Dec and Feb 16-Apr Wed–Mon 11am–6pm. Closed Jan–Feb 15.

Musée Eugène-Boudin ★★ MUSEUM Located in the former chapel of an Augustinian convent, this museum showcases the pastels and paintings of Honfleur's native son, Eugène Boudin. A fine collection of Impressionist artworks is also on display, including canvases by Dubourg, Monet, Courbet, and Dufy. Additional displays include local photographs (snapped between 1880–1920), Norman tourism posters, and antiques.

Rue de l'Homme de Bois. www.musees-honfleur.fr. (2) **02-31-89-54-00.** Admission 5.50€ adults, 2.50€ students and children 10 and over. Mar 15–June Wed–Mon 10am–noon and 2–6pm; July–Sept Wed–Mon 10am–noon and 2–6:30pm; Oct–Dec and Feb 16–Mar 14 Mon and Wed–Fri 2:30–5:30pm, Sat–Sun 10am–noon and 2:30–5:30pm. Closed Jan–Feb 15.

NaturoSpace ★★ MUSEUM Discovering France's largest tropical butterfly house in Honfleur is an unexpected delight. Thousands of colorful specimens—more than 50 species from South America, Asia, Africa, and Oceania—flutter through a greenhouselike labyrinth of exotic foliage, from orchids and birds of paradise to palms. Visit in the morning to watch chrysalises crack open and brand-new butterflies make their first flight.

Bd. Charles V. www.naturospace.com. (2) **02-31-81-77-00.** Admission 8.30€ adults, 6.50€ students and children 3 to 13, family package 33€. Apr–June and Sept daily 9:30am–1pm and 2–6:30pm; July–Aug daily 9:30am–6:30pm; Oct–Nov and Feb–Mar 9:30am–1pm and 2–5:30pm. Closed Dec and Jan.

DEAUVILLE ★★★

206km (128 miles) NW of Paris; 47km (29 miles) NE of Caen

Deauville has been associated with the rich and famous since the duc de Morny, Napoleon III's half-brother, founded it as an upscale resort in 1859. In 1913, it entered sartorial history when Coco Chanel launched her career here, opening a boutique selling tiny hats that challenged the fashion of huge-brimmed hats loaded with flowers and fruit. (Coco's point of view: "How can the mind breathe under those things?")

Coco Chanel cultivated a tradition of elegance that survives in Deauville and in its smaller neighbor Trouville, on the opposite bank of the River Touques (see "A Day Out in Trouville," below). Don't expect flash; in its way, restrained and ever-so-polite Deauville is the most British seaside resort in France. The crowds here tend to be urban, hip, and stylish. Deauville is also not—by anyone's definition—inexpensive.

Essentials

ARRIVING There are five to nine daily **rail** connections from Paris's Gare St-Lazare (trip time: 2 hr., 15 min.); prices start at 25€ one-way. The rail depot lies midway between Trouville and Deauville, within walking distance of both resorts. **Bus Verts du Calvados** (www.busverts.fr; (2) 08-10-21-42-14) serves the Normandy coast from Caen to Le Havre. To **drive** from Paris (trip time: 2½ hr.), take A13 west to Pont L'Evêque, and then follow D677 north to Deauville.

VISITOR INFORMATION The **Office de Tourisme** is at 112 rue Victor Hugo (www.deauville.org; (2) 02-31-14-40-00).

SPECIAL EVENTS For a week in September, the **Deauville Festival of American Film** (www.festival-deauville.com; (2) 02-31-14-40-00) honors movies made in the United States. Actors, producers, directors, and writers, from Brad Pitt to Steven Spielberg, flock here and briefly eclipse the high rollers at the casinos and the polo crowd.

[FastFACTS] DEAUVILLE

ATMs/Banks   A half-dozen banks cluster on and around rue Eugène-Colas.

Internet Access   Various bars and cafes offer free Wi-Fi, including **Le Morny's Café,** 6 place Morny (② **02-31-87-32-06**).

Mail & Postage   **La Poste,** 20 rue Robert Fossorier (② **36-31**).

Pharmacies   **Pharmacie de Garde,** 8 rue Désiré Le Hoc (② **02-31-14-61-70**).

Where to Stay

Hotel Royal Barrière ★★★   No single hotel epitomizes the epic grandeur of Deauville like the Hotel Royal Barrière. Push through its gilded revolving doors to find photo portraits of a thousand famous former guests: Sean Connery, Harrison Ford, Barack Obama, among them. Guest rooms and suites are a palatial medley of crushed red velvet, plush carpet, and cool marble. Lucky sojourners enjoy complimentary access to the Royal's beach club and Olympic-size pool or a golf lesson at the prestigious Golf Barrière Club. Even nonguests may sit at Deauville's top table by dining at **Restaurant l'Etrier** (set menus 67€/105€). This Michelin-starred temple of inventive seafood gastronomy is overseen by chef Eric Provost, a one-time understudy of Alain Ducasse and Joël Robuchon. In short, a very deserving member of the Leading Hotels of the World group.

Boulevard Cornuché, Deauville 14800. www.lucienbarriere.com. ② **02-31-98-66-22.** 252 units. 222€–650€ double; 635€–1,810€ suite. Parking 15€. **Amenities:** Restaurant; children's dining room; bar; babysitting; exercise room; heated outdoor pool; room service; steam room; 2 tennis courts; TV, hair dryer, minibar, Wi-Fi (10€/day).

L'Augeval ★   A rare Deauville bargain, this Norman-style villa sits just west of the Hippodrome de Deauville-La Touques, within easy walking distance of the beach. Guestroom decor is heartily French. Flowering gardens surround the property, and there's a petite heated outdoor pool on the grounds. Some units have air-conditioning and private balconies.

15 av. Hocquart-de-Turtot, Deauville 14800. www.augeval.com. ② **02-31-81-13-18.** 31 units. 72€–170€ double; 154€–340€ suite. Parking 8€. **Amenities:** Bar; babysitting; billiards and darts room; exercise room; outdoor pool; room service; free Wi-Fi.

Les Manoirs de Tourgéville ★★★   An inspired base for families touring the Normandy coast, Les Manoirs, a 4km (2½ miles) hop from downtown Deauville, is an ultra-friendly grand hotel built around an ancient Norman mansion. Tour its 7 hectares of verdant grounds, alive with rabbits and deer, on the hotel's free bikes. Or indulge your cinematic fantasy by playing your own DVD in the 50-person private screening room; staff are happy to deliver drinks while you watch a classic Hitchcock movie. Guestrooms in the mansion combine period features with some of the finest linens and furnishings known to man. Suites in the newer building are ultra-modern and can interlink to accommodate large families.

Chemin de l'Orgueil, Tourgéville, Deauville 14800. www.lesmanoirstourgeville.com. ② **02-31-14-48-68.** 57 units. 150€–310€ double; 260€–580€ suite. Closed Jan. **Amenities:** 2 restaurants; bar; bikes; cinema; health club; parking; pool; room service; sauna; TV, hair dryer, minibar; free Wi-Fi.

Where to Eat

Chez Miocque ★★ TRADITIONAL FRENCH   This classy brasserie is a favorite both with locals and Parisians *en vacances*. The wood-paneled interior is covered floor to ceiling in photos of celebrity patrons arm in arm with owner Jacques Miocque. Dishes are hearty: Dig into Bouchot mussels, local farm-raised chicken in Norman cream sauce, or sole *meunière*. The tipple of choice is local boy François David's unfiltered cider.

81 rue Eugène Colas. www.chez-miocque.fr. ℂ **02-31-88-09-52.** Reservations recommended. Main courses 19€–43€. Daily noon–2pm and 7–9pm. Closed Tues and Wed out of season.

Le Ciro's Barrière ★★★ FRENCH/SEAFOOD   Spilling directly onto the beach, Le Ciro's dishes up Deauville's best seafood. It may be pricey, but Norman chef Jérôme Taquet's superb cuisine is worth it. For a luxurious appetizer, try lobster salad with foie gras and white asparagus. If you're looking to really splurge, go for the *plateau de fruits de mer royal* (79€), a tower of local lobster, Isigny oysters, and super-fresh shellfish. The ambience is airy, stylish, and evocative of the city's Belle Epoque heyday.

Planches de Deauville, boulevard de la Mer. www.lucienbarriere.com. ℂ **02-31-14-31-31.** Reservations required. Main courses 33€–52€. Thurs–Mon noon–2:30pm and 7:30–10pm. Open daily July–Aug. Closed 2 weeks in Jan.

Exploring Deauville

With its golf courses, casinos, deluxe hotels, La Touques and Clairefontaine racetracks, regattas, yachting harbor, polo grounds, and tennis courts, Deauville hums with upper-class patronage. There's little better for soaking up the exclusive vibe than an afternoon spent people-watching, particularly along boutique-lined **rue Eugène-Colas, place Morny** (named for the resort's founder), and **place du Casino.**

Outdoor Activities

BEACHES   Deauville's boardwalk, **Les Planches,** is an impossibly pretty promenade running parallel to the town's 2km (1¼-mile) beach, **Plage de Deauville.** Beaux Arts and half-timbered Norman-inspired buildings line its edges. In summer, parasols dot the beach and oiled bodies cover every inch of these silken sands. Visitors parade past private bathing cabins, each one's entrance stenciled with the names of Hollywood film stars who have attended the Deauville Festival of American Film.

Access to every beach in Normandy is free, although beach clubs dot some stretches of sand. If you'd like to rent a beach umbrella and two sunloungers in Deauville, prices start at around 12€ per half day. Parking costs from 2€ per hour in the public lots beside the sea.

The **Piscine Municipale,** boulevard de la Mer (ℂ **02-31-14-02-17**), is a large indoor seawater pool. Depending on the season, bathers pay 4.50€ to 5€ per person.

HORSE RACES/POLO   You can watch horses—either racing or competing at polo—most days from late June to early September. The venues are the **Hippodrome de Deauville-La Touques,** 45 av. Hocquart de Turtot (www.france-galop.com; ℂ **02-31-14-20-00**), in the heart of town near the Mairie de Deauville (town hall); and the **Hippodrome de Deauville Clairefontaine,** route de Clairefontaine (www.hippodrome-deauville-clairefontaine.com; ℂ **02-31-14-69-00**), within the city limits, 2km (1¼ miles) west of the center. Tickets normally cost around 4€.

A day out IN TROUVILLE

Unlike its über-fashionable neighbor on the opposite banks of the Touques River (the carefully planned resort of Deauville), Trouville is this stretch of sand's original medieval fishing port. During the late 19th century, while Deauville attracted glitzy punters with its hippodrome and casino, Trouville secured its position as a family-friendly resort. Today it's far less dependent on tourist euros than Deauville; when the bathers leave its splendid sands in September, Trouville continues to thrive on its local commerce and a working fishing fleet.

Our recommendation? Spend a day wandering Trouville's friendly streets, absorbing the resort's low-key charm. The town is easy to access: A 2-minute **passenger ferry** zips back and forth across the Touques from Deauville at high tide (daily May–Sept; weekends and holidays only Oct–Apr; 1.20€), and there's a walkway to amble across when the water's low. (Alternatively, there are permanent bridges over the river farther south.) On the Trouville quay, **Les Trouvillaises** (www.lestrouvillaises.fr; © 02-31-98-54-11; mid-Mar to Oct) rents children's and adults' bikes,

tandems, and four-wheeler buggies by the hour.

Les Planches is a stretch of ocean-front boardwalk dotted with 19th-century mansions on one side and the sea on the other. There's only one beach, **Plage de Trouville,** where in midsummer you can expect to see vacationers ranging from groups of rambunctious schoolchildren to multigenerational picnickers.

Without a doubt one of Normandy's most delicious places to lunch, Trouville's **Marché aux Poissons,** or fish market, has been thriving since 1840. Stroll the dozen stalls and take your pick of fresh seafood—from lobster and oysters to Seine Bay scallops and sea snails—then have your choice shelled or cooked up on the spot. Grab a glass of Champagne, then perch at one of the high tables surrounding the market and devour. Pick of the bunch is **Poissonnerie Pillet Saiter,** bd. Fernand Moureaux (www.poissonnerie-pilletsaiter. fr, © 02-31-88-02-10).

Trouville's **Office de Tourisme** is at 32 quai Fernand-Moureaux (www. trouvillesurmer.org; © 02-31-14-60-70).

Shopping

This seaside town has a pedestrian shopping area between the polo field and the port; the main drags are **rue Mirabeau, rue Albert-Fracasse,** and the west end of **avenue de la République.** Big brand-name shops, from Hermès and Louis Vuitton to a lovely Norman-style Printemps department store, cluster on **rue Eugène-Colas, place Morny,** and **place du Casino. La Cave de Deauville,** 48 rue Mirabeau (© 02-31-87-35-36) has a wide selection of apple ciders, Calvados, and the apple aperitif known as *pommeau.*

For an overview of the bounty of the fertile Norman soil, head for the **Marché Publique** (open-air market) in place du Marché, adjacent to place Morny. In July and August, it's open daily 8am to 1pm. The rest of the year, market days are Tuesday, Friday, and Saturday, as well as Sunday March to June and September through October. In addition to fruits, vegetables, poultry, cider, wine, and cheese, you'll find cookware, porcelain tableware, and cutlery.

Nightlife

Opened in 1912, the **Casino de Deauville,** rue Edmond Blanc (www.lucienbarriere. com; ✆ **02-31-14-31-14**), is one of France's premier casinos. Its original Belle Epoque core now includes a theater, Le Brummel nightclub, three restaurants, two bars, and an extensive collection of slot machines *(machines à sous).* The casino distinguishes areas for slot machines from more formal zones containing such games as roulette, baccarat, blackjack, and poker. The slots are open daily 10am to 2am (to 3am Fri and 4am Sat) and have no dress code. The areas containing *les jeux de table* (table games) are open Monday to Thursday 4pm to 2am (to 3am Fri and 4am Sat) and Sunday 2:30pm to 2am. Entrance is free, and you must present a passport or I.D. to gain admission.

If it's a dance floor you're seeking, try **Le Chic,** 14 rue Désiré-le-Hoc (www. lechicdeauville.fr; ✆ **02-31-88-30-91**), a favorite with French actors and off-duty jockeys. Polo players frequent the perennially popular **Brok Café,** 14 av. du Général-de-Gaulle (✆ **02-31-81-30-81**)—if you're keen to join them, secure your entrance by hitting this Cuban-style venue before midnight.

Les Planches, Domain du Bois Lauret, Blonville (www.lesplanches.com; ✆ **02-31-87-58-09**), 4km (2½ miles) from Deauville, is a club with up-to-date music, a dance floor, and even a swimming pool adjacent to the indoor/outdoor bar. It's open from 11pm until dawn every Saturday night year-round and daily in July and August.

CAEN ★

238km (148 miles) NW of Paris; 119km (74 miles) SE of Cherbourg

Situated on the banks of the Orne, the port of Caen suffered great damage in the 1944 invasion of Normandy, though the twin abbeys founded by William the Conqueror and his wife, Mathilda, were spared. Today much of Caen is both cosmopolitan and commercial, boasting a vibrant, welcoming vibe. The capital of Lower Normandy, it's home to a student population of 30,000 and several great museums, and serves as an ideal staging base for the surrounding coast.

Essentials

ARRIVING From Paris's Gare St-Lazare, between 12 and 15 **trains** a day arrive in Caen (trip time: 2–2½ hr.). The fare is 35€ one-way. One-way fares from Rouen (trip time: 1 hr., 45 min.) start at 26€. To **drive** from Paris, travel west along A13 to Caen (drive time: 2½–3 hr.).

VISITOR INFORMATION The **Office de Tourisme** is on place St-Pierre in the 16th-century Hôtel d'Escoville (www.caen-tourisme.fr; ✆ **02-31-27-14-14**).

CITY LAYOUT Downtown Caen stretches from Abbaye aux Dames in the east to Abbaye aux Hommes in the west. The pedestrianized rue St-Pierre bisects the town's main shopping district. The train station is southeast of the city center. The towering ramparts of the hilltop Château make an ideal spot to get your bearings.

Getting Around

ON FOOT Caen's city center is small and largely pedestrianized. For short stays, it's easiest to explore the town on foot.

BY BICYCLE & MOTOR SCOOTER Caen has its own bike-sharing scheme, **V'eol** (www.veol.caen.fr). You can register online (where you can also download a handy map of the city's bike paths) or directly at one of Caen's 40 bike stands; fees are 1€ per day.

BY CAR   It's best to park your wheels and explore the city center on foot. The Tourist Office website offers a downloadable map (under "Transport"), clearly marked with the town's major parking lots. Among others, there is one behind the train station and three just south of the Château.

BY TAXI   **Taxis Abbeilles,** 54 place de la Gare (www.taxis-abbeilles-caen.com; ✆ **02-31-52-17-89**).

BY PUBLIC TRANSPORT   The **Twisto bus and tram network** (www.twisto.fr; ✆ **02-31-15-55-55**) crisscrosses the city. Most useful for visitors is the tram: The north-south two lines (A and B) overlap through the city center, passing all of Caen's major monuments en route. Tickets (1.35€) can be purchased from automatic kiosks at each station.

[FastFACTS] CAEN

ATMs/Banks   The city center has plenty of banks, including five on rue Jean Eudes.

Doctors & Hospitals   **Centre Hospitalier Universitaire de Caen,** av. de la Côte de Nacre (www.chu-caen.fr; ✆ **02-31-06-31-06**).

Internet Access   **Espace Micro,** 1 rue Basse (✆ **08-99-10-17-50**).

Mail & Postage   **La Poste,** 2 rue Georges Lebret (✆ **36-31**).

Pharmacies   **Pharmacie du Château,** 27 av. Libération (✆ **02-31-93-64-78**).

Where to Stay

Ivan Vautier Hotel ★   Set on the western edge of the city center, this five-star hotel offers spacious, contemporary guestrooms. It has an excellent restaurant as well as a small boutique selling local products. Note that the hotel embraces the modern rather than traditional French style. Easy access to the region's major roads makes this a good base for exploring farther afield.

3 ave. Henry Chéron, Caen 14300. www.ivanvautier.com. ✆ **02-31-73-32-71.** 19 units. 115€–190€ double; 235€–260€ suite. Parking free. **Amenities:** Restaurant; bar; room service; free Wi-Fi.

Le Clos St-Martin ★★   Sylvie and Jean Noël run this intimate, four-room *chambres d'hôtes*, or bed-and-breakfast. The three antique-splashed suites (one of which can be booked as a family room) and one double are set over three floors of a rambling

---

A Proustian Remembrance of "Balbec"

Torn from the pages of Marcel Proust's "Remembrance of Things Past," the resort of "Balbec" was really Cabourg, 24km (15 miles) northeast of Caen. Fans still come to this Second Empire resort, much of which looks as it did during the Belle Epoque. Guests can check into the 1907 **Grand Hôtel,** Les Jardins du Casino, promenade Marcel Proust, 14390 Cabourg (www.mgallery.com; ✆ **02-31-91-01-79**), a holdover from the opulent days of the 19th century. What used to be Marcel Proust's favorite room has been restored from a description in "Remembrance." A double room costs from 210€ to 350€.

16th-century mansion, just a short stroll from the Abbaye aux Hommes. Breakfast is superb, and often includes Sylvie's baked treats, such as *teurgoule*, Norman rice pudding.

18bis place Saint Martin, Caen 14000. www.leclosaintmartin.com. © **02-31-50-08-71.** 4 units. 105€ double; 115€–155€ suite. Public parking nearby. **Amenities:** Breakfast room; free Wi-Fi.

Where to Eat

A large student population helps make Caen's dining scene one of the most dynamic in Normandy. Sidewalk cafes and restaurants line rue du Vaugueux and the surrounding neighborhood, east of the Château.

A Contre Sens ★★ FRENCH/NORMAN   This Michelin-starred temple of gastronomy is run by innovative chef Anthony Caillot. Set menus depend heavily on morning market finds, from butternut squash *velouté* to John Dory served with artichokes infused with black cardamom and verbena leaves. **Note:** The restaurant's petite size means reservations should be made well in advance.

8 rue des Croisiers. www.acontresenscaen.fr. © **02-31-97-44-48.** Reservations required. Main courses 30€–32€; fixed-price lunch 24€–48€; fixed-price dinner 48€–60€. Wed–Sat noon–2pm; Tues–Sat 7:30–9:15pm.

Le Bouchon du Vaugueux ★★ FRENCH   A lively little bistro in Caen's buzzing bar-and-restaurant district, Le Bouchon du Vaugueux is a favorite with visitors and locals alike. Dishes—focusing on regional ingredients—are hearty: Try chicken braised in ginger, stuffed zucchini paired with snails, or bread pudding steeped in rum. The ambience is animated and the service is excellent.

12 rue Graindorge. www.bouchonduvaugueux.com. © **02-31-44-26-26.** Reservations recommended. Fixed-price lunch 15€–23€; fixed-price dinner 20€–30€. Tues–Sat noon–2pm, Tues–Thurs 7–10pm, Fri–Sat 7–10:30pm. Closed 2 weeks Sept.

Exploring Caen

A fun way to visit Caen's major sites, including both Abbayes and the Château, is to follow the self-guided **William the Conqueror Circuit.** Maps can be picked up at the Tourist Office, from which the walking tour departs.

Abbaye aux Dames ★ RELIGIOUS SITE   Founded by Mathilda, wife of William the Conqueror, around 1060, this abbey embraces Eglise de la Trinité, which is flanked by Romanesque towers. Its spires were destroyed in the Hundred Years' War. The 12th-century choir houses the tomb of Queen Mathilda.

Place Reine Mathilde. © **02-31-06-98-98.** Free admission. Daily 2–5:30pm. Free guided 1-hr. tour of choir, transept, and crypt (in French) daily 2:30 and 4pm.

Abbaye aux Hommes ★★ RELIGIOUS SITE   Founded by William the Conqueror in 1066 to ensure papal pardon for marrying his distant cousin Mathilda, this abbey is adjacent to the Eglise St-Etienne. During the height of the Allied invasion, residents of Caen flocked to St-Etienne for protection. Twin Romanesque towers 84m-tall (276 ft.) dominate the church. A marble slab inside the high altar marks the site of William's tomb. Hand-carved wooden doors and an elaborate wrought-iron staircase are exceptional.

Esplanade Jean-Marie Louvel. © **02-31-30-42-81.** 4.50€ adults, 3.50€ students, free for children 17 and under. Obligatory tours (50–90 min.; in English and/or French) July–Aug daily 9:30am, 10:15am, 11am, 2:30pm, 3:15pm, 4pm and 5:15pm; Feb–June and Sept–Nov daily 9:30am, 11am, 2:30pm and 4pm; Jan and Dec Mon–Fri 9:30am, 11am, 2:30pm and 4pm, Sat–Sun no tours but cloisters open Mon–Sat 9am–1pm and 2–6:30pm, Sun 2–6:30pm.

Le Château de Caen ★★ CASTLE This castle complex was built on the ruins of a fortress erected by William the Conqueror in 1060. Come summertime, locals picnic at sunset in the surrounding gardens. From the extensive ramparts, sublime views over Caen unfold. Within the medieval compound are two museums, as well as scattering of contemporary sculptures. The **Musée de Normandie** (www.musee-de-normandie.caen.fr; ✆ **02-31-30-47-60**) displays local archaeological finds, along with a collection of regional sculpture, paintings, and ceramics. Admission is 3.10€, and it's open daily 9:30am to 6pm (closed Tues Nov–May). Also within the walls is the **Musée des Beaux-Arts** (www.mba.caen.fr; ✆ **02-31-30-47-70**), a collection of Old Masters including Veronese, Tintoretto, and Rubens. Admission is free excluding temporary shows, which cost 3.10€ to 9€. It's open Wednesday through Monday 9:30am to 6pm. Both museums stage major exhibitions each summer.

Esplanade de la Paix, rue de Geôle, av. de la Libération. www.chateau.caen.fr.

Le Mémorial de Caen (Caen Memorial) ★★ MONUMENT/MEMORIAL The museum presents a journey through history from 1918 to the present. One wing is dedicated to a depiction of the American global role after World War II. Its photo documentaries and exhibits illustrate the Cold War, the construction and collapse of the Berlin Wall, and the assault of military weapons (especially nuclear testing) on the environment. In 2013, Nazi German General Richter's former command post and underground bunker opened to the public. History buffs can expect to spend around 2 hours at this memorial.

Esplanade Général Eisenhower. www.memorial-caen.fr. ✆ **02-31-06-06-45.** Admission Apr–Sept 19€ adults, 17€ students and children 10–18; Oct–Mar 19€ adults, 16€ students and children 10–18; free to World War II veterans, those with war disabilities, war widows, and children 9 and under. Feb 16–Nov 11 daily 9am–7pm; Oct 12–Feb 15 daily 9:30am–6pm. Closed Jan.

Shopping

Caen has some excellent boutique-lined shopping streets, including **boulevard du Maréchal-Leclerc, rue St-Pierre,** and **rue de Strasbourg. Antiques** hunters should check out the shops along **rue Ecuyère.** The **market** at place Courtonne on Sunday morning sells secondhand goodies.

For foodie souvenirs, **Hotot Chocolaterie,** 13 rue St-Pierre (✆ **02-31-86-31-90**), has a cornucopia of chocolate products, as well as local jams and jellies. Find regional items at **Le Comptoir Normand,** 7 rue de Geôle (✆ **02-31-86-34-13**), including Calvados, charcuterie products, and Caen-style tripe.

Nightlife

Take a walk down rue de Bras, rue St-Pierre, and rue Vaugueux to size up the action. Young hipsters go to **Le Chic,** rue des Prairies St-Gilles (✆ **02-31-94-48-72**), where dance music begins around 11:30pm. For offbeat international gigs, head to **Le Cargö,** 9 quai Caffarelli, Port de Caen (www.lecargo.fr; ✆ **02-31-86-79-31**).

Day Trip from Caen
MONT-ST-MICHEL ★★★
324km (201 miles) W of Paris; 129km (80 miles) SW of Caen; 48km (30 miles) E of St-Malo

A UNESCO World Heritage Site, Mont-St-Michel is one of the most alluring spots on France's Northern Coast. The fortified island seems to float on a meandering bed of sand and sea. Once a bastion marking the border between Normandy and Brittany, then a place of monastic retreat, this Disney-like castle now attracts 3 million visitors every year. In high summer it's exceptionally busy, but enthralling nevertheless.

Essentials

This being France—a nation that spends a full 6 percent of its taxes on culture and tourism—Mont-St-Michel is supremely accessible. A new visitor center, the **Tourist Information Centre,** Lieu-dit le Bas Pays, 50170 Beauvoir (www.bienvenueaumont-saintmichel.com; ℂ **02-14-13-20-15**), opened in summer 2013. Diagrams inside explain the history of the rock. To help return the site to its natural status, cars are now left in a giant parking lot by the visitor center, from which free shuttle buses depart across a new causeway to the island. Parking costs 6€ for 2 hours, or 12€ for 24 hours. Total driving time from Paris is about 4 hours.

From the parking lot, a new **pedestrian path** opened in 2014. This allows energetic visitors to take a 40-minute hike to the island across the shifting sands, much as pilgrims did in yesteryear. Those with their own bike can pedal over. A ride across in a horse-drawn carriage costs 5€ per person. An additional **Office de Tourisme** lies on the island itself, to the left of the town gates (www.ot-montsaintmichel.com; ℂ **02-33-60-14-30**). Both tourist centers are open daily year-round.

There are no direct **trains** between Paris and Mont-St-Michel. The best option is to take a local TER train from Paris's Gare Saint-Lazare to Caen, then another local TER train to Pontorson, where a 3€ shuttle bus ferries passengers directly to the new visitor center.

Exploring Mont-St-Michel

You'll have a steep climb up Grande Rue, lined with 15th- and 16th-century houses and many a souvenir store, to reach its famous **abbey** (http://mont-saint-michel. monuments-nationaux.fr; ℂ **02-33-89-80-00**). Ramparts encircle the church and a three-tiered ensemble of 13th-century buildings called **La Merveille** that rise up to the abbey's pointed spire. This terraced complex is one of Europe's most important Gothic monuments. On the second terrace of La Merveille is one of Mont-St-Michel's largest and most beautiful spaces, a 13th-century hall known as the **Salle des Chevaliers.** Crowning the mount's summit is the spellbindingly beautiful **Eglise Abbatiale** church.

The abbey is open daily May through August 9am to 7pm, and September to April 9:30am to 6pm. Entrance includes an English-language group tour when available, but you can also explore on your own. Admission is 9€ adults, 5.50€ students and ages 18 to 25, and free for children 17 and under.

Most visitors are content to wander around the medieval ramparts. Those seeking a little more sightseeing may head to the **Musée de la Mer,** Grande Rue (ℂ **02-33-89-02-02**), which showcases marine crafts throughout history; the ecology of the local tidal flats; and illustrations of the French government's project to return the mount to its original status. Another museum worth visiting is the **Logis Tiphaine,** Grande Rue (ℂ **02-33-89-02-02**), a 15th-century home originally under the control of the Duguesclin family. Both museums are open daily from 9am to 6pm, and cost 4€ for adults, free for children 18 and under.

Where to Stay & Eat

Better-value hotels can be found away from the island using an Internet search. But those eager to bed down on Mont-St-Michel itself can check-in to the **Auberge Saint-Pierre,** Grand Rue (www.auberge-saint-pierre.fr; ℂ **02-33-60-14-03**). Double rooms start from 190€. On the same winding street, **Crêperie La Sirène** (ℂ **02-33-60-08-60**) does a fine job serving savory galettes, fruit-filled crêpes, and flagons of Normandy cider.

BAYEUX ★★

267km (166 miles) NW of Paris; 25km (16 miles) NW of Caen

The *ducs de Normandie* sent their sons to this Viking settlement to learn the Norse language in the ninth century. Bayeux has changed a lot since then but was spared from bombardment in 1944. This was the first French town to be liberated, and the citizens gave de Gaulle an enthusiastic welcome when he arrived on June 14. The picturesque town is still filled with timbered houses, stone mansions, and cobblestone streets.

Essentials

ARRIVING   Nine **trains** depart daily from Paris's Gare St-Lazare. The 2½-hour trip to Bayeux costs 38€. Most journeys require a change in Caen. Travel time between Caen and Bayeux is about 15 minutes and costs 6.40€. To **drive** to Bayeux from Paris (trip time: 3 hr.), take A13 to Caen and E46 west to Bayeux.

VISITOR INFORMATION   The **Office de Tourisme** is at 3 rue St-Jean (www.bessin-normandie.com; ✆ **02-31-51-28-28**).

SPECIAL EVENTS   The town goes wild on the first weekend in July during **Fêtes Médiévales** (www.fetesmedievales.bayeux.fr; ✆ **02-31-92-03-30**); the streets fill with market stalls, medieval dress, and themed treats during 2 days of medieval revelry.

[FastFACTS] BAYEUX

ATMs/Banks   There are banks throughout town, particularly along rue Saint-Malo.

Internet Access   **Médiathèque Municipale,** Centre Guillaume Le Conquérant, rue aux Coqs (✆ **02-31-51-20-20**), has Internet access and Wi-Fi.

Mail & Postage   **La Poste** av Dubois de la Cotardière (✆ **36-31**).

Pharmacies   **Pharmacie St Martin,** 20 rue St Martin (✆ **02-31-92-00-22**).

Where to Stay

Hôtel Tardif ★★   Set within an 18th-century *hôtel particulier,* or private home, this luxurious guesthouse is just steps from Bayeux's town center. Within the elegant foyer, a suspended wooden staircase sweeps up to first-floor rooms, each one decked out in period furnishings and overlooking either the *cour d'honneur* courtyard or botanical gardens. Breakfast (9€) is a celebration of local delights, from buttery croissants to regional cheeses.

16 rue Nesmond or 57 rue Larcher, Bayeux 14400. www.hoteltardif.com. ✆ **02-31-92-67-72.** 6 units. 60€–195€ double; 170€–260€ suite. Free parking. **Amenities:** Lounge-library; free Wi-Fi.

Where to Eat

Le P'tit Resto ★ NORMAN   Tucked just behind the town's cathedral, this small restaurant stands out among Bayeux's more tourist-targeted eateries. Chef Yannick Yon's cuisine puts a creative spin on traditional Norman dishes. Think beef tartare with wasabi and roasted sesame seeds, or coconut-crusted cod and honey-caramelized leeks. It hosts just 20 place settings, plus eight more on a small outdoor terrace, so reservations are highly recommended.

2 rue du Bienvenu. www.restaurantbayeux.com. ✆ **02-31-51-85-40.** Reservations recommended. Main courses 17€; fixed-price menus 19€–33€. Mon 7–9pm, Tue–Sat noon–2pm and 7–9pm.

Le Volet qui Penche ★★ NORMAN   Combination wine bar, shop and cozy bistro, this unassuming venue offers limited—yet exceptional—regional cuisine. A daily home-style menu features dishes such as braised pork cheeks or *andouillette* sausage, and a selection of *tartines* (open-faced sandwiches) and salads. Equally tasty for a light aperitif of wine, cured meats, and local cheese.

3 impasse de l'Islet. www.levoletquipenche.com. ☏ **02-31-21-98-54.** Reservations recommended. Main courses 17€–25€; fixed-price menus 9.50€–16€. June–Sept Mon–Fri 10am–9pm, Sat 5–9pm; Oct–Dec and March–May Tues–Fri 10am–9pm, Sat 5–9pm. Closed Jan–Feb.

Exploring Bayeux

This compact town is best explored on foot. At its heart sits **Cathédrale Notre-Dame de Bayeux,** Rue du Bienvenu, a Norman medieval structure consecrated in 1077 in the presence of William the Conqueror. The Bayeux Tapestry is displayed to the public in the cathedral's nave for 2 weeks each year. It's open daily 9am to 6pm (until 5pm Jan–Mar; until 7pm July–Sept). Entrance is free.

Musée d'Art et d'Histoire Baron Gérard (MAHB) ★ MUSEUM   Brand-new for 2013, this bright and airy museum is set within the town's ancient bishop's palace, much of it constructed during the Middle Ages. Exhibitions range from local archaeological finds to regional lacework (displayed within the palace's former dressing rooms) and stacks of delicate porcelain, as well as more than 600 regional artworks created between the 15th and 20th centuries.

37 rue du Bienvenu. ☏ **02-31-92-14-21.** Admission 7€ adults, 4€ students and children, free for children 9 and under. May–Sept daily 9:30am–6:30pm; Oct–Apr daily 10am–12:30pm and 2–6pm. Closed Jan–Feb 15.

Musée de la Tapisserie de Bayeux ★★★ MUSEUM   The most famous tapestry in the world is actually an elaborate embroidery on linen, 69m (226 ft.) long and 50cm (20 in.) wide. It depicts 58 scenes in eight colors and was likely created in Kent between 1066 and 1077.

Housed in a 270-degree Plexiglas case that sweeps along a low-lit tunnel-like room, this masterpiece tells the story of the conquest of England by William the Conqueror. Scenes include the coronation of Harold as the Saxon king of England, William being told of the apparition of a comet (a portent of good fortune), the Battle of Hastings, and the death of Harold with an arrow through the eye. An excellent audioguide—essential for truly understanding the tapestry—is included in the admission price.

In 2013, the museum inaugurated a new area dedicated to the creation of the Bayeux Tapestry, as well as details of daily life during this period. Displays include maps, models, and a 16-minute film about the Battle of Hastings.

Centre Guillaume le Conquérant, 13 bis rue de Nesmond. www.bayeuxmuseum.com. ☏ **02-31-51-25-50.** Admission 9€ adults, 4€ students, free for children 9 and under. Mar 15–Nov 15 daily 9am–6:30pm (May–Aug until 7pm); Nov 16–Mar 14 daily 9:30am–12:30pm and 2–6pm. Closed 3 wks Jan.

Musée Memorial de la Bataille de Normandie ★ MUSEUM   On June 7, 1944, Bayeux was the first strategic town to be liberated during the Battle of Normandy (June 6–Aug 29, 1944). Here, in a low-slung bunkerlike building are window displays of military history, details of the beach landings, and examples of the tanks and weapons used to win the battle. A 25-minute documentary showcases film clips from the period. Across from the museum, the perfectly manicured **Commonwealth**

Cemetery contains 4,144 graves of soldiers from throughout the British Commonwealth, all of them killed during the Battle of Normandy.

Bd. Fabian Ware. ℂ **02-31-51-46-90.** www.bayeuxmuseum.com. Admission 6€ adults, 4€ students and children, free for children 9 and under. May–Sept daily 9:30am–6:30pm; Oct–Apr daily 10am–12:30pm and 2–6pm. Closed Jan–Feb 15.

THE D-DAY BEACHES

A visit to the beaches where the greatest invasion force of all time landed is a must-see for visiting Americans, Canadians, Brits, or any other nationality. The year 2014 marked the 70th anniversary of D-Day and the wider Allied liberation of northern France. A whole host of new museums, sights, and memorials marks this time-shattering event.

It was a rainy week in early June 1944 when the greatest armada ever—soldiers and sailors, warships, landing craft, tugboats, jeeps—assembled along the southern coast of England. High winds and heavy rains had delayed the invasion, and millions of restless men camped on Britain's shores. A full moon and cooperative tides were needed for the cross-Channel invasion. Delay the action now and it would be another month before conditions would be right.

But Britain's top meteorologist for the USAAF and RAF—Sir James Stagg—forecast a small window in the inclement weather. Over in northern France, Normandy's German occupiers lacked such a detailed weather forecast, so many Nazi officers drifted home for the weekend in the belief that no landing could take place for the foreseeable future. Furthermore, thanks to an entire year of British deception and ruse, the Nazis believed the eventual invasion would come farther north at Calais near the Belgian border.

Supreme Allied Commander Dwight D. Eisenhower believed Stagg's reports—and knew that further delays would hinder his element of surprise. With the British invasion commander, Field Marshal Montgomery, at his side, Eisenhower made the ultimate call.

At 9:15pm on June 5, the BBC announced to Normandy's French Resistance that the invasion was imminent by way of secret coded messages. The underground movement started dynamiting the region's railways to hinder German troop movement. Fake radio traffic from London kept up the ruse that this was a diversionary attack before a major invasion farther north.

Before midnight, Allied planes began bombing the Norman coast. By 1:30am on June 6 ("the Longest Day"), members of the 101st Airborne were parachuting to the ground on German-occupied French soil. At 6:30am, the Americans began landing on the beaches, code-named Utah and Omaha. An hour later, British and Canadian forces made beachheads at Juno, Gold, and Sword, swelling the number of Allied troops in Normandy to a massive 135,000 plus 20,000 vehicles. That evening a joint beachhead had been formed and yet more troops, tanks, trucks, and other *materiel* poured into Normandy. The push to Paris—and indeed the race to Berlin—had begun.

Transport & Accommodations

A **car** is practically essential to explore the D-Day Beaches at leisure. The coastal roads are simply stunning and seldom host much traffic. Each monument, museum, and beach has plenty of parking too. Alternatively, **Bus Verts** (www.busverts.fr; ℭ **08-10-21-42-14**) runs buses from Bayeux to Arromanches (no. 75) and from Bayeux to Omaha Beach and the American Cemetery (no. 70) every few hours for 1.70€ per trip. Several group tours also cover the D-Day Beaches. From Bayeux, **Normandy Tours,** Hotel de la Gare (www.normandy-landing-tours.com; ℭ **02-31-92-10-70**), runs a 4-hour tour (in English) to Arromanches, Omaha Beach, the American Military Cemetery, and Pointe du Hoc for 50€ adults and 43€ students and seniors from April to October. From Caen, the **Caen Memorial Museum,** Esplanade Général Eisenhower (www.memorial-caen.fr; ℭ **02-31-06-06-45**), conducts full day (114€) tours along the same route from April to December, including lunch and access to Caen's excellent museum. A half-day trip costs 64€, including museum access.

Although the D-Day beaches are easily served on a day trip, numerous B&Bs stud the surrounding countryside. In the pretty village of Port-en-Bessin, midway between Colleville and Arromanches, the **Mercure Omaha Beach** Chemin du Colombier (www.mercure.fr; ℭ **02-31-22-44-44**), is a great base for exploring the sites. Double rooms start from 90€. *Moules et frites* (mussels and fries) establishments abound across the coast.

Reliving the Longest Day

Few places in the world have a more concentrated—or more moving—selection of sights than Normandy's D-Day Beaches. More than 30 memorials, cemeteries, and museums, which range from coastal batteries to museums dedicated to underwater military finds, dot this 50km stretch of coast. The most spellbinding site for all nationalities is surely the **Normandy American Visitor Center ★★★,** behind Omaha beach at Colleville-sur-Mer (www.abmc.gov; ℭ **02-31-51-62-00**). The graves of 10,000 Allied heroes who liberated mainland France lie within 70 hectares (173 acres) of manicured grounds above the Normandy cliffs. Rarely has there been a better monument to liberty and sacrifice. The visitor center retells the dramatic story of the American landings—and those of British, Canadian, Polish, Free French, and other international allies—on the morning of June 6, 1944. Most dramatic of all are the personal tales, often told via video and interactive displays, of male and female soldiers from across the United States. Admission is free. The cemetery is open daily 9am to 5pm; the visitor center until 6pm. Visitors may also wander down to Omaha Beach itself, s dotted with bunkers, cenotaphs, and memorials of that fateful day.

The **Overlord Museum,** Colleville-sur-Mer (www.overlordmuseum.com; ℭ **02-31-22-00-55**), opened in summer 2013, just half a mile uphill from the Normandy American Visitor Center. More than 10,000 pieces of *materiel* and 35 military vehicles (including American Sherman tanks and German Panzer halftracks) are showcased in D-Day dioramas around a great hall. Admission is 6.90€ adults and 4.90€ students and children. From June to August, hours are daily 9:30am to 7pm (Oct–Mar daily 10am–6pm; closed Jan).

Eastward along the coast in the British invasion sector is the seaside resort of **Arromanches-les-Bains.** A deepwater port was deemed essential to Allied success, so in June 1944 a mammoth prefabricated port known as "Winston" was towed across the Channel. "Victory could not have been achieved without it," Eisenhower later said. Indeed, in 10 months this "temporary" artificial harbor delivered 2.5 million men and countless vehicles into northern France. The wreckage is still visible just off the beach. Arromanches's **Plage Musée du Débarquement,** place du 6-Juin (www.musee-arromaches.fr; ℭ **02-31-22-34-31**), illuminates the scale of the D-Day landings through maps, models, a cinema, photos, and a diorama of the landing beaches. Admission is 7.50€ adults and 5.50€ students and children. May to September, hours are daily 9am to 7pm (Oct–Apr daily 10am–12:30pm and 1:30pm–5pm; closed Jan).

Eastward again through the British and Canadian invasion sectors is **Musée Gold Beach ★★,** 2 place Amiral Byrd, Ver-sur-Mer (www.goldbeachmusee.fr; © 02-31-22-58-58). The museum focuses on the heroism of Britain's RAF and Royal Navy and the meticulous Allied coordination that went into the D-Day landings. The British and Commonwealth Cemetery in nearby Bayeaux is a moving testament to the invasion's sacrifice and eventual success. Admission to the museum is 4€ adults and 2.40€ students and children. From April to October, hours are daily 10:30am to 5:30pm (closed Tues Apr–June and Sept–Oct); open November to March only by prior appointment.

Just eastward along the coast in Courseulles-sur-Mer is the **Centre Juno Beach ★★,** voie des Français Libres (www.junobeach.org; © 02-31-37-32-17). This gem of a museum details Canada's entire war effort, with particular focus on the Battle of the Atlantic and the march through Germany, where Canadian troops acquitted themselves with aplomb. Widely reckoned to beach the most fearsome of all Allied troops, the Canadians pushed even deeper into occupied territory than both Americans and Brits on D-Day. Admission is 7€ adults and 5.50€ students and children. From April to September, hours are daily 9:30am to 7pm (Oct–May daily 10am–5pm; closed Jan).

THE LOIRE VALLEY

by Lily Heise

Just 2 hours south of Paris, the Loire Valley enchants visitors with a stunning landscape of castles and vineyards straight out of a fairy tale. King François I and his Renaissance court left a spectacular cultural legacy, earning the entire valley a place on the World Heritage Site list. History buffs can trace Joan of Arc from Orléans to Chinon; romantics fall in love with the storybook châteaux of Chenonceau, Azay-le-Rideau, and Ussé; garden lovers revel in the verdant paradise of Chaumont and Villandry; gastronomes tantalize their palates at Michelin-starred restaurants and rustic *auberges;* and outdoor adventurers can see it all by bike.

As its name would imply, the region's rolling hills and forests hug the winding Loire River, encompassing 800 sq. km (308 sq. miles) of land south of Île-de-France, from the city of Orléans and extending west to Nantes on the Atlantic coast. Most visitors use Tours or Orléans as their starting point; however, the towns of Blois, Amboise or Saumur make excellent bases for exploring the region.

Most visitors to the Loire arrive via Paris; there are about six direct trains daily from the TGV station at Charles de Gaulle airport to the Tours TGV station Saint-Pierre (1 hr., 40 min; 35€–68€ one-way). At least one high-speed train (TGV) an hour runs to both Orléans and Tours, convenient starting points for for anyone not renting a car directly in Paris.

The Loire Valley has **two regional tourist offices** that can help you plan your stay in advance: **Comité Régional de Tourisme Val de Loire,** 37 av. de Paris, Orléans 45000 (www.visaloire.com; ✆ **02-38-79-95-28**), and **SEM Régionale des Pays de la Loire,** 1 place de la Galarne, BP 80221, Nantes 44202 Cedex 2 (www.westernloire.com; ✆ **02-40-48-24-20**). Local tourist offices are listed throughout the chapter.

ORLEANS ★

119km (74 miles) SW of Paris; 72km (45 miles) SE of Chartres

Ever since **Joan of Arc** relieved the besieged city from the Burgundians and the English in 1429, the city has honored the "Maid of Orléans." This deliverance is celebrated every year on May 8, the anniversary of her victory, but even if you aren't in town for the celebration, it's impossible to overlook the city's affection for the warrior, her name adorning everything from streets and cafes to chocolates and candies. Though suffering damage

Sleep Like a King (or Queen)

As one of the most visited regions of France, it's not surprising to find a great variety of accommodation options. Sleep like a king or queen in one of the Loire's many châteaux hotels, from the medieval **Hostellerie Gargantua** (p. 152) to the opulence of the **Château d'Artigny** (p. 145) or the **Chateau de Marçay** (p. 152). The valley is dotted with thousands of unique *gîtes* **(B&Bs)** including medieval towers, houseboats, and even troglodyte caves. For details and reservations, go to http://en.gites-de-france.com.

BIKING YOUR WAY through THE LOIRE

Trains serve some towns, but the best way to see this relatively flat region is by car or bike. Ten years and several million euros later, the vast program called **La Loire à Vélo ("The Loire on a Bike";** www.cycling-loire.com) has completed the 800km-long (496-mile) **Loire à Vélo trail,** meaning you can now safely pedal from Sancerre to the sea on a dedicated bike path past châteaux, villages, and natural areas or easily bike from one château to another. Relatively flat, the path was designed primarily for low-key cycling with family and friends and is linked to cycling-friendly hotels and bike-rental outfits along the way (look for the ACCUEIL VÉLO signs). More paths are added every year, and the trail will hook up to an even more massive project called **EuroVelo 6,** a cycling path that leads all the way to the Black Sea.

La Loire à Vélo has partnered with various tourist offices and travel agencies to offer a range of bike-trip packages that include hotel, meals, bike rental, and baggage transport (very important if you don't want to haul extra weight). For more information, visit **www.cycling-loire.com,** or one of the two regional

tourist offices (listed above). The website also has detailed information on dozens of bike-rental outfits along the route, as well as brochures and links to guide-books on various sections of the path.

One of the better-known outfitters is **Detours de Loire,** 35, rue Charles Gille, Tours (www.locationdevelos.com; (℃) **02-47-61-22-23**), which has three other shops in Blois, Saumur, and Nantes, as well as 20 or so associated outlets up and down the Loire à Vélo cir-cuit. This means that you can pick up your bike in one town and leave it in any partner outlet along the way without having to worry about returning the bike to the place you rented it from. If you are arriving in the Loire Valley by train, the four main shops are all located close to the town station. Prices for all-pur-pose bikes run from 15€ to 22€ per day, with discounts for multi-day rentals. A 300€ deposit (usually a credit card imprint) is required. Detours de Loire can also organize hotel-bike packages, deliver your bike to your accommoda-tions, and store your baggage while you are out pedaling. **Note:** Most outlets are open only from April to October.

in World War II, the city's downtown still remains quaint; however, it has gradually been losing its regional prominence to the more prosperous Tours.

Essentials

GETTING THERE About two **trains** per hour arrive from Paris's Gare d'Austerlitz (1 hr., 10 min; 20€ one-way); there are also a dozen connections from Tours (50–70 min.). The one-way fare from Tours to Orléans is about 20€. Orléans lies on the road between Paris and Tours. If you're **driving** from Paris, take A10 south; from Tours, take A10 north.

VISITOR INFORMATION The **Office de Tourisme** is at 2 place de L'Etape (www.tourisme-orleans.com; (℃) **02-38-24-05-05**).

Where to Stay

Hôtel de l'Abeille ★ It's best to stay overnight in a smaller town or in the coun-tryside, but if you need to overnight in Orléans, this is the city's most charming hotel.

A touch of the 19th century lingers in these cozy lodgings—bedrooms are decorated in period prints and antique armoires, and even the façade of the building has a certain fin-de-siècle flourish. The hotel has been in the family for four generations, and the feeling here is of a grand old house that is open to visitors. A pretty roof garden with a view of the cathedral is ideal for lazing about on sunny days. You'll notice a Joan of Arc theme on the walls; the hotel owners collect artworks that celebrate Orléans' favorite liberator.

64 rue Alsace-Lorraine. www.hoteldelabeille.com. ✆ **02-38-53-54-87.** 27 units. 89€–98€ double; 140€–160€ family suite. Parking 7€. **Amenities:** Bar; room service; TV, hair dryer, free Wi-Fi.

Where to Eat

Chez Jules ★ TRADITIONAL FRENCH   This small bistro may not look like much, but it serves some of the best regional cuisine in the city, prepared and served by the friendly Isabelle et Yvan Cardinaux. Tables are limited, so try to reserve in advance. Given the quality of the cuisine, prices are very reasonable. The menu is seasonally adjusted; you may sample eggplant caviar with ratatouille, marinated mussels and beets, or a goat cheese pastry to start, with a changing array of seafood dishes as well as hardier dishes such as parmentier of pigeon with foie gras.

136 rue de Bourgogne. ✆ **02-38-54-30-80.** Reservations highly recommended. Main courses 18€–22€; fixed-price lunch 20€, dinner 26€–43€. Tues–Sat noon–2pm and 7–9:30pm. Closed 2–3 weeks in July.

La Vieille Auberge ★ MODERN FRENCH   Take a trip to the French countryside in the heart of the city at this charming restaurant housed in a 17th-century building. You can dine inside in a stylish room or, if the weather's right, order your food in a lovely garden. The menu changes with the season to take advantage of the freshest available ingredients and may include foie gras with succulent Chartentais cantaloupe, *involtini* of free-range chicken, or smoked beef with *garrigue* seasoned potatoes.

2 rue du Faubourg St-Vincent. www.lavieilleauberge45.com. ✆ **02-38-53-55-81.** Main courses 18€–35€; fixed-price lunch 25€, dinner 35€–49€. Mon–Thurs noon–2pm and 7–9:30pm; Fri–Sat noon–2pm and 7–10pm; Sun noon–2pm.

Exploring the Town

Orléans, pop. 116,000, is the chief town of Loiret, on the Loire, and beneficiary of many associations with the French aristocracy. It gave its name to the dukes and duchesses of Orléans. Wander the narrow lanes of the city center to get the feel for what the city might have been like during Joan of Arc's time. Note the equestrian statue of Jeanne d'Arc on place du Martroi. From the square, you can drive past the elegant arched galleries on rue Royal (rebuilt in 18th-c. style) across pont George-V (erected in 1760). A simple cross marks the site of the Fort des Tourelles, which Joan of Arc and her men captured.

Cathédrale Ste-Croix ★ CATHEDRAL   Begun in 1287, after an earlier Romanesque church here collapsed from old age, the cathedral was burned by the Huguenots in 1568. Henri IV laid the first stone of the present building in 1601, and work continued until 1829. The cathedral boasts a 17th-century organ and woodwork from the early 18th century in its chancel, the masterpiece of Jules Hardouin-Mansart and other artists associated with Louis XIV.

Place Ste-Croix. ✆ **02-38-77-87-50.** Free admission. May–Sept daily 9:15am–6pm; Oct–Apr daily 9:15am–noon and 2–6pm.

Eglise St-Aignan ★ CHURCH One of the most frequently altered churches in the Loire Valley, St-Aignan was consecrated in 1509 in the form you see today. It possesses one of France's earliest vaulted hall crypts, complete with polychromed capitals. Scholars of pre-Romanesque art view are interested in its rare 10th- and 11th-century aesthetics. Above ground, the church's Renaissance-era choir and transept remain, but the Protestants burned the nave during the Wars of Religion. In a wood-carved shrine are the remains of the church's patron saint.

Place St-Aignan. No phone. Crypt can be visited only on a guided tour; sign up at the tourist office.

Hôtel Groslot ★ HISTORIC HOME This brick Renaissance mansion was begun in 1550 and embellished in the 19th century. François II (the first husband of Mary, Queen of Scots) lived here during the fall of 1560 and died on December 5. It was here that his brother and successor Charles IX met his lovely Marie Touchet. Between the Revolution and the mid-1970s, it functioned as the town hall. Marriage ceremonies, performed by the town's magistrates, are still held here. The statue of Joan of Arc praying was the work of Louis-Philippe's daughter, Princesse Marie d'Orléans. In the garden, you can see the remains of the 15th-century Chapelle St-Jacques.

Place de l'Etape (northwest of the cathedral). ✆ **02-38-79-22-30.** Free admission. July–Sept Mon–Fri and Sun 9am–6pm, Sat 5–8pm; Oct–June Mon–Fri and Sun 10am–noon and 2–6pm, Sat 5pm–7pm.

Musée des Beaux-Arts ★★ MUSEUM The best art museum in the region, this collection is made up of mostly French, but also Italian, Dutch, and Flemish works dating from the 15th to 20th centuries. It includes some impressive treasures by Tintoretto, Boucher, Van Dyke, and Vélasquez as well as a fine array of portraits, including one of Mme. de Pompadour by Drouais. The museum also boasts one of the largest collections of pastels in French, includes works by Quentin de la Tour and Chardin.

Place Saint-Croix. www.coeur-de-france.com/orleans-beauxarts.html. ✆ **02-38-79-21-55.** Admission 4€ adults, 2€ students, free for children 18 and under and for all visitors on the 1st Sun of the month; Tues–Sun 10am–6pm.

BEAUGENCY

150km (93 miles) SW of Paris; 85km (53 miles) NE of Tours

On the right bank of the Loire, the charming town of Beaugency boasts many medieval sites including a long 12th-century bridge with 23 arches, said to have been built by the Devil himself.

Essentials

GETTING THERE If you're **driving** from Blois to Beaugency, take N152 northeast. About 20 **trains** per day run between Beaugency and either Blois or Orléans; each trip takes about 20 minutes, and the one-way fare is 6€. For railway information, visit www.voyages-sncf.com or dial ✆ **36-35.** From Orléans, about four to eight **buses** a day go to Beaugency. For bus schedules and information, visit www.ulys-loiret.com or contact the tourist office (see below).

Where to Eat & Stay Nearby

For lunch in the center of Beaugency, the **Relais du Ch**âteau (8 rue du Pont; ℰ **02-38-44-55-10**), at the foot of the castle, serves up satisfying traditional dishes and lunch menus from 16€.

La Tonnellerie ★ About 1.5km (1 mile) south of the center of Beaugency, this well-managed hotel is intimate and charming. It was originally built as a manor house in the 19th century and retains its original L-shaped design, walled garden, and sense of the era of Balzac and Flaubert. Rooms are comfortable and traditional, furnished with reproduction antiques and period prints. The restaurant serves regional classics (main courses from 19€) and is open to nonguests, though reservations are required.

12 rue des Eaux-Bleues, Tavers, Beaugency 45190. www.tonelri.com. ℰ **02-38-44-68-15.** 20 units. 108€–180€ double; 180€–199€ suite. Closed Dec 13–Jan 31. Take A10, exit at Beaugency, and then take N152 to Beaugency/Tavers. **Amenities:** Restaurant; bar; outdoor pool; bike rental; TV; hair dryer; free Wi-Fi.

Princess de la Loire Youth Hostel ★ The best bargain for bikers on a budget, this youth hostel near Beaugency offers the most reasonable accommodation in the whole of the Loire. Clean and bright, the hostel has dormitories with four to six beds, a common kitchen, and laundry facilities. Share your Loire touring routes with other travelers at the sociable barbecue and picnic areas. Bike rentals are available directly from the hostel or in town at the Détours shop near the train station.

152 rue de Châteaudun (2km from Beaugency on the D925). www.hihostels.com. ℰ **02-38-44-61-31.** 116 beds. 16€ shared dormitory. A Hostelling International card is required. Closed mid-Nov to mid-March. **Amenities:** Shared kitchen; laundry room; barbecue and picnic area; bike rental; free Wi-Fi.

Exploring the Town

A major medieval event took place here: the 1152 annulment of the marriage of Eleanor of Aquitaine and her cousin, Louis VII. She then married Henry II of England, bringing southwestern France as her dowry, an act that set off the Hundred Years War. This remarkable woman was the mother of Richard the Lion-Hearted. (The film "The Lion in Winter" dramatizes these events.)

The 15th-century **Château Dunois** is currently closed for renovations and may not reopen again into 2015 or beyond, so you'll have to see it from its exterior. The château is brooding and impressive, its historical links stretching back to almost-mystical medieval antecedents. The current castle was built by Jean d'Orléans, who fought alongside Joan of Arc in the siege of Orléans, on the foundations of an earlier 10th-century fortress that belonged to the lords of Beaugency, whose feudal power extended throughout the region. Astride the street (la rue du Pont) that leads to one of the château's secondary entrances, the **Voûte St-Georges (St. George's Vault)** is an arched gateway from the earlier château.

More medieval moodiness is on hand at **La Tour César,** a 36m-tall (118-ft.) castle keep that is all that remains of an 11th-century citadel. It's a fine example of Romanesque military architecture, but the interior is in ruins.

Eglise Notre-Dame, place Saint-Fermin, a 12th-century abbey, was rebuilt after it was burned during the Wars of Religion (1562–98). You can still see traces of its original Romanesque architecture in the chancel and transept. Nearby, the 16th-century

Tour St-Fermin, a bell tower with a panoramic view of the valley, is famous for bells that ring out a traditional tune three times a day.

The 10th-century **Eglise St-Etienne,** place du Martroi, is one of the oldest churches in France. Now deconsecrated, it is owned by the municipality and is open only for temporary exhibitions of painting and sculpture.

BLOIS

180km (112 miles) SW of Paris; 60km (37 miles) NE of Tours

The star attraction in this town of 52,000 is unquestionably the **Château de Blois,** but if time remains after a chateau visit, you may want to wander around the quaint historic core to get a feel for a real Loire Valley town.

Essentials

GETTING THERE   A dozen or so **trains** run from Paris's Gare de Austerlitz every day (1 hr., 45 min.; 28€ one-way), and several others depart from the Gare Montparnasse, which involves a change in Tours (around 1 hr., 50 min.; 30€–68€). From Tours, trains run almost every hour (trip time: 40 min.), at a cost of 11€ one-way. For information and schedules, visit www.voyages-sncf.com or dial ✆ **36-35.** From June to September, you can take a **bus** (www.tlcinfo.net; ✆ **02-54-58-55-44**) from the Blois train station to tour châteaux in the area, including Chambord, Chaumont, Chenonceau, and Amboise. If you're **driving** from Tours, take RN152 east to Blois, which runs along the Loire; if you want to get there fast, take the A10 autoroute. If you'd like to explore the area by **bike,** check out **Traineurs de Loire,** 1 rue Chemonton (www.traineurs deloire.com; ✆ **02-54-79-36-71**). Rentals start at 6€ per hour, 13€ per day.

VISITOR INFORMATION   The **Office de Tourisme** is at 23 place du Château (www.bloispaysdechambord.com; ✆ **02-54-90-41-41**).

Where to Stay

Some of the best rooms in town are at **Le Médicis** (see "Where to Eat," above) or in the surrounding area.

Côté Loire–Auberge Ligérienne ★   About a 5-minute walk from Blois Castle, these B&B–like lodgings include impeccably maintained rooms decorated with an interesting mix of antique headboards, country throw rugs, and 1930s shipping posters. There is a low-key maritime theme here, which makes sense for a hotel that sits on the edge of a river that served as a major transportation link up until the 19th century. Parts of this small inn were constructed in the 12th, 15th, and 16th centuries, which explains

---

Lights, Sound, Action!

Many of the Loire châteaux present *son-et-lumière* (sound and light) shows on summer nights. The **Château de Blois** hosts one of the best nightly from April to September (around 10–10:30pm; on Wed nights, the show is in English). As a taped lecture plays, colored lights and readings evoke the age in which the château was built. Admission 7.50€ adults, 6€ students, 4€ children 6 to 17, and free for children 5 and under (www. chateaudeblois.fr).

the narrow stairways and exposed beams. A tiny restaurant on the ground floor is open to outside guests, with one of the owners doing double duty as chef. His love of the region shines in such culinary creations as savory blancmange with goat cheese and tomatoes confit or local Sandre fish with butter sauce.

2 place de la Grève. www.coteloire.com. ℰ **02-54-78-07-86.** 8 units. 57€–92€ double. Restaurant fixed-price menu 30€ main course 18€ Open Tues–Sat. **Amenities:** Bar; restaurant; TV; hair dryer; free Wi-Fi. Closed Jan.

Where to Eat

Le Médicis ★ TRADITIONAL FRENCH   Members of the Garanger family maintain one of the most sophisticated inns in Blois, just 1km (½ mile) from the château. It's ideal for a gourmet meal or an overnight stop. Typical dishes are swordfish with spinach "lasagna" and pistou emulsion, pigeon suprême with gnocchi of green peas and beans, and veal sweetbreads *meunière* with white asparagus. Chocolate in many manifestations is the dessert specialty. The Garangers rent 10 elegant rooms with air-conditioning, TV, minibar, and hair dryer. Double rates are 87€ to 150€.

2 allée François 1er. www.le-medicis.com. ℰ **02-54-43-94-04.** Reservations required. Main courses 19€–25€; fixed-price menu 25€–75€. AE, MC, V. Daily noon–1:15pm and 7–9pm. Closed Jan and Sun night and Mon Nov–Mar. Bus: 2.

L'Orangerie du Château ★★★ TOURAINE   Next to the château, one of the castle's former outbuildings holds the grandest and best restaurant in the area, with a floral-themed dining room. Faithful customers and the most discerning foodies visiting Blois delight in the filet mignon with truffles. You can also sample frogs' legs with rosemary sauce, a freshly caught monkfish flavored with fresh thyme, or French "surf and turf": veal with lobster. Everything tastes better with a sauvignon de Touraine. Junior *gastronomes* can satisfy their palates with the special children's menu.

1 av. Jean-Laigret. www.orangerie-du-chateau-fr. ℰ **02-54-78-05-36.** Main courses 25€–40€; fixed-price menu 38€–80€; children's menu 15€. Tues–Sat noon–1:30pm and 7:15–9:15pm. Closed mid-Feb to mid-Mar.

Exploring the Town & the Chateau

Blois is a piece of living history, with cobblestone streets and restored white houses with slate roofs and redbrick chimneys. Some of its "streets" are mere alleyways originally laid out in the Middle Ages or lanes linked by a series of stairs. If you have time for **shopping,** head for the area around **rue St-Martin** and **rue du Commerce** for high-end items such as clothing, perfume, shoes, and jewelry. On Saturday, a daylong **food market** is on place Louis XII and place de la République, lining several blocks in the center of town at the foot of the château.

Château de Blois ★★★ CASTLE   A wound in battle earned him the name Balafré (Scarface), but he was quite a ladies' man. In fact, on the misty morning of December 23, 1588, Henri I, the duc de Guise, had just left a warm bed and the arms of one of Catherine de Médicis's ladies-in-waiting. His archrival, King Henri III, had summoned him, but when the duke arrived, only the king's minions were about. The guards approached with daggers. Wounded, the duke made for the door, where more guards awaited him. Staggering, he fell to the floor in a pool of his own blood. Only then did Henri emerge from behind the curtains. "Mon Dieu," he reputedly exclaimed, "he's taller dead than alive!" The body couldn't be shown: The duke was too popular. Quartered, it was burned in a fireplace.

The murder of the duc de Guise is only one of the events associated with the Château de Blois, begun in the 13th century by the comte de Blois. Blois reached the apex of its power in 1515, when François I moved to the château. For that reason, Blois is often called the "Versailles of the Renaissance," the second capital of France, and the "City of Kings." But Blois soon became a palace of exile. Louis XIII banished his mother, Marie de Médicis, to the château, but she escaped by sliding into the moat down a mound of dirt left by the builders.

If you stand in the courtyard, you'll find that the château is like an illustrated story-book of French architecture. The Hall of the Estates-General is a beautiful 13th-century work; Louis XII built the Charles d'Orléans gallery and the Louis XII wing from 1498 to 1501. Mansart constructed the Gaston d'Orléans wing between 1635 and 1637. Most remarkable is the François I wing, a French Renaissance masterpiece containing a spiral staircase with ornamented balustrades and the king's symbol, the salamander.

41000 Blois. www.chateaudeblois.fr. ✆ **02-54-90-33-33.** Admission 9.50€ adults, 7€ students, 4€ children 6–17, free for children 5 and under. Additional fees for light shows and special events. July–Aug daily 9am–7pm; Apr–June and Sept daily 9am–6:30pm; Oct daily 9am–6pm; Nov–Mar daily 9am–12:30pm and 1:30–5:30pm.

CHAMBORD ★★★

91km (118 miles) SW of Paris; 18km (11 miles) E of Blois

The Château de Chambord, the grandest of the region's castles, is the culmination of François I's two biggest obsessions: hunting and architecture. It's a must for any Loire castle itinerary.

Essentials

GETTING THERE It's best to **drive** to Chambord. Take D951 northeast from Blois to Saint Dyé, turning on to the rural road to Chambord. You can also rent a **bicycle** in Blois and ride the 18km (11 miles) to Chambord, or take a **tour** to Chambord from Blois in summer. From May to September, **Transports du Loir et Cher** (www.tlcinfo. net; ✆ **02-54-58-55-44**) operates bus service to Chambord.

Exploring the Château

The Château de Chambord ★★★ Built as a "hunting lodge," this colossal edifice is a masterpiece of architectural derring-do. Some say Leonardo da Vinci had something to do with it, and when you climb the amazing double spiral staircase, that's not too hard to believe. The staircase is superimposed upon itself so that one person may descend and a second ascend without ever meeting. While da Vinci died a few months before construction started in 1519, what emerged after 20 years was the pinnacle of the French Renaissance, the largest château in the Loire Valley. The castle's proportions are of an exquisite geometric harmony, and its fantastic arrangement of turrets and chimneys makes it one of France's most recognizable chateaux.

Construction continued for decades; François I actually stayed at the chateau for only a few weeks during hunting season, though he insured Chambord would forever carry his legacy by imprinting his "F" emblem and symbol, the Salaman-der, wherever he could. After he died, his successors, none too sure what to do with the vast, unfurnished, and unfinished castle, basically abandoned it. Finally, Louis XIII gave it to his brother, who saved it from ruin; Louis XIV stayed there on several occasions and saw to restorations, but not a single monarch ever really moved in. The state acquired Chambord in 1932, and restoration work has been ongoing ever since.

Four monumental towers dominate Chambord's facade. The three-story keep has a spectacular terrace from which the ladies of the court watched the return of their men from the hunt. While many of the vast rooms are empty, several have been restored and filled with an impressive collection of period furniture and objects, giving an idea of what the castle looked like during the periods when parts of it were occupied. The château lies in a park of more than 5,260 hectares (12,992 acres), featuring miles of hiking trails and bike paths, as well as picnic tables and bird-watching posts.

www.chambord.org. ℂ 02-54-50-40-00. Admission 11€ adults and free 17 and under accompanied by an adult. Open daily April to Sept 9am–6pm, and Oct–Mar 9am–5pm.

CHEVERNY ★

192km (119 miles) SW of Paris; 19km (12 miles) SE of Blois

Unlike most of the Loire castles, Cheverny is the residence of the original owner's descendants, offering a rare glimpse into the normally very private life of French aristocrats.

Essentials

GETTING THERE   Cheverny is 19km (12 miles) south of Blois, along D765. It's best reached by **car** or on a **bus tour** (Apr–Aug only) from Blois with **TLC Transports du Loir et Cher** (www.tlcinfo.net; ℂ 02-54-58-55-44). Bus no. 4 leaves from the railway station at Blois once or twice per day; see the TLC website for the schedule. You can also take a **taxi** (ℂ 02-54-78-07-65) from the railway station at Blois.

Exploring the Château

Château de Cheverny ★   The family of the vicomte de Sigalas can trace its lineage from Henri Hurault, the son of the chancellor of Henri III and Henri IV, who built the château in 1634. Designed in classic Louis XIII style, it is resolutely symmetrical, with square pavilions flanking the central pile. Its elegant lines and sumptuous furnishings provoked the Grande Mademoiselle, otherwise known as the Duchess of Montpensier, to proclaim it an "enchanted castle."

You, too, will be impressed by the antique furnishings, tapestries, and objets d'art. A 17th-century French artist, Jean Mosnier, decorated the fireplace with motifs from the legend of Adonis. The Guards' Room contains a collection of medieval armor; also on display is a Gobelin tapestry depicting the abduction of Helen of Troy. In the king's bedchamber, another Gobelin traces the trials of Ulysses. Most impressive is the stone stairway of carved fruit and flowers. To complete the regal experience, your arrival or departure from the chateau might be heralded by red-coated trumpeters accompanied by an enthusiastic pack of hunting hounds.

www.chateau-cheverny.fr. ℂ 02-54-79-96-29. Admission 9€ adults, 6€ students under 25 and children 7–18, and free children 6 and under (additional fee for exhibits). Daily Nov–Mar 9:45am–5pm; April–June and Sept 9:15am–6:15pm; July–Aug 9:15am–6:45pm; and Oct 9:45am–5:30pm.

VALENÇAY ★★

233km (144 miles) SW of Paris; 56km (35 miles) S of Blois

One of the Loire's most handsome Renaissance châteaux, Valençay combines the wonders of châteaux-hopping and family fun, and even has a special museum for car lovers.

Essentials

GETTING THERE If you're **driving** from Tours, take A85 east, turning south on D956 (exit 13 to Selles-sur-Cher) to Valençay. From Blois, follow D956 south.

Where to Eat & Stay in Nearby Blois

St-Hubert ★ TRADITIONAL FRENCH   About 500m (1,640 ft.) from the Château de Cheverny, this inn was built in the 1950s in the provincial style. Excellent value for money, it offers fixed-price menus of regional specialties such as Muscadet-infused rabbit terrine with pear compote; local free-range Touraine Géline chicken with *pommes darphin* (thick potato pancake), topped with a tomato caviar; and for "dessert" Ste. Maure goat cheese or Sologne strawberry melba. While it's a far cry from the luxury of the Cheverny castle, the St-Hubert offers economic no-frills **lodging** with 20 conservatively decorated rooms for 57€ to 65€ for a double.

122 rte. Nationale. www.hotel-sthubert.com. ✆ **02-54-79-96-60.** Main courses 18€–22€; fixed-price menu 19€–39€; children's menu 12€. Daily noon–2pm and 7–9pm. Closed Sun night off-season.

Exploring the Château & Park

Château de Valençay ★★ CASTLE   Talleyrand acquired it in 1803 on the orders of Napoleon, who wanted his minister of foreign affairs to receive dignitaries in style. The d'Estampes family built Valençay in 1520. The dungeon and west tower are of this period, as is the main body of the building, but other wings were added in the 17th and 18th centuries. The effect is grandiose, all domes and turrets. The apartments are sumptuously furnished, mostly in the Empire style, but with Louis XV and Louis XVI trappings as well. A star-footed table in the main drawing room is said to have been the one on which the final agreement of the Congress of Vienna was signed in June 1815 (Talleyrand represented France).

After your visit to the château, take a walk through the garden and deer park. There are plenty of activities here for kids, including a giant labyrinth, a miniature farm, a playground, a golf cart circuit through the forest, and, in high season, historic reenactments (at 3pm, 4pm, and 5pm). A few nights each summer the château and its grounds return to the Renaissance, decked out with thousands of candles, costumed performers, and musical entertainment (see website for details).

Within 200m (656 ft.) of the château is the **Musée de l'Automobile de Valençay,** an impressive collection of some 60 antique automobiles. Of special interest is a Bédélia (ca. 1914). The tandem-style automobile (the driver rode behind the passenger) with a pulley-operated two-speed gearshift is the rarest car in the collection. Like 80 percent of the cars here, the Bédélia was made in France.

2 rue de Blois. www.chateau-valencay.fr. ✆ **02-54-00-10-66.** The Automobile Museum is located at 12 av. de la Résistance (www.musee-auto-valencay.fr; ✆ **02-54-00-07-74**), Admission for castle, automobile museum, and park 12€ adults, 8.50€ students, 3€ children 4–6, and free ages 5 and under. Open daily mid-March to April 10:30am–6pm; May 10am–6pm; June 9:30am–6:30pm; July–Aug 9:30am–7pm; Sept 10am–6pm; Oct–Nov 9 10:30am–5:30pm.

AMBOISE ★★

219km (136 miles) SW of Paris; 35km (22 miles) E of Tours

Amboise is on the banks of the Loire in the center of vineyards known as Touraine-Amboise. The good news: This is a real Renaissance town. The bad news: Because it is so beautiful, tour buses overrun it, especially in summer. Other than the myriad of notable royal residences, the town has also played host to Leonardo da Vinci, who spent his last years here, and more recently, royal rocker Mick Jagger, lord of a nearby château.

Essentials

GETTING THERE About a dozen **trains** per day leave from both Tours and Blois. The trip from Tours takes 20 minutes and costs 5.40€ one-way; from Blois, it takes 20 minutes and costs 6.80€ one-way. Several conventional trains a day leave from Paris's Gare d'Austerlitz (trip time: about 2 hr., 15 min.), and several TGVs depart from the Gare Montparnasse, with a change to a regular train at St-Pierre-des-Corps, next to Tours (trip time: 1 hr., 30 min.). Fares from Paris to Amboise start at 25€. For information, visit www.voyages-sncf.com or call ⓒ **36-35.**

If you prefer to travel by bus, **Fil Vert Buses** (www.tourainefilvert.com), which operates out of Gare Routière in Tours, just across from the railway station, runs about six to eight **buses** every day between Tours and Amboise. The one-way trip takes about 45 minutes and costs 2€.

If you're **driving** from Tours, take the D751, following signs to Amboise.

VISITOR INFORMATION The **Office de Tourisme** is on quai du Général-de-Gaulle (www.amboise-valdeloire.com; ⓒ **02-47-57-09-28**).

Where to Eat & Stay

Le Choiseul ★★★ Composed of three mansions dating from the 15th through 18th centuries and nestled on the banks of the Loire River, Le Choiseul is the best hotel in Amboise and serves its best cuisine. Guest rooms are luxurious; though modernized, they retain their old-world charm. Be sure to explore the grounds, where an outdoor pool is surrounded by Italian sculptures; ask the staff about visiting the impressive "Greniers de César" troglodyte caves nearby. The formal dining room has a view of the Loire and welcomes nonguests who phone ahead. The restaurant is superb, with a menu featuring classic and regional dishes made with the freshest ingredients. Lunch ranges from 28€ to 60€, with dinner going for 47€ to 82€.

36 quai Charles-Guinot. www.le-choiseul.com. ⓒ **02-47-30-45-45.** 32 units. 110€–315€ double; 295€-370€ suite. **Amenities:** Restaurant; bar; bicycles; outdoor pool; room service; A/C; TV; hair dryer; minibar; free Wi-Fi.

Le Fleuray ★★ One of the most appealing hotels in the region is this well-maintained ivy-covered manor house, run by a family of English expatriates, a short drive from Amboise. Guest rooms have been recently renovated and evoke an elegant but not terribly formal English country house, several have private terraces. With peaceful surroundings and plenty to do on the extensive grounds, this is an excellent base for château touring and unwinding. The hotel also has an excellent restaurant serving food infused with regional and international flavors. Items on the fixed-price menus (29€–39€) might include lobster risotto with fennel, saffron, and zucchini; filet of beef with purple-potato purée and baby artichokes with Loire Valley red-wine sauce; or a vegetarian-friendly soba-noodle and seasonal-vegetable stir-fry.

Route D74, near Amboise. www.lefleurayhotel.com. ℭ **02-47-56-09-25.** Fax 02-47-56-93-97. 23 units. 88€–148€ double. MC, V. Free parking. From Amboise, take the D952 on the north side of the river, following signs to Blois; 12km (7½ miles) from Amboise, turn onto D74, in the direction of Cangey. **Amenities:** Restaurant; bar; free bikes; golf course; Jacuzzi; massage; outdoor pool; room service; tennis court; TV; hair dryer.

Le Manoir Les Minimes ★★ Centrally located on the river's edge in the shadow of the château, this restored 18th-century mansion is a welcoming and reasonably priced hotel built on the foundations of an ancient convent. Inside, furnishings are elegant in both the public and private rooms, with much use made of antiques. The most desirable rooms are in the main building; a comfortable, well-furnished trio of units is in an annex, although these lack character. Many of the second-floor bedrooms open onto views of the Loire. The best-value rooms are smaller and on the third floor. Each room has unique decor and comes with an elegant bathroom with tub.

34 quai Charles Guinot. www.manoirlesminimes.com. ℭ **02-47-30-40-40.** 15 units. 135eu]–210€ double; 290€–500€ suite. MC, V. **Amenities:** Breakfast room; A/C; TV; minibar; free Wi-Fi.

Where to Eat

For finer dining, the restaurants at the hotels **Le Choiseul and Le Fleuray** (see above) are excellent.

Brasserie de l'Hotel de Ville ★ FRENCH If you need a quick lunch in the town's historic core, this bustling Paris-style brasserie is a good option, particularly in pleasing hungry little bellies. Expect a noisy environment focused on rows of banquettes, hassled waiters, and steaming platters that emerge relatively quickly from the overworked kitchen. Menu items include a full range of old-fashioned dishes that locals may remember from their childhoods, like sausage splashed with Vouvray sparkling wine; standard grilled beefsteak with french fries; and duck with honey and rosemary—as well as lighter salads and omelets.

1 and 3 rue François 1er. ℭ **02-47-57-26-30.** Main courses 7€–18€; fixed-price menu 15€–26€; children's menu 6.90€. Daily noon–2pm and 7–9:30pm.

Exploring the Town

Château du Clos-Lucé ★ HISTORIC HOME/MUSEUM Within 3km (1¾ miles) of the base of Amboise's château, this brick-and-stone building was constructed in the 1470s. Bought by Charles VII in 1490, it became the summer residence of the royals and also served as a retreat for Anne de Bretagne, who, according to legend, spent a lot of time praying and meditating. Later, François I installed "the great master in all forms of art and science," Leonardo himself. Da Vinci lived here for 3 years, until his death in 1519. Today the site functions as a small museum, where you can step back into the life and imagination of da Vinci. The manor contains furniture from his era; examples of his sketches; models for his flying machines, bridges, and cannon; and temporary exhibits.

2 rue de Clos-Lucé. www.vinci-closluce.com. ℭ **02-47-57-00-73.** Mar–Nov 15 admission 14€ adults, 8.50€ students and children 6–18, 37€ family ticket (2 adults, 2 children), free children 5 and under. Jan daily 10am–6pm; Feb–June daily 9am–7pm; July–Aug daily 9am–8pm; Sept–Oct daily 9am–7pm; Nov–Dec daily 9am–6pm.

Château d'Amboise ★★ CASTLE On a rocky spur above the town, this medieval château was rebuilt in 1492 by Charles VIII, the first in France to reflect the Italian Renaissance.

Visitors enter on a ramp that opens onto a panoramic terrace fronting the river. At one time, buildings surrounded this terrace, and fêtes took place in the enclosed courtyard. The castle fell into decline during the Revolution, and today only about a quarter of the once-sprawling edifice remains. You first come to the Flamboyant Gothic **Chapelle de St-Hubert,** distinguished by its lacelike tracery, which holds the **tomb of Leonardo da Vinci,** who died in Amboise. Tapestries cover the walls of what's left of the château's grandly furnished rooms, which include **Logis du Roi (King's Apartment).** The vast **Salle du Conseil,** book-ended by a Gothic and a Renaissance fireplace, was once the venue of the lavish fêtes. Exit via the **Tour des Minimes** (also known as the Tour des Cavaliers), noteworthy for a ramp up which horsemen could ride. The other notable tower is the Heurtault, which is broader than the Minimes, with thicker walls.

www.chateau-amboise.com ✆ **02-47-57-00-98.** Admission 11€ adults, 9€ students, 7.20€ ages 7–14, free children 7 and under. Open daily Jan 9am–12:30pm and 2–4:45pm; Feb 9am–12:30pm and 1:30–5pm; Mar 9am–5:30pm; Apr–June 9am–6:30pm; July–Aug 9am–7pm; Sept–Oct 9am–6pm; Nov 2–15 9am–5:30pm; Nov 16–Dec 31 9am–12:30pm and 2–4:45pm.

CHENONCEAUX ★★★

224km (139 miles) SW of Paris; 26km (16 miles) E of Tours

Chenonceau is one of the most remarkable castles in France. Its impressive setting, spanning a whole river, along with an intriguing history and renowned residents, make it many visitors' favorite château in the whole country. (**Note:** The village, whose year-round population is less than 300, is spelled with a final *x,* but the château isn't.)

Essentials

GETTING THERE   About a dozen daily **trains** run from Tours to Chenonceaux (trip time: 30 min.), costing 6.60€ one-way. The train deposits you at the base of the château; from there, it's an easy walk. For information, visit www.voyages-sncf.com or call ✆ **36-35.** If you're **driving,** from the center of Tours follow the signs to the D40 east, which will take you to the signposted turnoff for Chenonceaux.

Exploring the Château, Museum & Gardens

Château de Chenonceau ★★★ CASTLE   A Renaissance masterpiece, the château is best known for the dames de Chenonceau, who once occupied it. Built first for Katherine Briçonnet, the château was bought in 1547 by Henri II for his mistress, Diane de Poitiers. For a time, this remarkable woman was virtually queen of France, infuriating Henri's dour wife, Catherine de Médicis. Diane's critics accused her of using magic to preserve her celebrated beauty and keep Henri's attentions from waning. Apparently, Henri's love for Diane continued unabated, and she was in her 60s when he died in a jousting tournament in 1559.

When Henri died, Catherine became regent (her eldest son was still a child), and one of the first things she did was force Diane to return the jewelry Henri had given her and abandon her beloved home. Catherine added her own touches, building a two-story gallery across the bridge—obviously inspired by her native Florence. The gallery, which was used for her opulent fêtes, doubled as a military hospital in WWI. It also played a crucial role in WWII, serving as the demarcation line between Nazi-occupied France and the "free" zone.

Gobelin tapestries, including one depicting a woman pouring water over the back of an angry dragon, and several important paintings by Poussin, Rubens, and Tintoretto adorn the château's walls. The chapel contains a marble Virgin and Child by Murillo, as well as portraits of Catherine de Médicis in black and white. There's even a portrait of the stern Catherine in the former bedroom of her rival, Diane de Poitiers. In François I's Renaissance bedchamber, the most interesting portrait is that of Diane as the huntress Diana.

The women of Chenonceau are the subject of the **Musée de Cire (Wax Museum),** located in a Renaissance-era annex a few steps from the château.

The château boasts vast grounds that include a maze, a vegetable garden, and a beautiful *jardin à la française,* open on summer evenings for an illuminated "night walk" accompanied by Italian classical music (weekends in June; nightly July–Aug 9:30pm–11:30pm).

www.chenonceau.com. ℰ **02-47-23-90-07.** Admission 11€ adults and 8.50€ students and children 7–17; combination ticket château and wax museum 13€ adults, 11€ children 7–17, free 6 and under; admission for evening garden light show 5€ adults, free children under 7. Daily 9am–8pm July–Aug; 9am–7pm for the last 2 weeks of March; 9am–7:30pm June and Sept; 9am–6pm Oct; 9am–5pm rest of the year.

CHAUMONT-SUR-LOIRE ★★

200km (124 miles) SW of Paris; 40km (25 miles) E of Tours

The connections of this lesser-visited castle to Diane de Poitiers make it an excellent château to pair with a visit to the Château de Chenonceau (see above). It is also a wonderful stop for garden enthusiasts.

Essentials

GETTING THERE Several **trains** a day travel to Chaumont from Blois (trip time: 10–15 min.) and Tours (about 40 min.). The one-way fare is 3.50€ from Blois, 8.40€ from Tours. The railway station serving Chaumont is in Onzain, a nice 1½-mile walk north of the château. For train schedules and ticketing information, visit www.voyages-sncf.com or call ℰ **36-35.**

Where to Eat & Stay Near Amboise

Au Gâteau Breton ★ TRADITIONAL FRENCH   Just a short walk from the Château de Chenonceau, this restaurant makes a refreshing stop for a casual lunch or tea. The pretty 18th-century inn was once a grocery store run by an "immigrant" from the distant land of Brittany. Gravel paths run among beds of pink geraniums and lilacs, and bright umbrellas adorn red tables. In cool months, meals are served in the rustic dining rooms. Worthwhile dishes include homey favorites like *boudin* (blood sausage) with apples; *poulet Tourangelle* (sautéed chicken with mushroom and cream sauce); and steak with *beurre maître d'hôtel* (butter mixed with parsley, garlic, and lemon).

16 rue du Dr. Bretonneau. ℰ **02-47-23-90-14.** Main courses 14€–18€; fixed-price menus 15€–27€. Apr–Sept daily noon–2:30pm, daily 7–10pm; Nov–Mar daily noon–2:30pm.

Le Domaine des Hauts de Loire ★★   Less than 3km (1¾ miles) from the Château de Chaumont, this property sits on the opposite side of the Loire. The manor house was built by the owner of a Paris-based newspaper in 1840 and is called, rather coyly, a "hunting lodge." It's the most appealing stopover in the neighborhood, with rooms decorated in Louis Philippe or Empire style. More than half the rooms are in the slightly less desirable half-timbered annex that was originally the stables.

Treat yourself to an incredible meal at its Michelin-two-starred restaurant. The creative menu may offer pan-fried *sandre* fish with tarragon-infused seasonal vegetables drizzled in beetroot dressing, or young pigeon with crispy potatoes, turnip puree, and a side of cocoa-flavored sauce. Main courses range from 58€ to 69€, with fixed-price menus ranging from 60€ to 160€.

Rte. d'Herbault. www.domainehautsloire.com. ℰ **02-54-20-72-57.** 36 units. 190€–315€ double; 350€–690€ suite. Closed Dec–Feb. **Amenities:** Restaurant; bar; outdoor pool; room service; TV; hair dryer; minibar; Wi-Fi (10€/hour).

Exploring the Château & Garden

Château de Chaumont ★★ CASTLE   On the morning when Diane de Poitiers first crossed the drawbridge, the Château de Chaumont looked grim. Henri II, her lover, had recently died. The king had given her Chenonceau, but his angry widow, Catherine de Médicis, forced her to trade her favorite château for Chaumont, a comparatively virtual dungeon for Diane, with its medieval battlements and pepper-pot turrets and position perched high above the Loire.

The château belonged to the Amboise family for 5 centuries. In 1465, when one of them, a certain Pierre, rebelled against the rule of Louis XI, the king had the castle burned to the ground as a punishment. Pierre and his descendants rebuilt for the next few decades. The castle's architecture spans the period between the Middle Ages and the Renaissance, and the vast rooms still evoke the 16th and 17th centuries. In the bedroom occupied by Catherine de Médicis, you can see a portrait of the Italian-born queen. The superstitious Catherine housed her astrologer, Cosimo Ruggieri, in one of the tower rooms (a portrait of him remains). He reportedly foretold the disasters awaiting her sons.

The château passed through the hands of various owners and was eventually acquired and restored by the eccentric Marie Say and Amédée de Broglie in the late 18th century, who also added elaborate stables, a farm, and gardens. Since 1992, the latter has hosted the **International Garden Festival,** a world-renowned gathering of cutting-edge landscape designers that lasts from mid-April to mid-October and is open to the public. Each year, a dozen different gardens are created, using thousands of different plants and innovative garden designs. Since 2008, the château has also been a site for contemporary art and photography exhibits; check the website for this year's program.

www.domaine-chaumont.fr; ℰ **02-54-51-26-26.** Admission is 10€ adults, 6€ children 12–18, 4€ children 6-11, and free ages 5 and under. Full pass including the festival 16€ adults, 11€ children 12–18, 5:50€ children 6–11, and free 5 and under. Open daily Nov–Mar 10am–5pm; April–June 10am–6:30pm; July–Aug 10am–7pm; Sept 10am–6:30pm; and Oct 10am–6pm.

TOURS ★

232km (144 miles) SW of Paris; 113km (70 miles) SW of Orléans

Though it doesn't have a major château, Tours (pop. 137,000), at the junction of the Loire and Cher rivers, is known for its food and wine. Many of its buildings were bombed in World War II, and 20th-century apartment towers have taken the place of castles. But the downtown core is quite charming, and because Tours is at the doorstep of some of the most magnificent châteaux in France, it makes a good base from which to explore.

Essentials

GETTING THERE   As many as 14 high-speed TGV **trains** per day depart from Paris's Gare Montparnasse and arrive at St-Pierre des Corps station, 6km (3¾ miles) east of the center of Tours, in an hour. Free *navettes,* or shuttle buses, await your arrival to take you to the center of town (the Tours Centre train station). A limited number of conventional trains also depart from Gare d'Austerlitz and arrive in the center of Tours, but these take twice as long (about 2¼ hr.). One-way fares range from 20€ to 62€. For information, visit www.voyages-sncf.com or call ☎ **36-35.** If you're **driving,** take highway A10 to Tours.

GETTING AROUND   It's easy to walk from one end of central Tours to the other, and many of the good hotels are near the train station. For taxi service, call **Taxi Radio** (☎ **02-47-20-30-40**). You can rent a car at **Avis** (www.avis.fr; ☎ **02-47-20-53-27**), located in the Tours Centre train station, or **Europcar,** at the St-Pierre des Corps station (www.europcar.fr; ☎ **02-47-63-28-67**). You can rent a bike at **Detours de Loire,** 35 rue Charles Gilles (www.locationdevelos.com; ☎ **02-47-61-22-23**), at a cost of 15€ per day. A deposit is required.

VISITOR INFORMATION   The **Office de Tourisme** is at 78–82 rue Bernard-Palissy (www.ligeris.com; ☎ **02-47-70-37-37**).

Where to Stay

Best Western Le Central ★   Off the main boulevard, this old-fashioned hotel is within walking distance of the train station, the river, and the cathedral. Despite its central location, its has plenty of greenery. The back of the hotel looks out onto a leafy garden, and the front is set off by a lawn, which helps reduce street traffic noise, though it makes the hotel a little tricky to find. The decor is classic and conservative and meshes well with the building's 19th-century bones.

21 rue Berthelot, Tours 37000. www.bestwesterncentralhoteltours.com. ☎ **800/528-1234** in the U.S. and Canada, or 02-47-05-46-44. Fax 02-47-66-10-26. 37 units. 104€–160€ double; 200€–260€ suite. AE, DC, MC, V. Parking 10€. **Amenities:** Bar; babysitting; room service; A/C; TV; hair dryer; minibar; free Wi-Fi.

Where to Eat

Restaurants in Tours can be pricey, but you can keep costs low by dining at **La Souris Gourmande,** 100 rue Colbert (http://lasourisgourmande.com; ☎ **02-47-47-04-80**), where the chef is respected for the diversity of his cheese selection. Try it in half-dozen fondues. You may be asked to join a communal table. Main courses cost 13€ to 15€. At the raffish but cheerful bistro **Le Lapin qui Fume,** 90 rue Colbert (☎ **02-47-66-95-49**), a fixed-price menu costs 10€ to 15€ at lunch and 15€ to 26€ at dinner and features standard bistro fare and, as the name suggests, rabbit.

La Roche le Roy ★★ MODERN FRENCH   Gastronomes will delight in Alain Couturier's creative blends. Housed in a gabled 18th-century manor south of the town center, the picturesque setting adds to this sensorial experience. Couturier's repertoire includes lobster risotto, foie gras with caramelized apples, bass with champagne cream sauce, and *matelote* (stew) of eel with Vouvray wine. His masterpiece is *suprême* of pigeon with "roughly textured" sauce. For dessert, try a warm orange soufflé flavored with Grand Marnier.

55 rte. St-Avertin. www.rocheleroy.com. ☎ **02-47-27-22-00.** Main courses 25€–38€, lunch menu 34€, dinner menu 782eu]. Tues–Sat noon–1:30pm and 7:30–9:30pm. Closed 2 weeks in Feb and 3 weeks in Aug. From the center of town, take av. Grammont south (follow signs to St-Avertin–Vierzon).

Rive Gauche ★ MODERN FRENCH This gourmet restaurant and wine bar touts "responsible gastronomy," which takes into consideration both taste and environmental impact. The talented young chef, Gaëtan Evrard, uses his lively imagination and high-quality local and/or artisanal products to create surprising dishes like tiger prawns flambéed in Grand Marnier; scallop sashimi with black truffle from Touraine and roasted hazelnuts; and "Roi Rose" pork tenderloin with candied turnip, fennel and apple salad. Be sure to save room for the decadent white chocolate and tonka beans Saint Honoré. You can savor these delicacies in either of two cozy dining rooms or, in warm weather, outdoors on the terrace.

23 rue du Commerce. www.tours-rivegauche.com. ℂ **02-47-05-71-21.** Main courses 15€–32€; fixed-price menu 29€–69€. Tues–Sun 12:30pm–2pm and 7:30–10pm.

Where to Stay & Eat Near Tours

Château d'Artigny ★★★ This is perhaps the grandest address in the Loire Valley. About 1.5km (1 mile) west of the hamlet of Montbazon and 15km (9¼ miles) south of Tours, the château was built between 1912 and 1920 for the perfume and cosmetics king François Coty, who lived and entertained lavishly. Set in a forest and overlooking formal gardens, the château combines Jazz Age ostentation with 18th-century French aesthetics. The drawing room and corridors are furnished with fine antiques, Louis XV–style chairs, and bronze statuary. The grounds contain acres of parks and a large garden with a reflecting pool. Guest rooms are outfitted in period style, with many antiques, comfortable mattresses, and all the perks of upscale country living. Only 31 units are in the main building; the others are in four annexes: a former chapel, gatehouse, mill, and staff dormitory. The château experience continues in the Artigny's regal restaurant **L'Origan** (lunch menu from 29€, dinner from 55€).

Rte. des Monts (D17). www.artigny.com. ℂ **02-47-34-30-30.** 65 units. 180€–415€ double; 424€–530€ junior suite. From Tours, take N10 south for 11km (6¾ miles) to Montbazon, and then take D17 1.5km (1 mile) southeast. **Amenities:** Restaurant; bar; babysitting; exercise room; outdoor pool; room service; sauna; spa; 2 tennis courts; A/C; TV; hair dryer; minibar; free Wi-Fi (in some).

Exploring the City

Pilgrims en route to Santiago de Compostela in northwest Spain once stopped here to pay homage at the tomb of St-Martin, the "Apostle of Gaul," and bishop of Tours in the 4th century. One of the most significant conflicts in European history, the 732 Battle of Tours, checked the Arab advance into Gaul. In the 15th century, French kings set up shop here, and Tours became the capital of France, a position it held for more than 100 years.

Most Loire Valley towns are rather sleepy, but Tours is where the action is, where streets and cafes bustle with a large student population. The heart of town is **place Jean-Jaurès.** The principal street is **rue Nationale,** running north to the Loire River. Head west along rue du Commerce and rue du Grand-Marché to Vieux Tours/Vieille Ville (old town). If you turn left on rue du Commerce toward the old town center, you can explore the streets and courtyards for regional specialties, books, toys, and crafts. A hotbed for antiques is east of rue Nationale (toward the cathedral), along **rue de la Scellerie.** Up rue Nationale toward the river are more shops and upscale boutiques and a small mall with chain stores.

Place Plumereau (often shortened to "place Plume"), a square of medieval buildings, houses a concentration of restaurants and bars. In the warmer months, the square explodes with tables that fill with people who like to people-watch (and be watched

If you aren't renting a car, several tour companies in Tours arrange full- and half-day visits to nearby castles, and three of them offer minibus tours that leave daily from the tourist office. **Acco-Dispo** (www.accodispo-tours.com; ℭ **06-82-00-64-51**), **Saint-Eloi Excursions** (http://saint-eloiexcursions.com; ℭ **06-70-82-78-75**), and **Quart de Tours** (www.quartdetours.com; ℭ **06-30-65-52-01**) all offer minibus tours that depart around 9am; you can reserve on the tourist office website (www.visaloire.com) or directly on the company websites. Costs range from 20€ to 52€ per person. The price does not include meals or admission to the châteaux, but participation in the tour qualifies you for reduced group rates. Keep in mind that less is sometimes more when it comes to castle viewing; after two or three, you may not be able to remember which was which.

themselves). This is a good place to start if you're going out in the evening; otherwise venture to the trendy bars on **rue Colbert,** which lies in the heart of Tours, midway between the place Plumereau and the cathedral. Allow a morning, afternoon, or evening to see Tours.

Cathédrale St-Gatien ★ CATHEDRAL   This cathedral honors a 3rd-century evangelist and has a Flamboyant Gothic facade flanked by towers with bases from the 12th century. The lanterns date from the Renaissance. The choir is from the 13th century, with new additions built in each century through the 16th. Sheltered inside is the handsome 16th-century tomb of Charles VIII and Anne de Bretagne's two children. Some of the glorious stained-glass windows are from the 13th century.

5 place de la Cathédrale. ℭ **02-47-70-21-00.** Free admission. Daily 9am–7pm.

Musée des Beaux-Arts ★ ART MUSEUM   This fine provincial museum is worth a visit just to see the lovely rooms and gardens of the former Archbishop's Palais, parts dating as far back as the 12th century. Old Masters are here as well, including works by Rubens, Delacroix, Rembrandt, and Boucher. The sculpture collection includes works by Houdon and Bourdelle.

18 place François Sicard. www.mba.tours.fr/. ℭ **02-47-05-68-73.** Admission 5€ adults, 2:50€ seniors and students, free for children 12 and under. Wed–Mon 9am-12:45 and 2pm–6pm. Bus: 3.

VILLANDRY ★★★

253km (157 miles) SW of Paris; 32km (20 miles) NE of Chinon; 18km (11 miles) W of Tours; 8km (5 miles) E of Azay-le-Rideau

The Renaissance Château de Villandry should be top of the list for any garden lover. Its 16th-century-style *jardins* are celebrated throughout Touraine and amaze visitors from around the world with their beauty and faithful historic preservation.

Essentials

GETTING THERE   Three daily **buses** operate from Tours from July to October only; the trip takes about 30 minutes and costs 2€. For bus information, visit www. touraine-filvert.com or call ℭ **02-47-05-30-49.** Villandry has no train service. The nearest connection from Tours is in the town of Savonnières; the trip takes around

15 minutes and costs 3.40€ one-way. For information, visit www.voyages-sncf.com or call ℂ **36-35.** From Savonnières, you can walk along the Loire for 4km (2½ miles) to reach Villandry, rent a **bike** at the station, or take a **taxi.** You can also **drive,** following D7 from Tours.

Where to Eat

Le Cheval Rouge MODERN FRENCH   The well-known dining stopover near the Château de Villandry extends a congenial welcome. The conservatively decorated dining room lies about 91m (298 ft.) from the banks of the Cher. Specialties include fois gras profiteroles with fig jam; bass poached in sparkling Vouvray wine; rump steak with goat cheese sauce; and roast lamb with thyme. The inn also rents 41 recently renovated rooms, decorated with modern appeal and furnishings. A double is 66€; the hotel also has several family rooms renting for 76€ to 97€.

9 rue Principale. www.lecheval-rouge.com. ℂ **02-47-50-02-07.** Main courses 15€–18€; fixed-price menu 20€–36€. Daily noon–2:30pm and 7–9pm.

Exploring the Gardens & Château

Château de Villandry ★★★ CASTLE/GARDENS   Every square of the gardens is like a geometric mosaic. Designed on a trio of superimposed cloisters with a water garden on the highest level, the gardens were restored by the Spanish doctor and scientist Joachim Carvallo, great-grandfather of the present owner. The grounds contain 17km (11 miles) of boxwood sculpture, which the gardeners cut to style in only 2 weeks each September. The borders symbolize the faces of love: tender, tragic (represented by daggers), and crazy (with a labyrinth that doesn't get you anywhere). The vine arbors, citrus hedges, and walks keep six men busy full-time. The French vegetable garden is being reverted to all-organic.

A feudal castle once stood at Villandry. In 1536, Jean le Breton, François I's Finance Minister and former Ambassador to Italy, acquired the property and built the present château with strong influences of the Italian Renaissance. The buildings form a U and are surrounded by a moat. Near the gardens is a terrace from which you can see the small village and its 12th-century church. A tearoom on-site, **La Doulce Terrasse** (www.chateauvillandry.com; ℂ **02-47-50-02-10;** closed mid-Nov to mid-Feb), serves regional cuisine, including vegetables from the garden, fresh-baked bread, and homemade ice cream. For a more gourmet meal, try **Le Cheval Rouge** (above).

www.chateauvillandry.com. ℂ **02-47-50-02-09.** Admission to gardens and château 9.50€ for adults, 5.50€ children 8 to 18, and free for children 7 and under, entrance to gardens only 6.50€ adults and 4€ for children 8 to 18. Gardens open daily 9am–5 or 7:30pm, depending on the hour of sunset; château open daily 9am–:30 or 6:30pm, depending on a complicated seasonal schedule.

LANGEAIS ★

259km (161 miles) SW of Paris; 26km (16 miles) W of Tours

Dominating the town on a steep slope, this medieval fortress is one of the few châteaux actually on the Loire. Crossing over its drawbridge and through its massive towers takes you back 500 years to the start of the golden age of the Loire.

Essentials

GETTING THERE   Several **trains** per day stop here en route from Tours or Saumur. The one-way fare from Saumur is 7.90€; the one-way fare from Tours 5.40€. Transit time from both cities is around 20 minutes. For schedules and information, visit www. voyages-sncf.com or call ⓒ **36-35.** If you're **driving** from Tours, take D952 southwest to Langeais.

Exploring the Château

Château de Langeais ★★ CASTLE   On December 6, 1491, 15-year-old Anne de Bretagne was wed to Charles VIII at Langeais, permanently attaching Brittany to France. The original castle was built in the 10th century when Fulk III (972–1040), count of Anjou, sometimes called the "Black Falcon," seized Langeais from the Count of Blois. He erected the first keep, the ruins of which can still be seen. The present structure was built in 1465 in the late medieval style. The interior is well preserved and furnished, thanks to Jacques Siegfried, who not only restored it over 20 years, but also bequeathed it to the Institut de France in 1904.

The rooms re-create the ambience of a regal residence of the late Middle Ages, rich with ornamental fireplaces and tapestries. A remarkable 15th-century millefleurs tapestry decorates the Chambre de la Dame, and seven superb tapestries known as the "Valiant Knights" cover the walls of the Salle des Preux.

The Banquet Hall features a mantelpiece carved to resemble a fortress, complete with crenellated towers. The Wedding Hall includes a re-creation of the marriage of Anne de Bretagne and Charles VIII with lavishly costumed wax figures. In the Luini Room is a large 1522 fresco by that artist, removed from a chapel on Lake Maggiore, Italy. It depicts Saint Francis of Assisi and Saint Elizabeth of Hungary with Mary and Joseph. Kids can learn medieval castle construction with interactive displays, or have some fun exploring the treehouse and the two playgrounds.

www.chateau-de-langeais.com. ⓒ **02-47-96-72-60.** Admission 8.80€ adults, 7.20€ students and ages 18–25, 5€ for children 10–17, free for 9 and under. Daily Apr–June and Sept to mid-Nov 9:30am–6:30pm; mid-Nov to Jan 10am–5pm; Feb–Mar 9:30am–5:30pm; July–Aug 9am–7pm.

AZAY-LE-RIDEAU ★★

261km (162 miles) SW of Paris; 21km (13 miles) SW of Tours

With its idyllic location and fairy-tale turrets, the Renaissance Château d'Azay-le-Rideau was deemed by neighboring writer Honoré de Balzac to be "a facetted diamond set in the Indre."

Essentials

GETTING THERE   To reach Azay-le-Rideau, take the **train** from Tours or Chinon. From either starting point, the trip time is about 30 minutes; the one-way fare is 5€ from Chinon, 5.60€ from Tours. For the same fare, the SNCF railway also operates a bus between Tours and Azay; the trip takes 50 minutes. For schedules and information, visit www.voyages-sncf.com or call ⓒ **36-35.** If you're **driving** from Tours, take D751 southwest to Azay-le-Rideau.

Where to Eat

L'Aigle d'Or ★ TRADITIONAL FRENCH   This excellent restaurant near the Château d'Azay-le-Rideau is set in a century-old house in the village center. The service is professional, the welcome charming, and the food the best in town. In a dining room accented with ceiling beams, a fireplace, and pastel colors, you can savor dishes including chilled asparagus soup with a poached egg; filet of beef Chinon; and a

As you drive along the Loire something other than castles may catch your eye along the riverbanks. The region of Anjou holds the largest concentration of troglodyte caves in all of France. The beige limestone of the area was put to good use building the many châteaux, and the empty caverns from the excavated stone were not left abandoned.

Not surprisingly, the caves were first used to store bottles of the region's bubbly wine; more recently, however, many have been converted into homes, art galleries, and even restaurants. For a true troglodyte experience, stop in at the bustling and mainly underground artist town of **Turquant,** 10 km (6 miles) east of Saumur (www.turquant.fr).

blanquette (stew) of Loire Valley whitefish prepared with local white wine. Desserts include baked apple with rice pudding mousse and chocolate cake with sour cherry coulis. In summer, dining extends onto an outdoor terrace.

10 av. Adélaïde-Riché. www.laigle-dor.fr. © **02-47-45-24-58.** Main courses 15€–25€; fixed-price menus lunch 20€, dinner 28€–56€. Mon–Tues and Thurs–Sat noon–1:30pm and 7:30–9pm Sun noon–1:30pm, closed Jan to mid-Feb.

Exploring the Château

Château d'Azay-le-Rideau ★★ CASTLE   Its machicolated towers and blue-slate roof pierced with dormers give it a medieval air, however, its defensive-fortress like appearance is all for show. The chateau was actually commissioned in the early 1500s for Gilles Berthelot, François I's finance minister, and his wife, Philippa, who supervised its construction. They didn't have long to enjoy their elegant creation: In 1527, Berthelot was accused of misappropriation of funds and forced to flee, and the château reverted to the king. He didn't live here, but granted it to Antoine Raffin, one of his high-ranking soldiers. It became the property of the state in 1905.

Before you enter, circle the château and note the perfect proportions of the crowning achievement of the Renaissance in the Touraine. Check out its most fancifully ornate feature, the bay enclosing a grand stairway with a straight flight of steps. From the second-floor Royal Chamber, look out at the gardens. This lavish bedroom housed Louis XIII when he came through in 1619. The private apartments are lined with rich tapestries dating from the 16th and 17th centuries and feature examples of rare period furniture, like the Spanish *bargueno,* a carved wooden chest that held writing materials. Azay hosts a sound-and-light show most nights in July and August (details below).

http://azay-le-rideau.monuments-nationaux.fr/. © **02-47-45-42-04.** Admission 8.50€ adults, 5.50€ youth 18-25, and free 17 and under, Open daily July–Aug 9:30am–7pm; April–June and Sept 9:30am–6pm; and Oct–Mar 10am–12:30pm and 2–5:30pm. Admission to the evening sound-and-light show 9€ adults, 4€ children 5–12, free 4 and under; show is nightly mid July to late Aug 8:30pm–midnight.

SAUMUR

299km (185 miles) SW of Paris; 53km (33 miles) SE of Angers

Saumur lies in a region of vineyards, where the Loire separates to encircle an island. It makes one of the best bases for exploring the western Loire Valley. A small but thriving town, it doesn't entirely live off its past: Saumur produces some 100,000 tons per year of the mushrooms the French adore. Balzac left us this advice: "Taste a mushroom and delight in the essential strangeness of the place." The cool tunnels for the *champignons* also provide the ideal resting place for the region's celebrated sparkling wines. Enjoy both of these local favorites at a neighborhood cafe.

Essentials

GETTING THERE **Trains** run frequently between Tours Centre and Saumur. Some 20 trains per day arrive from Tours (trip time: 30–40 min.); the one-way fare is 12€. From the station, take bus A into town. For schedules and information, visit www. voyages-sncf.com or call ✆ **36-35.** If you're **driving** from Tours, follow D952 or the A85 autoroute southwest to Saumur.

VISITOR INFORMATION The **Office de Tourisme** is on place de la Bilange (www.ot-saumur.fr; ✆ **02-41-40-20-60**).

Where to Stay

Hôtel St-Pierre ★ Nestled among tiny winding streets and built against the Eglise St-Pierre, this hotel overflows with character. Recent renovations have retained the building's traditional character while adding modern conveniences. Appointments include finely upholstered antiques, half-timbered walls, beamed ceilings, stone fireplaces, and spiral staircases. Guest rooms are individually decorated in the same rich style; even the bathroom walls showcase custom-tile designs. Overall, the hotel is an appealing middle-bracket choice in a historic location. The intimate breakfast room opens onto a small garden terrace.

Rue Haute-Saint-Pierre. www.saintpierresaumur.com. ✆ **02-41-50-33-00.** 14 units. 100€–180€ double. **Amenities:** Babysitting; room service; A/C; TV; hair dryer; minibar; free Wi-Fi.

Where to Eat

If you're just breezing through town or looking for a casual bite, try **Les Tontons** (www.bistrotlestontons-saumur.blogspot.fr; ✆ **02-41-49-49-50**), a welcoming English-friendly bistro with great-value daily lunch specials and a fabulous local wine list. If you're visiting the equestrian center, you can rub shoulders with the riders at nearby **Le Carrousel** (www.le-resto-du-carrousel.com; ✆ **02-41-51-00-40**), showcasing regional cuisine for 13€ for lunch and 18€ at dinner.

Le Gambetta ★★ MODERN FRENCH This is certainly not the cheapest restaurant in Saumur, but if you want to enjoy cutting-edge cuisine made with top-quality ingredients, it's the place to go. The Michelin-starred cuisine is creative and absolutely delicious—the menu includes dishes like baked wild bass and asparagus crumble, local pigeon breast with Oriental spices and bergamot jus, and the adventurous Gorgozola *croque-monsieur* with pears and Java pepper.

12 rue Gambetta. www.restaurantlegambetta.com. ✆ **02-41-67-66-66.** Main courses 20€–30€; lunch menu 25€, dinner menu 31€–97€. Tues and Thurs–Sun noon–2pm; Tues and Thurs–Sat 7–9pm. Closed 2 weeks in Jan, 3 weeks in Aug.

Exploring the Area

Of all the Loire cities, Saumur remains the most bourgeois; perhaps that's why Balzac used it for his classic characterization of a smug little town in "Eugénie Grandet." Saumur is also famous as the birthplace of the *couturière* Coco Chanel.

The men of Saumur are among the best equestrians in the world. Founded in 1768, the city's riding school, **Cadre Noir de Saumur ★**, avenue de l'Ecole Nationale d'Equitation (www.cadrenoir.fr; ✆ **02-41-53-50-50**), is one of the grandest in Europe, rivaling Vienna's, enough so to be deemed a UNESCO World Heritage Site in 2011. The stables house some 350 horses. Mid-February to October, 1-hour tours (9€ adults, 6€ children) run from 9:30 to 11am and 2pm to 4pm from Monday afternoon to Saturday afternoon. Tours depart about every 20 minutes. Some 48km (30 miles) of specialty tracks wind around the town—to see a rider carry out a curvet is a thrill. The performances peak during the **Carrousel de Saumur ★★** on the third weekend in July.

After lengthy restoration work, the **Château de Saumur** (www.chateau-saumur.com; ✆ **02-41-83-31-31**) has reopened to the public. The 12th-century château was the royal residence of Philippe II in the early 13th century and hasn't changed much since being immortalized in the September scene of the famous illuminated manuscript "Les Très Riches Heures" in 1410. The interior or the castle has displays recounting the history of the château as well as examples of tapestries, porcelain, furniture, and other decorative arts. An evening equestrian-and-light show is held in July and August in front of the château (Thurs–Sat; admission 18€ adult, 14€ children). Admission to the château museum from June to September is 9€ adult, 5€ children 7–16, free under 7; spring and autumn 5€ adult, 3€ children (daily Apr to mid-June and mid-Sept to Oct 10am–1pm and 2pm–5:30pm; mid-June to mid-Sept 10am–6:30pm; closed Nov–Apr).

The area surrounding the town has become famous for its delicate sparkling wines. In the center of Saumur, you can wander the many aisles of **La Maison du Vin,** 7 quai Carnot (www.vinsvaldeloire.fr; ✆ **02-41-38-45-83**), and choose from a large stock direct from the many surrounding vineyards.

An alternative is to travel east of Saumur to the village of **St-Hilaire,** where you'll find a host of vineyards. One of the better ones is **Veuve Amiot,** 21 rue Jean-Ackerman (www.veuveamiot.fr; ✆ **02-41-83-14-14**), where you can tour the wine cellars, taste different vintages, and buy bottles right in the showroom.

Mushrooms enthusiasts can learn about the cultivation of the local fungi first-hand at the **Musée du Champignon** (www.musee-du-champignon.com; ✆ **02-41-50-31-55**). Don't miss the annual mushroom festival in October. Admission to the museum is 8€ adult, 6€ under 18 (daily Feb to mid-Nov 10am–7pm).

CHINON ★★

283km (175 miles) SW of Paris; 48km (30 miles) SW of Tours; 31km (19 miles) SW of Langeais

In the film "Joan of Arc," Ingrid Bergman identified the dauphin as he tried to conceal himself among his courtiers. This took place in real life at the Château de Chinon, one of the oldest fortress-châteaux in France. Charles VII centered his government at Chinon from 1429 to 1450. In 1429, with the English besieging Orléans, the Maid of Orléans prevailed upon the dauphin to give her an army. The rest is history. The seat of French power stayed at Chinon until the end of the Hundred Years' War.

Essentials

GETTING THERE The SNCF runs about seven **trains** and four **buses** every day to Chinon from Tours (trip time: 45 min. by train; 1 hr., 15 min. by bus); the one-way fare is 8.90€. For schedules and information, visit www.voyages-sncf.com or call ✆ **36-35**.

Both buses and trains arrive at the train station, which lies at the edge of the very small town. If you're **driving** from Tours, take D751 southwest through Azay-le-Rideau to Chinon.

VISITOR INFORMATION   The **Office de Tourisme** is at place Hofheim (www. chinon-valdeloire.com; ✆ **02-47-93-17-85**).

Where to Stay

Château de Marçay ★★★   This property close to Chinon began in the 1100s as a fortress and took its present form during the Renaissance. The centerpiece of the wine-producing hamlet of Marçay, it's sumptuously decorated. The main building houses more opulent lodgings; a handful of less-expensive, less-dramatic rooms are in an annex a short walk away. Menu specialties change with the season at the restaurant, and the chef works hard to maintain high standards. The garden terrace and elegantly rustic dining room afford a panoramic view.

Marçay. www.chateaudemarcay.com. ✆ **02-47-93-03-47.** Fax 02-47-93-45-33. 33 units. 105€–225€ double; 240€–290€ suite. AE, DC, MC, V. Closed mid-Jan to mid-Mar. Take D116 for 7km (4¼ miles) southwest of Chinon. **Amenities:** Restaurant; bar; outdoor pool; room service; tennis court; TV; hair dryer; minibar; free Wi-Fi.

Hostellerie Gargantua ★   This 15th-century building in Chinon was once a courthouse where the father of writer François Rabelais (see "Musée Rabelais–La Devinière," below) worked as a lawyer. Art historians admire the structure's early Renaissance staircase and chiseled-stone details. As one would expect of a building this age, the hotel has some quirks, but its large guest rooms have plenty of charm, with high ceilings and canopy beds; a few have stone fireplaces and/or views of the castle. Try to stop here for a meal, served in a medieval hall, where you can sample Loire *sandre* prepared with Chinon wine or duckling with dried pears and smoked lard, followed by a medley of seasonal red fruits in puff pastry.

73 rue Haute St. Maurice. www.hotel-gargantua.com. ✆ **02-47-93-04-71.** Fax 02-47-93-08-02. 7 units. 56€–84€ double. AE, MC, V. Closed Dec **Amenities:** Restaurant; bar; TV; free Wi-Fi.

Where to Eat

Les Années 30 ★ FRENCH   On the oldest street in Chinon, you'll find the town's most innovative restaurant. If the charming 16th-century building doesn't entice you, the excellent-value menu certainly will. In summer, savor grilled sea bass with fruit and fennel puree on the shady terrace, and in winter, feast on braised sweetbreads accompanied by potato pancakes topped with artichokes beside the cozy fireplace.

78 Rue Haute St Maurice. www.lesannees30.com. ✆ **02-47-93-37-18.** Main courses 18€–32€; fixed-price lunch menu during the week 18€, dinner menus 28€–44€. Thurs–Mon 12:15–2:00pm; Thurs-Tues 7:30–10pm.

Exploring the Town & the Château

On the banks of the Vienne, the winding streets of Chinon are lined with many medieval turreted houses, built in the heyday of the court. The most typical street is **rue Voltaire,** lined with 15th- and 16th-century townhouses. At no. 44, Richard the Lion-Hearted died on April 6, 1199, from a wound suffered during the siege of Chalus in Limousin. The Grand Carroi, in the heart of Chinon, was the crossroads of the Middle Ages. For the best view, drive across the river and turn right onto quai

IN PURSUIT OF THE grape

Chinon is famous for its wines, which crop up on prestigious lists around the world. Supermarkets and wine shops throughout the region sell them; families that have been in the business longer than anyone can remember maintain the two most interesting stores. At **Caves Plouzeau,** 94 rue Haute-St-Maurice (www.plouzeau.com; ✆ **02-47-93-32-11**), the 12th-century cellars were dug to provide building blocks for the foundations of the château. The present management dates from 1929; bottles of red or white wine cost from 6€ to 12€. You're welcome to climb down to the cellars (open for visits and wine sales Apr–Sept Tues–Sat 11am–1pm and 3–7pm and Oct–Mar Thurs–Sat 2–6pm).

The cellars at **Couly-Dutheil,** 12 rue Diderot (www.coulydutheil-chinon.com; ✆ **02-47-97-20-20**), are suitably medieval; many were carved from rock. This company produces largely Chinon wines (mostly reds); the popularity of its Bourgueil and St-Nicolas de Bourgueil has grown in North America in recent years. Tours of the caves and a *dégustation des vins* (wine tasting) require an advance call and cost 4€ to 6€ per person. Visits are conducted year-round 8am to noon and 1:45 to 5:45pm.

Danton. From this vantage point, you'll be able to see the castle in relation to the town and the river.

Chinon is known for its delightful red wines. After you visit the attractions, stop for a glass on one of Chinon's terraced cafes or visit a few local vineyards.

Château de Chinon ★★ CASTLE   The château, which was more or less in ruins, has undergone a massive excavation and restoration that started in 2003 and so far has resulted in beautifully restored ramparts, castle keep, and royal apartments, which now look more or less as they did in the good old days. After being roofless for 200 years, the apartments sport pitched and gabled slate roofs and wood floors, and the keep is once again fortified. The restoration, while not exact (due to the state of the original building), gives the overall impression of what the castle looked like around the time of Joan of Arc's visit. The buildings are separated by a series of moats, adding to its medieval look. A new building has been construction on the foundations of the Fort of St-George, which serves as an entrance hall and museum, featuring new archeological finds discovered during the restoration, as well as objects and interactive displays that recount the story of Joan of Arc, Charles VII, and the history of the castle.

Btw. rue St-Maurice and av. Francois Mitterrand. www.forteressechinon.fr. ✆ **02-47-93-13-45.** Admission 7.50€ adults, 5.50€ students, free for children 12 and under. Open daily May–Aug 9:30am–7pm; Mar, Apr and Sept 9am–6pm; Oct–Feb 9:30am–5pm.

Musée Rabelais–La Devinière ★ MUSEUM   The most famous son of Chinon, François Rabelais, the earthy humanist Renaissance writer, lived in town on rue de la Lamproie. (A plaque marks the spot where his father practiced law and maintained a home and office.) The museum in his honor, just outside the hamlet of Seuilly, 5.5km (3½ miles) west of Chinon, was an isolated cottage at the time of his birth. Spending the early years of his life here profoundly affected the writer, and the area served as inspiration for parts of his most famous work "Gargantua." The museum has three floors of exhibition space, each focusing on an aspect of Rabelais, his times, and his role in Chinon.

La Devinière, just outside of Seuilly off the N751. www.monuments-touraine.fr ✆ **02-47-95-91-18.** Admission 5€ adults, 4€ students, free for children 11 and under. Open daily Apr–June 10am–12:30pm and 2–6pm; July–Aug 10am–7pm; Sept 10am–12:30pm and 2–6pm; Oct–Mar Wed–Mon 10am–12:30pm and 2–5pm. From Chinon, follow the road signs pointing to Saumur and the D117.

USSE ★

295km (183 miles) SW of Paris; 14km (8¾ miles) NE of Chinon

The Château d'Ussé is truly a fairy-tale castle. At the edge of the dark forest of Chinon in Rigny-Ussé, it was the inspiration for Perrault's legend of "The Sleeping Beauty" ("La Belle au Bois Dormant").

Essentials

GETTING THERE   The château is best visited by car or on an organized bus tour from Tours. If you're driving from Tours or Villandry, follow D7 to Ussé.

Exploring the Château

Château d'Ussé ★ CASTLE   Conceived as a fortress in 1424, this complex of steeples, turrets, towers, and dormers was erected at the dawn of the Renaissance on a hill overlooking the Indre River. The terraces, laden with orange and lemon trees, were laid out by the royal gardener Le Nôtre. When the need for a fortified château passed, the north wing was demolished to open up a greater view. The château was later owned by the duc de Duras and then by Mme. de la Rochejacquelin; its present owner, the marquis de Blacas, has opened many rooms to the public, most recently the private dining room and the dungeon. The visit begins in the Renaissance chapel, with its sculptured portal and handsome stalls. You then proceed to the royal apartments, furnished with tapestries and antiques. One gallery displays an extensive collection of swords and rifles. A spiral stairway leads to a tower with a panoramic view of the river and a waxwork Sleeping Beauty waiting for her prince to come.

www.chateaudusse.fr. ✆ **02-47-95-54-05.** Admission 14€ adults, 4€ students and children 8–16, and free children 7 and under. Open daily mid-Feb to March 10am–6pm; April–Aug 10am–7pm; and Sept–Nov 10am–6pm; closed the rest of the year.

FONTEVRAUD-L'ABBAYE ★★

304km (188 miles) SW of Paris; 16km (10 miles) SE of Saumur

The Plantagenet dynasty is buried in the Abbaye Royale de Fontevraud. The kings, whose male line ended in 1485, were also the comtes d'Anjou, and they wanted to be buried in their native soil. This regal patronage led to the building of one of Europe's largest medieval monastery complexes.

Essentials

GETTING THERE   If you're **driving,** take D147 about 4km (2½ miles) from the village of Montsoreau. In season, you can take a **bus** (Line 1) from Saumur; schedules vary according to school holidays—visit the bus company's website, www.agglobus. fr, to download the schedule or call (✆ **02-41-51-11-87**). The one-way fare for the 30-minute trip is 1.50€.

LOIRE FOR kids

The Loire is a wonderful family holiday destination, and the highlights, of course, are the castles (**Valençay, Langeais,** and **Loches** being the best to include for children; see specific chapter listings). But the two most frequently visited attractions for families are located at the same address: the **Aquarium du Val de Loire** and the **Parc des Mini-Châteaux** (www.decouvrez-levaldeloire.com; ϕ **02-47-23-44-44**), 9.5km (6 miles) west of Amboise, near the village of village of Lussault-sur-Loire.

The **Parc des Mini-Châteaux** holds replicas of France's most famous castles, built at ⅓₀ the size of the originals. Chambord, for example, is less than 3.5m (11 ft.) tall. It's all very patriotic—a sort of learning game that teaches French schoolchildren the glories of their *patrimoine* (heritage) and collects some of the most celebrated architecture in Europe. Admission is 14€ adults, 9.50€ students and children 4 to 14, and free children 3 and under; ask about the discounted joint ticket with Aquarium (daily Apr–May 10:30am–7pm; 10am–7pm/8pm June–Aug; 10:30am–6pm Sept–Nov 14; closed mid-Nov to early Apr). The **aquarium** is home to some 10,000 freshwater and saltwater fish. Admission is 14€ adults and 9.50€ children 4 to 14 (daily Jan–Mar and Sept–Dec 10:30am–6pm; Apr–May 10:30am–7pm; June–July 10am–7pm; and late July to mid-Aug 10am–8pm; closed 2 weeks in Nov and Jan)

Where to Eat

La Licorne ★ MODERN FRENCH   For the perfect combination of medieval history and culinary sensuality, visit the Fontevraud Abbey and then dine at this 35-seat restaurant on a linden-lined walkway between the abbey and a nearby parish church. Its symmetrical proportions and neoclassical pilasters, built in the 1700s just before the French Revolution, evoke the *ancien régime* at its most graceful and opulent. In summer, guests sit in the garden or in the elegantly rustic dining room. Service can be a tad slow, but the excellent-value menu is well worth the wait. It includes refined dishes such as filet of local Féra freshly caught from lake Léman; royal Maine d'Anjou pigeon topped with Chinon truffles; scampi ravioli with wild morel mushroom sauce; and such luscious desserts as local Alienor pastries.

Allée Ste-Catherine. www.restaurant-gastronomique-licorne.fr. ϕ **02-41-51-72-49.** Main courses 15€–30€; fixed-price menu 29€–65€. Nov–Apr Tues–Sun noon–2pm; Tues and Thurs–Sat 7–9pm; May–Oct daily noon–2pm and 7–9pm. Closed 1 week in Dec.

Exploring the Abbey

Fontevraud-l'Abbaye ★★ ABBEY   In this 12th-century Romanesque church—with four Byzantine domes—lie the remains of two English kings or princes, including Henry II of England, the first Plantagenet king, and his wife, Eleanor of Aquitaine, the most famous woman of the Middle Ages. Her crusading son, Richard the Lion-Hearted, is also entombed here. The Plantagenet line ended with the death of Richard III at the 1485 Battle of Bosworth. The tombs fared badly during the Revolution, when mobs desecrated the sarcophagi and scattered their contents on the floor.

More intriguing than the tombs is the octagonal **Tour d'Evraud,** the last remaining Romanesque kitchen in France. Dating from the 12th century, it contains five of its original eight *apsides* (half-rounded indentations originally conceived as chapels), each crowned with a conically roofed turret. A pyramid tops the conglomeration, capped by an open-air lantern tower pierced with lancets. Robert d'Arbrissel, who spent much of his life as a recluse, founded the abbey in 1101. Aristocratic ladies occupied one part; many, including discarded mistresses of kings, had been banished from court. The four youngest daughters of Louis XV were educated here. Since 1975, the abbey has also functioned as a cultural center, offering expositions, concerts, and seminars.

www.abbaye-fontevraud.com. © **02-41-51-73-52.** Admission 9€ adults, 6€ students, free 8 and under. Open daily April–June and Sept–Oct 9:30am-6pm; daily July–Aug 9:30am–7pm; daily Nov–Dec 10am–5:30pm; and Feb–Mar Tues–Sun 10am–5:30pm; closed Jan.

PROVENCE

by Kathryn Tomasetti

The ancient Greeks left their vines, the Romans their monuments, but it was the 19th-century Impressionists who most shaped the romance of Provence today. Cezanne, Gauguin, Chagall, and countless others were drawn to the unique light and vibrant spectrum brought forth by what van Gogh called "the transparency of the air." Modern-day visitors will delight in the region's culture, colors and world-class museums. And they will certainly dine well too.

Provence, perhaps more than any other part of France, blends past and present with an impassioned pride. It has its own language and customs, and some of its festivals go back to medieval times. The region is bounded on the north by the Dauphine River, on the west by the Rhône, on the east by the Alps, and on the south by the Mediterranean. In chapter 8, we focus on the part of Provence known as the Côte d'Azur, or the French Riviera.

AVIGNON ★★★

691km (428 miles) S of Paris; 83km (51 miles) NW of Aix-en-Provence; 98km (61 miles) NW of Marseille

In the 14th century, Avignon was the capital of Christendom. What started as a temporary stay by Pope Clement V in 1309, when Rome was deemed too dangerous even for clergymen, became a 67-year golden age. The cultural and architectural legacy left by the six popes who served during this period makes Avignon one of Europe's most alluring medieval destinations.

Today this walled city of some 95,000 residents is a major stop on the route from Paris to the Mediterranean. In recent years, it has become known as a cultural center, thanks to its annual international performing-arts festivals and wealth of experimental theaters and art galleries.

Essentials

ARRIVING   Frequent TGV **trains** depart from Paris's Gare de Lyon. The ride takes 2 hours and 40 minutes and arrives at Avignon's modern TGV station 10 minutes from town by shuttle bus. The one-way fare is around 80€ depending on the date and time, although it can also be as cheap as 25€ if booked well in advance. Regular trains arrive from Marseille (trip time: 70 min.; 20€ one-way) and Arles (trip time: 20 min.; 7.30€ one-way), arriving at either the TGV or Avignon's central station. Hourly trains from Aix-en-Provence (trip time: 20 min.; 25€ one-way) shuttle exclusively between the two towns' TGV stations. For rail information, visit www.voyages-sncf. com or call ℂ **36-35**. The regional **bus** routes (www.info-ler.fr; ℂ **08-21-20-22-03**) go from Avignon to Arles (trip time: 1 hr., 10 min.; 7.10€ one-way) and Aix-en Provence (trip time: 1 hr., 15 min.; 17€ one-way). The bus station at Avignon is the **Gare Routière,** 5 av. Monclar (ℂ **04-90-82-07-35**). If you're **driving** from Paris, take A6 south to Lyon, and then A7 south to Avignon.

VISITOR INFORMATION The **Office de Tourisme** is at 41 cours Jean-Jaurès (www.avignon-tourisme.com; ℂ **04-32-74-32-74**).

CITY LAYOUT Avignon's picturesque Old Town is surrounded by 14th-century ramparts. Within the walls is a mix of winding roads, medieval townhouses, and pedestrianized streets. To the west of the city is the Rhône River, and beyond, Villeneuve les Avignon. Just south of the Old Town sits the Gare d'Avignon Centre train station.

SPECIAL EVENTS The international **Festival d'Avignon** (www.festival-avignon. com; ℂ **04-90-14-14-14**), held for 3 weeks in July, focuses on avant-garde theater, dance, and music. Tickets are 17€ to 40€. Prices for rooms skyrocket during this period, so book yours well in advance. An edgier alternative festival, the **Avignon OFF** (www.avignonleoff.com; ℂ **04-90-85-13-08**), takes place almost simultaneously in July, with theater performances in various improbable venues.

Getting Around

ON FOOT All of Avignon's major sights—as well as its infinitely enchanting back streets—are easily accessible on foot. The helpful tourist office's free maps are marked with four easy walking routes, ideal for getting a feel for the city.

BY BICYCLE & MOTOR SCOOTER The **Vélopop** bicycle-sharing scheme (www.velopop.fr, from 1€ per day) lets registered riders borrow any of the city's 200 bikes for up to 30 minutes at a time for free. To get out of town and explore the surrounding countryside, **Provence Bike,** 7 av. St-Ruf (www.provence-bike.com; ℂ **04-90-27-92-61**), rents different models for around 12€ to 40€ per day. It's possible to reserve a bike online.

BY CAR Traffic and a labyrinthine one-way system means it's best to park once you've arrived in Avignon's town center. Seven fee-paying parking lots and two free ones are dotted around the city. See the Avignon tourist office website for details.

BY TAXI Taxis Avignon (www.taxis-avignon.fr; ℂ **04-90-82-20-20**).

BY PUBLIC TRANSPORT Eco-friendly **Baladine** vehicles (www.tcra.fr; Mon–Sat 10am–1pm and 2–6pm; during July and Aug Mon–Sat 10am–8pm) zip around within the city walls for 0.50€ per ride.

[FastFACTS] AVIGNON

ATMs/Banks Avignon's town center is home to banks aplenty, including three along cours Jean-Jaurès.

Doctors & Hospitals Hôpital Général Henri Duffaut, 305 rue Raoul Follereau (www.ch-avignon.fr; ℂ **04-32-75-33-33**).

Internet Access Chez M@W, 41 rue de Vieux Sextier (ℂ **04-90-86-19-03**).

Mail & Postage La Poste, 4 cours Président Kennedy (ℂ **36-31**).

Pharmacies Pharmacie des Halles, 48 rue Bonneterie (ℂ **04-90-82-54-27**).

Where to Stay

For travelers on a budget, the friendly **Hôtel Le Colbert** (www.avignon-hotel-colbert. com) is an excellent town center option.

La Banasterie ★   This oh-so-pretty B&B is situated in a 16th-century property just opposite the Palais des Papes. It's owned by gregarious chocolate lovers Françoise and Jean-Michel—and their candy-fueled passion permeates throughout. The traditionally decorated bedrooms (exposed stone walls, sumptuous fabrics) are named for varieties of chocolate, and decadent cups of cocoa are offered at bedtime. The indulgent breakfast alone (included in the rate) makes this spot unmissable. Note that there is no elevator.

11 rue de la Banasterie. www.labanasterie.com. ℂ **06-87-72-96-36.** 5 units. 100€–145€ double; 145€–190€ suite. Parking 10€. **Amenities:** Breakfast room; free Wi-Fi.

Le Prieuré ★   Those who perceive Provence as breakfast under an arbor, a set of tennis on a leaf-strewn court, a lazy lunch, then a doze by the pool—all topped of by chilled rosé at sunset—have found the right place. What could be calmer than staying in a former 14th-century convent ringed by lavender-scented gardens in the historic suburb of Villeneuve? Individually styled rooms and suites are casually arranged over three ancient buildings. Original floors, hardwood furniture, and locally purchased antiques blend with marble bathrooms, fine linens, and modernist Louis XIV chairs. Lunch (set menu 42€) and dinner (set menus 72€–115€) in the herb-filled gardens are prepared by young head chef Fabien Fage from Arles. Luxurious locally sourced cuisine includes strawberries from Beaucaire, pigeon from Nimes, and rockfish from the Mediterranean near Marseille.

7 Place du Chapitre. www.leprieure.com. ℂ **04-90-15-90-15.** 37 units. 200€–450€ double; from 350€ suite. Free parking. **Amenities:** Restaurant; bar; concierge; outdoor pool; room service; tennis; free Wi-Fi. Closed Nov–Mar.

ALTERNATIVE ACCOMMODATIONS

Thames Résidences ★★   This handful of superbly equipped apartments lies a short stroll from both the train station and Avignon's city center. Decor is Provençal-themed, and each residence possesses either its own private balcony or panoramic views over the town's medieval ramparts. In addition to kitchenettes and Nespresso Pixie espresso machines, there's also free satellite television, speedy Wi-Fi, and unlimited free telephone calls abroad. Note that apartments may also be rented (at a discount) by the week.

36 bd. Saint Roch. www.thames-residences.com. ℂ **04-32-70-17-01.** 9 units. 114€–296€ 2-person apartments. Free parking. **Amenities:** Free Wi-Fi.

Where to Eat

La Fourchette ★★ PROVENÇAL   Set a block back from the bustling place de l'Horloge, this upscale bistro has been a local favorite since it opened its doors in 1982. Philippe Hiély, the restaurant's sixth-generation chef, dishes up a cuisine that's sophisticated yet hearty: Think saffron-infused salt cod *brandade* served with crusty bread, or seared scallops atop fennel puree. Walls are adorned with an eclectic collection of antique cutlery (*la fourchette* translates as "the fork"), making the ambience as alluring as the food.

17 rue Racine. www.la-fourchette.net. ℂ **04-90-85-20-93.** Reservations recommended. Main courses 20€; fixed-price menu 33€. Mon–Fri 12:15–1:45pm and 7:15–9:45pm. Closed 3 weeks in Aug.

Map legend:

0 — 200 y / 0 — 200 m

Information ⓘ

Rhône

ÎLE DE LA BARTHELASSE

ÎLE PIOT

pont St-Bénézet

Porte du Rocher

bd. du Quai de la Ligne

Porte de la Ligne

bd. du Quai St-Lazare

Porte St-Joseph

r. St-Joseph

pont Daladier

Musée du Petit-Palais

Rocher des Doms

Notre-Dame des Doms

r. des Infirmières

Carreterie

Porte de l'Oulle

r. St-Etienne

pl. du Palais

Palais des Papes

bd. Banasterie

r. Ste-Catherine

rue Portail Matheron

r. Louis Pasteur

rue Limas

bd. du Rhône

r. Racine

r. Petite Fusterie

pl. de l'Horloge

rue de la Croix

rue Carnot

r. Paul Sain

Hôtel de Ville

pl. Carnot

place Pie

pl. Pignotte

rue Thiers

r. Joseph Vernet

r. Félix Gras

r. Bouquerie

r. Victor Hugo

rue d'Annanelle

rue de la République

pl. de la Principale

rue Bonneterie

r. de Roi René

r. Philonarde

Porte St-Dominique

bd. de l'Oulle

Musée Calvet

Musée Angladon

r. des Études

Lices

Collection Lambert

r. Joseph Vernet

r. H. Fabre

ⓘ

rue des

Paris ✪

FRANCE

Avignon •

bd. Saint-Dominique

r. Veloutene

bd. Raspail

r. St-Charles

cours J. Jaures

r. du Rempart St-Roch

cours Prés. Kennedy

rue St-Michel

r. du Rempart St-Michel

Porte St-Roch

Porte St-Charles

av. du 7e Génie

bd. St-Michel

Porte St-Michel

Gare d'Avignon–Centre

5 — Porte de la République

HOTELS ■
La Banasterie **4**
Le Prieuré **1**
Thames Résidences **5**
RESTAURANTS ◆
La Fourchette **2**
Restaurant Christian Etienne **3**

Restaurant Christian Etienne ★★★ PROVENÇAL   This Michelin-starred temple of gastronomy is perched atop a 12th-century stone edifice—complete with 15th-century frescoes—just next door to the Palais des Papes. Avignon-born Chef Etienne is wildly innovative, and many of his dishes have a more than a hint of molecular influence. Fixed-price menus are themed around single ingredients such as duck, lobster, truffles, or (summertime only) heavenly heirloom tomatoes.

10 rue de Mons. www.christian-etienne.fr. Ⓒ **04-90-86-16-50.** Reservations required. Main courses 30€–50€; fixed-price lunch 35€, dinner 75€–120€. Tues–Sat noon–1:15pm and 7:30–9:15pm. Closed 2wks Nov.

Exploring Avignon

Avignon is undoubtedly one of the prettiest towns in France. From its impressively imposing skyline to the verdant Île de la Barthelasse opposite, it's a delight to simply amble along aimlessly, perhaps stopping at a sidewalk café or two en route. Countless hidden gems crop up along the way, including the sun-dappled courtyard of the **Hôtel d'Europe** (www.heurope.com). This luxury hotel has been in operation since 1799, welcoming luminaries from Charles Dickens to Jacqueline Kennedy.

Poking westward from the grassy banks of the Rhône River, **Pont St-Bénézet** ★★ (www.palais-des-papes.com; ✆ **04-32-74-32-74**) was constructed between 1177 and 1185. Once spanning the Rhône and connecting Avignon with Villeneuve-lèz-Avignon, it is now a ruin, with only 4 of its original 22 arches remaining (half of it fell into the river back in 1669). The remains of the bridge have the same opening hours as those of the Palais des Papes (see below). Admission is 4.50€ adults, 3.50€ seniors and students, and free children 7 and under.

Collection Lambert ★★ MUSEUM This contemporary art space is housed within an 18th-century private home that once belonged to collector and gallery owner Yvon Lambert. It stages three groundbreaking exhibitions each year. Works may range from video and photography to conceptual installations. Major artists such as Anselm Kiefer, Jenny Holzer, and Cy Twombly have all featured.

5 rue Violette. www.collectionlambert.fr. ✆ **04-90-16-56-20.** Admission changes according to exhibition, free for children 5 and under. Tues–Sun July–Aug 11–7pm; Sept–June 11–6pm.

Musée Angladon ★★ MUSEUM Haute-couture designer Jacques Doucet (1853–1929) didn't limit himself to the appreciation of finely cut fabrics. His former home is now a showcase for the international artworks that he and his wife collected over their lifetimes—from 16th-century Buddhas and Louis XVI chairs to Degas's famous dancers and canvases by Cézanne, Sisley, and Modigliani.

5 rue Laboureur. www.angladon.com. ✆ **04-90-82-29-03.** Admission 6€ adults, 4€ students and children 13–17, 1.50€ children 7–12, free for children 6 and under. Tues–Sun 1–6pm. Closed Tues in winter.

Musée du Petit-Palais ★ MUSEUM An ideal complement to the Palais des Papes' architectural austerity, this museum's artworks were originally part of a collection belonging to 19th-century art lover Giampietro Campana. Today the museum exhibits a myriad of paintings from the Italian and Provençal schools of the 13th to 16th centuries. Botticelli's "Madonna with Child" is a particular highlight.

Palais des Archevêques, place du Palais des Papes. www.petit-palais.org. ✆ **04-90-86-44-58.** Admission 6€ adults, 3€ students, free for children 11 and under. Wed–Mon 10am–1pm and 2–6pm.

Palais des Papes ★★★ PALACE Dominating Avignon from a hilltop is one of the most famous, or notorious, palaces in the Christian world. Headquarters of a schismatic group of cardinals who came close to destroying the authority of the popes in Rome, this fortress is the city's most popular monument. Because of its massive size, you may be tempted to opt for a guided tour—but these can be monotonous. The detailed audioguide, included in the price of admission, will likely suffice.

A highlight is the **Chapelle St-Jean,** known for its frescoes of John the Baptist and John the Evangelist, attributed to the school of Matteo Giovanetti and painted between 1345 and 1348. The **Grand Tinel (Banquet Hall)** is about 41m (134 ft.) long and 9m (30 ft.) wide; the pope's table stood on the south side. The walls of the **Pope's Bedroom,** on the first floor of the Tour des Anges, are painted with foliage, birds, and squirrels. The **Studium (Stag Room)**—the study of Clement VI—was frescoed in 1343 with hunting scenes. The **Grande Audience (Great Receiving Hall)** contains frescoes of the prophets, also attributed to Giovanetti and painted in 1352.

Note that the 12th-century **Cathédrale Notre-Dame des Doms cathedral,** just next door on the main square, contains the elaborate tombs of popes Jean XXII and Benoît XII.

Place du Palais des Papes. www.palais-des-papes.com. ℰ **04-32-74-32-74.** Admission (including audioguide) 11€ adults, 8.50€ seniors and students, free for children 7 and under. Daily Nov-Feb 9:30am-5:45pm; Mar 9am-6:30pm; Apr-June and Sept-Nov 9am-7pm; July 9am-8pm; Aug 9am-8:30pm

Shopping

The chain boutique **Souleiado,** 19 rue Joseph-Vernet (ℰ **04-90-86-32-05**), sells reproductions of 18th- and 19th-century Provençal fabrics by the meter or made into clothing and linens. There is also a large selection of housewares and gifts.

Hervé Baume, 19 rue Petite Fusterie (ℰ **04-90-86-37-66**), is the place to buy a Provençal table—or something to put on it. A massive inventory includes French folk art and hand-blown hurricane lamps.

A covered market with 40 different merchants is **Les Halles,** place Pie, open Tuesday through Sunday (6am–1:30pm). The **flower market** is on place des Carmes on Saturday (8am–1pm), and the **flea market** occupies the same place each Sunday morning (6am–1pm).

Nightlife

Le Grand Café, 4 rue des Escaliers-Sainte-Anne (www.legrandcafe-avignon.fr; ℰ **04-90-86-86-77**), is a restaurant-bar-café and one of the town's most popular watering holes. Behind the Palais des Papes, it's in an entertainment complex in a former military supply warehouse. Avignon's beautiful people frequent **Les Ambassadeurs,** 27 rue Bancasse (www.clublesambassadeurs.fr; ℰ **04-90-86-31-55**), an upscale dance club.

Behind the Hôtel d'Europe, disco-bar **L'Esclave,** 12 rue du Limas (www.esclavebar.com; ℰ **04-90-85-14-91**), is a focal point of the city's gay scene.

DAY TRIP FROM AVIGNON

Orange ★

31km (19 miles) N of Avignon

Antiquities-rich Orange was not named for citrus fruit, but as a dependency of the Dutch House of Orange-Nassau during the Middle Ages. It is home to two UNESCO World Heritage sites: Europe's third-largest **triumphal arch** and its best-preserved **Roman theater.** Louis XIV, who once considered moving the theater to Versailles, claimed: "It is the finest wall in my kingdom." The Théâtre Antique is now the site of **Les Chorégies d'Orange** (www.choregies.fr), a summertime opera and classical music festival.

Just 10km (6 miles) south along the D68 is **Châteauneuf-du-Pape,** a prestigious appellation known for its bold red wines. Spend an afternoon visiting the village's numerous tasting rooms, winding your way up to the ruins of a castle that served as a summer residence for Pope John XXII.

ESSENTIALS

Frequent **trains** (trip time: 20 min.; 6€ one-way) and **buses** (www.sudest-mobilites.fr; ℰ **04-32-76-00-40;** trip time: 1 hr.; 2€ one-way) connect Avignon and Orange. If you're **driving** from Avignon, take A7 north to Orange. The **Office de Tourisme** is at 5 cours Aristide-Briand (www.otorange.fr; ℰ **04-90-34-70-88**).

EXPLORING ORANGE & AROUND

The carefully restored **Théâtre Antique ★★★**, rue Madeleine Roch (www.theatre
-antique.com; ℂ **04-90-51-17-60**), dates from the days of Augustus. Built into the side
of a hill, it once held 9,000 spectators in tiered seats. Nearly 105m-long (344 ft.) land
37m high (121 ft.), it's open daily November to February 9:30am to 4:30pm; March
and October 9:30am to 5:30pm; April, May, and September 9am to 6pm; and June to
August 9am to 7pm. Admission (which includes a free audioguide) is 9€ adults, 7€
students and children 8 to 17, and free children 7 and under.

The imposing **Arc de Triomphe ★**, avenue de l'Arc-de-Triomphe, comprises a trio
of arches held up by Corinthian columns embellished with military and maritime
emblems. Also built during the reign of Augustus, it was once part of the original
town's fortified walls.

WHERE TO EAT

At **Au Petit Patio,** 58 cours Aristide Briand (ℂ **04-90-29-69-27**), contemporary Provençal cuisine is served on a petite outdoor terrace. Sample honey-glazed sea bass or
summery strawberry tartare.

GORDES ★★★

720km (446 miles) S of Paris; 38km (24 miles) E of Avignon; 77km (48 miles) N of Aix-en-Provence;
92km (57 miles) N of Marseille

Hilltop Gordes is a supremely chic rocky outcrop deep in Provence. From afar, this
gorgeous *village perché* (perched village) is a pastiche of beiges, grays, and terra cotta
that blushes golden at sunrise and sunset.

Essentials

ARRIVING   Gordes is difficult to reach via public transportation. The closest train
station is Cavaillon, where trains arrive from Avignon's central station (trip time:
35 min.; 6.80€ one-way). From here, bus nr. 15.3 departs three times daily for place du
Château in Gordes (www.sudest-mobilites.fr; trip time: 35 min.; 2€ one-way). Another
option is to take a 1-day coach tour from either Avignon or Aix-en-Provence. **Autocars
Lieutaud** (www.excursionprovence.com; ℂ **04-90-86-36-75;** from 55€ per person)
offers this service in Avignon, as does the Aix-en-Provence tourist office (www.aixen-
provencetourism.com; ℂ **04-42-16-11-61;** from 115€ per person). By car, Gordes is a
38km (24-mile) drive east of Avignon via D900.

VISITOR INFORMATION   The **Office de Tourisme** is at Le Château (www.
gordes-village.com; ℂ **04-90-72-02-75**).

[FastFACTS] GORDES

Mail & Postage   **La Poste,** place du Jeu de Boules (ℂ **36-31**). Note that the post
office also offers an ATM.

Pharmacies   **Pharmacie de Gordes,** 2 rue de l'Eglise (ℂ **04-90-72-02-10**).

Where to Stay

La Ferme de la Huppe ★★   This combination bed-and-breakfast, and its superb
Provençal restaurant (also open to nonguests), spills over a pristinely renovated

18th-century farmhouse. Country-style guest rooms are named after their former functions, such as Hay Loft or Wine Cellar, and all boast cute modern bathrooms. An abundant buffet breakfast (croissants, fresh juices, local cheeses) is served on the poolside terrace. La Ferme's location, just down the road from Gordes itself, makes it perfectly positioned for exploring the wider Luberon region, including the pretty villages of Bonnieux and Roussillon.

R.D. 156, Les Pourquiers. www.lafermedelahuppe.com. ⓒ **04-90-72-12-25.** 10 units. 110€–185€ double. Breakfast (mandatory) 16€ per person. Half-board available. Free parking. **Amenities:** Restaurant, outdoor pool; free Wi-Fi. Closed Nov to mid Mar.

Where to Eat

L'Artegal PROVENÇAL   A standout venue among Gordes' handful of eateries, this family-run restaurant prides itself on its creative local cuisine. Well-conceived dishes include lentil and salmon tartare, rich lamb *navarin* stew, and the restaurnt's own generous adaptation of duck-heavy *salade Landaise*. Tucked into the shadow of the Château de Gordes, L'Artegal is a romantic spot to dine, particularly in the evening when the town's daytrippers have disappeared.

Place du Château. ⓒ **04-90-72-02-54.** Main courses 16€–26€; fixed-price lunch 24€; fixed-price dinner 36€. Thurs–Tues noon–1:45pm; Thurs–Mon 7:15–8:45pm. Closed mid-Jan to mid-Mar.

Exploring Gordes

Gordes is best explored on foot. Its primarily pedestrianized streets unwind downhill from the Château de Gordes, the Renaissance rehabilitation of a 12th-century fortress. Its windows still bear grooves from bows and arrows used to protect Gordes during Gallo-Roman times, when it was a border town. Today Gordes is more likely to be invaded by easels. Its austere beauty has drawn many artists, including Marc Chagall and Hungarian painter Victor Vasarely, who spent summers here gathering inspiration for his geometric abstract art.

Caves du Palais St. Firmin ★ RUINS   Steep Gordes lacks an abundance of surface area, so early settlers burrowed into the rock itself, creating an underground network of crude rooms and stairways over seven levels. Over the centuries, these rooms have housed the village's production of olive oil and grain. Though the tunnels are adequately lit, children are provided with a small headlamp to let them feel like true explorers.

Rue du Belvédère. www.caves-saint-firmin.com. ⓒ **04-90-72-02-75.** Admission 6€ adults, 4.50€ students. Free audioguide. May–Sept Wed-Mon 10am–6pm. Oct–Apr by reservation only.

Château de Gordes ★ HISTORIC HOME/ART MUSEUM   Access to the ancient château is reserved for visitors of its small museum, dedicated to contemporary Flemish painter Pol Mara (1920–98), a former resident of Gordes. More than 200 of the artist's works are on display, along with temporary shows, such as 2013's popular "Planete Ocean" photo exhibition.

Place Genty Pantaly. ⓒ **04-90-72-98-64.** Admission 4€ adults, 3€ children 10–17, free for children 9 and under. Daily 10am–1pm and 2–6:30pm.

Outlying Attractions

Gordes is part of the **Parc Naturel Régional du Luberon,** made up of three mountain ranges and their common valley. Author Peter Mayle brought attention to the area with his "A Year in Provence" series extolling the virtues of picturesque villages such as

THE LAST HOME OF albert camus

Author of "The Stranger," among many other works, Algerian-born Albert Camus (1913–60) moved to France at the age of 25. A member of the French Resistance, political journalist, and philosopher, he was awarded the Nobel Prize for Literature in 1958 "for his important literary production, which with clear-sighted earnestness illuminates the problems of the human conscience in our times."

That same year, drawn by its "solemn and austere landscape despite its bewildering beauty," Camus and his wife moved to Lourmarin, 30km (18 miles) southeast of Gordes along D36. Just 2 years later, Camus was killed in a car accident near Paris. According to his wishes, he was buried in Lourmarin's cemetery.

In 1999, French president Nicolas Sarkozy—with whom Camus would have had little in common philosophically or politically—proposed moving the writer's ashes to the Pantheon in Paris, to rest aside such literary giants as Alexander Dumas, Victor Hugo, and Emile Zola. His descendants politely declined.

Bonnieux, Lourmarin, and Menerbes, where Mayle restored his first French home. Most of these are within 12km (7½ miles) of each other, making the Luberon well worth an afternoon's exploration.

For avid cyclists, **Vélo Loisir en Luberon** (www.veloloisirluberon.com) has marked hundreds of kilometers of bike routes throughout the region's vineyards and lavender fields. See the website for maps and bicycle rental agencies, as well as suggestions of bucolic dining spots en route.

Abbaye Nôtre Dame de Sénanque ★★★ MONASTERY One of the prettiest sights in the Luberon—indeed, in all of Provence—is the Abbaye Nôtre Dame de Sénanque, even more so when the lavender is in bloom. Five kilometers (3 miles) down the road from Gordes, it was built by Cistercian monks in 1148. Just a handful of monks continue to live on the premises today. The structure is noted for its simple architecture and unadorned stone—though standing in a sea of lavender purple, from June to late July, it's dramatic indeed. The abbey is open daily to visitors. A gift shop sells items made by the resident monks, as well as lavender honey.

D177. www.senanque.fr. ✆ **04-90-72-17-92.** Admission 7€ adults, 5€ students and ages 19–25, 3€ children 6–18, 20€ families, free children 5 and under. Hours vary; call or see website.

Village des Bories ★ RUINS Bories are beehive-shaped dwellings made of intricately stacked stone—and not an ounce of mortar. They date back as far as the Bronze Age and as recently as the 18th century in Provence. An architectural curiosity, their thick walls and cantilevered roofs beg the question: How did they do that? The Village des Bories is the largest group of these structures in the region, comprising 30 huts grouped according to function (houses, stables, bakeries, silkworm farms, and more). Traditional tools are on display, along with an exhibit on the history of dry-stone architecture in France and around the world.

1.5km (1 mile) west of Gordes on the D15. ✆ **04-90-72-03-48.** Admission 6€ adults, 4€ children 12–17, free children 11 and under. Daily 9am to sundown.

ST-RÉMY-DE-PROVENCE ★

710km (440 miles) S of Paris; 24km (15 miles) NE of Arles; 19km (12 miles) S of Avignon; 10km (6¼ miles) N of Les Baux

Though the physician and astrologer Nostradamus was born here in 1503, most associate St-Rémy with Vincent van Gogh, who committed himself to a local asylum in 1889 after cutting off his left ear. "Starry Night" was painted during this period, as were many versions of "Olive Trees" and "Cypresses."

Come to sleepy St-Rémy not only for its history and sights, but also for an authentic experience of daily Provençal life. The town springs into action on Wednesday mornings, when stalls bursting with the region's bounty, from wild-boar sausages to olives, elegant antiques to bolts of French country fabric, huddle between the sidewalk cafes beneath the plane trees.

Essentials

ARRIVING   A regional bus, the Cartreize, runs four to nine times daily between Avignon's Gare Routière and St-Rémy's place de la République (trip time: 45 min.; 3.30€ one-way). For bus information, see www.lepilote.com or call ✆ **08-10-00-13-26.** The St-Rémy Tourist Office also provides links to up-to-date bus schedules on their website (see below). Drivers can head south from Avignon along D571.

VISITOR INFORMATION   The **Office de Tourisme** is on place Jean-Jaurès (www.saintremy-de-provence.com; ✆ **04-90-92-05-22**).

[FastFACTS] ST-RÉMY-DE-PROVENCE

ATMs/Banks   Société Marseillaise de Crédit, 10 bd. Mirabeau (✆ 04-90-92-74-00).

Mail & Postage   La Poste, 5 rue Roger Salengro (✆ 36-31).

Pharmacies   Pharmacie Cendres, 4 bd. Mirabeau (✆ 04-90-92-08-05).

Where to Stay

Château des Alpilles ★★★   A former castle situated at the heart of magnolia-studded parkland, Château des Alpilles was constructed by the Pichot family in 1827. Françoise Bon converted the mansion in 1980, creating luxurious double rooms inside the castle itself, with additional private accommodation in the property's former chapel, farm, and washhouse. Decor throughout encompasses a confident mix of antiques (plush upholstery, local artworks) and cool amenities (deep travertine-trimmed bathtubs, iPod docks). It's 2km (1¼ miles) from the center of St-Rémy.

Route de Rougadou. www.chateaudesalpilles.com. ✆ **04-90-92-03-33.** 21 units. 200€–330€ double; 300€–430€ suite; 270€–395€ apartment. Free parking. Closed Jan to mid-Mar. **Amenities:** Restaurant; bar; outdoor pool; room service; sauna; 2 tennis courts; free Wi-Fi.

L'Amandière ★   Tucked into the Provençal countryside around 1.5km (1 mile) north of town, this budget bolthole is justly favored by visitors who would rather splurge on the region's gourmet restaurants. L'Amandière's accommodation may be simple, but bedding down here is certainly no hardship. Rooms are spacious, all boast their own balcony or private patio, and there's a large outdoor pool. Breakfast is served under citrus trees in the lavender-trimmed gardens.

Av. Théodore Aubanel. www.hotel-amandiere.com. © **04-90-92-41-00.** 26 units. 72€–95€ double; 95€ triple. Free parking. **Amenities:** Outdoor pool; free Wi-Fi in common areas.

Where to Eat

La Maison Jaune ★ FRENCH/PROVENÇAL Within an 18th-century village home in St-Rémy's Old Town, handsome tables spill over two chic dining rooms, as well as a terrace overlooking the neighboring Hôtel de Sade's lush gardens. It's here that creative chef François Perraud concocts his Michelin-starred cuisine, relying almost exclusively on local ingredients. Mediterranean anchovies may be doused in a parsley pesto, Provençal lamb seared with smoky eggplant, or the darkest chocolate cake paired with frozen lemon parfait.

15 rue Carnot. www.lamaisonjaune.info. © **04-90-92-56-14.** Reservations required. Main courses 36€–38€; fixed-price lunch 32€; fixed-price dinner 42€–72€. Tues–Sat noon–1:30pm; daily 7:30–9pm. Closed Nov to mid Mar.

L'Estagnol ★★ MEDITERRANEAN This popular eatery (which translates as "little pond" in the regional dialect) is owned and operated by the Meynadier family, third-generation restaurateurs. Hearty local cuisine ranges from Camargue bull hamburger topped with goat cheese and eggplant to Provençal gazpacho with basil sorbet. Dining takes place either in the ancient *orangerie* (private greenhouse) or in the sun-dappled courtyard adjacent.

16 bd. Victor Hugo. www.restaurant-lestagnol.com. © **04-90-92-05-95.** Reservations recommended. Main courses 13€–35€; fixed-price lunch 14€, dinner 27€–34€. May–Sept Tues–Sun noon–2:30pm and 7:15–10pm; Oct–Apr Tues–Sun noon–2:30pm, Tues–Sat 7:15–10pm.

Shopping

St-Rémy is a decorator's paradise, with many antiques shops and fabric stores on the narrow streets of the Old Town and surrounding boulevards. **Broc de Saint Ouen,** route d'Avignon (© **04-90-92-28-90**), is a 6,000-sq.-m (64,583-sq.-ft.) space selling everything from architectural salvage to vintage furniture. The town's famous Provençal market is held Wednesday mornings.

Exploring St-Rémy

St-Rémy's pale stone Old Town is utterly charming. Scattered among its pedestrianized streets are 18th-century private mansions, art galleries, medieval church towers, bubbling fountains, and Nostradamus's birth home. Note that St-Rémy's two major sites (below) lie around 1km (0.6 miles) south of the town center.

Le Site Archéologique de Glanum ★★ RUINS Kids will love a scramble around this bucolically sited Gallo-Roman settlement, which thrived here during the final days of the Roman Empire. Its monuments include a triumphal arch from the time of Julius Caesar, all garlanded with sculptured fruits and flowers. Another interesting feature is the baths, which had separate chambers for hot, warm, and cold. Visitors can see entire streets and foundations of private residences from the 1st-century town, plus the remains of a Gallo-Greek town of the 2nd century B.C.

Route des Baux-de-Provence. http://glanum.monuments-nationaux.fr. © **04-90-92-23-79.** Admission 7.50€ adults, 4.50€ students, free for European nationals 18-25 and children 17 and under. Apr–Aug daily 9:30am–6:30pm; Sept Tues–Sun 9:30am–6:30pm; Oct–Mar Tues–Sun 10am–5pm.

Saint Paul de Mausole ★ MONASTERY   This former monastery and clinic is where Vincent Van Gogh was confined from 1889 to 1890. It's now a psychiatric hospital for women, which specializes in art therapy. You can't see the artist's actual cell, but there is a reconstruction of his room. The Romanesque chapel and cloisters are worth a visit in their own right, as Van Gogh depicted their circular arches and beautifully carved capitals in some of his paintings. A waymarked path between the town center and the site (east of ave. Vincent Van Gogh) is dotted with 21 reproductions of Van Gogh's paintings from the period he resided here.

Chemin Saint-Paul. www.saintpauldemausole.fr. © **04-90-92-77-00.** Admission 4.50€ adults, 3.20€ students, free for children 12 and under. Apr–Sep daily 9:30am–6:45pm; Mar, Oct–Dec daily 10:30am–4:45pm. Closed Jan–Mar.

Nightlife

Located in a former Art Deco movie theater, **Le Cocktail Bar,** Hôtel Image, 36 bd. Victor Hugo (© **04-90-92-51-50**), is an unusual destination in this laid-back town. In summertime, it is open Tuesday to Saturday until 1am.

LES BAUX ★★★

720km (446 miles) S of Paris; 18km (11 miles) NE of Arles; 85km (53 miles) N of Marseille

Les Baux de Provence's location and geology are extraordinary. Cardinal Richelieu called the massive, 245m-high (804-ft.) rock rising from a desolate plain "a nesting place for eagles." A real eagle's-eye view of the outcropping would be part moonscape, dotted with archeological ruins and a vast plateau, and part civilization, with boxy stone houses stacked like cards on the rock's east side. The combination is so cinematic that it seems like a living, breathing movie set.

Baux, or *baou* in Provençal, means "rocky spur." The power-thirsty lords who ruled the settlement took this as their surname in the 11th century, and by the Middle Ages had control of 79 other regional fiefdoms. After they were overthrown, Les Baux was annexed to France with the rest of Provence, but Louis XI ordered the fortress demolished. The settlement experienced a rebirth during the Renaissance, when structures where restored and lavish residences built, only to fall again in 1642 when, wary of rebellion, Louis XIII ordered his armies to destroy it once and for all. Today the fortress compound is nothing but ruins, but fascinating ones.

Now the bad news: Because of its dramatic beauty, plus a number of quaint shops and restaurants in the village, Les Baux is often overrun with visitors at peak times, so time your visit wisely.

Essentials

ARRIVING   Les Baux is best reached by car. From St-Rémy, take D27 south; from Arles, D17 east. Alternatively, on weekends in June and September, and every day during July and August, **bus** nr. 59 (35 min.; 2.20€ one-way) runs between Arles and St-Rémy, stopping at Les Baux en route. For bus information, see www.lepilote.com or call © **08-10-00-13-26.** You can also book 1-day coach tours through **Autocars**

Lieutaud (www.excursionprovence.com; ✆ **04-90-86-36-75;** from 200€ per person) in Avignon or the tourist office in Aix-en-Provence (www.aixenprovencetourism.com; ✆ **04-42-16-11-61;** from 109€ per person).

VISITOR INFORMATION The **Office de Tourisme** (www.lesbauxdeprovence. com; ✆ **04-90-54-34-39**) is at Maison du Roy, near the northern entrance to the old city.

FAST FACTS Note that you'll need to head to the nearby town of Maussane-les-Alpilles for access to a bank, pharmacy, or post office.

Where to Stay

Hotel Benvengudo ★ This ancient Provençal *bastide* is surrounded by 3 hectares (7½ acres) of lavender fields and olive groves near the foot of Les Baux. From here it's a long walk—or a short drive—to the village summit. A luxurious medley of rooms and suites dots the scented grounds (although bear in mind that Wi-Fi doesn't reach every room and you're charged for the capsules used in your in-room Nespresso machine). All in all, it's a true taste of Provence, from the pétanque court to the on-site cooking school. It also hosts a gourmet restaurant (fixed-price menus 57€–70€).

Quartier de l'Arcoule. www.benvengudo.com. ✆ **04-93-54-32-34.** 27 units. 185€–250€ double; from 450€ suite. Free parking. **Amenities:** Restaurant; bar; babysitting; bike rental; outdoor pool; room service; sauna; spa; tennis courts; free Wi-Fi. Closed mid Oct to Mar.

Where to Eat

La Cabro d'Or ★★★ PROVENÇAL The Cabro d'Or delivers intelligent, innovative Provençal cuisine with a lightness of touch on the most bucolic restaurant terrace in southern France. Chef Michel Hulin diners savor the unctuousness of Mediterranean langoustines, the crispness of roasted red mullet, the froth of fresh pea velouté, and the crunch of slow-cooked suckling pig. More important, the restaurant is part of a truly fabulous trio of luxury hotels surrounding Les Baux. Together they form the most magical resort in all Provence. These include the **Hotel Cabro d'Or** (www.lacabrodor.com; ✆ **04-90-54-33-07;** doubles 200€–460€), which has enchanting grounds, an organic garden, and a vast swimming pool; the **Le Manoir** annex next door, which looks like a rural French movie set; and **Oustau de Baumanière,** at the foot of the village (www.oustaudebaumaniere.com; ✆ **04-90-54-33-21;** doubles 220€–588€), which has hosted the likes of Queen Elizabeth and Johnny Depp and also purveys an even more acclaimed (and more expensive) restaurant than the Cabro d'Or.

In the Hotel Cabro d'Or, Chemin départemental 27. www.maisonsdebaumaniere.com. ✆ **04-90-54-33-21.** Reservations recommended. Main courses 48€–56€; fixed-price lunch 56€; fixed-price dinner 78€–125€. Daily midday–2pm and 7:30–10pm. Closed winter.

Exploring Les Baux

Les Baux's windswept ruins, **Château des Baux** ★★★ (www.chateau-baux-provence.com; ✆ **04-90-54-55-56**), cover an area of 7 hectares (17 acres), much larger than the petite hilltop village itself. Consider visiting them early in the morning before the sun gets too strong.

The medieval compound is accessed via the 15th-century **Hôtel de la Tour du Brau.** Beyond this building are replicas of wooden military equipment that would have been used in the 13th century. Built to scale—that is to say, enormous—are a battering ram and various catapults capable of firing huge boulders. From April to September, these are fired every day at 11am and 1:30pm, 3:30pm, and 5:30pm, with an extra show during July and August at 6:30pm. Medieval jousting demonstrations (noon, 2:30pm, and 4:30pm) are held in summer.

Other stopping points include the **Chapel of St-Blaise** (inside which a film of aerial views of Provence is shown), a windmill, the skeleton of a hospital built in the 16th century, and a cemetery. The **Tour Sarrazin,** so named because it was used to spot Saracen invaders coming from the south, yields a sweeping view. Alongside each of the major points of interest, illustrated panels show what the buildings would have originally looked like and explain how the site has evolved architecturally.

Admission to the Château (including audioguide) is 8€ adults, 6€ children 7 to 17 from October to March. The rest of the year, it costs 9.50€ adults, 7.50€ children 7 to 17 (daily Apr–June and Sept 9am–7:15pm; July and Aug 9am–8:15pm; Mar and Oct 9:30am–6:30pm; Nov–Feb 10am–5pm).

Carrières de Lumières ★★ MUSEUM   A 10-minute stroll downhill from Les Baux, this temporary exhibition space occupies the site of a former limestone quarry. It's here that images of modern artworks (such as audiovisual exhibitions dedicated to Monet, Renoir, Van Gogh, or Gauguin) are projected against the 7m to 9m (23- to 30-ft.) columns. The museum's Cubist-style entrance featured in Jean Cocteau's final film, "The Testament of Orpheus."

Route de Maillane. www.carrieres-lumieres.com. © **04-90-54-47-37.** Admission 9.50€ adults, 7.50€ children 7–17, free children 6 and under. Daily March–Sept 9:30am–7pm; Oct–Jan 10am–6pm. Closed Feb.

ARLES ★★

744km (461 miles) S of Paris; 36km (22 miles) SW of Avignon; 92km (57 miles) NW of Marseille

On the banks of the Rhône River, Arles (pop. 53,000) attracts art lovers, archaeologists, and historians. To the delight of visitors, many of the vistas van Gogh painted remain luminously present today. Here the artist was even inspired to paint his own bedroom ("Bedroom in Arles," 1888).

Julius Caesar established a Roman colony here in the 1st century. Constantine the Great named Arles the second capital of his empire in A.D. 306, when it was known as "the little Rome of the Gauls." The city was incorporated into France in 1481.

Arles's ancient streets are not as pristinely preserved as, say, Avignon's, but are stunningly raw instead, with excellent restaurants, and summer festivals to boot. Its position on the river makes it a gateway to the Camargue, giving the town a healthy dose of Spanish and gypsy influence.

Essentials

ARRIVING   Trains run almost every hour between Arles and Avignon (trip time: 20 min.; 7.30€ one-way) and Marseille (trip time: 1 hr.; 15€). Be sure to take local trains from city center to city center, not the TGV, which, in this case, takes more time. If **driving,** head south along D570N from Avignon.

VISITOR INFORMATION   The **Office de Tourisme** is on bd. des Lices (www.arlestourisme.com; © **04-90-18-41-20**).

SPECIAL EVENTS   Les **Rencontres d'Arles** (www.rencontres-arles.com; © **04-90-96-76-06**), held from early July until late September, focuses on contemporary international photography. Tickets range from free to 8€ per exhibition, although passes are also available for 28€ to 48€. The ticket office is located in place de la République for the duration of the festival.

[FastFACTS] ARLES

ATMs/Banks   There are more than a dozen banks in downtown Arles, including three in place de la République.

Internet Access   CyberSaladelle Informatique Arles, 17 rue de la République (www.cybersaladelle.fr; ☏ **04-90-93-13-56**).

Mail & Postage   La Poste, 5 bd. des Lices (☏ **36-31**).

Pharmacies   Pharmacie des Arènes, 17 rue du 4 Septembre (☏ **04-90-96-02-77**).

Where to Stay

Hôtel de l'Amphitheatre ★★   This delightful hotel is a firm favorite with regular visitors to Arles. Tucked into the heart of the Old Town, the building itself was originally constructed in the 17th century and retains its historical atmosphere. Guest rooms feature reproduction Provençal furniture, and some—including the plush Belvedere Suite—offer views over the terra-cotta roofs of historic Arles.

5–7 rue Diderot. www.hotelamphitheatre.fr. ☏ **04-90-96-10-30.** 33 units. 69€–119€ double; 109€–119€ triple; 129€–139€ quadruple; 129€–139€ suite. Parking 8€. **Amenities:** Free Wi-Fi.

Le Cloitre ★★   Perfectly positioned in Arles' Old Town, midway between Les Arènes and place de la République, Le Cloitre is a unique medley of ancient stone features and funky 1950s furnishings. Each room is individually decorated in bright tones, with wooden ceiling beams, mosaic floors, and designer knickknacks. Free bikes are available for guest use. Organic breakfast is served up on the rooftop terrace.

18 rue du Cloître. www.hotel-cloitre.com. ☏ **04-88-09-10-00.** 19 units. 90€–160€ double. Parking 10€. **Amenities:** Bar; free Wi-Fi.

Where to Eat

L'Atelier Jean-Luc Rabanel ★★★ MODERN PROVENÇAL   Put simply, this is the finest restaurant that I have ever had the pleasure of experiencing. And that's saying something. Double-Michelin-starred chef Jean-Luc Rabanel pairs organic ingredients from his own garden with locally reared bull, pork, and game (and even herbs, mushrooms, and flowers). Delivery combines the deftness of touch of a Japanese samurai (an Asian influence pervades Rabanel's set menus) with the creative vision of a Parisian fashion designer. A wine-accompaniment option offers a unique and passionate oenophilic tour of France. The chef also purveys two adjoining restaurants. The **Bistro Acote** (www.bistro-acote.com; ☏ **04-90-91-07-69**) is softer on the wallet and serves Provençal classics on a 29€ set menu; and **Iode** (www.iode-rabanel.com; ☏ **04-90-91-07-69**) specializes in "hyper-fresh" crustaceans and shellfish. Wow.

7 rue des Carmes. www.rabanel.com ☏ **04-90-91-07-69.** Reservations recommended. Fixed-price lunch 65€–185€; fixed-price dinner 125€–185€. Wed–Sun noon–1:30pm and 8pm–9pm.

Le Criquet ★ MODERN PROVENÇAL   Tiny, charming, and worth reserving well in advance, Le Criquet is a classic local restaurant on the back streets of Arles. Friendly service meets unpretentious dishes like *bourride* of salt cod and spices, bowls of local

7

PROVENCE
Fast Facts: Arles

172

mussels, and stew made from local Camargue bull. Sit outside amid a romantic street setting or in the rather cramped—but undeniably cozy—interior.

21 rue Porte de Laure. ✆ **04-90-96-80-51.** Reservations recommended. Main courses 11€–19€. Tue–Sun noon–2:30pm and 7pm–9pm.

Exploring Arles

The **Place du Forum,** shaded by plane trees, stands around the old Roman forum. The Terrasse du Café le Soir, immortalized by Van Gogh, is now the square's Café Van Gogh. Visitors keen to follow on in the footsteps of the great artist may pick up a **Van Gogh walking map** (1€), which takes in 10 important sites around the city, from the tourist office. On a corner of place du Forum sits the legendary **Grand Hôtel Nord-Pinus:** Bullfighters, artists, and A-listers have all stayed here. Three blocks south, the **Place de la République** is dominated by a 15m-tall (49-ft.) red granite obelisk.

One of the city's great classical monuments is the Roman **Théâtre Antique ★**, rue du Cloître (✆ **04-90-49-59-05**). Augustus began the theater in the 1st century; only two Corinthian columns remain. The "Venus of Arles" (now in the Louvre in Paris) was discovered here in 1651. The theater is open May through September daily 9am to 7pm; March, April, and October daily 9am to 6pm; and November through February daily 10am to 5pm. Admission is 6.50€ adults, 5€ students, and free children 17 and under. The same ticket admits you to the nearby **Amphitheater (Les Arènes) ★★**, rond-pont des Arènes (✆ **04-90-49-59-05;** same opening hours), also built in the 1st century. Sometimes called Le Cirque Romain, it seats almost 25,000. For a good view, climb the three towers that remain from medieval times, when the amphitheater was turned into a fortress.

Le Cloître et l'Église St-Trophime ★ CHURCH   This church is noted for its 12th-century portal, one of the finest achievements of the southern Romanesque style. Frederick Barbarossa was crowned king of Arles here in 1178. In the pediment, Christ is surrounded by the symbols of the Evangelists. The pretty cloister, in Gothic and Romanesque styles, possesses noteworthy medieval carvings: During July's Les Rencontres d'Arles festival, contemporary photographs are also exhibited here.

East side of place de la République. ✆ **04-90-49-59-05.** Free admission to church; cloister 3.50€ adults, 2.60€ students, free for children 17 and under. Church daily 10am–noon and 2–5pm; cloister May–Sept daily 9am–7pm; Mar, Apr, and Oct daily 9am–6pm; Nov–Feb daily 10am–5pm.

Les Taureaux

Bulls are a big part of Arlesien culture. It's not unusual to see bull steak on local menus, and *saucisson de taureau* (bull sausage) is a local specialty. The first bullfight, or *corrida*, took place in the amphitheater in 1853. Appropriately, Arles is home to a bullfighting school (the **Ecole Taurine d'Arles**). Like it or loathe it, *corridas* are still held during the Easter Feria and in September, during the Feria du Riz. The bull is killed only during the Easter *corrida;* expect a few protestors. The Easter event begins at 11am, the September events around 6pm. A seat on the stone benches of the amphitheater costs 18€ to 97€. Tickets are usually available a few hours beforehand at the ticket office on **Les Arenes d'Arles** (1 rond-pont des Arènes). For information or advance tickets, go to www.arenes-arles.com or contact ✆ **08-91-70-03-70.**

Les Alyscamps ★ RUINS   Perhaps the most memorable sight in Arles, this once–Roman necropolis became a Christian burial ground in the 4th century. Mentioned in Dante's "Inferno," it has been painted by both Van Gogh and Gauguin. Today it is lined with poplars and studded with ancient sarcophagi. Arlesiens escape here with a cold drink to enjoy a respite from the summer heat.

Avenue des Alyscamps. ℭ **04-90-49-59-05.** Admission 3.50€ adults, 2.60€ students, free children 17 and under. May–Sept daily 9am–7pm; Mar, Apr, and Oct daily 9am–noon and 2–6pm; Nov–Feb daily 10am–noon and 2–5pm.

Musée Départemental Arles Antiques ★★ MUSEUM   Set within a sleek compound around 1km (½ mile) south of Arles' town center, this archaeological museum hosts finds uncovered throughout the region's rich territories. Vast, airy rooms present Roman sarcophagi, sculptures, mosaics, and inscriptions from ancient times through the 6th century A.D. Temporary exhibitions, such as 2013's Rodin show, highlight the inspiration antiquity has had on artists through the ages.

Avenue 1ere Division France Libre, presqu'île du Cirque Romain. www.arles-antique.cg13.fr. ℭ **04-13-31-51-03.** Admission 8€ adults, 5€, free children 17 and under. Wed–Mon 10am–6pm.

Musée Réattu ★★ ART MUSEUM   Exhibited over the labyrinthine rooms of the 15th-century Grand Priory of the Order of Malta, this museum was opened in 1868 to showcase artworks previously owned by local painter Jacques Réattu. Over the past 150 years, the collection has swollen with donations and annual acquisitions, including dozens of Picasso drawings and close to 4,000 photographs. The building's former archives room is now dedicated to the history of the Order of the Knights Hospitaller. The museum also stages some three temporary exhibitions each year.

10 rue du Grand-Prieuré. www.museereattu.arles.fr. ℭ **04-90-49-37-58.** Admission 8€ adults, 6€ students, free children 17 and under. Tues–Sun 11am–7pm.

Outlying Attractions

Abbaye de Montmajour ★★ MONASTERY   This medieval monastery, founded in the leafy countryside 6km (3½ miles) northeast of Arles during the 10th

---

Mistral, Two Ways

Born just north of Arles, Frédéric Mistral (1830–1914) dedicated his life to defending and preserving the original Provençal language known as Occitan. The poet won the Nobel Prize for his epic work "Mirèio" and his overall contributions to French literature. Mistral joined six other Provençal writers in 1854 to found Félibrige, an association for the promotion of Occitan language and literature. He is the author of "Lo Tresor dóu Félibrige," the most comprehensive dictionary of the Occitan language to this day. Many think Mistral lent his name to the notorious glacial wind that roars through Provence every year. However, in this case, *mistral* is the Occitan word for "master"—and those who experience the phenomenon regularly say it's a cruel one. Tearing through the Rhône River Valley toward the Mediterranean, the mistral reaches speeds of 100km (62 miles) per hour and can blow up to 100 days per year. Most of these occur in winter, but it is also common in the spring and, in unlucky years, can persist until early summer.

A day out IN THE CAMARGUE

A marshy delta south of Arles, the Camargue is located between the Mediterranean and two arms of the Rhône. With the most fragile ecosystem in France, it has been a nature reserve since 1970. You cannot drive into the protected parts, and some areas are accessible only to the Gardians, the local cowboys. Their ancestors may have been the first American cowboys, who sailed on French ships to the port of New Orleans, where they rode the bayous of Louisiana and east Texas, rounding up cattle—in French, no less.

The Camargue is also cattle country. Black bulls are bred here both for their meat and for the regional bullfighting arenas. The whitewashed houses, plaited-straw roofs, plains, sandbars, and pink flamingos in the marshes make this area different, even exotic. There's no more evocative sight than the snow-white horses galloping through the marshlands, with hoofs so tough that they don't need shoes. The breed was brought here by the Arabs long ago, and it is said that their long manes and bushy tails evolved over the centuries to slap the region's omnipresent mosquitoes. Exotic flora and fauna abound. The birdlife here is among the most luxuriant in Europe. Looking much like the Florida Everglades, the area is known for its colonies of pink flamingos *(flamants roses)*, which share living quarters with some 400 other bird species, including ibises, egrets, kingfishers, owls, wild ducks, swans, and ferocious birds of prey. The best place to see flamingo colonies is at the **Parc Ornithologique de Pont de Gau,** D570 (www.parcornithologique. com; ✆ **04-90-97-82-62**), 4km (3 miles), north of Camargue's capital, Stes-Maries-de-la-Mer.

You can explore the Camargue's rugged terrain by boat, bike, jeep, or horse. The latter can take you along beaches and into the interior, fording waters to places where black bulls graze and wild birds nest. Dozens of stables are located along the highway between Arles to Stes-Maries. Virtually all charge the same rate (around 40€ for 2 hr.). The rides are aimed at the neophyte, not the champion equestrian.

For details, visit Arles' Office de Tourisme (see above) or head to the **Office de Tourisme,** 5 av. Van Gogh, Ste-Maries-de-la-Mer (www.saintesmaries. com; ✆ **04-90-97-82-55**).

century, is now an innovative exhibition venue. Temporary shows, ranging from 2013's Christian Lacroix installation to annual photographic displays as part of Les Rencontres d'Arles, are dotted throughout the atmospheric ruins. A wonderful outdoor restaurant is tucked under the trees at the back of the parking lot opposite.

Route de Fontvieille. http://montmajour.monuments-nationaux.fr. ✆ **04-90-54-64-17.** Admission 7.50€ adults, 4.50€ students, free children 17 and under. July–Sept daily 10am–6:30pm; Apr–June daily 9:30am–6pm; Oct–Mar Tues–Sun 10am–5pm.

Nightlife

Because of its relatively small population, Arles doesn't offer as many nightlife options as Aix-en-Provence, Avignon, or Marseille. The town's most appealing spot is the organic wine bar–café **L'Ouvre-Boîte,** 22 rue du Cloître (no phone). Open June to September only, it's set under a majestic canopy of trees in one of the Old Town's loveliest squares.

AIX-EN-PROVENCE ★★

760km (471 miles) S of Paris; 84km (52 miles) SE of Avignon; 34km (21 miles) N of Marseille; 185km (115 miles) W of Nice

One of the most surprising aspects of Aix is its size. Frequently guidebooks proclaim it the very heart of Provence, evoking a sleepy town filled with flowers and fountains. Which it is—in certain quarters. But Aix is also a bustling university town of nearly 143,000 inhabitants (the Université d'Aix dates from 1413).

Founded in 122 B.C. by Roman general Caius Sextius Calvinus, who conveniently named the town Aquae Sextiae, after himself, Aix originated as a military outpost. Aix's most celebrated son, Paul Cézanne, immortalized the Aix countryside in his paintings. Just as he saw it, the Montagne Ste-Victoire looms over the town today.

Time marches on, but there are still plenty of decades-old, family-run shops on the narrow streets of the Old Town. A lazy summer lunch at one of the bourgeois cafes on the cours Mirabeau is an experience not to be missed.

Essentials

ARRIVING **Trains** arrive frequently from Marseille (trip time: 45 min.; 7.60€ one-way) and Nice (trip time: 3½ hr.; 39€ one-way). High-speed TGV trains—from Paris as well as Marseille and Nice—arrive at the modern station near Vitrolles, 18km (11 miles) west of Aix. Bus transfers to the center of Aix cost 3.60€ one-way. There are **buses** from Marseille, Avignon, and Nice; for information, see www.lepilote.com or call ☎ **08-10-00-13-26.** If you're **driving** to Aix from Avignon or other points north, take A7 south to A8 and follow the signs into town. From Marseille or other points south, take A51 north.

VISITOR INFORMATION The **Office de Tourisme** is at Les Allées Provençales, 300 av. Giuseppe Verdi (www.aixenprovencetourism.com; ☎ 04-42-16-11-61).

CITY LAYOUT Aix's **Old Town** is primarily pedestrianized. To the south, it's bordered by the grand **cours Mirabeau,** which is flanked by a canopy of plane trees. The city was built atop thermal springs, and forty fountains still bubble away in picturesque squares around town.

SPECIAL EVENTS The **Festival d'Aix,** created in 1948 (www.festival-aix.com; ☎ **08-20-92-29-23**), mid-June through late July, features music and opera from all over the world.

Aix Through the Eyes of Cézanne

One of the best experiences in Aix is a walk along the well-marked *route de Cézanne.* From the east end of cours Mirabeau, take rue du Maréchal-Joffre across boulevard Carnot to boulevard des Poilus, which becomes avenue des Ecoles-Militaires and D17. The stretch between Aix and the hamlet of Le Tholonet is full of twists and turns where Cézanne used to set up his easel. The route also makes a lovely 5.5km (3½-mile) stroll. Le Tholonet has a cafe or two where you can refresh yourself while waiting for one of the frequent buses back to Aix.

HOTELS ■
Hôtel Cezanne **6**
Hôtel du Globe **2**
La Villa Gallici **1**

RESTAURANTS ◆
Brasserie Les
Deux Garçons **5**
Lavault **3**
Le Mille Feuille **4**

[FastFACTS] AIX-EN-PROVENCE

ATMs/Banks   There are scores of banks in downtown Aix, including three along cours Mirabeau.

Internet Access   **Pasyl,** 52 rue Aumône Vieille (📞 **04-42-26-60-41**).

Mail & Postage   **La Poste,** place de l'Hôtel de Ville (📞 **36-31**).

Pharmacies   **Pharmacie Victor Hugo,** 16 av. Victor Hugo (📞 **04-42-26-24-93**).

Where to Stay

In a city where expensive is the norm, the budget option **Hôtel du Globe** (www.hotel duglobe.com) is also recommended.

Hôtel Cézanne ★★   This super-chic—and enormously friendly—boutique hotel is best suited to guests seeking a more unusual spot to snooze. Conceived by one of the designers of both Villa Gallici and sophisticated *hotel particulier* **28 à Aix** (www.28-a-aix.com), the Cézanne is a mélange of colorful decor and hip designer touches. Baroque furnishings, unique artworks, and an honesty bar all add to the atmosphere. The hotel's location—midway between the train station and Aix's Old Town—makes it ideal for visitors planning day trips farther afield.

40 av. Victor Hugo. http://cezanne.hotelaix.com. ℭ **04-42-91-11-11.** 55 units. 250€ double; 350€ junior suite; 450€ suite. Parking 16€. **Amenities:** Bar; business center; free Wi-Fi.

La Villa Gallici ★★★ This 18th-century Provençal house is one of Aix's most luxurious getaways. It also boasts a 7-acre garden and a gastronomic restaurant on-site. It may be just a 5-minute stroll from the town center, yet the countrified ambience makes it feel miles away. Guest rooms are swathed in pastel printed fabrics, while suites have their own private patios. Days may be spent lounging by the terra-cotta-trimmed pool; candlelit dinners are served alfresco under the stars.

Av. de la Violette. www.villagallici.com. ℭ **04-42-23-29-23.** 22 units. 230€–690€ double; 440€–970€ suite. Free parking. Closed Jan. **Amenities:** Restaurant; bar; babysitting; outdoor pool; room service; free Wi-Fi.

Where to Eat

Lavault ★ FRENCH This innovative restaurant spills over the charming 15th-century premises. The atmospheric stone vaulted cellar is a favorite dining venue on hot summer evenings. The cuisine is affordable yet creative and may include lemongrass-spiked gazpacho with avocado, duck ravioli tossed in a morel mushroom sauce, or the hugely popular foie-gras club sandwich pinched into a sweet brioche. The extensive wine list features a top selection of vintages from the local region.

4 rue Felibre Gaut. www.lavault.net. ℭ **04-42-38-57-28.** Reservations recommended. Main courses 15€–23€; fixed-price lunch 16€; fixed-price dinner 28€–35€. Thurs–Sat noon–2:30pm and Tues–Sat 7–11:30pm.

Le Mille Feuille ★★ PROVENÇAL Nestled into a quiet corner of Aix's Old Town, this excellent eatery stands out against the often-average local dining scene. Little surprise, as the restaurant is the brainchild of chef Nicolas Monribot and sommelier Sylvain Sendra, both former staff at the famous l'Oustau de Baumanière in Les Baux (p. 169). The market-fresh menu changes daily but may include yellow and green zucchini crumble with *cœur de bœuf* tomatoes, Sisteron lamb atop an almond and apricot tajine, or a delectable vanilla bourbon *millefeuille* pastry. You can dine either on the small outdoor terrace or indoors, where the classy decor features crimson walls and chartreuse upholstered furnishings.

8 rue Rifle-Rafle. www.le-millefeuille.fr. ℭ **04-42-96-55-17.** Dinner reservations essential. Main courses 15€; fixed-price lunch 23€–28€, dinner 35€–39€. Tues–Sat noon–1:30pm and Wed–Sat 8–10:30pm.

Exploring Aix-en-Provence

Aix's main street, **cours Mirabeau ★**, is one of Europe's most beautiful. A double row of plane trees shades it from the Provençal sun and throws dappled daylight onto its rococo fountains. Shops and sidewalk cafes line one side; 17th- and 18th-century sandstone *hôtels particuliers* (private mansions) take up the other. Stop into **Brasserie Les Deux Garçons,** 53 cours Mirabeau, for a coffee or a glass of rosé. The brasserie was founded in 1792 and frequented by the likes of Emile Zola, Cézanne, Picasso, and Sir Winston Churchill. Boulevard Carnot and cours Sextius circle the heart of the old quarter (Vieille Ville), which contains the pedestrian-only zone.

One fun way to check out the lay of the land is aboard an eco-friendly **Diabline** (www.la-diabline.fr; Mon–Sat 8:30am–7:30pm; 0.50€/ride). These vehicles operate three routes along cours Mirabeau and through most of the Old Town.

Atelier de Cézanne ★★ MUSEUM   A 10-minute (uphill) stroll north of Aix's Old Town, Cézanne's studio offers visitors a unique glimpse into the artist's daily life. Because the building remained untouched for decades after Cézanne's death in 1906, the studio has remained perfectly preserved for close to a century. Note the furnishings, vases, and small figurines on display, all of which feature in the modern master's drawings and canvases. Cézanne aficionados should also enjoy both **Jas de Bouffan,** the artist's family manor, and the inspirational Cubist landscape of the **Bibémus Quarries.** The **Cézanne Pass** (12€) allows entry to all three sites.

9 av. Paul-Cézanne. www.atelier-cezanne.com. © **04-42-21-06-53.** Admission 5.50€ adults, 2€ students and children 13–25, free for children 12 and under. July–Aug daily 10am–6pm, English tour at 5pm; Apr–June and Sept daily 10am–noon and 2–6pm, English tour at 5pm; Oct–Mar daily 10am–noon and 2–5pm, English tour at 4pm. Closed Sun Dec–Feb.

Musée Granet ★★ MUSEUM   One of the South of France's top art venues, this popular museum displays a permanent collection of paintings and sculpture ranging from 15th-century French canvases to 20th-century Giacometti sculptures. However, it's the large-scale temporary exhibitions that truly impress, such as the 2013 "Le Grand Atelier du Midi: De Cézanne a Matisse," a show that featured every major artist inspired by the region.

Place Saint Jean de Malte. www.museegranet-aixenprovence.fr. © **04-42-52-88-32.** Admission 11€ adults, 9€ students and children 13–25, free children 12 and under. Tues–Sun June–Sept 10am–7pm; Oct–May noon–6pm.

Shopping

Opened more than a century ago, **Béchard,** 12 cours Mirabeau (© **04-42-26-06-78**), is the most famous bakery in town. It specializes in the famous *Calissons d'Aix,* a candy made from ground almonds, preserved melon, and fruit syrup. **Chocolaterie de Puyricard,** 7 rue Rifle-Rafle (www.puyricard.fr; © **04-42-21-13-26**), creates sensational chocolates filled with candied figs, walnuts, or local lavender honey.

Founded in 1934 on a busy boulevard just east of the center of town, **Santons Fouque,** 65 cours Gambetta (www.santons-fouque.com; © **04-42-26-33-38**), stocks close to 2,000 traditional *santons* (crèche figurines).

For a range of truly useful souvenirs, including copper pots and pocket knives by famous French forgers such as Laguiole, try **Quincaillerie Centrale,** 21 rue de Monclar (© **04-42-23-33-18**), a hardware/housewares store that's been offering a little bit of everything since 1959.

To the Markets We Will Go

Aix offers the best markets in the region. Place Richelme holds a **fruit and vegetable market** every morning from 8:30am to 12:30pm. Come here to buy exquisite products such as olives, lavender honey, and regional local cheeses. There's a **flower market** every day, with the same hours, at either place de l'Hôtel de Ville or place des Prêcheurs (the former on Tues, Thurs, and Sat; the latter on Mon, Wed, Fri, and Sun). The **fish market** takes place every morning on the south side of place Richelme.

Nightlife

Open daily from 8am until 2am, **La Rotonde,** 2A place Jeanne d'Arc (www.larotonde-aix.com; ℭ **04-42-91-61-70**), is a bar, cafe, and historic hangout. Aix's countless students kick off their evenings at **Le Sextius Bar,** 13 cours Sextius (ℭ **04-42-26-07-21**).

Under-30s who like thumping beats should head for **Le Mistral,** 3 rue Frédéric Mistral (www.mistralclub.fr; ℭ **04-42-38-16-49**), where techno and house pumps long and loud for a cover charge of around 20€. **Le Divino,** 4039 route de Sisteron (ℭ **04-42-21-28-28**), draws a lively gay/straight crowd for weekend boogeying until 6am (cover charge 8€–16€).

For jazz produced by a changing roster of visiting musicians, head for the **Scat Club,** 11 rue de la Verrerie (ℭ **04-42-23-00-23**), a preferred venue for more mature local patrons.

MARSEILLE ★★

776km (481 miles) S of Paris; 203km (126 miles) SW of Nice; 32km (20 miles) S of Aix-en-Provence

Marseille, with nearly 1.5 million inhabitants, is the second-largest city in France. It's also the country's oldest metropolis, founded as a port by the Greeks in the 6th century B.C.

Author Alexandre Dumas called teeming Marseille "the meeting place of the entire world." It's an industrial city with many faces, both figuratively and literally. A view from high up reveals the colorful Vieux Port, with its elegant old buildings, boat-filled harbor, and the Mediterranean beyond. The city is sprawling and can be down at heel in parts, but it's also a cosmopolitan nexus of vibrant sounds, smells, and sights—unlike any other place in France.

Marseille's age-old problems may include unemployment, the Mafia, and racial tension (around a quarter of the population is of North African descent, with significant Armenian, Jewish, and Asian communities too), but civic pride is strong, and the city is firmly focused on the future, evidenced by the ongoing **Euroméditerranée urban regeneration project** (www.euromediterranee.fr). Marseille proudly held the title of **European Capital of Culture 2013** (www.mp2013.fr), sparking the construction of a flurry of new cultural venues, the creation of landmark museums, and the completion of long-term architectural projects, particularly in the old docklands neighborhood north of the Vieux Port. Marseille's second city has finally come of age.

Essentials

ARRIVING   **Marseille-Provence Airport** (www.marseille-airport.com; ℭ **04-42-14-14-14**), 27km (17 miles) northwest of the city center, receives international flights from all over Europe. From the airport, shuttle buses (*navettes;* www.navettemarseilleaeroport.com; ℭ **08-92-70-08-40**) make the trip to Marseille's St-Charles rail station, near the Vieux-Port, for 8€, 5.60€ passengers 12 to 26, and 4€ children under 12. The shuttle buses run daily every 20 minutes from 5am until midnight; the trip takes 25 minutes.

Marseille has **train** connections from all over Europe, particularly to and from Nice, and on to Italy. It's also linked to Paris via the TGV bullet train, which departs almost every hour from the Gare de Lyon (trip time: 3 hr., 20 min.; 45€–110€ one-way). **Buses** serve the **Gare Routière,** rue Honnorat (ℭ **04-91-08-16-40**), adjacent to the St-Charles railway station. Several buses run daily between Aix-en-Provence and Marseille (trip time: 40 min.; 5.20€ one-way). If you're **driving** from Paris, follow A6 south to Lyon, and then continue south along A7 to Marseille. The drive takes about 8 hours. From Provence, take A7 south to Marseille.

VISITOR INFORMATION The **Office de Tourisme** is at 11 la Canebière (www. marseille-tourisme.com; ℂ **08-26-50-05-00;** Métro: Vieux-Port).

CITY LAYOUT Marseille is a large, sprawling metropolis. Unlike any of the other towns mentioned in this chapter, if you're keen to explore different parts of the city, you'll probably need to take advantage of its comprehensive public transport.

NEIGHBORHOODS IN BRIEF The major arteries divide Marseille into 16 *arrondissements.* Like Paris, the last two digits of a postal code tell you within which *arrondissement* an address is located. Visitors tend to spend most of their time in four main neighborhoods. The first is the **Vieux Port,** the atmospheric natural harbor that's a focal point for the city center. From here, the wide La Canebière boulevard runs eastwards, bisected by Marseille's most popular shopping avenues. To the north lies **Le Panier,** the original Old Town, crisscrossed by a pastel network of undulating alleyways. This neighborhood's western edge is trimmed by former docklands, which have been completed redeveloped over the past few years. Southeast of the Vieux Port, the alternative neighborhood around **cours Julien** is home to convivial restaurants and one-off boutiques aplenty. And come summertime, action shifts to the **Plages du Prado,** a strip of beaches due south of the city center.

Getting Around

ON FOOT Each of Marseille's neighborhoods is easily navigable on foot. However, unless you're an avid walker, you may want to rely on either the Métro or the tramway (see below) to zip you around town.

BY CAR Parking and car safety are so problematic that your best bet is to park in a garage and rely on public transport. The website **www.parking-public.fr** lists Marseille's public parking lots and hourly fees.

BY TAXI Taxis Radio Marseille (✆ **04-91-02-20-20**).

BY PUBLIC TRANSPORT **Métro** lines 1 and 2 both stop at the main train station, Gare St-Charles, place Victor Hugo. Line 1 makes a U-shaped circuit from the suburbs into the city and back again; Line 2 runs north and south in the downtown area. Also with two lines, the tramway services the Canabière and the refurbished Joliette Docks district, as well as continuing out to the suburbs. Individual tickets are 1.50€; they're valid on Métro, tram, and bus lines for up to 60 minutes after purchase. If you plan to take public transport several times during your stay, buy a **pass journée,** valid for 1 day for 5€ or 3 days for 11€.

Alternatively, it's also possible to purchase a 1-day (22€) or 2-day (29€) **City Pass** from the Marseille Tourist Office. The pass covers all public transport, including the round-trip ferry trip to **Château d'If** (p. 186), as well as entrance to more than a dozen of the city's museums and a ride on the *petit-train* (p. 186) up to the **Basilique Notre-Dame de la Garde** (p. 184).

[FastFACTS] MARSEILLE

ATMs/Banks Marseille's banks are plentiful, including three along La Canebière.

Doctors & Hospitals **Hopital Saint Joseph,** 26 bd. de Louvain (www.hopital-saint-joseph.fr; ✆ **04-91-80-65-00**).

Embassies & Consulates **British Consulate Marseille,** 24 av. du Prado (www.gov.uk; ✆ **04-91-15-72-10**); **Consulate General of the United States Marseille,** place Varian Fry (http://marseille.usconsulate.gov; ✆ **04-91-54-92-00**).

Internet Access In 2013, Marseille's municipality installed 50 free Wi-Fi hotspots around the city. Central locations (including Jardin du Pharo, the square outside the Hôtel de Ville, and La Vieille Charité) are indicated on the free maps distributed by the tourist office.

Mail & Postage **La Poste,** 1 cours Jean Ballard (✆ **36-31**).

Newspapers & Magazines Bilingual **"COTE Magazine"** (www.cotemagazine.com) offers a good selection of tried-and-true Marseille tips, as well as local interviews and recent openings.

Pharmacies **Leader Santé,** 37 la Canebière (✆ **04-91-91-32-06**).

Safety As in any big city, it's wise to keep to keep a close eye on your belongings and avoid poorly lit areas at night.

Where to Stay

Although slightly removed from the city center, the iconic **Hôtel le Corbusier** (www.gerardin-corbusier.com) is a must for architecture aficionados. In 2013, local French designers transformed the hotel's rooftop gym into a brand-new contemporary art space, **MAMO** (www.mamo.fr).

Casa Honoré ★   Interior designer Annick Lestrohan, creator of the Honoré brand of homewares, has transformed this former print shop into an ultra-stylish bed-and-breakfast. Unsurprisingly, guest rooms are decorated with Lestrohan's exquisite creations, from sleek designer furnishings to quality linens (and all are for sale too). An oasis of tranquility just south of Marseille's Vieux Port, the B&B's four rooms all center around a courtyard splashed with tropical foliage and a small swimming pool. Book as far in advance as you dare.

123 rue Sainte. www.casahonore.com. ✆ **04-96-11-01-62.** 4 units. 150€–200€ double. No credit cards. Métro: Vieux-Port. **Amenities:** Breakfast room; outdoor pool; free Wi-Fi.

Hôtel-Dieu ★★   Another 2013 addition to the local scene, the luxurious Hotel Dieu is perched just behind Marseille's Hôtel de Ville, overlooking the Vieux Port from Le Panier. This five-star hotel occupies what was once an 18th-century hospital. It's now managed by the InterContinental Group with aplomb. As well as modern, minimalist guest rooms with superb views, guest may enjoy the indoor pool, the Clarins Spa, brasserie **Les Fenêtres,** and gastronomic restaurant **Alcyone** onsite.

1 place Daviel. www.ihg.com. ✆ **04-13-42-42-42.** 194 units. 275€–485€ double; 585€–1,400€ suite. Parking 25€. Métro: Vieux-Port. **Amenities:** Restaurant; bar; business center; fitness center; indoor pool, room service; spa. Free internet.

Mama Shelter ★★   Tucked into the hipster cours Julien district, this unique hotel is the brainchild of designer Philippe Starck. Rooms are bright and contemporary, from the modular furnishings to the wall-mounted iMacs offering dozens of free on-demand movies. Downstairs, Egyptian graffiti artist Tarek has tagged the industrial-chic restaurant's ceiling. And outdoors, Mama Shelter's yellow-striped courtyard hosts a pastis bar where guests can sip their way through more than four dozen variants of the city's beloved anise-flavored tipple. An excellent bet for a true taste of France's second city.

64 rue de la Loubière. www.mamashelter.com. ✆ **04-84-35-20-00.** 127 units. 49€–109€ double; 129€ family room; 199€ suite. Parking 17€. Métro: Notre Dame du Mont. **Amenities:** Restaurant; bar; free Wi-Fi.

Where to Eat

For diners interested in re-creating Marseille's famous *bouillabaisse* fish stew at home, **Miramar Restaurant** (www.lemiramar.fr) offers cooking classes (120€/5-hr. lesson including lunch). Contact the tourist office for details.

See also the delectable **La Table du Môle** (p. 185), which opened atop the MuCEM in 2013.

La Kahena TUNISIAN   Among Marseille's many Tunisian restaurants, this 35-year-old eatery stands out from the crowd. Named for a 6th-century-B.C. Tunisian princess, La Kahena's specialty is couscous: Among the 10 varieties are versions with lamb, *merguez* spicy sausages, and cod. Other Tunisian classics such as *mechoua* salad (spicy grilled vegetables), tajines, and crispy *brick* pastry stuffed with shrimp are also served up in the ornate blue-tiled dining room. A solid budget choice.

2 rue de la République. ✆ **04-91-90-61-93.** Reservations recommended. Main courses 10€–18€. Daily noon–2:30pm and 7:30–10:30pm. Métro: Vieux-Port.

Le Grain du Sel ★★ MODERN MEDITERRANEAN Marseille-born chef Pierre Giannetti concocts what many locals consider to be the city's most creative bistro cuisine. Dishes are infinitely innovative, often taking inspiration from Giannetti's years of cooking in Barcelona. Following morning market finds, the daily menu may include Sardinian gnocchi with clams, mussel *escabèche*, or Spanish rice with shellfish harvested from the Camargue seaside town of Saintes-Maries-de-la-Mer. The wine list is carefully considered, and you can dine outside on sunny days in the petite courtyard.

39 rue de la Paix Marcel Paul. ℂ **04-91-54-47-30.** Reservations recommended. Main courses 16€–35€; fixed-price lunch 16€–19€. Tues–Sat noon–2pm, Fri-Sat 8–10pm. Closed Aug. Métro: Vieux-Port.

L'Epuisette ★★ SEAFOOD/MEDITERRANEAN This Michelin-starred option is undoubtedly the premier place in Marseille to sample *bouillabaisse* stew. Pack your appetite: Fresh fish is poached in saffron-infused soup; the final product is served as two separate courses, accompanied by *rouille,* a mayonnaise-like sauce flavored with garlic, cayenne pepper, and saffron. L'Epuisette's setting is as sublime as the cuisine: The seaside dining room overlooks Château d'If from the picturesque fishing port of Vallon des Auffes, 2.5km (1½ miles) south of Marseille's Vieux Port.

Vallon des Auffes. www.l-epuisette.fr. ℂ **04-91-52-17-82.** Reservations required. Main courses 18€–60€; fixed-price dinner 70€–125€. Tues–Sat noon–1:30pm and 7:30–9:30pm. Closed Aug. Bus: 83.

Exploring Marseille

Immerse yourself in local life with a wander through Marseille's busy streets, including along the famous **La Canebière.** Lined with hotels, shops, and restaurants, it used to be a very seedy street indeed, saturated with sailors from every nation. With Marseille's ongoing urban regeneration, however, it has become the heart and soul of the city.

La Canebière joins the **Vieux Port** ★★, dominated at its western end by the massive neoclassical forts of St-Jean and St-Nicolas. The harbor is filled with fishing craft and yachts and ringed by seafood restaurants. For a panoramic view, head to the **Jardin du Pharo,** a promontory facing the entrance to the Vieux-Port. From the terrace of the Château du Pharo, built by Napoleon III, you can clearly see the city's old and new cathedrals, as well as the recently redeveloped docklands, now the **Cité de la Méditerranée,** which includes **Fort Saint-Jean** and the **MuCEM** (Museum of European and Mediterranean Civilizations), which opened in June 2013.

North of the old port is **Le Panier,** Marseille's Old Town. Small boutiques and designer ateliers now populate these once-sketchy streets. To the south, the **corniche Président-J.-F.-Kennedy** is a 4km (2½-mile) promenade. You'll pass villas and gardens facing the Mediterranean, before reaching the popular **Plages du Prado.** Patrolled by lifeguards in the summer, these spacious, sandy beaches have children's playgrounds, sunloungers, and waterside cafes. Serious hikers can continue south of here into the **Parc National des Calanques** (www.calanques-parcnational.fr), France's newest national park. This series of stunning limestone cliffs, fjords, and rocky promontories stretches along the coast for 20km (12 miles) southeast of Marseille; the postcard-perfect **Calanque d'En Vau** in particular is well worth seeking out.

Basilique Notre-Dame-de-la-Garde ★ CHURCH This landmark church crowns a limestone rock overlooking the southern side of the Vieux-Port. It was built in the Romanesque-Byzantine style popular in the 19th century and topped by a 9.7m (32-ft.) gilded statue of the Virgin. Visitors come for the views (best at sunset) from its terrace. Spread out before you are the city, the islands, and the shimmering sea.

Rue Fort-du-Sanctuaire. www.notredamedelagarde.com. $©$ **04-91-13-40-80.** Free admission. Daily Apr–Sept 7am–7:15pm, Oct–Mar 7am–6.15pm. Métro: Estrangin-Préfecture. Bus: 60.

MuCEM (Museum of European and Mediterranean Civilizations) ★★

MUSEUM   Opened in summer 2013, the long-anticipated MuCEM is the first national gallery in France to be located outside of Paris. More than 250,000 objects have been collected from throughout the Mediterranean region and are exhibited here, along with local prints, photographs, and historical postcards. Architect Rudy Ricciotti designed the museum's contemporary form, which is encased in unique concrete lace. The premises encompass the 12th-century **Fort Saint-Jean,** its suspended gardens, and Michelin-starred-chef Gérard Passédat's primarily organic restaurant, **La Table du Môle** (www.passedat.fr).

1 esplanade du J4. www.mucem.org. $©$ **04-84-35-13-13.** Admission 5€ adults, 3€ seniors and students, free children 17 and under. Additional fee for temporary exhibitions. Summer Wed–Thurs and Sat–Mon 11am–7pm, Fri 11am–10pm; winter Wed–Thurs and Sat–Mon 11am–6pm, Fri 11am–10pm. Métro: Vieux-Port. Bus: 49, 60, or 82.

Musée Cantini ★ ART MUSEUM

Fully renovated in honor of Marseille's European Capital of Culture 2013 festivities, this 17th-century *hôtel particulier* (private mansion) organizes outstanding modern art exhibitions. Recent shows have been dedicated to Chilean surrealist Roberto Matta and native Marseillaise sculptor César. The museum also houses a permanent collection, particularly strong on masterpieces (by Picasso, Dufy, de Staël, Ernst, and others) created during the first half of the 20th century.

19 rue Grignan. $©$ **04-91-54-77-75.** Admission 5€ adults, 3€ seniors, free for children 17 and under. Tues–Sun 11am–6pm. Métro: Estrangin/Préfecture.

Musée des Beaux-Arts ★ MUSEUM

Reopened in 2013 after extensive renovations, the 150-year-old Museum of Fine Arts is Marseille's oldest exhibition venue. Its permanent collection ranges from 16th-century Italian works to 19th-century French masterpieces, including Rodin's sculpture "La Voix Intérieure" ("The Inner Voice"). Summer 2013 saw the museum dedicated entirely to the blockbuster show "Le Grand Atelier du Midi: Van Gogh a Bonnard," held in tandem with the **Musée Granet** in Aix (p. 179).

Palais Longchamp. http://musee-des-beaux-arts.marseille.fr. $©$ **04-91-14-59-30.** Admission varies according to exhibition. Fri–Wed 9am–7pm; Thurs noon–11pm. Métro: Longchamp. Tram: Longchamp.

La Marseillaise

Few know that France's national anthem was actually composed in Strasbourg. Originally titled "War Song of the Army of the Rhine," it was written in 1 night by army captain Claude-Joseph Rouget de Lisle in 1792. That same year, revolutionaries from Marseille (who had been given printed copies) marched into Paris singing it. In their honor, the song became known as "La Marseillaise" and was quickly adopted as the rallying cry of the French Revolution. It was officially declared the national anthem of France in 1795, only to be banned by Napoleon during the Empire, Louis XVIII in 1815, and Napoleon III in 1830. The anthem was reinstated for good in 1879.

Outlying Attractions

You can take a 25-minute ferry ride to the **Château d'If** (http://if.monuments-nation aux.fr), a national monument built by François I as a fortress to defend Marseille. Alexandre Dumas used it as a setting for the fictional adventures of "The Count of Monte Cristo." The château is open daily May 16 to September 16 9:30am to 6:10pm; September 17 to March 31 Tuesday to Sunday 9:30am to 4:45pm; and April 1 to May 31 daily 9:30am to 4:45pm. Entrance to the island is 5.50€ adults, free children 17 and under. Boats leave approximately every 45 to 60 minutes, depending on the season; the round-trip transfer is 10€. For information, contact the **Frioul If Express** (www.frioul-if-express.com; ✆ **04-96-11-03-50**; Métro: Vieux-Port).

Organized Tours

One of the easiest ways to see Marseille's centrally located monuments is aboard the fleet of open-top **Le Grand Tour Buses** (www.marseillelegrandtour.com; ✆ **04-91-91-05-82**; Métro: Vieux-Port). You can hop off at any of 13 different stops en route and back on to the next bus in the day's sequence, usually arriving between 1 and 2 hours later, depending on the season. The buses run four to eight times a day during each month except January. A 1-day pass costs 18€ adults and 16€ seniors and students with ID; the fare for children ages 4 to 11 is 8€. Two-day passes are also available.

The motorized **Trains Touristiques de Marseille** (www.petit-train-marseille.com; ✆ **04-91-25-24-69**; Métro: Vieux-Port), or *petit-trains,* make circuits around town too. Year-round, train no. 1 drives a 75-minute round-trip to Basilique Notre-Dame-de-la-Garde and Basilique St-Victor. From April to mid-November, train no. 2 makes a 65-minute round-trip of old Marseille by way of the cathedral, Vieille Charité, and the Quartier du Panier. Both trains make a 30-minute stop for sightseeing en route. The trains depart from the quay just west of the Hôtel de Ville. The fare for train no. 1 is 8€ adults and 4€ children; train no. 2 is 1€ less for both.

Boat tours to the **Parc National des Calanques** are popular. Many tour operators with different prices and formulas (for example, three Calanques in 2 hr./22€, or eight in 3 hr./28€) can be found on the quai des Belges at the Vieux-Port.

Shopping

Only Paris and the French Riviera can compete with Marseille for its breadth and diversity of merchandise. Your best bet is a trip to the streets just southeast of the **Vieux-Port,** crowded with stores of all kinds.

Rue Paradis and **rue Saint Ferréol** have many of the same upscale fashion boutiques found in Paris, as well as a Galeries Lafayette, France's largest chain department store. For more bohemian wear, try **cours Julien** and **rue de la Tour** for richly brocaded and beaded items on offer in North African boutiques. **Le Panier** is now home to a vibrant range of unique boutiques. Try **5.7.2,** 23 rue du Panier (www.5-7-2. com; ✆ **06-07-14-62-92**) for 1950s to 1970s homewares, or **Les Baigneuses,** 3 rue de l'Eveche (www.lesbaigneuses.com; ✆ **09-52-68-67-64**), which sells a gorgeous range of retro-styled swimwear.

Navettes, small cookies that resemble boats, are a Marseillaise specialty. Flavored with secret ingredients that include orange zest and orange flower water, they were invented in 1791 and are still sold at **Le Four des Navettes,** 136 rue Sainte (www. fourdesnavettes.com; ✆ **04-91-33-32-12**), for around 8.50€ per dozen.

One of the region's most authentic fish markets at **Quai des Belges** (daily 8am– 1pm), on the old port, is partially sheltered under the new Norman Foster–designed

Ombrière mirrored canopy. On **cours Julien,** you'll find a market with fruits, vegetables, and other foods (Tues, Thurs, and Sat 8am–1pm); exclusively organic produce (Wed 8am–1pm); stamps (Sun 8am–1pm); and secondhand goods (3rd Sun of the month 8am–1pm).

Nightlife

For an amusing and relatively harmless exposure to the town's saltiness, walk around the **Vieux-Port,** where cafes and restaurants angle their sightlines for the best view of the harbor.

L'Escale Borély, avenue Pierre Mendès France, is 20 minutes south of the town center (take bus no. 83). With a dozen animated bars and cafés, plus restaurants of every possible ethnicity, you'll be spoiled for choice.

Marseille's dance clubs are habitually packed out, especially **Trolley Bus,** 24 quai de Rive-Neuve (www.letrolley.com; ℭ **04-91-54-30-45;** Métro: Vieux-Port), known for techno, house, hip-hop, jazz, and salsa. Equally buzzing is **l'Exit,** 12 quai de Rive-Neuve (ℭ **04-91-54-29-43;** Métro: Vieux-Port), a bar/disco with a terrace that profits from Marseille's sultry nights and two floors of seething nocturnal energy (happy hour starts at 5pm). The **New Can Can,** 3–7 rue Sénac (www.newcancan.com; ℭ **04-91-48-59-76;** Métro: Noailles), is a lively, sprawling bar and disco that identifies itself as a gay venue but attracts many straight folks too. It's open Friday through Sunday midnight until 7am.

For jazz right on the port, head to **La Caravelle,** 34 quai du Port (www.lacaravelle -marseille.com; ℭ **04-91-90-36-64;** Métro: Vieux-Port), an aperitif bar and dinner club that serves a different flavor almost every night, including *manouche,* the French gypsy style most associated with guitarist Django Reinhardt.

ÎLES D'HYÈRES ★★

39km (24 miles) SE of Toulon; 119km (74 miles) SW of Cannes

Bobbing off the French Riviera in the Mediterranean Sea, a small group of islands encloses the eastern boundary of Provence. During the Renaissance, they were coined the Îles d'Or (Golden Islands), named for the glow the rocks give off in sunlight. As might be expected, their location only half an hour from the French coast means the islands are often packed with tourists in summer—but there is still space on its breathtaking beaches for everyone.

If you have time for only one island, choose the beautiful, lively **Île de Porquerolles.** The **Île de Port-Cros** is quieter—and perhaps better for an overnight stay in order to take advantage of the great hiking, exploring, and snorkeling that would be too rushed for a 6-hour day trip. As for the **Île du Levant,** 80 percent belongs to the French army and is used for missile testing; the remainder is a nudist colony.

Essentials

GETTING TO ÎLE DE PORQUEROLLES Ferries leave from several points along the Côte d'Azur. The most frequent, cheapest, and shortest trip is from the harbor of La Tour Fondue on the peninsula of Giens, a 32km (20-mile) drive east of Toulon. Depending on the season, there are 5 to 19 departures per day. The round-trip fare for the 15-minute crossing is 19€ adults and 17€ children 4 to 10. For information, contact **TLV-TVM,** La Tour Fondue, Giens 83400 (www.tlv-tvm.com; ℭ **04-94-58-21-81**). **Bateliers de la Côte d'Azur** (www.bateliersdelacotedazur.com; ℭ **04-94-05-21-14**) and **Les Vedettes Île d'Or & Le Corsaire** (www.vedettesilesdor.fr; ✆ **04-94-71-01-02**) also offer services from La Londe-les-Maures and Le Lavandou respectively.

GETTING TO ÎLE DE PORT-CROS The most popular ferry route to the island is the 35-minute crossing that departs from Le Lavadou 3 to 7 times daily, depending on the season (27€ adults, 22€ children 4–12 round-trip). For information, contact **Les Vedettes Île d'Or & Le Corsaire** (see above). The **TLV-TVM** and **Bateliers de la Côte d'Azur** (see above) also service Île de Port-Cros. Some of the former's services travel onwards to Île de Levant.

VISITOR INFORMATION Other than temporary, summer-only kiosks that distribute brochures and advice near the ferry docks in Porquerolles and Port-Cros, there are no tourist bureaus on the islands. For further information, contact the **Office de Tourisme de Hyères, Bureau de Porquerolles,** Rotonde du Park Hôtel, av. de Belgique, Hyères (www.hyeres-tourisme.com; ✆ **04-94-58-33-76**). Information can also be found at www.porquerolles.com and www.portcrosparcnational.fr.

MAIL/POSTAGE & MONEY The post office, **La Poste,** place d'Armes, Porquerolles (✆ **36-31**), also has an ATM, but it's best to bring petty cash. Most establishments accept credit cards.

Exploring Île de Porquerolles ★★

Île de Porquerolles is the largest and westernmost of the Îles d'Hyères. It has a rugged south coast, but the northern strand, facing the mainland, boasts a handful of pristine white-sand beaches. The island is about 8km (5 miles) long and 2km (1¼ miles) wide, and is 4.8km (3 miles) from the mainland. The permanent population is only 400.

The island is said to receive 275 days of sunshine annually. The landscape is one of rocky capes, pine forests twisted by the mistral, sun-drenched vineyards, and pale ochre houses. It's best explored on foot or by bike (look for plenty of bike-rental agencies just behind the harbor). The **place d'Armes,** former site of the garrison, is home to several quaint cafes—your best bet for lunch if you're here for a day trip.

The island has a history of raids, attacks, and occupation by everyone from the Dutch and the English to the Turks and the Spaniards. Ten forts, some in ruins, testify to its fierce past. The most ancient is **Fort Ste-Agathe,** built in 1531 by François I. In time, it was a penal colony and a retirement center for soldiers of the colonial wars.

In 1971, the French government purchased a large part of the island and turned it into a national park. Indigenous trees such as fig, mulberry, and olive are protected, as well as plants that attract butterflies.

WHERE TO EAT & STAY

Hotel et Residence Les Medes (www.hotel-les-medes.fr) also offers good-value guest rooms and apartments.

Mas du Langoustier ★★ This Provençal-style hotel is far and away Porquerolles' most luxurious accommodation. Located on the island's western tip, it's set in a 40-hectare park shaded by eucalyptus and Aleppo pines, and overlooks a lovely pine-ringed bay. Elegant rooms are decorated with classic local textiles; many have their own private patio. And come evening time, there's no need to leave paradise. The onsite **Restaurant L'Olivier** (open to nonguests) is Michelin-starred: Prepare for unique pairings like steamed crayfish and fig ravioli or foie gras with hibiscus jelly.

www.langoustier.com. ✆ **04-94-58-30-09.** 50 units. 215€–310€ double; 335€–345€ suite; 320€–330€ apartment. Rates include half-board. Closed Oct to late Apr. **Amenities:** 2 restaurants; bar; babysitting; outdoor pool; tennis court; free Wi-Fi.

Exploring Île de Port-Cros ★★

The most mountainous island of the archipelago, Port-Cros has been France's smallest national park since 1963. It's just 5km (3 miles) long and 2km (1¼ miles) wide. It's blanketed with beautiful beaches, pine forests, and subtropical vegetation (birders flock here to observe nearly 100 different species). A hiker's paradise, it also has a number of well-marked trails. The most popular and scenic is the easy, 1-hour *sentier des plantes*. The more adventurous and athletic take the 10km (6¼-mile) *circuit de Port-Man* (and pack their lunch). There is even a 274m (899-ft.) "underwater trail" along the coast where you can snorkel past laminated signs identifying the plants and fish you'll see.

WHERE TO EAT & STAY

Le Manoir de Port-Cros Port-Cros's only hotel sits within an 18th-century whitewashed building. Accommodation may be simple—crisp white sheets, oversized copper vases, terra-cotta tiled floors—but guests stay here to truly switch off. Paddle in the pool, head out for a hike, or simply amble the surrounding palm and eucalyptus-studded gardens. Rates are half-board, although plenty of day-trippers visit for the restaurant's hearty three-course lunch (58€).

www.hotel-lemanoirportcros.com. *©* **04-94-05-90-52.** 21 units. 165€–265€ double; 210€–240€ suite; 230€–265€ bungalows for 4. Closed Nov–Mar. **Amenities:** Restaurant; bar; outdoor pool; room service; free Wi-Fi in common areas.

THE FRENCH RIVIERA

by Tristan Rutherford

The fabled real estate known as the French Riviera, also called the Côte d'Azur (Azure Coast), ribbons for 200km (125 miles) along the sun-kissed Mediterranean. The region has long attracted artists and jetsettters alike with its clear skies, blue waters, and carefree cafe culture. Chic, sassy, and incredibly sexy, the Riviera can be explored by bus, train, boat, bikes, Segway, electric car, or in a dozen novel ways.

A trail of modern artists captivated by the region's light and setting has left a rich heritage: Matisse at Vence, Cocteau at Villefranche, Léger at Biot, Renoir at Cagnes, and Picasso at Antibes and seemingly everywhere else. The finest collection of contemporary artworks is at the Foundation Maeght in St-Paul-de-Vence. New museums dedicated to Jean Cocteau in Menton and Pierre Bonnard near Cannes offer a vivid introduction to the Riviera's storied art scene.

A century ago, winter and spring were considered high season on the Riviera. In recent decades, July and August have become the most crowded months, and reservations are imperative. The region basks in more than 300 days of sun per year, and even December and January are often clement and bright.

The ribbonlike corniche roads stretch across the western Riviera from Nice to Menton, scenic stars in scores of films including Cary Grant's "To Catch a Thief" and Robert de Niro's "Ronin." The lower road, the 32km (20-mile) Corniche Inférieure, takes in the resorts of Villefranche, Cap-Ferrat, Beaulieu, Monaco, and Cap-Martin. The 31km (19-mile) Moyenne Corniche (Middle Road) winds in and out of mountain tunnels and takes in the picture-perfect village of Eze. Napoleon built the Grande Corniche—the most panoramic roadway—in 1806. La Turbie is the principal town along the 32km (20-mile) stretch, which reaches more than 480m (1,574 ft.) high at Col d'Eze.

ST-TROPEZ ★★★

874km (542 miles) S of Paris; 76km (47 miles) SW of Cannes

This sun-kissed town has an air of hedonism. But Tropezian style is blissfully understated—it's not in-your-face. St-Tropez attracts artists, musicians, models, writers, and an A-lister movie colony each summer, with a flamboyant parade of humanity trailing behind. In winter it morphs back into a boho fishing village, albeit one with modern art galleries and some of the best restaurants along the coast.

The Brigitte Bardot movie "And God Created Woman" put St-Tropez on the tourist map. Droves of decadent tourists baring almost all on the peninsula's white-sand beaches trailed in her wake. In 1995, Bardot pronounced St-Tropez dead, "squatted by a lot of no-goods, drugheads, and villains." But 1997 saw her return, followed in recent years by celebrity A-listers including Keith Richards, David Beckham, Paris Hilton, Jay-Z, and Beyoncé.

Essentials

ARRIVING The nearest rail station is in St-Raphaël, a neighboring coastal resort. **Boats** depart (www.bateauxsaintraphael.com; ℃ **04-94-95-17-46**) from its Vieux Port for St-Tropez (trip time: 1 hr.) five times a day in high summer, reducing to once- or twice-daily sailings in winter. The one-way fare is 15€. Year-round, 10 to 15 Varlib **buses** per day leave from the Gare Routière in St-Raphaël (www.varlib.fr; ℃ **04-94-24-60-00**) for St-Tropez. The trip takes 1½ to 2 hours, depending on the bus and the traffic, which during midsummer is usually horrendous. A one-way ticket is 3€. Buses also run from Toulon train station 56km (35 miles) away.

If you **drive,** note that parking in St-Tropez is tricky, especially in summer. For parking, follow the signs for **Parking des Lices** (℃ **04-94-97-34-46**), beneath place des Lices, or **Parking du Nouveau Port,** on waterfront avenue Charles de Gaulle (℃ **04-94-97-74-99**). To get here from **Cannes,** drive southwest along the coastal highway (D559), turning east when you see signs to St-Tropez.

VISITOR INFORMATION The **Office de Tourisme** is on quai Jean-Jaurès (www.ot-saint-tropez.com; ℃ **08-92-68-48-28**). Note that it charges 2€ for a town map. Meanies.

[FastFACTS] ST-TROPEZ

ATMs/Banks **Crédit Agricole,** 17 place des Lices (℃ **32-25**).

Internet Access There's free WiFi—as well as a handy table and stools—at the **Casino Supermarket,** av. Genéral Leclerc.

Mail & Postage **La Poste,** rue de la Poste (℃ **36-31**).

Pharmacies **Pharmacie du Port,** 9 quai Suffren (℃ **04-94-97-00-06**).

Where to Stay

Hôtel Byblos ★★★ Opened in 1967 on a hill above the harbor, this hamlet of pastel-hued, Provençal-style houses is opulence personified. Inspired by the legendery Phoenician city of the same name, Byblos is favored by visiting celebrities, rock stars, aristocrats, and the über-rich. Its patios and private spaces are splashed with antiques, rare objects, bubbling fountains, and ancient olive trees. Rooms range in size from medium to mega; some units have such special features as four-posters with furry spreads or sunken whirlpool tubs. In 2013, Alain Ducasse's brand-new restaurant **Rivea** (℃ **04-94-56-68-20**) opened on the premises. Ingredients, used to create tapas-style sharing dishes, are sourced exclusively from the French and Italian Rivieras. It's the best place to sample Brangelina's exclusive Château Miraval wine.

20 av. Paul Signac. www.byblos.com. ℃ **04-94-56-68-00.** 96 units. 420€–1,180€ double; 840€–2,960€ suite. Parking 35€. Closed Nov to mid Apr. **Amenities:** 2 restaurants; 1 bar; nightclub; babysitting; concierge; exercise room; massage; outdoor pool; room service; sauna; spa; free Wi-Fi.

The Riviera

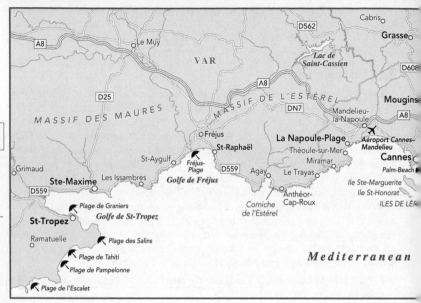

Hôtel Les Palmiers ★ In a town packed with pricey accommodation options, this friendly, family-run hotel is a real find. Apart from its fanatasic location—directly astride place des Lices in the center of St-Tropez—Les Palmiers boasts compact Provençal-style rooms and a sun-dappled courtyard garden. Part of the hotel dates from the late 18th century and gives the place a cozy, vintage feel.

24–26 bd. Vasserot (place des Lices). www.hotel-les-palmiers.com. ℂ **04-94-97-01-61.** 25 units. 80€–260€ double. **Amenities:** Bar; free Wi-Fi.

Pastis Hôtel-St-Tropez ★★ This portside Provençal house feels more like a sophisticated, eclectic home than a hotel—albeit one decorated with a phenomenal eye for design. British owners John and Pauline Larkin have arranged their private collection of Matisse prints, vintage photographs, 1970s framed album artwork, and Provençal antiques in and around the guest-only lounge and inspired guestrooms surrounding the courtyard swimming pool. Each unique unit is spacious yet intimate and possesses its own balcony or breakfast terrace. Highly recommended.

75 av. du Général Leclerc. www.pastis-st-tropez.com. ℂ **04-98-12-56-50.** 10 units. 175€–675€ double. Free parking. Closed mid-Nov to Dec. **Amenities:** Bar; outdoor pool; free Wi-Fi.

Where to Eat

St-Tropez's dining scene is both expensive and exclusive—particularly during the summer season. Reserve well in advance; alternatively be prepared to dine very early or very late. In addition to the suggestions below, the long-established Moroccan restaurant **Salama,** 1 rue Tisserands (ℂ **04-94-97-59-62**), cooks up a fine selection of couscous, pastilla, and tajines; **Chez Madeleine,** 4 place aux Herbes (℗ **04-94-96-59-81**), behind the fish market, serves stellar seafood platters; and **Barbarac,** 2 rue Allard (www.barbarac.fr; ℗ **04-94-97-67-83**), scoops up the finest ice cream in town.

Auberge des Maures ★★ PROVENÇAL   A local favorite since it opened in 1931, this vintage restaurant is tucked into one of the Old Town's rambling back streets. Over the years, celebrities from Charlie Chaplin to Colette have dined here—and with good reason. The seasonal menu is littered with southern French specialties, including artichokes *à la barigoule, gigot d'agneau* lamb with rosemary confit, and *petits farcis* (stuffed vegetables). The restaurant is decorated in regional murals (the St-Tropez bay, rolling fields of lavender) and lashings of traditional Provencal fabrics; in summertime the roof rolls back to reveal the star-studded sky.

4 rue du Docteur Boutin. www.aubergedesmaures.fr. ℗ **04-94-97-01-50.** Reservations recommended. Main courses 42€–60€; fixed-price menu 52€. Daily 7:30pm–1am. Closed mid-Nov to Mar.

Pizzeria Bruno ★ ITALIAN   Proving that not all good meals in St-Tropez have to break the bank, this casual joint has been turning out thin, crispy, wood-fired pizzas since 1959. Even Bardot was a regular. The menu includes a handful of creative salads, pasta dishes, and grilled meats. Note that the restaurant's copious wood-paneled and overly snug seating isn't the comfiest—but the atmosphere is among the liveliest in town.

2 rue de l'Eglise. ℗ **04-94-97-05-18.** Main courses 11€–18€. Daily noon–2pm and 7–11pm. Closed Oct–Apr.

Exploring St-Tropez

During summertime, St-Tropez's pleasure port is trimmed with superyachts, each one berthing stern-to after a day of hedonistic excess at nearby Plage de Pampelonne. Yacht owners, their lucky guests, spectators, and celebrity-seekers all intermingle along the town's chic quays.

In the Old Town, one of the most interesting streets is **rue de la Miséricorde.** It's lined with stone houses that hold boutiques and evokes medieval St-Tropez better than any other in town. At the corner of rue Gambetta is **Chapelle de la Miséricorde,** with a blue, green, and gold tile roof. Towering above town is the **Citadelle (✆ 04-94-54-84-14),** a fortified castle complete with drawbridges and stunning views across the Bay of St-Tropez. In July 2013, a brand-new **Maritime Museum** opened within the Citadelle, charting famous local historical figures and their travels around the world. From April to September, the entire complex is open daily from 10am to 6:30pm; October through March from 10am to 12:30pm and 1:30pm to 5:30pm. Admission is 3€; entrance is free for those 8 and under.

Musée de l'Annonciade (Musée St-Tropez) ★★★ MUSEUM   Set in a 16th-century chapel just off the harbor, this petite museum showcases a collection of superb post-Impressionist paintings (1890–1950). Many of the artists, including St-Tropez's adopted son, Paul Signac, painted the port of St-Tropez, a backdrop that lies right outside the building. The museum includes such masterpieces as Bonnard's Nu devant la Cheminée as well as artworks by Matisse, Braque, Dufy, Marquet, and Derain. Temporary shows, like recent exhibits showcasing Modigliani drawings or works by 20th-century artists from Marseille (the Ecole Marseillaise), are held on the ground floor.

Place Grammont. ✆ **04-94-17-84-10.** Admission 6€ adults, 4€ children 11 and under. July–Oct Wed–Mon 10am–noon and 2–6pm. Closed Nov.

Outdoor Activities

BEACHES   The hottest Riviera beaches are at St-Tropez. The best for families are closest to the center, including **Plage de la Bouillabaisse, Plage des Graniers,** and **Plage des Salins.** More daring is the 5km (3-mile) crescent of **Plage de Pampelonne,** about 10km (6¼ miles) from St-Tropez. Here around 35 hedonistic beach clubs dot the sand. Overtly decadent is **Club 55** (www.club55.fr; ✆ **04-94-55-55-55),** a former Bardot hangout, while the American-run **Nikki Beach** (www.nikkibeach.com; ✆ **04-94-79-82-04)** is younger and more understated, if painfully chic. Gay-friendly **Aqua Club (✆ 04-94-79-84-35)** and bare-all **Plage de Tahiti** (www.tahiti-beach.com; ✆ **04-94-97-18-02)** are extremely welcoming.

You'll need a car, bike, or scooter to get from town to Plage de Pampelonne. Parking is around 10€ for the day. More than anywhere else on the Riviera, topless bathing is the norm.

BOATING   In St-Tropez port, **Octopussy** (www.octopussy.fr; ✆ **04-94-56-53-10)** rents boats 5 to 16m (16–52 ft.) long. Larger ones come with a captain at the helm. Prices begin at 320€ per day.

DIVING   Multilingual scuba tuition and equipment hire is available from the **European Diving School** (www.europeandiving.com; ✆ **04-94-79-90-37),** on Plage de Pampelonne. Regular dives, including all equipment, cost 38€.

Map legend:

HOTELS ■
Hôtel Byblos **8**
Hôtel Les
Palmiers **7**
Pastis Hôtel-
St-Tropez **4**

RESTAURANTS ◆
Auberge des
Maures **6**
Barbarac **3**
Chez Madeleine **2**
Pizzeria Bruno **1**
Rivea **8**
Salama **5**

Information ⓘ

Golfe de St-Tropez

Shopping

St-Tropez is awash in stylish shops. The merchandise is Mediterranean, breezy, and sophisticated. Dotted throughout the town's *triangle d'or,* the rough triangle formed by place de la Garonne, rue François Sibilli and place des Lices, chic labels include Hermès, Sonia Rykiel, and Louis Vuitton. For the past 4 years, a summer pop-up shop has occupied the old Hotel la Mistralée at 1 av. du Général Leclerc, while nearby, Michelin-starred chef Yannick Alléno dishes up delights at **Dior des Lices,** 13 rue François Sibilli, the fashion house's own summertime pop-up eatery. There are also scores of unique boutiques around the Vieille Ville (Old Town), including **Chichou 88,** 27 rue Georges Clémenceau (ⓒ **04-94-96-48-93**), which stocks Indian-inspired homewares and neon handbags; **Truffaux Chapelier,** 44 rue de la Citadelle (ⓒ **04-94-45-33-14**), packed with Panama hats; and **K. Jacques,** 25 rue Allard (www.lestropeziennes. com; ⓒ **04-94-97-41-50**), with its iconic *tropéziennes* sandals. Place des Lices hosts an excellent **outdoor market,** Marché Provençal, with food, clothes, and *brocante,* on Tuesday and Saturday mornings.

FRENCH boules

A game of *pétanque*, or French boules, is seriously cool for kids. Hop to **Le Café** (www.lecafe.fr; ℂ **04-94-97-44-69**), one of many alfresco bars in place des Lices, and request a handful of *pétanque* boules to toss around the tree-dappled square. The game was created down the coast and is about as Provençal as it gets. Pick up some tips by watching the locals. Games begin with a toss of the jack, or *bouchon*. Teams then take turns to throw. Whoever is farthest away keeps trying to get closest to the *bouchon*, with any remaining balls tossed in at the end. A point is awarded for each steel ball that's closer to the jack than any balls from the opposing team.

Nightlife

On a lower level of the Hôtel Byblos' grounds, **Les Caves du Roy,** 20 avenue Paul-Signac (www.lescavesduroy.com; ℂ **04-94-56-68-00**), is the most self-consciously chic nightclub in St-Tropez. Entrance is free, but drink prices are eye-wateringly high. It's open nightly from Easter to early October from 11:30pm until dawn. Brand-new for 2013 was **White 1921,** place des Lices (www.white1921.com; ℂ **04-94-45-50-50**), a champagne and cocktail bar set within a jasmine-cloaked courtyard garden. **Le Papagayo,** port de St-Tropez (www.papagayo-st-tropez.com; ℂ **04-94-97-95-95**), is one of the largest nightclubs in town. The decor is inspired by the psychedelic 1960s. Entrance is around 20€ and includes one drink, although those dining at the attached restaurant can routinely sneak in for free. Adjacent to Le Papagayo is **Le VIP Room,** in the Résidence du Nouveau-Port (www.st-tropez. viproom.fr; ℂ **06-38-83-83-83**), a younger yet similarly chic version of Les Caves du Roy. Paris Hilton and Snoop Dogg have been known to drop by. Cocktails hover around the 20€ mark.

Under new ownership in 2013, **Le Pigeonnier,** 19 rue de la Ponche (ℂ **06-33-58-92-45**), rocks, rolls, and welcomes a mostly gay or lesbian crowd between 20 and 50. **L'Esquinade,** 2 rue de Four (ℂ **04-94-56-26-31**), equally gay-friendly, is the habitual sweaty follow-up club.

Below the Hôtel Sube in the port, **Café de Paris** (www.cafedeparis.fr; ℂ **04-94-97-00-56**), is one of the most popular—and friendly—hangouts in town. It has 1900s-style globe lights, masses of artificial flowers, and a long zinc bar. **Café Sénéquier,** quai Jean Jaurès (www.senequier.com; ℂ **04-94-97-20-20**), is historic, venerable, snobbish by day, and off-puttingly stylish by night.

CANNES ★★★

905km (561 miles) S of Paris; 163km (101 miles) E of Marseille; 26km (16 miles) SW of Nice

When Coco Chanel came here and got a suntan, returning to Paris bronzed, she shocked the milk-white society ladies—who quickly began to copy her. Today the bronzed bodies, clad in nearly nonexistent swimsuits, line the beaches of this chic resort and continue the late fashion designer's example. A block back from the famed promenade de la Croisette are the boutiques, bars, and bistros that make Cannes the Riviera's capital of cool.

Essentials

ARRIVING By **train,** Cannes is 10 minutes from Antibes, 30 minutes from Nice, and 45 minutes from Monaco. The TGV from Paris reaches Cannes in an incredibly scenic 5 hours. The one-way fare from Paris is 55€ to 125€, although advance purchase bargains can be has for as low as 26€. For rail information and schedules, visit www.voyages-sncf. com or call ℂ **36-35. Lignes d'Azur** (www.lignesdazur.com; ℂ **08-10-06-10-06**) provides bus service from Cannes' Gare Routière (place Bernard Cornut Gentille) to Antibes every 20 minutes during the day (trip time: 25 min.). The one-way fare is 1.50€.

The **Nice international airport** (www.nice.aeroport.fr; ℂ **08-20-42-33-33**) is a 30-minute drive east. **Buses** pick up passengers at the airport every 30 minutes during the day (hourly at other times) and drop them at Cannes' Gare Routière. The one-way fare is 20€.

By **car** from Marseille, take A51 north to Aix-en-Provence, continuing along A8 east to Cannes. From Nice, follow A8 or the coastal D6007 southwest to Cannes.

VISITOR INFORMATION The **Office de Tourisme** is at 1 bd. de la Croisette (www.cannes-destination.fr; ℂ **04-92-99-84-22**).

SPECIAL EVENTS Cannes is at its most frenzied in mid-May during the **International Film Festival** (www.festival-cannes.com) at the Palais des Festivals, on promenade de la Croisette. It attracts not only film stars (you can palm the cement molds of their handprints outside the Palais des Festivals), but also seemingly every photographer in the world. You have a better chance of being named prime minister of France than you do attending one of the major screenings, although if you're lucky, you may be able to swing tickets to screenings of one of the lesser films. (Hotel rooms and tables at restaurants are equally scarce during the festival.) But the people-watching is absolutely fabulous!

Getting Around

ON FOOT Cannes' small town center is a labyrinth of one-ways and serious traffic—which makes it best explored on foot.

BY BICYCLE & MOTOR SCOOTER Despite the summertime commotion, the flat landscapes between Cannes and satellite resorts such as La Napoule and Juan-les-Pins are well suited for bikes and motor scooters. At **Daniel Location,** 7 rue de Suffern (www.daniel-location-2roues.com; ℂ **04-93-99-90-30**), *vélos tout terrain,* or VTT (mountain bikes) cost 16€ a day. Motorized bikes and scooters cost from 30€ per day. For larger motorbikes, you must present a valid driver's license. Another bike shop is **Mistral Location,** 4 rue Georges Clémenceau (www.mistral-location.com; ℂ **04-93-39-33-60**), which charges 16€ per day.

BY CAR The Cannes Tourist Office website offers a downloadable document (under "Cannes Practical," then "Useful Information") listing all of the town's **public parking lots** and their hourly fees.

BY TAXI Allô Taxi Cannes (www.allo-taxis-cannes.com; ℂ **08-90-71-22-27**).

BY PUBLIC TRANSPORT Bus Azur (www.busazur.info; ℂ **08-25-82-55-99**) operates all public transport in and around Cannes. There's little need for public transport in the city center—although the open-top nr.8, which runs along the seafront from the port in the west to the Palm Beach peninsula in the east, makes for a fun and scenic ride. Tickets cost 1.50€ and can be purchased directly aboard any bus.

[FastFACTS] CANNES

ATMs/Banks   Banks are dotted throughout the city, including more than a dozen along the central rue d'Antibes.

Dentists   For emergency dental services, contact **SOS Dentaire** (✆ **04-93-68-28-00**).

Doctors & Hospitals   **Hopital de Cannes,** 15 av. Broussailles (www.ch-cannes.fr; ✆ **04-93-69-70-00**).

Internet Access   Cannes is in the process of blanketing the city with free Wi-Fi. The first area with coverage is the Jardins de l'Hotel de Ville, just behind the port; the network is "Cannes sans fil."

Mail & Postage   **La Poste,** 22 rue Bivouac Napoléon (✆ **36-31**).

Pharmacies   **Pharmacie du Casino,** 9 bis square Mérimée (✆ **04-93-39-25-48**).

Where to Stay

Five Seas Hôtel ★★   The newest, coolest hotel in Cannes harks back to a Gatsby era of Art Deco furnishings and no-limits lavishness. The style is Louis Vuitton meets vintage liner. The furniture design is based on classic traveling cases, albeit with Apple computers and Nespresso machines thrown into the mix. New for 2013 is the bespoke **Carita spa.** The top-floor terrace features a small infinity pool, a cocktail bar, and linen-shaded sun loungers. It's also the location of the acclaimed **Sea Sens** modern Mediterranean restaurant (fixed-price lunch 19€–39€ Tues–Fri; dinner menu 40€–120€ Thurs–Sat) under the direction of head chef Arnaud Tabarec. And boy, what a view it has. Desserts come courtesy of 28-year-old World Pastry Champion Jérôme de Oliveira, who also maintains **Intuitions by J,** a tea and pastry shop on the ground floor.

1 rue Notre Dame. www.five-seas-hotel-cannes.com. ✆ **04-63-36-05-05.** 45 units. 295€–805€ double; from 595€ suite. **Amenities:** Restaurant; bar; concierge; outdoor pool; room service; spa; free Wi-Fi.

Grand Hyatt Hotel Martinez ★★★   The Martinez has been the socialite hub of the South of France for a century. The great and good have marched through its revolving doors including—during the 2013 Cannes Film Festival—Eva Longoria, Nicole Kidman, and Steven Spielberg. This Art Deco masterpiece is more than just an ultra-luxe hotel. Nonguests can mingle with celebrities in the **l'Amiral** cocktail bar, bathe next to A-listers in the **ZPlage** beach club, or dine alongside minor royalty in one of the finest restaurants in the South of France, **La Palme d'Or** (p. 199). Hotel management was taken over by Hyatt in 2013, which ushered in a sleek refurbishment and a bicycle-sharing scheme—and what deliciously cool bikes they are.

73 bd. de la Croisette. cannesmartinez.grand.hyatt.com. ✆ **04-93-90-12-34.** 409 units. 750€–990€ double; from 3,300€ suite. Parking 40€. **Amenities:** 3 summer restaurants, 2 winter restaurants; bar; babysitting; private beach; free bikes; children's center; concierge; exercise room; outdoor pool; room service; sauna; spa; free Wi-Fi.

Hôtel Pruly ★★   New on the local scene, this delightful hotel spills from a renovated century-old townhouse. Charming rooms are decorated in bright colors and Provençal textiles; some boast traditional terra-cotta *tomette* floors or private balconies. An afternoon nap on a sun lounger in the hotel's palm-splashed private garden is a welcome respite from Cannes' summertime crowds. It's located just behind the train station.

32 bd. d'Alsace. www.hotel-pruly.com. ✆ **04-93-38-41-28.** 12 units. 70€–200€ double; 130€–245€ triple. **Amenities:** Garden; free Wi-Fi.

Where to Eat

Cannes' dining scene is all-encompassing: expect to stumble across everything from Michelin-starred gastronomy to traditional Provençal peasant cuisine. Restaurants are scattered across the city center, with a particularly heavy concentration around Le Suquet, Cannes' Old Town.

EXPENSIVE

La Palme d'Or ★★★ MODERN FRENCH Double-Michelin-starred chef Christian Sinicropi has presided over this theater of fine dining for more than a decade. Yet his level of innovation knows no bounds. Think algae lollipops, flavored smoke, herb perfume. Guests are greeted at the table by the man himself. Diners are then taken on an intensely seasonal 5- to 10-course gastronomic journey in a dining room so rococo that even Liberace would feel at home. Sinicropi also serves the Cannes Film Festival jury a special set dinner each spring. Spellbinding dishes created for recent festival presidents, like Tim Burton and Woody Allen, can be sampled from the menu. Unforgettable.

In the Grand Hyatt Hotel Martinez, 73 bd. de la Croisette. cannesmartinez.grand.hyatt.com. ℂ **04-92-98-74-14.** Reservations required. Jacket and tie recommended. Main courses 58€–82€; fixed-price menu 69€–185€. Tues–Sat 12:30–2pm and 8–10pm. Closed Jan–Feb.

Le Park 45 ★★★ MEDITERRANEAN One of the most inventive—and least expensive—Michelin-starred restaurants on the Riviera is run by one of the coast's youngest chefs, baby-faced Sebastien Broda. Nicknamed the "Petit Prince de la Croisette," Broda scooped up his first Michelin star before the age of 30, after a career at La Palme d'Or in Cannes and L'Amandier in Mougins, two dens of fine Riviera dining. Locally grown vegetables and Atlantic seafood sparkle with additions of yuzu condiment, ponzu cream, Parmesan bouillon, and zingy Granny Smith apple *jus*. Surrounding Le Park 45 is the modernist splendor of **Le Grand Hotel** (www.grand-hotel-cannes. com; ℂ **04-93-38-15-15**). Originally the first hotel on the Croisette, this current 1960s incarnation boasts the best sea views in Cannes and perfectly preserved period features—from funky plastic telephones to Art Decl lampshades. Prices run 140€ to 500€ for a double and from 450€ for a suite, including free Wi-Fi.

In Le Grand Hotel, 45 bd. de la Croisette. ℂ **04-93-38-15-15.** Reservations recommended. Main courses 22€–35€; fixed-price lunch 50€, dinner 50€–110€. Daily midday–2pm and 7:30–10pm.

MODERATE

La Table du Chef ★ FRENCH/PROVENÇAL Just off Cannes' premier shopping street, rue d'Antibes, this unassuming little bistro serves up some of the city's tastiest cuisine. Chef Bruno Gensdarme (who spent almost 20 years working alongside superchef Guy Savoy in Paris) puts his own spin on traditional French dishes, such as Muscadet-infused rabbit terrine, or eggplant *millefeuilles* drizzled in goat's cheese cream and olives. Picky eaters beware: Menus are either fixed or offer very limited choice.

5 rue Jean Daumas. ℂ **04-93-68-27-40.** Reservations recommended. Fixed-price menu 18€–39€. Tues–Sat noon–2pm; Thurs–Sat 7–10pm.

INEXPENSIVE

Aux Bons Enfants ★ PROVENÇAL You could easily miss this old-fashioned eatery, tucked among a crowd of mediocre tourist-targeted restaurants. But what an oversight that would be. Family-run for three generations, the authentic Aux Bons Enfants today is headed up by Chef Luc Giorsetti. Dishes are traditional: *daube de* *canard,* slow-cooked *duck à la niçoise;* zucchini flower fritters; or house-cured salmon gravlax. Seasonal ingredients are sourced each morning from Marché Forville, just around the corner. Note that the restaurant has no telephone and does not accept reservations or credit cards.

80 rue Meynadier. www.aux-bons-enfants.com. No telephone; no reservations. Main courses 16€–23€; fixed-price menus 22€. No credit cards. Tues–Sat noon–2pm and 7–10pm.

Exploring Cannes

Far and away, Cannes' most famous street is the **promenade de la Croisette**—or simply La Croisette—which curves along the coast. It's lined by grand hotels (some dating from the 19th c.), boutiques, and exclusive beach clubs. It's also home to temporary exhibition space **La Malmaison,** 47 La Croisette (✆ **04-97-06-44-90**), which holds three major modern art shows—featuring artists ranging from Miró to Picasso—each year. It's open Tuesday to Sunday July to mid-September 11am to 8pm, and mid-September to mid-April Tuesday to Sunday 10am to 1pm and 2 to 6pm. Above the harbor, the Old Town of Cannes sits on Suquet Hill, where visitors can climb the 14th-century **Tour de Suquet.**

Musée Bonnard ★★ ART MUSEUM   The only museum in the world dedicated to the Impressionist painter Pierre Bonnard is located 3km (1¾ miles) north of Cannes, in the suburb of Le Cannet. Portraits, sculptures, and sketches on display in this petite museum were created primarily between 1922 and 1947, the period during which the artist was a local resident. The museum's audio guide comes embedded inside an iPod Touch.

16 bd. Sidi Carnot, Le Cannet. www.museebonnard.fr. ✆ **04-93-94-06-06.** Admission 5€–7€ adults, 3.50€–5€ ages 12–18, free for children 11 and under. June–Sept Tues–Sun 10am–8pm (Thurs until 9pm); Oct–May Tues–Sun 10am–6pm (Thurs until 8pm). Closed 3 wks. in Jan. Bus nrs 1 and 4 from Cannes city center.

Musée de la Castre ★ MUSEUM   Perched above Cannes' Old Town within the medieval Château de la Castre, this museum focuses primarily on ethnographic finds from around the world. Spears from the South Seas and Tibetan masks are interspersed with Sumerian cuneiform tablets and 19th-century paintings of the Riviera. Many visitors, however, will be most impressed by the astounding views from the museum's viewing tower—accessed via 109 steeps steps. The shady Mediterranean gardens, just outside the museum's entrance, are a welcome respite for tired sightseers.

Le Suquet. ✆ **04-93-38-55-26.** Admission 6€ adults, 3€ ages 18–25, free for children under 17. July–Aug daily 10am–7pm (Wed until 9pm); Sept and Apr–June Tues–Sun 10am–1pm and 2–6pm (June and Sept Wed 10am–1pm and 2–9pm); Oct–Mar Tues–Sun 10am–1pm and 2–5pm.

Organized Tours

One of the best ways to get your bearings in Cannes is to climb aboard the **Petit Train touristique de Cannes** (www.cannes-petit-train.com; ✆ **06-22-61-25-76**). The vehicles operate every day from 9 or 10am to between 7 and 11pm, depending on the season. Three itineraries are offered: Modern Cannes, with a ride along La Croisette and its side streets (35 min.); Historical Cannes, which weaves through the narrow streets of Le Suquet (35 min.); or the Big Tour, a combination of the two (1 hr.). All trains depart from outside the Palais des Festivals every 30 to 60 minutes. Shorter tours cost 7€ for adults and 3€ for children aged 3 to 10; the Big Tour costs 10€ for adults and 5€ for children aged 3 to 10.

Outdoor Activities

BEACHES   Beachgoing in Cannes has more to do with exhibitionism than actual swimming. **Plage de la Croisette** extends between the Vieux Port and the Port Canto. The beaches along this billion-dollar stretch of sand are *payante,* meaning entrance costs between 15€ to 30€. You don't need to be a guest of the Martinez, say, to use the beaches associated with a high-end hotel (see "Where to Stay," above), and Cannes has heaps of buzzing beach clubs dotted around, including sassy **3.14 Beach** (www.314cannes.com; © **04-93-94-25-43**). Why should you pay an entry fee at all? Well, the fee includes a full day's use of a mattress, a chaise longue (the seafront is more pebbly than sandy), and a parasol, as well as easy access to freshwater showers. There are also outdoor restaurants and bars (some with organic menus, others with gourmet burgers and sushi) where no one minds if you dine in your swimsuit. Every beach allows topless bathing. Looking for a free public beach without chaises or parasols? Head for **Plage du Midi,** just west of the Vieux Port, or **Plage Gazagnaire,** just east of the Port Canto. Here you'll find families with children and lots of RV-type vehicles parked nearby.

BOATING   Several companies around Cannes's Vieux Port rent boats of any size, with or without a crew, for a day, a week, or even longer. An outfit known for short-term rentals of small motorcraft is **Elco Marine,** 110 bd. du Midi (www.elcomarine.fr; © **04-93-47-12-62**). For kayak rental and guided tours of the coastline by canoe, try **SeaFirst,** Place Franklin Roosevelt (www.seafirst.fr; © **04-93-65-06-14**).

GOLF   Cannes is ringed by 10 golf courses, almost all within a 20-minute drive of the city. The **Old Course,** 265 route de Golf, Mandelieu (www.golfoldcourse.com; © **04-92-97-32-00**), is a leafy gem dating from 1891. Greens fees start at 90€, with big reductions for lunch deals and afternoon tee-offs. The prestigious **Royal Mougins Golf Club,** 424 av. du Roi, Mougins (www.royalmougins.fr; © **04-92-92-49-69**), also boasts a gourmet restaurant and spa. Greens fees start at 175€, including buggy hire; it's half-price for 9 holes.

PADDLEBOARDING   Cannes is nothing if not cutting edge. And like the rest of the world, this city has fallen in love with stand-up paddleboarding (SUP). Rent your own from **Cannes Standup Paddle Location,** Plage du Mouré Rouge, bd. Gazagnaire, Palm Beach (www.cannesstanduppaddle.fr; © **06-82-17-08-77**). Fees start at 12€ per hour.

TENNIS   Some resorts have their own courts. The city of Cannes also maintains 16 synthetic courts and 6 clay-topped ones at the **Garden Tennis Club,** 99 av. Maurice Chevalier (© **04-93-47-29-33**). You'll pay from 13€ to 17€ per hour, plus 3.70€ per hour for floodlights.

Shopping

Cannes achieves a blend of resort-style leisure, glamour, and media glitz more successfully than many of its neighbors. You'll see every big-name designer you can think of (Saint Laurent, Rykiel, and Hermès), plus a legion of one-off designer boutiques and shoe stores. There are also real-people shops; resale shops for star-studded castoffs; flea markets for fun junk; and a fruit, flower, and vegetable market.

BOOKS   **Ciné-Folie,** 14 rue des Frères-Pradignac (© **04-93-39-22-99**), is devoted entirely to film. Called "La Boutique du Cinema," it is the finest film bookstore in the south of France; vintage film stills and movie posters are also for sale. **Cannes English Bookshop,** 11 rue Bivouac Napoleon (www.cannesenglishbookshop.com; ℰ **04-93-99-40-08**), stocks locally based classics from Peter Mayle and Carol Drinkwater, plus bestselling novels, travel guides, and maps.

DESIGNER SHOPS   Most of the big names in fashion line promenade de la Croisette, the main drag running along the sea. Among the most prestigious are **Dior,** 38 La Croisette (ℰ **04-92-98-98-00**), and **Hermès,** 17 La Croisette (ℰ **04-93-39-18-23**). The stores stretch from the Hôtel Carlton almost to the Palais des Festivals, with the top names closest to the **Gray-d'Albion,** 38 rue des Serbes (www.lucienbarriere.com; ℰ **04-92-99-79-79**), both a mall and a hotel (how convenient). Near the train station, department store **Galeries Lafayette** has all the big-name labels crammed into one smallish space at 6 rue du Maréchal-Foch (ℰ **04-97-06-25-00**).

Young hipsters should try **Bathroom Graffiti,** 52 rue d'Antibes (ℰ **04-93-39-02-32**), for sexy luggage, bikinis, and designer homeware. The rue d'Antibes is also brilliant for big-brand bargains (Zara and MaxMara), as well as one-off boutiques.

FOOD   The Marché Forville (see below) and the surrounding streets are unsurprisingly the best places to search for picnic supplies. For bottles of Côtes de Provence, try **Cave du Marché,** 5 place Marché Forville (ℰ **04-93-99-60-98**). It also serves up glasses of local rosé and olive crostini on tables outside. **La Compagnie des Saumons,** 12 place Marché Forville (ℰ **04-93-68-33-20**), brims with caviar, bottles of fish soup, and slabs of smoked salmon. Local cheese shop **Le Fromage Gourmet,** 8 rue des Halles (ℰ **04-93-99-96-41**), is a favorite of celebrated chef Alain Ducasse. Closer to the seafront, World Pastry Champion Jérôme Oliveira creates fairy-tale desserts in bite sizes—from flower-topped tarts to a pastel rainbow of *macarons*—at **Intuitions by J,** 22 rue Bivouac Napoléon (www.patisserie-intuitions.com; ℰ **04-63-36-05-07**).

MARKETS   The **Marché Forville,** in place Marché Forville just north of the Vieux Port, is a covered stucco structure with a few arches but no walls. From Tuesday to Sunday, 7am to 1pm, it's the fruit, vegetable, and flower market that supplies the dozens of restaurants in the area. Monday (8am–6pm) is *brocante* day, when the market fills with dealers selling everything from Grandmère's dishes and bone-handled carving knives to castaways from estate sales.

Tuesdays to Sundays, 8am to 12:30pm, the small **Marché aux Fleurs** (Flower Market) takes place outdoors along the edges of the allée de la Liberté, across from the Palais des Festivals.

Nightlife

BARS & CLUBS   A strip of sundowner bars stretches along rue Félix Faure. Most are chic, some have happy hour cocktails, and several have DJs after dinner. New tapas bar **Le Bivi,** 7 rue des Gabres (www.lebivi-cannes.com; ℰ **04-93-39-97-90**), is a convivial spot to sample more unusual South of France wines. For an aperitif with history, the **Bar l'Amiral,** in the Hôtel Martinez, 73 La Croisette (ℰ **04-93-90-12-34**), is where deals have always gone down during the film festival. The bar comes complete with the nameplates of stars that once propped it up, Humphrey Bogart among them. At **Le Bâoli,** Port Pierre Canto, La Croisette (www.lebaoli.com; ℰ **04-93-43-03-43**), Europe's partying elite, from Prince Albert of Monaco to Jude Law, dance until dawn. Dress to the nines to slip past the über-tight security and into this Asian-inspired wonderland.

CASINOS Cannes is invariably associated with easygoing permissiveness, film-making glitterati, and gambling. If the latter is your thing, Cannes has world-class casinos loaded with high rollers, voyeurs, and everyone in between. The better established is the **Casino Croisette,** in the Palais des Festivals, 1 espace Lucien Barrière (www.lucienbarriere.com; © **04-92-98-78-00**). A well-respected fixture in town since the 1950s, a collection of noisy slot machines it is most certainly not. Its main competitor is the newer **Palm Beach Casino,** place F-D-Roosevelt, Pointe Croisette (www.casinolepalmbeach.com; © **04-97-06-36-90**), on the southeast edge of La Croisette. It attracts a younger crowd with a summer-only beachside poker room, a beach club with pool, a restaurant, and a disco that runs until dawn. Both casinos maintain slots that operate daily from lunchtime to 4 or 5am. Smarter dress is expected for the *salles des grands jeux* (blackjack, roulette, craps, poker, and chemin de fer), which open nightly 8pm to 4am. The casino also pulls in daytime visitors with tasty inexpensive lunches and Sunday brunches, both of which come with free gaming chips.

DAY TRIPS FROM CANNES

Îles de Lerins ★★

Short boat ride from Cannes

Floating in the Mediterranean just south of Cannes' southern horizon, the Lérins Islands are an idyllic place to escape the Riviera's summertime commotion. Head for Cannes port's western quai Laubeuf, where ferryboats operated by **Trans-Côte d'Azur** (www.trans-cote-azur.com; © **04-92-98-71-30**) offer access to Île Ste-Marguerite. To visit Île St-Honorat, head for the same quay, to the **Transports Planaria** (www.cannes-ilesdelerins.com; © **04-92-98-71-38**) ferryboats. Both companies offer frequent service to the islands at intervals of between 30 and 90 minutes depending on the season, and operate daily and year-round. Round-trip transport to Île Ste-Marguerite costs 13€ per adult and 8€ for children 5 to 10; round-trip transport to Île St-Honorat costs 14€ per adult and 6.50€ for children 5 to 10. Travel to both islands is free for children 4 and under. As dining options on the islands are limited, pack up a picnic lunch from Cannes' Marché Forville before you set off.

EXPLORING ÎLE STE-MARGUERITE

Île Ste-Marguerite is one big botanical garden—cars, cigarettes, and all other pollutants are banned—ringed by crystal-clear sea. From the dock, you can stroll along the island to Fort Royal, built by Spanish troops in 1637 and used as a military barracks and parade ground until World War II. The infamous "Man in the Iron Mask" was allegedly imprisoned here, and you can follow the legend back to his horribly spooky cell.

Musée de la Mer, Fort Royal (© **04-93-38-55-26**), traces the history of the island, displaying artifacts of Ligurian, Roman, and Arab civilizations, plus the remains discovered by excavations, including paintings, mosaics, and ancient pottery. Temporary exhibitions, often showcasing contemporary French artists, are also held on the premises. The museum is open Tuesday to Sunday, June to September 10am to 5:45pm, and October to May 10:30am to 1:15pm and 2:15 to 4:45pm (closing at 5:45pm Apr–May). Admission is 6€.

EXPLORING ÎLE ST-HONORAT ★★

Only 1.6km (1 mile) long, the Île St-Honorat is much quieter than neighboring Ste-Marguerite. But in historical terms, it's much richer than its island sibling and is the site of a monastery whose origins date from the 5th century. The **Abbaye de St-Honorat** ★ (www.abbayedelerins.com; © **04-92-99-54-00**) is a combination of medieval ruins and early-20th-century ecclesiastical buildings, and is home to a community of about 25 Cistercian monks. Most visitors content themselves with a wander through the pine forests on the island's western side, a clamber around the ruined monastery on the island's southern edge, and a bathe on its seaweed-strewn beaches.

Grasse ★

18km (11 miles) N of Cannes

Grasse, a 20-minute drive from Cannes, has been renowned as the capital of the world's perfume industry since the Renaissance. It was once a famous resort, attracting such royals as Queen Victoria and Princess Pauline Borghese, Napoleon's lascivious sister.

Today some three-quarters of the world's essences are produced here from thousands of tons of petals, including violets, daffodils, wild lavender, and jasmine. The quaint medieval town, which formed the backdrop for the 2006 movie "Perfume," has several free perfume museums where visitors can enroll in workshops to create their own scent.

ESSENTIALS

Trains run to Grasse from Cannes, depositing passengers a 10-minute walk south of town. From here, a walking trail or shuttle bus leads visitors into the center. One-way train tickets cost 4.20€ from Cannes. **Buses** pull into town every 10 to 60 minutes daily from Cannes (trip time: 50 min.), arriving at the Gare Routière, place de la Buanderie (© **04-93-36-37-37**), a 5-minute walk north of the town center. The one-way fare is 1.50€. Visitors arriving by **car** may follow RN85 from Cannes. The **Office de Tourisme** is at place du cours Honoré Cresp (www.grasse.fr; © **04-93-36-66-66**).

EXPLORING GRASSE

Musée International de la Parfumerie ★ MUSEUM   This comprehensive museum chronicles both Grasse's fragrant history, as well as worldwide perfume development over the past 4,000 years. Wander among raw materials, ancient flasks (including Marie Antoinette's 18th-c. toiletry set) and scented soaps, all set against a backdrop of contemporary artworks. Kids age 7 and older have their own dedicated pathway, lined with interactive exhibits to touch—and, of course, smell.

2 bd. du Jeu-de-Ballon. www.museesdegrasse.com. © **04-97-05-58-00.** Admission 4€ adults, free for children under 18. May–Sept daily 10am–7pm; Oct—Apr Wed–Mon 11am–6pm. Closed Nov.

WHERE TO EAT & SHOP

For light lunch or an afternoon snack, pop into **Le Péché Gourmand,** 8 rue de l'Oratoire (© **06-62-69-61-57**), a combination mini-restaurant, tearoom and ice cream parlor. Try the goat's cheese and candied tomato crumble, or order up a bowl of the decadent chocolate sorbet.

Both **Parfumerie Molinard,** 60 bd. Victor Hugo (www.molinard.com; © **04-93-62-90-50**), and **Parfumerie Fragonard,** 20 bd. Fragonard (www.fragonard.com; © 04-93-36-44-65), offer factory tours, where you'll get a firsthand peek into scent extraction and perfume and essential oil production. You can also purchase their products on-site.

Vallauris ★

Once simply a stopover along the Riviera, Vallauris's ceramics industry was in terminal decline until it was "discovered" by Picasso just after World War II. The artist's legacy lives on both in snapshots of the master in local galleries and in his awesome "La Paix et La Guerre" fresco.

ESSENTIALS

Envibus **bus** (www.envibus.fr; ✆ **04-89-87-72-00**) connects Cannes' train station with Vallauris every 30 minutes (journey time 20 min.). Tickets cost 1€ each way. There's an **Office de Tourisme** (www.vallauris-golfe-juan.fr) on square du 8 Mai 1945 (✆ **04-93-63-82-58**).

EXPLORING VALLAURIS

In Vallauris, Picasso's **"l'Homme au Mouton"** ("Man and Sheep") is the outdoor statue at place Paul Isnard in front of which Prince Aly Kahn and screen goddess Rita Hayworth were married. The local council had intended to enclose this statue in a museum, but Picasso insisted that it remain on the square, "where the children could climb over it and dogs piss against it."

Musée Magnelli, Musée de la Céramique & Musée National Picasso La Guerre et La Paix ★★ ART MUSEUM

Three museums in one, this petite cultural center developed from a 12th-century chapel where Picasso painted "La Paix" ("Peace") and "La Guerre" ("War") in 1952. Visitors can physically immerse themselves in this tribute to pacifism. Images of love and peace adorn one wall; scenes of violence and conflict the other. Also on site is a permanent exposition of works by Florentine-born abstract artist Alberto Magnelli, as well as a floor dedicated to traditional and innovative ceramics from potters throughout the region.

Place de la Libération. www.musees-nationaux-alpesmaritimes.fr. ✆ **04-93-64-71-83.** Admission 4€ adults, free for children 15 and under. July–Aug daily 10am–7pm; June 15–30 and Sept 1–15 Wed–Mon 10am–12:15pm and 2–6pm; Sept 16–June 14 Wed–Mon 10am–12:15pm and 2–5pm.

WHERE TO EAT & SHOP

Join the locals for lunch at **Le Cafe du Coin,** 16 place Jules Lisnard (www.cafe-du-coin.com; ✆ **04-92-90-27-79**), where a small selection of market-fresh specials are scribbled on the chalkboard daily. For souvenirs, head around the corner to avenue Georges-Clemenceau, lined with small shops selling brightly glazed, locally made ceramics. Be on the lookout for the **Galerie Madoura,** rue Georges et Suzanne Ramié: Vallauris' municipality purchased Picasso's former studio in 2013, and it is now being redeveloped into a cultural center.

Mougins ★★

A fortified hill town, Mougins preserves the quiet life in a postcard-perfect manner. The town's artsy legacy—Picasso, Jean Cocteau, Paul Eluard, Fernand Léger, Isadora Duncan, and Christian Dior were all previous residents—has blessed the town with must-see galleries. Real estate prices are among the highest on the Riviera, and the wealthy residents support a dining scene that also punches well above its weight. The **Etoile des Mougins food festival** (www.lesetoilesdemougins.com), held each

September, is a highbrow gastronomic love-in featuring Michelin-starred chefs from across the globe.

ESSENTIALS

From Cannes, the best way to get to Mougins is to **drive** north of the city along D6285. By bus, **Société Tam** (www.cg06.fr; © **08-00-06-01-06**) runs bus no. 600 from Cannes to Val-de-Mougins, a 10-minute walk from the center of Mougins. One-way fares cost 1.50€. The **Office de Tourisme** is at 18 bd. Courteline (www.mougins.fr; © **04-93-75-87-67**).

EXPLORING MOUGINS

Picasso discovered Mougins' tranquil maze of flower-filled lanes in the company of his muse, Dora Marr, and photographer Man Ray, in 1935. The Vieux Village's pedestrianized cobblestone streets—each corner prettier than the last—have changed little over the decades since. After the highlights below, it's well worth seeking out the romantic **Chapelle Notre-Dame de Vie,** Chemin de la Chapelle, and its tree-dappled grounds, once painted by Sir Winston Churchill. Just 1.5km (1 mile) southeast of Mougins, it was built in the 12th century and reconstructed in 1646. The priory next door was Picasso's studio and residence for the last 12 years of his life. It's still a private home occupied intermittently by the Picasso heirs.

Musée d'Art Classique de Mougins ★★ MUSEUM   The newest addition to Mougins' art scene is wonderfully quirky: Egyptian, Greek, and Roman artifacts are juxtaposed alongside similarly themed modern artworks, including sculptures, drawings, and canvases from Matisse, Dufy, Cézanne, Dali, and Damien Hirst. A personal favorite pairing matches an ancient statue of Venus with Yves Klein's neon-blue "Venus" sculpture.

32 rue Commandeur. www.mouginsmusee.com. © **04-93-75-18-65.** Admission 12€ adults, 5€ children 10–17, free for children 9 and under. Daily 10:30am–8pm (Thurs until 10pm).

Musée de la Photographie André Villers ★ ART MUSEUM   Picasso's close friend, photographer André Villers, chronicled the artist's Mougins years in black-and-white photos. Images line the walls of an ancient medieval home: Some are hilarious, such as the photo showing Picasso sitting down for breakfast in his trademark Breton shirt, pretending he has croissants for fingers. Additional portraits by Villars—including snaps of Dali, Catherine Deneuve, and Edith Piaf—are frequently on display, along with three major temporary exhibitions each year.

Porte Sarrazine. © **04-93-75-85-67.** Free admission. Tues–Fri 10am–12:30pm and 2–7pm; Sat–Sun 11am–7pm.

WHERE TO EAT

Le Moulin de Mougins, Notre Dame de Vie (www.moulindemougins.com; © **04-93-75-78-24;** menus 85€ and 120€), is a place of foodie pilgrimage. Inside an enchanting 16th-century mill, talented chef Erwan Louaisil follows in the footsteps of founder Roger Vergé and previous head chef Alain Llorca with modern twists on culinary traditions from both Provence and his native Brittany. The restaurant is closed Monday all day, and Tuesday and Wednesday at lunch. It also rents six double rooms (150€–200€) and three suites (200€–350€) on site.

On a budget? Try the traditional bistro **Le Resto des Arts,** 2 rue Maréchal Foch (© **04-93-75-60-03**), which dishes up hearty specials like basil-spiked *soupe au pistou,* red mullet doused in tomato sauce, or seared steak with morel mushrooms.

JUAN-LES-PINS ★★

913km (566 miles) S of Paris; 9.5km (6 miles) S of Cannes

Just west of the Cap d'Antibes, this Art Deco resort burst onto the South of France scene during the 1920s, under the auspices of American property developer Frank Jay Gould. A decade later, Juan-les-Pins was already drawing a chic summer crowd, as the Riviera "season" flipped from winter respites to the hedonistic pursuit of summer sun, sea, and sensuality. It has been attracting the young and the young-at-heart from across Europe and the U.S. ever since. F. Scott Fitzgerald decried Juan-les-Pins as a "constant carnival." His words ring true each and every summer's day.

Essentials

ARRIVING Juan-les-Pins is connected by **rail** to most nearby coastal resorts, including Nice (trip time: 30 min.; 3.80€ one-way), Antibes, and Cannes. A **bus** (www. envibus.fr; ℂ **04-89-87-72-00**) leaves for Juan-les-Pins from Antibes' Gare Routière (bus station) daily every 20 minutes and costs 1€ one-way (trip time: 10 min.). To **drive** to Juan-les-Pins from Nice, travel along coastal D6007 south; from Cannes, follow the D6007 north.

VISITOR INFORMATION The **Office de Tourisme** is at 51 bd. Charles-Guillaumont (www.antibes-juanlespins.co.uk; ℂ **04-97-23-11-10**).

SPECIAL EVENTS The town offers some of the best nightlife on the Riviera. The action reaches its peak during the annual 10-day **Festival International de Jazz** (www.jazzajuan.com) in mid-July. It attracts jazz, blues, reggae, and world music artists who play nightly on the beachfront Parc de la Pinède. Recent performers have included George Benson, Maceo Parker, Norah Jones, and B. B. King. Tickets cost 25€ to 75€ and can be purchased at the Office de Tourisme in both Antibes and Juan-les-Pins, as well as online.

[Fast FACTS] JUAN-LES-PINS

ATMs/Banks   **BNP Paribas,** 14 av. Maréchal Joffre (ℂ **08-20-82-00-01**).

Internet Access   **Mediterr@net-phone.com,** av. du Dr Fabre (ℂ **04-93-61-04-03**).

Mail & Postage   **La Poste,** 1 av. Maréchal Joffre (ℂ **36-31**).

Pharmacies   **Pharmacie Provençale,** 144 bd. Président Wilson (ℂ **04-93-61-09-23**).

Where to Stay

Hôtel Belles-Rives ★★★   This luxurious hotel is one of the Riviera's most fabled addresses. It started life in 1925 as a holiday villa rented by Zelda and F. Scott Fitzgerald (as depicted in Fitzgerald's semi-autobiographical novel "Tender Is the Night"). Today, 85 years after her grandparents first opened the Belles-Rives' doors, the elegant Madame Estène-Chauvin owns and oversees this waterside gem. Guestrooms are sumptuous yet eclectic—each one its own unique size and shape. The lower terraces hold garden dining rooms, an elegant bar and lounge, as well as a private jetty. Also on site is the superb **La Passagère** restaurant and a private beach. If you're daring, you can even try waterskiing at the waterside aquatic club where, almost a century ago, the sport was invented.

33 bd. Edouard Baudoin. www.bellesrives.com. ⓒ **04-93-61-02-79.** 43 units. 192€–880€ double; 800€–2,000€ suite. Parking 30€. Closed Jan–Feb. **Amenities:** 2 summer restaurants; 1 winter restaurant; 2 bars; private beach; room service; free Wi-Fi.

Le Grand Pavois ★   Nestled in an unbeatable location between the base of the Cap d'Antibes and Juan-les-Pins' center, this Art Deco edifice is literally a 2-minute walk to the beach. The elegant period lobby has been perfectly restored, and a live pianist often graces the ground-floor **La Rotonde** bar with jazzy tunes. Guestrooms are simply decorated with Provençal furnishings; many possess private balconies and sea views. Breakfast is served in the palm-fringed garden outside.

5 av. Saramartel. www.bestwestern-legrandpavois.com. ⓒ **04-92-93-54-54.** 60 units. 74€–190€ double; 110€–270€ suite. Parking 8€. **Amenities:** Bar; restaurant; room service; free Wi-Fi.

Where to Eat

Le Perroquet ★ PROVENÇAL   One of the best restaurants in Juan-les-Pins, Le Perroquet attracts both casual visitors and longtime locals. The *assortiment de poissons grillés*—grilled sea bream, John Dory, giant prawns, and red mullet—is an excellent introduction to the best of the Mediterranean. The pretty sidewalk seating looks out over La Pinède's Aleppo pines, and a good-value fixed-price lunch menu changes daily.

Av. Georges-Gallice. www.restaurantleperroquet.fr. ⓒ **04-93-61-02-20.** Reservations recommended. Main courses 16€–32€; fixed-price lunch 18€; fixed-price dinner 30€–39€. Daily noon–2pm and 7–10pm. Closed Nov–Dec.

Les Pirates ★★ ITALIAN/MEDITERRANEAN   For the ultimate in toes-in-the-sand dining, head to this family-friendly seaside restaurant. Within the palm-trimmed oasis, Les Pirates' summery menu is perfect for punctuating lazy days on the beach. There's a very good range of salads, including La Jazz (local baby-leafed mesclun, violet artichokes, Parma ham, and avocado), as well as more extravagant offerings, such as seared scallops or *fritto misto* (Italian-style fried fish). *Tiramisu della Mamma* is whipped up in the kitchen by true Italian mamma Anna.

23 bd. Baudoin. www.plage-les-pirates.fr. ⓒ **04-93-61-00-41.** Reservations recommended. Main courses 12€–38€. Daily noon–3pm and 8–10pm. Closed Nov–Jan.

Exploring Juan-les-Pins

Spilling over from Antibes' more residential quarter, Juan-les-Pins is petite—which makes the resort town best navigated on foot. Be sure to swing by the shady square known as **La Pinède** (square Frank Jay Gould) to check out the legions of local *pétanque* players. At sunset, stroll the long, beachside promenade to Golfe-Juan, where Napoleon kicked off his march to Paris and famous Hundred Days in power in 1815. Alternatively, pick a beach bar, order a glass of rosé, and watch the sun drop over the Îles de Lérins.

Outdoor Activities

BEACHES   Part of the reason people flock to Juan-les-Pins is for the town's wealth of sandy beaches, all lapped by calm waters. The town also basks in a unique microclimate, making it one of the warmest places on the Riviera to soak up the sun, even in winter. **Plage de Juan-les-Pins** is the most central beach, although quieter stretches of sand wrap around the Cap d'Antibes and include family-friendly **Plage de la Salis** and chic **Plage de la Garoupe.** If you do want to stretch out on a sunlounger, go to any of the beach-bar concessions that line the bay, where you can rent a mattress for around 12€ to 20€. Topless sunbathing and overt shows of cosmetic surgery are the norm.

WATERSPORTS   If you're interested in scuba diving, try **Easy Dive,** bd. Edouard Baudouin (www.easydive.fr; ✆ **04-93-61-26-07**). A one-tank dive costs 30€ to 55€, including all equipment. **Sea kayaking, pedalos, parascending,** and **donuts** are available at virtually every beach in Juan-les-Pins. **Waterskiing** was invented at the Hôtel des Belles-Rives in the 1920s, and it's still a great place to try out the sport.

Nightlife

For a faux-tropical-island experience, head to **Le Pam Pam,** 137 bd. Wilson (www. pampam.fr; ✆ **04-93-61-11-05**), a time-honored "rhumerie" where guests sip rum and people-watch while reggae beats drift around the bar. More modern is **La Réserve,** av. Georges Gallice (✆ **04-93-61-20-06**), where a younger crowd sips rosé on leopard-print seats under a large plane tree.

If you prefer high-energy partying, you're in the right place. The entire Riviera descends upon Juan-les-Pins' discos every night in summer, and it's best to follow the crowds to the latest hotspot. **Le Village,** 1 bd. de la Pinède (✆ **04-92-93-90-00**), is one of the more established clubs and boasts an action-packed dance floor with DJs spinning summer sounds from salsa to soul. The cover charge is usually 16€ including one drink; more for themed evenings. For top jazz, head to **Le New Orleans,** 9 av. Georges Gallice (✆ **04-93-67-41-71**), a new addition to the local live music scene in 2013.

ANTIBES & CAP D'ANTIBES ★★

913km (566 miles) S of Paris; 21km (13 miles) SW of Nice; 11km (6¾ miles) NE of Cannes

Antibes has a quiet charm unique to the Côte d'Azur. Its harbor is filled with fishing boats and pleasure yachts. The likes of Picasso and Monet painted its oh-so-pretty streets, today thronged with promenading locals and well-dressed visitors. A pedestrianized town center makes it a family-friendly destination as well, and a perfect place for an evening stroll. An excellent covered market is also located near the harbor, open every morning except Mondays.

Spiritually, Antibes is totally divorced from Cap d'Antibes, a peninsula studded with the villas of the super-rich. But the less affluent are welcome to peek at paradise, and a lovely 6km (3¾ miles) coastal path rings the headland, passing picnic and diving spots en route.

Essentials

ARRIVING   **Trains** from Cannes arrive at the rail station, place Pierre-Semard, every 20 minutes (trip time: 15 min.); the one-way fare is 2.80€. Around 25 trains arrive from Nice daily (trip time: 20 min.); the one-way fare is 4.40€. The **bus** station, or Gare Routière, place Guynemer (www.cg06.fr or www.envibus.fr; ✆ **04-89-87-72-00**), offers bus service throughout Provence. Bus fares to Nice, Cannes, or anywhere en route cost 1.50€ one-way.

To **drive** to Antibes from Nice, travel along coastal D6007 south; from Cannes, follow the D6007 north. The Cap d'Antibes is clearly visible from most parts of the Riviera. To drive here from Antibes, follow the coastal road south—you can't miss it

VISITOR INFORMATION   The **Office de Tourisme** is at 11 place du Général de Gaulle (www.antibes-juanlespins.co.uk; ✆ **04-97-23-11-11**).

[FastFACTS] ANTIBES

ATMs/Banks   Among others, there are half a dozen banks dotted along av. Robert Soleau.

Internet Access   **Wilson.net,** 74 bd. Wilson (✆ **04-92-90-25-34**).

Mail & Postage   **La Poste,** 2 av. Paul Doumer (✆ **36-31**).

Pharmacies   **Grande Pharmacie d'Antibes,** 2 place Guynemer (✆ **04-93-34-16-12**).

Where to Stay

Hôtel du Cap-Eden-Roc ★★★   This legendary hotel was first launched in 1887, serving as a Mediterranean getaway for visitors seeking winter sunshine. Over the intervening years, it's played host to the world's most famous clientele, from the Duke and Duchess of Windsor (who escaped here after the former king's abdication) to the Hollywood superstars who cavort at the "Vanity Fair" Cannes Film Festival party. Surrounded by a maze of manicured gardens, accommodation is among the most sumptuous on the Riviera. Guest rooms recently benefitted from a thorough renovation completed in 2013 that outfitted every room with sleek modern fittings, iPod docks, and LED screens. Guests lounge by the seawater swimming pool, carved from natural basalt rock, while evenings are spent at the panoramic **Restaurant Eden-Roc** or the **Bellini Bar.** Looking to splurge? Pick up an exclusive Eden-Roc-label beach sarong. Alternatively, signature treatments at the onsite spa come courtesy of luxury Swiss brand La Prairie.

Bd. J.F. Kennedy. www.hotel-du-cap-eden-roc.com. ✆ **04-93-61-39-01.** 118 units. 800€–1,400€ double; 1,630€–6,120€ suite; villa rates available upon request. Closed mid-Oct to mid-Apr. **Amenities:** 2 restaurants; 2 bars; babysitting; exercise room; massage; outdoor pool; room service; spa; free Wi-Fi.

La Jabotte ★★   Literally a 5-minute stroll from one of Antibes' sandy beaches, this cozy little bed-and-breakfast is a favorite with regular visitors. Eight rooms, each with its own small terrace, cluster around a jasmine-splashed courtyard garden, and a suite and another double are upstairs. Guestrooms may be petite, but rooms are brightly decorated and beds are all brand-new. Nathalie and Pierre—new owners in 2013—make warm and welcoming hosts.

13 av. Max Maurey. www.jabotte.com. ✆ **04-93-61-45-89.** 10 units. 80€–169€ double; 129€–249€ suite (sleeps up to 4). Parking 10€. **Amenities:** Garden; bar; free Wi-Fi.

Where to Eat

The Zelda and Scott Fitzgeralds of today head for the **Restaurant Eden-Roc** at the Hôtel du Cap-Eden-Roc for grand service and grand cuisine. Alternatively, the excellent **Restaurant de Bacon,** bd. de Bacon (www.restaurantdebacon.com; ✆ **04-93-61-50-02**), has served the best seafood around for more than 6 decades. For light bites and unusual local wines, stop into **Entre 2 Vins,** 2 rue James Close (✆ **04-93-34-46-93**).

Bistro Le Rustic ★ FRENCH/PIZZA For hearty local dishes on a budget, it's hard to beat family-run Le Rustic. The menu here focuses on wood-fired pizzas and rich pots of fondue, with plenty of Riviera classics (fish soup, a fresh shrimp platter, slow-roasted duck) thrown in too. The restaurant is located at the heart of Antibes' Old Town, with spacious (and kid-friendly) outdoor seating in the square.

33 place Nationale. ℂ **04-93-34-10-81.** Main courses 10€–18€; fixed-price menu 14€–19€. Daily noon–3pm and 7–11pm.

L'Armoise ★★ PROVENÇAL Talented chef Laurent Parrinello, who honed his skills at Eze's Chèvre d'Or à Eze and the nearby Hôtel du Cap–Eden-Roc, crafts modern adaptations of traditional dishes, such as pestro-drizzled asparagus, fennel, and goat-cheese salad, or sea bream served with curry-infused red cabbage. Fresh ingredients come from Antibes' daily market; cheeses and wines are sourced from local producers. Note that reservations at this tiny restaurant are required in advance.

2 rue de la Tourraque. ℂ **04-92-94-96-13.** Reservations required. Main courses 22€–24€; fixed-price menu 45€–80€. Tues–Fri & Sun 12:30–2pm and 7:30–9:30pm. Closed 2 wks. in July & 2 wks. in Dec.

Exploring Antibes

Antibes' largely pedestrianized Old Town—all pale stone homes, weaving lanes, and window boxes of colorful flowers—is easily explored on foot. A dip into Picasso's former home, now a museum, and a stroll along the bling-tastic pleasure port, where artist Jaume Plensa's giant "Nomad" sculpture shimmers against the night sky, are undoubtedly its highlights. Visitors keen to escape the crowds may head to the Cap d'Antibes' **Espace du Littoral et du Milieu Marin**, bd. J.F. Kennedy (ℂ **04-93-61-45-32**). This small, kid-friendly space showcases a permanent Jacques Cousteau exhibition, and it has a seaside park (which overlooks the grounds of the ultra-exclusive Hôtel du Cap–Eden-Roc!) to explore too. It's open Tuesday to Saturday 10am to 4:40pm; entrance is 3€ for adults, free for children under 18.

Musée Picasso ★★ ART MUSEUM Perched on the Old Town's ramparts, the 14th-century Château Grimaldi was home to Picasso in 1946, when the Spanish artist lived and worked here at the invitation of the municipality. Upon his departure, he gifted all the work he'd completed to the chateau museum: 44 drawings and 23 paintings, including the famous "La Joie de Vivre." In addition to this permanent collection, contemporary artworks by Nicolas de Staël, Arman and Modigliani, among many others, are also on display.

Château Grimaldi, Place Mariejol. ℂ **04-92-90-54-28.** Admission 6€ adults, 3€ students and seniors, free for children 18 and under. Mid-June to mid-Sept Tues–Sun 10am–6pm (July–Aug Wed and Fri until 8pm); mid-Sept to mid-June Tues–Sun 10am–noon and 2–6pm.

DAY TRIPS FROM ANTIBES

Biot ★

6.5km (4 miles) NW of Antibes

Biot has been famous for its pottery since merchants began to ship earthenware jars to Phoenicia and throughout the Mediterranean. It's also where Fernand Léger painted until the day he died, leaving a magnificent collection of his work on display just outside town.

ESSENTIALS

Bus lines no. 7 and no. 10 from Antibes's Gare Routière, place Guynemer (www.envibus.fr; ✆ **04-89-87-72-00**), run to Biot's town center. Tickets cost 1€. To **drive** to Biot from Antibes, follow D6007 east, then head west on the D4. Biot's **Office de Tourisme** is at 46 rue St-Sébastien (www.biot-tourisme.com; ✆ **04-93-65-78-00**).

EXPLORING BIOT

Exploration of Biot's small historic center begins at **place des Arcades,** where you can see the 16th-century gates and the remains of the town's ramparts. The **Musée d'Histoire et Céramique Biotoise,** 8 rue St-Sebastien (www.musee-de-biot.fr; ✆ **04-93-65-54-54**), has assembled the best works from local artists, potters, ceramists, painters, and silver- and goldsmiths. Hours are mid-June to mid-September Wednesday to Monday 10am to 6pm and mid-September to mid-June Wednesday to Sunday 2 to 6pm. Admission is 4€, free ages 16 and under.

Outside of town, the excellent **Musée National Fernand Léger,** 316 chemin du Val de Pôme (www.musees-nationaux-alpesmaritimes.fr/fleger; ✆ **04-92-91-50-20**), displays a comprehensive collection of the artist's colorful creations, from 1930s Cubist ladies to circus scenes of the 1950s. Hours are Wednesday to Monday May to October 10am to 6pm, November to April 10am to 5pm. Admission is 5.50€, 4€ for students and children. There are temporary exhibitions and a café garden on site.

WHERE TO EAT & SHOP

For a Provençal take on crêpes—such as summery tomato, olive tapenade with basil or the house speciality, crêpe-pizza—stop in to **Crêperie Auberge du Village,** 29 rue Saint Sébastien (www.creperie-aubergeduvieuxvillage.com; ✆ **04-93-65-72-73**). This low-key lunch spot sits at the northern end of Biot's main shopping street. In the late 1940s, local glassmakers created a bubble-flecked glass known as *verre rustique.* In brilliant cobalts and emeralds, it's displayed in many store windows here. Or head down to **Verrerie Guyot Pascal,** 16 rue Saint-Sébastien (www.verrerieguyot.com; ✆ **04-93-65-06-50**), where you can see a master glass-blower work on unique vases and tableware most afternoons.

ESPECIALLY FOR KIDS

Just south of Biot sits a kid-tastic complex of theme parks. **Marineland** offers the chance to get personal with penguins, polar bears, and sharks. **Aqualand** boasts more than 2km (1¼ miles) of waterslides, including toboggan-style Le Draguéro and the Rainbow Cannon. The Wild West–themed **La Ferme du Far West** caters to animal-loving little ones, with pony rides and a petting zoo. And **Adventure Golf** is criss-crossed by two dinosaur-dotted miniature golf courses. Admission is as follows: Marineland 38€, 30€ children between 3 and 12; Aquasplash 26€, 20€ children between 3 and 12; Adventure Golf 11€, 9€ children between 3 and 12; and La Ferme du Far West 13€, 10€ children between 3 and 12. All are free for children 2 and under; combination entrance tickets are also available. It's open daily July and August 10am to 11pm, mid-April to June and September 10am to 7pm, and mid-March to mid-April 10am to 6pm.

ST-PAUL-DE-VENCE ★★

926km (574 miles) S of Paris; 23km (14 miles) E of Grasse; 28km (17 miles) E of Cannes; 31km (19 miles) N of Nice

Of all the hilltop villages of the Riviera, St-Paul-de-Vence is by far the most famous. It gained popularity in the 1940 and '50s, when artists including Picasso, Chagall, and

Matisse frequented the town, trading their paintings for hospitality at the Colombe d'Or inn. Art is now the town's principal attraction, and the winding streets are studded with contemporary galleries and museums. Circling the town are magnificent old ramparts (allow about 30 min. to walk the full loop) that overlook flowers and olive and orange trees.

Essentials

ARRIVING   The nearest **rail** station is in Cagnes-sur-Mer. Some 20 **buses** per day (no. 400) leave from central Nice, dropping passengers off in St-Paul-de-Vence (1.50€ one-way, journey time 1 hr.), then in Vence 10 minutes later. For information, contact Ligne d'Azur (www.lignesdazur.com; © **08-10-06-10-06**). If you're **driving** from Nice, take either the A8 highway or the coastal route du Bord du Mer west, turn inland at Cagnes-sur-Mer, and follow signs north to St-Paul-de-Vence.

VISITOR INFORMATION   The **Office de Tourisme** is at 2 rue Grande (www. saint-pauldevence.com; © **04-93-32-86-95**).

Getting Around

St-Paul's Old Town is entirely pedestrianised, and most of the narrow streets are paved in cobblestones. Note that driving a car here is prohibited, except to drop off luggage at an Old Town hotel, and by prior arrangement only. The Fondation Maeght is around half a mile out of town.

[FastFACTS] ST-PAUL-DE-VENCE

ATMs/Banks   **BNP Paribas,** rd-pt Sainte Claire (© **08-20-82-00-01**).
Mail & Postage   **La Poste,** rd-pt Sainte Claire (© **36-31**).
Pharmacies   **Pharmacie Saint Paul,** rd-pt Sainte Claire (© **04-93-32-80-78**).

Where to Stay

La Colombe d'Or rents deluxe rooms (see "Where to Eat," below).

La Vague de Saint-Paul ★★★   La Vague opened in 2013 to fill a glaring gap in the St-Paul accommodations market: an affordable hotel for art lovers seeking country tranquillity and wow-factor design. It delivers with aplomb. The wavelike main hotel building was originally conceived by far-out architect André Minangoy in the 1960s. Color-coded guestrooms now look out onto a vast garden complete with *pétanque* run, tennis court, bar, and pool. The attached (almost 100 percent organic) restaurant delivers five daily starters and mains on 22€ and 29€ set menus. The complex sits a short walk from the Fondation Maeght contemporary art museum—and a longer stroll through the forest to St-Paul-de-Vence village via a secret trail. Highly recommended.

Chemin des Salettes. www.vaguesaintpaul.com. © **04-920-11-20-00.** 37 units. 106€–240€ double; from 390€ suite. Free parking. Amenities: Restaurant; bar; concierge; outdoor pool; room service; spa; tennis; free Wi-Fi.

Where to Eat

St-Paul's petite size means that dining options are limited and may also be pricey. That said, the views and the ambience of pretty much any local eatery often make up for these shortcomings.

La Colombe d'Or ★★ PROVENÇAL   This celebrated restaurant opened its doors in 1920. At the time it was little more than a scattering of tables overlooking an overgrown artichoke patch. It was Paul Roux, the restaurant's art-adoring owner, who encouraged the era's struggling artists, such as Raoul Dufy, Paul Signac, and Chaime Soutine, to swap a canvas or two for generous room and board. Picasso, Braque, and Miró followed—and today La Colombe d'Or's art collection is one of the finest in the world. For a peek at these masterpieces, you'll need to dine here, either indoors beneath works by the likes of Signac, Matisse, and Braque or outdoors on the fig-trimmed terrace. The house specials include a selection of fresh hors-d'oeuvres (such as *crudités* and *anchoïade*, a traditional anchovy dip), and crispy roast chicken. It also offers 25 luxurious doubles and suites sprawling over the original 16th-century stone house and the two 1950s wings. Prices are 250€ for a double, 430€ for a suite.

1 place du Général-de-Gaulle. www.la-colombe-dor.com. ✆ **04-93-32-80-02.** Reservations required. Main courses 17€–35€. Daily noon–2pm and 7:30–10pm. Closed late Oct–3rd wk Dec and 10 days in Jan.

Les Terrasses ★ PROVENÇAL   A few minutes' stroll downhill from the Fondation Maeght, this laidback eatery offers classic regional cuisine and superb views over St-Paul's Old Town. Opt for *aïoli*, steamed vegetables, and cod served alongside a garlic-spiked mayonnaise dip; *secca d' Entrevaux,* a locally cured beef dished up with grilled goat cheese; or one of a dozen different pizzas. Prices are the best in the area, and the atmosphere is convivial—do note, however, that the restaurant is a favorite with large groups.

20 chemin des Trious. www.laterrassesursaintpaul.com. ✆**04-93-32-85-60.** Main courses 10€–22€; fixed-price menu 28€. Thurs–Tue 9am–10pm. Closed 2 weeks in Nov.

Exploring St-Paul

Perched at the top of the village, the **Collégiale de la Conversion de St-Paul** ★ was constructed in the 12th and 13th centuries and has been much altered over the years. The Romanesque choir is the oldest part, containing some remarkable stalls carved in walnut in the 17th century. Look to the left as you enter: You'll see the painting "Ste-Cathérine d'Alexandrie," which has been attributed to Tintoretto. The **Trésor de l'Eglise** is one of the most beautiful in the Alpes-Maritimes, with a spectacular ciborium. Look also for a low relief of the "Martyrdom of St-Clément" on the last altar on the right. It's open daily 9am to 6pm (to 7pm July–Aug). Admission is free.

Just around the corner is the light-flooded **Chapelle des Pénitents Blanc.** The artist Jean-Michel Folon, who worked on this unmissable masterpiece until his death in 2005, decorated the church with stained-glass windows, shimmering mosaics, and rainbow-hued frescos. It's open April to September daily 11am to 1pm and 3 to 6pm, and October to March daily from 2 to 5pm. Admission is 3€ adults, 2€ students and children 6 to 18, and free for children 5 and under.

Foundation Maeght ★★★ ART MUSEUM   Established by Parisian art dealers Aimé and Marguerite Maeght in 1964, this avant-garde building houses one of the most impressive modern-art collections in Europe. It was Spanish architect José Luis Sert who designed the pagoda-like exhibition space, ensuring the artwork it displays sits in perfect harmony with the surrounding pine-studded woods. In the gardens, colorful Alexander Calder installations are clustered with skinny bronze sculptures by

Alberto Giacometti. A rotating selection of artworks is displayed over the various levels inside, showcasing key pieces by artists like Matisse, Chagall, Bonnard, and Léger. Each summer the museum stages a large seasonal show, such as 2013's "Adventures of Truth," curated by philosopher Bernard-Henri Lévy. There's also a library, a cinema, a cafeteria, and a magnificent museum store on-site.

623 chemin des Gardettes, outside the town walls. www.fondation-maeght.com. ✆ **04-93-32-81-63.** Admission 15€ adults, 10€ students and ages 10–18, free for children 9 and under, 5€ fee for photographs. July–Sept daily 10am–7pm; Oct–June daily 10am–6pm.

Organized Tours

With advance booking, the local tourist office offers 10 different walking tours of the town's historic core and outskirts. **Themed tours** (5€, free for children under 12) last around an hour and a half and range from following in the footsteps of former resident Marc Chagall to trying your hand at the beloved Provençal pastime of *pétanque* (also known as *boules*) under the instruction of accomplished locals.

In nearby La Colle sur Loup, culinary legends Alain and Jean-Michel Llorca offer cooking workshops for adults and children at their **Ecole de Cuisine** (www.alainllorca. com; 60€–170€ per person). Lessons are in French and English and are often followed by an informal dinner.

Shopping

The pedestrian-only **rue Grande** is St-Paul's most evocative street, running the length of the town. Most of the stone houses along it are from the 16th and 17th centuries, and several still bear the coats of arms placed there by the original builders. Today many of the houses are antiques shops, arts-and-crafts galleries, and souvenir and gift shops; some are still artists' studios.

Galerie du Vieux Saint-Paul, 16–18 rue Grande (www.galeries-bartoux.com; ✆ 04-93-32-74-50), is the place to pick up serious art, from sculptures by local artist Arman to bronze works by Salvador Dali. Just down the road, **Galerie Capricorne,** 64 rue Grande (www.galeriecapricorne.com; ✆ 04-93-58-34-42), offers a colorful array of prints, including a selection by Marc Chagall. **Galerie Paul Rafferty,** 67 rue Grande (www.raffertyart.com; ✆ 06-08-33-93-65), purveys paintings inspired by the local village life. Stock up on olive oils, fruit vinegars, and olive-wood chopping boards at **Premier Pression Provence,** 68 rue Grande (www.ppp-olive.com; ✆ 04-93-58-07-69). It's worth plunging into the town's winding streets, too: **Saint Georges Editions,** 5 montée de l'Eglise (✆ 09-71-57-68-21), stocks superb, unique handbags, each one created from lengths of unusual antique textiles. Nearby **Atelier Silvia B** (www.silviabertini.com) is packed with bright collages of St-Paul.

VENCE ★

926km (574 miles) S of Paris; 31km (19 miles) N of Cannes; 24km (15 miles) NW of Nice

Often bypassed in favor of nearby St-Paul-de-Vence, the pretty village of Vence is well worth a detour. Its pale stone Old Town is atmospheric yet untouristy, splashed with shady squares and pavement cafés. The highlight is undoubtedly Matisse's Chapelle du Rosaire, set among a countryside studded with cypresses, olive trees, and oleanders.

Essentials

ARRIVING Frequent **buses** (no. 94 or 400) originating in Nice take 65-80 minutes to reach Vence, passing the nearest **rail** station in Cagnes-sur-Mer, about 10km (6¼ miles) southwest from Vence, en route. The one-way fare is 1.50€. For bus information, contact contact **Ligne d'Azur** (www.lignesdazur.com; *(C)* **08-10-06-10-06**). For train information, visit www.voyages-sncf.com or call *(C)* **36-35**. To **drive** to Vence from Nice, take D6007 west to Cagnes-sur-Mer, and then D36 north to Vence.

VISITOR INFORMATION The **Office de Tourisme** is on place due Grand-Jardin (www.ville-vence.fr; *(C)* **04-93-58-06-38**).

[FastFACTS] VENCE

ATMs/Banks Many banks are dotted around Vence, including **BNP Paribas,** 28 place du Grand-Jardin (*(C)* **08-20-82-00-01**).

Internet Access **SIMS,** 165 av. des Poilus (www.secretariat-services-vence.weebly.com; *(C)* **04-93-58-23-27**), offers high-speed Internet access, but no Wi-Fi.

Mail & Postage **La Poste,** place Clemenceau (*(C)* **36-31**).

Pharmacies **Pharmacie du Grand-Jardin,** 30 place du Grand-Jardin (*(C)* **04-93-58-00-39**).

Where to Stay

Note that St-Paul-de-Vence's hotels also make an excellent base for exploring Vence.

Cantermerle Hotel ★ Just south of Vence's Old Town, this hotel, restaurant, and spa is set within 3 acres of lush gardens. Spacious guestrooms feature terra-cotta tile floors and Provençal fabrics; many also boast their own private terrace. At the gourmet restaurant **La Table du Cantemerle,** chef Jérôme Héraud dishes up grilled Aveyron lamb in a parsley crust and lobster ravioli in the newly renovated dining room or outdoor alongside the pool. Use of the spa's heated indoor pool, mosaic Turkish baths, and fitness area is complimentary for guests.

258 chemin Cantemerle. www.cantemerle-hotel-vence.com. *(C)* **04-93-58-08-18.** 27 units. 175€–290€ double; 520€–570€ suite. Closed Nov–Mar. **Amenities:** Restaurant; 2 bars; outdoor pool; spa; free Wi-Fi.

Château Saint-Martin & Spa ★★★ Just 20 minutes from the Nice airport, amid 14 hectares (35 acres) of enchanting gardens, lies one of the most sumptuous hotels in the world. Take, for example, the Château Saint-Martin's spa. In addition to massages, it offers La Prairie and Bamford signature treatments, yoga lessons, color chromotherapy, and a wellness shower than can emulate the misting breeze of a tropical storm. Moreover, the hotel complex is shared by a mere handful of guests. Visitor favorites include the vast infinity pool, the outdoor **Oliveraie** grill restaurant set in an ancient olive grove, and mammoth chateau suites that overlook the shimmering sea below. Six independent villas are larger and more luxurious still. The double-Michelin-starred signature restaurant lies under the accomplished command of Yannick Franques, a protégé of Alain Ducasse. The cuisine switches from modern French fare to infused foam creations and desserts chilled with nitrogen steam. And it sits atop a wine cellar worth far more than the average Riviera mansion.

2490 av. des Templiers. www.chateau-st-martin.com. ℭ **04-93-58-02-02.** 39 units, 6 villas. 360€–585€ double; 470€–780€ suite; 930€–3,250€ villa. Rates include breakfast. Closed Oct to mid-Apr. **Amenities:** 3 restaurants; bar; babysitting; outdoor pool; room service; sauna; spa; tennis; free Wi-Fi.

Where to Eat

Vence's unpretentious attitude is also evident in the local cuisine. It tends to be traditional and tasty, occasionally Michelin-starred, and often dished up in a sublime setting. For homemade hot chocolate or artisanal sweets, **Entre Mes Chocolats,** 12 av. Marcellin Maurel (www.entre-mes-chocolats.com; ℭ **09-81-82-34-59**), is highly recommended.

The **Le Château du Domaine St-Martin** (see review in "Vence's Hotels," below) also offers award-winning dining.

Le Pigeonnier ★ PROVENÇAL   One of the Old Town's most welcoming eateries, Le Pigeonnier spills across the dining rooms of a 14th-century building and a sunny square, the latter perfect for people-watching. The restaurant menu is traditional. Linger over slow-cooked *daube* (a classic Niçois beef stew), a generous steak, or fish soup served with garlic croutons and *rouille,* saffron mayonnaise.

3 place du Peyra. ℭ **04-93-58-03-00.** Main courses 11€–19€; fixed-price menu 23€. July–Aug daily noon–2:30pm and 7:30–10pm; Sept–June Tues–Sat noon–2:30pm and 7:30–10pm, Sun noon–2:30pm.

Les Bacchanales ★★ PROVENÇAL   A short stroll from the Chapelle du Rosaire, Les Bacchanales is located inside a century-old villa, overlooking chef Christophe Dufau's enchanting kitchen garden. The creative menu uses almost exclusively local ingredients, transforming them into strikingly innovative versions of traditional Provençal cuisine. Mediterranean bream may be paired with apricots and Italian Taggiasche olives; sweet cantaloupe melon is grilled and served with fresh almonds and Corsican *brousse* cheese. Note that the market-fresh weekly menu is limited: Diners may simply select their preferred number of courses (two at lunch only, five to seven at dinner). The restaurant holds one Michelin star.

247 av. de Provence. www.lesbacchanales.com. ℭ **04-93-24-19-19.** Reservations recommended. Fixed-price menus 28€–85€. July–Aug Wed–Fri & Mon 7:30–9:30pm, Sat–Sun 12:30–2pm and 7:30–9:30pm; Sept–June Thurs–Mon 12:30–2pm and 7:30–9:30pm. Closed last 2 wks. of Dec, 3 wks. in Jan.

Exploring Vence

Vence's medieval **Vieille Ville (Old Town)** is compact, making it easy to explore on foot. A poke around its picturesque squares reveals place du Peyra's bubbling **Vieille Fontaine (Old Fountain),** while nearby the **Chateau de Villeneuve/Fondation Émile Hugues,** 2 place du Frêne (www.museedevence.com; ℭ **04-93-58-15-78**), is a temporary exhibition space dedicated to 20th-century art. Recent exhibits have showcased works by Matisse, Cézanne, and Jean-Michel Basquiat. Hours are Tuesday to Sunday 10am to 12:30pm and 2 to 6pm. Admission is 7€, 5€ for students, and free for children under 12. Also in the Old Town is **place Godeau,** where the **mosaic** "Moses saved from the Nile" by Marc Chagall adorns the 11th-century **cathedral**'s baptistery (free).

Vence's main draw, however, lies just outside the fortified main town. The Chapelle du Rosaire represents one of Matisse's most remarkable achievements.

Chapelle du Rosaire ★★ RELIGIOUS SITE   From the age of 47, Henri Matisse made Nice his home. But Vence held a special place in the artist's heart: It was his place of residence during World War II, as well as home to Dominican nun Sister Jacques-Marie, Matisse's former nurse and muse. So in 1947, when Matisse discovered that the sisters were planning the construction of a new chapel, he offered not only to design it, but fund the project as well. Matisse was 77 at the time.

The Chapelle du Rosaire was completed in 1951. A beautifully bright space, it offers the exceptional possibility of stepping into a three-dimensional artwork. Matisse described his creation: "What I have done in the chapel is to create a religious space . . . in an enclosed area of very reduced proportions and to give it, solely by the play of colors and lines, the dimensions of infinity."

From the front of the chapel, you may find the structure unremarkable and pass it by—until you spot a 12m (39-ft.) crescent-adorned cross rising from a blue-tile roof. Within, dozens of stained-glass windows shimmer cobalt blue (symbolizing the sea), sapphire green (the landscape), and golden yellow (the sun). Most remarkable are the 14 black-and-white-tile Stations of the Cross, featuring Matisse's self-styled "tormented and passionate" figures.

The bishop of Nice came to bless the chapel in the late spring of 1951; Matisse died 3 years later.

466 av. Henri-Matisse. ℂ **04-93-58-03-26.** Admission 3.50€ adults, 1.50€ children under 16; contributions to maintain the chapel are welcome. Mon, Wed, and Sat 2–5:30pm; Tues and Thurs 10–11:30am and 2–5:30pm. Closed mid-Nov to mid-Dec.

NICE ★★★

929km (576 miles) S of Paris; 32km (20 miles) NE of Cannes

The largest city on this fabled stretch of coast, Nice is known as the "Queen of the Riviera." It's also one of the most ancient, founded by the Greeks, who called it Nike (Victory). By the 19th century, Russian aristocrats and the British upper class—led by Queen Victoria herself—were sojourning here. These days, however, Nice is not as chi-chi as Cannes or St-Tropez. In fact, of all the major French resorts, Nice is the most down-to-earth, with an emphasis on fine dining and high culture. Indeed, it has more museums than any other French city outside Paris. In 2013 it inaugurated a new city center urban park, one of the largest public spaces in the South of France.

Nice is also the best place to base yourself on the Riviera, especially if you're dependent on public transportation. You can go to San Remo, a glamorous town over the Italian border, for lunch and return to Nice by nightfall. From Nice airport, the second largest in France, you can travel by train or bus along the entire coast to resorts such as Antibes, Juan-les-Pins, and Monaco.

Because of its brilliant sunshine and liberal attitude, Nice has long attracted artists and writers, among them Dumas, Nietzsche, Flaubert, Hugo, Sand, and Stendhal. Henri Matisse, who made his home in Nice, said, "Though the light is intense, it's also soft and tender." The city averages 300 sunny days a year.

Essentials

ARRIVING   Trains arrive at the city's main station, Gare Nice-Ville, avenue Thiers. From here you can take trains to Cannes for 5.60€, Monaco for 3.20€, and Antibes for

Nice

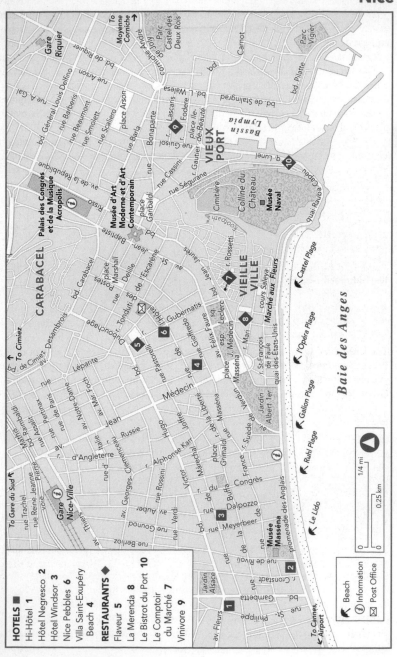

HOTELS ■
Hi-Hôtel **1**
Hôtel Negresco **2**
Hôtel Windsor **3**
Nice Pebbles **6**
Villa Saint-Exupéry
Beach **4**
RESTAURANTS ◆
Flaveur **5**
La Merenda **8**
Le Bistrot du Port **10**
Le Comptoir
du Marché **7**
Vinivore **9**

Beach
ℹ Information
☒ Post Office

1/4 mi
0.25 km

Baie des Anges

219

3.50€, with easy connections to Paris, Marseille, and anywhere else along the Mediterranean coast.

Buses (www.lignesdazur.com; ℂ **08-10-06-10-06**) to towns east, including Monaco (no. 100) depart from place Garibaldi; to towns west, including Cannes (no. 200) from Jardin Albert I.

Transatlantic and intercontinental flights land at **Aéroport Nice–Côte d'Azur** (www.nice.aeroport.fr; ℂ **08-20-42-33-33**). From there, municipal bus nos. 98 and 99 depart at 20-minute intervals for the port and Gare Nice-Ville, respectively; the one-way fare is 6€. A **taxi** from the airport to the city center costs between 30€ and 40€ each way. Trip time is about 20 minutes.

Ferryboats operated by **Trans-Côte d'Azur** (www.trans-cote-azur.com; ℂ **04-92-00-42-30**), on quai Lunel on Nice's port, link the city with Île Ste-Marguerite (see p. 203) from June to September and St-Tropez from June through August.

VISITOR INFORMATION Nice maintains three **tourist offices.** The largest is at 5 promenade des Anglais, near place Masséna (www.nicetourisme.com; ℂ **08-92-70-74-07**). Additional offices are in the arrivals hall of the Aéroport Nice–Côte d'Azur and outside the railway station on avenue Thiers.

CITY LAYOUT The city is divided into five main neighborhoods: the Italianate Old Town; the vintage port; the commercial city center between place Masséna and the main train station; the affluent residential quarter known as the Carré d'Or, just inland from the promenade des Anglais; and hilltop Cimiez. All are easy to navigate on foot, with the exception of Cimiez. For more, see "Exploring Nice," p. 224.

SPECIAL EVENTS The **Nice Carnaval** (www.nicecarnaval.com), known as the "Mardi Gras of the Riviera," runs from mid-February to early March, celebrating the return of spring with 3 weeks of parades, *corsi* (floats), *veglioni* (masked balls), confetti, and battles in which young women toss flowers at the audience.

The **Nice Festival du Jazz** (www.nicejazzfestival.fr) runs for a week in mid-July, when jazz, funk, and reggae artists perform in the Jardins Albert I near the seafront. Recent performers have included Herbie Hancock and George Benson.

Getting Around

ON FOOT Nice is very walkable, and no point of interest downtown is more than a 10-minute walk from place Massena, including the seafront promenade des Anglais, Old Town, and harbor.

BY BICYCLE & MOTOR SCOOTER Like many French cities, Nice has its own bike-sharing scheme, **Vélo Bleu** (www.velobleu.org). You can register directly at one of Nice's 175 bike stands (difficult) or online (much easier); fees range from 1€ for 1 day to 5€ for a week. Alternatively, you can rent bikes (from 12€ per day) and scooters (from 26€ per day; driver's license and deposit required) from **Holiday Bikes,** 23 rue de Belgique (www.holiday-bikes.com; ℂ **04-93-16-01-62**).

BY CAR A novel addition to the Nice transport scene is **Auto Bleue** (www.auto bleue.org; ℂ **09-77-40-64-06**). The scheme allows visitors to rent an electric Peugeot car from one of 50 vehicle stands around Nice for 45€ per day, inclusive of electricity, parking, and insurance. Sign-up online in advance.

BY TAXI **Taxis Niçois Indépendants** (www.taxis-nicois-independants.fr; ℂ **04-93-88-25-82**) will pick up within 5 minutes across town.

BY PUBLIC TRANSPORT Most local buses leave from the streets around place Masséna. Municipal buses charge 1.50€ for rides within the entire Alpes-Maritime province, even as far as Monaco or Cannes. The same ticket can also be used on Nice's tramway, which connects the Old Town with Gare Nice-Ville and northern Nice. Tickets and day passes (5€) can be bought directly onboard buses (although not trams) or at electronic kiosks around the city. For further information, see www.lignesdazur.com.

[FastFACTS] NICE

ATMs/Banks Nice is home to dozens of banks; **LCL Banque,** 15 av. Jean Médecin (© 04-93-82-84-61), is one of the most central.

Dentists SOS Dentaire (© 04-93-01-14-14).

Doctors & Hospitals Hôpital Saint-Roch, 5 rue Pierre Dévoluy (www.chu-nice.fr; © 04-92-03-33-33).

Embassies & Consulates U.S. Consular Agency Nice, 7 av. Gustave V (© 04-93-88-89-55); **Consulate of Canada,** 2 place Franklin (© 04-93-92-93-22).

Internet Access As of 2013, various public squares and streets (such as the cours Saleya) throughout Nice offer free Wi-Fi. Look for the network "NiceGOWEXFREEWiFi".

Local Information The **"Riviera Times"** (www.rivieratimes.com) and the **"Riviera Reporter"** (www.rivierareporter.com) both cover news, art, culture, and events in and around Nice. Alternatively, **"Angloinfo French Riviera"** (http://riviera.angloinfo.com) is an invaluable resource.

Mail & Postage La Poste, 6 rue Louis Gassin (© 36-31).

Pharmacies Pharmacie Masséna, 7 rue Masséna (© 04-93-87-78-94).

Safety Nice is generally a very safe place. However, as in any big city, it's important to keep an eye on your valuables, in particular anywhere that's crowded. Avoid poorly lit streets at night, including in Nice's Old Town.

Where to Stay
EXPENSIVE

Hi-Hôtel ★★ Tucked into a residential neighborhood, yet just minutes from the beach, this seven-story, former 1930s boardinghouse is a tribute to contemporary architecture. Designed by Matali Crasset, a one-time colleague of Philippe Starck, the hotel's 10 high-tech room concepts are utterly unconventional. They range from Indoor Terrasse, a vision of wooden decking and bamboo, to the brand-new Utop-Hi, sleek with polished concrete and a glass cube shower. Onsite there's an organic restaurant, a REN spa, Turkish baths, and a rooftop swimming pool with its own honesty bar. The Hi's nearby beach club, **Hi-Beach** (p. 227), is a hip hangout in its own right.

3 av. des Fleurs. www.hi-hotel.net. © 04-97-07-26-26. 38 units. 119€–469€ double; 159€–679€ suite. Parking 24€. **Amenities:** Restaurant; 24-hr. bar and snack bar; outdoor swimming pool; Turkish bath; free Wi-Fi.

Hôtel Negresco ★★ For more than a century, the Negresco has been Nice's most iconic hotel. Its flamingo-pink dome crowns the promenade des Anglais, its Belle Epoque façade turned towards the sea. Guestrooms—a mix of Louis XIV antiques and state-of-the-art wetrooms—have hosted each era's most noted celebrities, from the Beatles and Salvador Dali to Michael Jackson. Public areas are decorated with works from an exceptional collection of private art, which kicks off with the shimmering Nikki de St-Phalle jazz musician welcoming guests at the hotel's entrance. Dining ranges from the exquisite (the double-Michelin-starred **Chantecler** and its 15,000-bottle wine cellar) to the playful (the kooky merry-go-round-style brasserie, **La Rotonde**).

37 promenade des Anglais. www.hotel-negresco-nice.com. ✆ **04-93-16-64-00.** 117 units. 225€–600€ double; 620€–2,500€ suite. Parking 28€. **Amenities:** 2 restaurants; bar; babysitting; exercise room; massage; room service; free Wi-Fi.

MODERATE

Hôtel Windsor ★★★ The coolest, funkiest, and most friendly hotel in Nice is also one of its best-value lodging. This *maison bourgeoise* was built by disciples of Gustav Eiffel in the 1890s and has remained a family-run hotel for three generations. Current proprietor Mme Payen-Redolfi has ushered in an artsy era where a different acclaimed artist decorates another guest room each year. As of 2013 the hotel had 30 contemporary-art rooms, including one painted entirely in gold leaf by Claudio Parmigiani. Art and color stream outside into the unkempt bamboo garden—**WiJungle**—where alfresco breakfasts are also served. Back indoors, **WiLounge** serves dinner and chilled rosé. **WiZen** is the fifth-floor health club, hammam, sauna, and meditation zone.

11 rue Dalpozzo. www.hotelwindsornice.com. ✆ **04-93-88-59-35.** 57 units. 102€–175€ double. Parking 15€. **Amenities:** Restaurant; bar; babysitting; health club; outdoor pool; room service; sauna; free Wi-Fi.

INEXPENSIVE

Villa Saint Exupéry Beach ★ Just outside Nice's Old Town, this upscale hostel makes an ideal base for budget travelers of all ages. Accommodation ranges from dormitory-style beds to private twin rooms, and includes an abundant free buffet breakfast. Also onsite is a communal kitchen, gym with sauna, daily happy hour, and quality meals at backpacker prices. Its award-winning sister hostel, **Villa Saint Exupéry Gardens,** 22 ave Gravier (✆ **04-93-84-42-83**), is located in a converted monastery just north of the city center. A former chapel with stained-glass windows now serves as its buzzing bar.

6 rue Sacha Guitry. www.villahostels.com. ✆ **04-93-16-13-45.** 60 units. 35€–80€ per person in a single or twin-bedded room; 18€–40€ per person for dormitory bed. Rates include continental breakfast, sheets and towels. **Amenities:** Bar, cooking facilities, computers, luggage room, TV lounge; free WiFi.

ALTERNATE ACCOMMODATIONS

Nice Pebbles ★★★ A short-term rental of one of these holiday apartments allows you time to truly immerse yourself in local life, from cooking up morning-market bounty to sipping sunset aperitifs on your private terrace. More than 100 carefully selected properties (from studios to 10-bed homes) are dotted throughout the city's central neighborhoods, including the Old Town and harbor and along the promenade des Anglais. Apartments boast first-class amenities (iPod docks, high-def TVs, and designer bathrooms are common), yet weigh in at just a fraction of the price of a hotel room. Demand is high, so book well in advance. Sister agency **Riviera Pebbles** (www.rivierapebbles.com) manages additional properties along the coast.

23 rue Gioffredo. www.nicepebbles.com. ℭ **04-97-20-27-30.** 90€–350€ per apartment per night. **Amenities:** Babysitting; free Wi-Fi.

Where to Eat

Boasting more Michelin stars than Marseille, France's second-largest city, Nice is teeming with exquisite restaurants, from the high end to the downright local. Excellent eateries are scattered across the city—although beware of many of the Old Town's careless offerings, keen to lure in tourists for a single night only. In addition to the suggestions below, the portside **Le Bistrot du Port,** 28 quai Lunel (www.lebistrotdu-portdenice.fr; ℭ **04-93-55-21-70**), is where the Orsini family has been dishing up top-quality fish and creative seafood concoctions for over 30 years.

EXPENSIVE

Flaveur ★★ MODERN FRENCH   Brothers Gaël et Mickaël Tourteaux (whose last name, almost unbelievably, translates as "cake") are a pair of very talented chefs. They may be relatively young—38 and 34 respectively—yet they've already spent decades in the kitchens of the Riviera's top restaurants. Little surprise, then, that in 2011 their contemporary bistro, Flaveur, earned its first Michelin star. A childhood growing up on the tropical islands of Réunion and Guadeloupe means their modern French cuisine is laced with exotic flavors: Plump scallops are seasoned with Japanese *gomasio;* artistically displayed lemongrass and bubbles of lemon caviar sit atop risotto. Note that meals are variations on fixed-price menus only; there's no ordering à la carte, although lunchtime menus allow for gourmet bites on a budget.

25 rue Gubernatis. www.flaveur.net. ℭ **04-93-62-53-95.** Reservations required. Fixed-price lunch 28€–65€; fixed-price dinner 50€–80€. Tues–Fri noon–2pm and 7:30–11pm; Sat 7:30–11pm. Closed early Jan.

MODERATE

La Merenda ★★★ NIÇOIS   Top chef Dominique Le Stanc left the world of *haute cuisine* far behind to take over this tiny, traditional, family-run bistro. And how lucky we all are. La Merenda is now one of most authentic and unpretentious eateries along the French Riviera. Market-fresh specials are scribbled on a small chalkboard; depending on the season, they may include stuffed sardines, tagliatelle drenched in delicious basil pesto, or a delectable *tarte au citron.* Note that the restaurant has no phone, so you'll need to make reservations in person.

4 rue Raoul Bosio. www.lamerenda.net. No phone. Reservations required. Main courses 14€–29€. No credit cards. Mon–Fri noon–2pm and 7:30–10pm.

Le Comptoir du Marché ★★ TRADITIONAL FRENCH   A fabulous new addition to the local dining scene, Le Comptoir du Marché sits snugly within Nice's atmospheric Old Town. Dishes make use of hearty ingredients, yet chef Lois Guenzati has a light touch. The ever-changing menu may include seared tuna with coco beans, baby artichokes stewed with lardons, or grilled duck breast. There's an authentic vintage feel to the place. Request a table in the back room, where you'll have clear views into the open kitchen action. Le Comptoir's sister restaurant, **Bistrot d'Antoine,** 27 rue de la Préfecture (ℭ) **04-93-85-29-57**), is also superb.

8 rue du Marché. ℭ **04-93-13-45-01.** Reservations recommended. Main courses 16€–31€. Tues–Sat noon–2pm and 7–10:30pm.

INEXPENSIVE

Vinivore ★★ MODERN FRENCH   This vibrant eatery, located just behind the port, mixes fresh Provençal ingredients with Cantonese flair. Each day, Hong Kong–born chef Chun Wong's changing menu features just four appetizers, four main courses, and four desserts. Recent highlights include beef *tataki* with garlic flowers, wild rice risotto with grilled scallops, and vanilla-infused candied pineapple. Québécois sommelier Bonaventure Blankstein has handpicked some 200 vintages—carefully noted on the large chalkboards—from often-organic wineries across southern France. In 2013 the small **Vinivore wine bar** opened next door to the main restaurant.

10 rue Lascaris. www.vinivore.fr. ⓒ **04-93-14-68-09.** Reservations recommended. Main courses 10€–18€; fixed-price lunch 15€. Tues–Fri noon–2pm, Tues–Sat 7:30–10:30pm.

Exploring Nice

In 1822, Nice's orange crop had an awful year. The workers faced a lean time, so the English residents employed them to build the **promenade des Anglais ★★**, today a wide boulevard fronting the bay that stretches for 7km (4¼ miles), all the way to the airport. Along the beach are rows of grand cafes, the Musée Masséna, and the city's most glamorous hotels.

Crossing this boulevard in the tiniest bikinis are some of the world's most attractive bronzed bodies. They're all heading for the **beach.** Tough on tender feet, *le plage* is made not of sand, but of pebbles (and not small ones, either).

Rising sharply on a rock at the eastern end of the promenade is the **Colline du Château.** Once a fortified bastion, the hill has since been turned into a wonderful public park complete with a waterfall, cafés, and a giant children's play area, as well as an incredibly ornate cemetery. Head up aboard an elevator from the quai des Etats-Unis; more athletic visitors can walk up one of five sets of steep steps. The park is open daily from 8am to dusk.

Continuing east of the Colline, you reach the **Vieux Port,** or harbor, where the restaurants are filled with locals. While lingering over a drink at a sidewalk cafe, you can watch the ferries depart for Corsica and the yachts for St-Tropez. Just inland, the neighborhood around rue Bonaparte and place Garibaldi has become one of the hippest in town: head here for authentic eateries, hip bars, and the superb **MAMAC Museum of Contemporary Art,** place Yves Klein (www.mamac-nice.org; ⓒ **04-97-13-42-01;** free admission; closed Mon).

The **Vieille Ville ★★**, or Old Town, begins at the foot of the Colline and stretches to place Masséna. Sheltered by red-tiled roofs, many of the Italianate facades suggest 17th-century Genoese palaces, including the free museum **Palais Lascaris,** 15 rue Droite (ⓒ **04-93-62-72-40**). The Old Town is a maze of narrow streets teeming with local life, flower-strewn squares, and traditional *boulangeries:* sample a Niçois-style onion pizza *(pissaladière)* here. Many of the buildings are painted a faded Roman gold, and their banners are laundry flapping in the sea breeze.

From Tuesday through Sunday (8am–1pm), the Old Town's main pedestrianized thoroughfare, the **cours Saleya,** is crowded with local producers selling seasonal fruits and vegetables, cured meats, and artisanal cheeses. At the market's western end is the **Marché aux Fleurs.** A rainbow of violets, lilies and roses, the market operates Tuesday to Sunday from 8am to around 6pm. On Monday (8am–6pm) the cours Saleya is occupied by a superb **antiques market,** with vendors carting wares in from across France and Italy.

Nice's centerpiece is **place Masséna,** with rococo buildings and bubbling fountains, as well as a **parkway** that stretches from the MAMAC down to the **Jardin Albert-1er.** This verdant strip was renovated and newly pedestrianized in 2013. With palms and exotic flowers, it's one of the prettiest places in town.

Cathédrale Orthodoxe Russe St-Nicolas à Nice ★ CATHEDRAL   Ordered

built by none other than Tsar Nicholas II, this recently renovated cathedral is the most beautiful religious edifice of the Orthodoxy outside Russia. It dates from the Belle Epoque, when some of the Romanovs and entourage turned the Riviera into their stomping ground (everyone from grand dukes to ballerinas walked the promenade). The cathedral is richly ornamented and decorated with icons. You'll spot the building from afar because of its collection of ornate onion-shaped domes.

Av. Nicolas II (off bd. Tzaréwitch). www.cathedrale-russe-nice.fr. ✆ **04-93-83-94-08.** Free admission. Tues–Sun 9am–noon and 2–6pm. From the central rail station, bus nr. 71, or head west along av. Thiers to bd. Gambetta, and then go north to av. Nicolas-II.

Musée des Beaux-Arts ★★ ART MUSEUM   Housed in the fabulous former

residence of the Ukrainian Princess Kotchubey, this fine collection of 19th- and 20th-century art includes works by Rodin and Dufy, as well as works by a dynasty of painters, the Dutch Vanloo family. One of its best-known members, Carle Vanloo, born in Nice in 1705, was Louis XV's premier *peintre.* High drama hit the museum in 2007, when armed robbers broke into the museum on a quiet summer Sunday, stealing priceless canvases by Monet and Sisley. The artworks were recovered less than a year later in Marseille.

33 av. des Baumettes. www.musee-beaux-arts-nice.org. ✆ **04-92-15-28-28.** Free admission. Tues–Sun 10am–6pm. Bus: 3, 9, 10, 22, or 38.

Musée Masséna ★★★ MUSEUM   Riviera aficionados will adore this astound-

ing history museum. Located within an imposing Belle Epoque villa, it exhibits a quirky range of objects charting local life in Nice and its surrounds, from the first Victorian visitors through the roaring 1920s. Elegantly printed menus, train tickets from London to Nice, period maps, and snapshots of the promenading rich on vacation bring the past to life. Of additional note are the paintings and *objets d'art* donated by the Masséna family, a noble set of locals who constructed the villa. Botanist Edouard Ardre, who also designed the verdant greenery in front of the Casino de Monte-Carlo, landscaped the museum's neatly manicured gardens.

65 rue de France or 35 promenade des Anglais. ✆ **04-93-91-19-10.** Free admission. Wed–Mon 9am–6pm.

Outlying Attractions in Cimiez

In the once-aristocratic hilltop quarter of Cimiez, 5km (3 miles) north of Nice, Queen Victoria wintered at the Hôtel Excelsior. Half the English court traveled down from Calais with her on a luxurious private train. Be sure to stroll over to the adjacent **Monastère de Cimiez** (Cimiez Convent), which offers panoramic views over Nice and the Baie des Anges; artists Matisse and Dufy are buried in the cemetery nearby. To reach this suburb and its attractions, take bus no. 15 from bd. Dubouchage.

Musée Matisse ★★ ART MUSEUM   In 1963, this beautiful old Italian villa was transformed into a museum honoring Henri Matisse, one of the 20th century's greatest painters. Matisse came to Nice for the light and made the city his home, living in the Hotel Beau Rivage and on the cours Saleya, and dying in Cimiez in 1954. Most of the pieces in the museum's permanent collection—including "Nude in an Armchair with a Green Plant" (1937) and "Blue Nude IV" (1952)—were created in Nice. Artworks are interspersed with Matisse's personal possessions, such as ceramic vases and antique furniture, as well as scale models of his architectural masterpiece, Vence's **Chapelle du Rosaire** (p. 218).

164 av. des Arènes de Cimiez. www.musee-matisse.nice.org. ⓒ **04-93-81-08-08.** Free admission. Wed–Mon 10am–6pm.

Musée National Message Biblique Marc Chagall ★★ ART MUSEUM   Surrounded by pools and a garden, this handsome museum is devoted to Marc Chagall's treatment of biblical themes. Born in Russia in 1887, Chagall became a French citizen in 1937 and painted with astonishing light and color until his death in St-Paul-de-Vence in 1985. This museum's focal set of artworks—12 large paintings, illustrating the first two books of the Old Testament—was originally created to adorn the central cathedral in Vence. The church's high humidity nixed the artist's original plans, and Chagall assisted in planning this purpose-built space instead. The 200 additional artworks include gouaches, a mosaic, sculptures, and prints.

Av. du Dr. Ménard. www.musee-chagall.fr. ⓒ **04-93-53-87-20.** Admission 8€ adults, 6€ students, free for children 17 and under. May–Oct Wed–Mon 10am–6pm; Nov–Apr Wed–Mon 10am–5pm.

Organized Tours

One of the most enjoyable ways to quickly gain an overview of Nice is aboard a **Nice–Le Grand Tour** (www.nicelegrandtour.com; ⓒ **04-92-29-17-00**) double-decker bus. Between 10am and 6pm year-round, one of a flotilla of this company's buses departs from a position adjacent to the Jardin Albert I. The panoramic 90-minute tour takes in the harbor, the museums of Cimiez, the Russian church, and the promenade. Per-person rates for the experience are 21€ adults, 18€ students, and 5€ children 4 to 11. Participants can get off at any of 11 stops en route and reboard any other buses, which follow at 30- to 60-minute intervals, depending on the season. Advance reservations aren't necessary, and commentary is piped through to headsets in seven different languages. Tickets are valid the entire day of purchase.

Another easy way to see the city is by the small **Train Touristique de Nice** (www.trainstouristiquesdenice.com; ⓒ **06-08-55-08-30**), which also departs from the promenade des Anglais, opposite Jardin Albert I. The 45-minute ride passes many of Nice's most-heralded sites, including place Masséna, the Old Town, and the Colline du Château. Departing every 30 minutes, the train operates daily 10am to 5pm (until 6pm Apr–May and Sept, until 7pm June–Aug). The round-trip price is 8€ adults and 4€ children 4 to 12.

Possibly the coolest way to get around Nice is by Segway, the two-wheeled electronic scooters. Bespoke tours are run by **Mobilboard**, 2 rue Halévy (www.mobilboard.com; ⓒ **04-93-80-21-27**). Children 14 (minimum age) to 17 must be accompanied by an adult. An hour-long tour of Nice costs 30€ per person.

Outdoor Activities

BEACHES   Along Nice's seafront, beaches extend uninterrupted for more than 7km (4¼ miles), going from the edge of Vieux-Port (the old port, or harbor) to the international airport. Tucked between the public areas are several rather chic private beaches. Many of these beach bars provide mattresses and parasols for 12€ to 22€. The coolest clubs include **Hi-Beach** (www.hi-beach.net; ℭ 04-97-14-00-83), which has a sushi bar, blanket Wi-Fi, and family-friendly playpens; and **Castel Plage** (www.castelplage. com; ℭ 04-93-85-22-66), a celebrity hangout in summer.

SCUBA DIVING   Of the many diving outfits in Nice harbor, **Nice Diving,** 13 quai des Deux Emmanuel (www.nicediving.com; ℭ 06-14-46-04-06), offers bilingual instruction and *baptêmes* (dives for first-timers) around Nice and Cap Ferrat. A dive for experienced divers, equipment included, costs around 50€; appropriate diver's certification is required.

Shopping

CLOTHES   Nice's densest concentrations of fashionable French labels are clustered around **rue Masséna** and **avenue Jean-Médecin.** For more high-end couture, the streets around **place Magenta,** including **rue de Verdun, rue Paradis,** and **rue Alphonse Karr** are a credit card's worst nightmare. A shop of note is **Cotelac,** 12 rue Alphonse Karr (ℭ 04-93-87-31-59), which sells chic women's clothing. Men should try **Façonnable,** 7–9 rue Paradis (www.faconnable.com; ℭ 04-93-88-06-97). This boutique is the original site of a chain with several hundred branches worldwide; the look is conservatively stylish. For more unusual apparel, **Lucien Chasseur,** 2 rue Bonaparte (ℭ 04-93-55-52-14), is the city's coolest spot for Italian-designed shoes, scarves, and soft leather satchels.

FOOD   The winding streets of Nice's Old Town are the best place to find local crafts, ceramics, gifts, and foodie purchases. If you're thinking of indulging in a Provençale *pique-nique,* **Nicola Alziari,** 14 rue St François de Paule (www.alziari. com.fr; ℭ 04-93-62-94-03), will provide everything from olives, anchovies, and pistous to aiolis and tapenades. For an olive-oil tasting session—and the opportunity to buy the goods afterward—check out **Oliviera,** 2 rue Benoit Bunico (www. oliviera.com; ℭ 04-93-11-06-45), run by the amiable Nadim Beyrouti. In the port, **Confiserie Florian,** 14 quai Papacino (www.confiseriflorian.com; ℭ 04-93-55-43-50), has been candying fruit, chocolate-dipping roasted nuts, and crystalizing edible flowers since 1949.

SOUVENIRS   The best selection of Provençal fabrics is at **Le Chandelier,** 7 rue de la Boucherie (ℭ 04-93-85-85-19), where you'll see designs by two of the region's best-known producers of cloth, Les Olivades and Valdrôme. For antiquarian books, contemporary art, kitsch, and comic books, wander north of place Garibaldi to **rue Delille,** just past the MAMAC modern art gallery. And for offbeat gifts, **Chambre Cinquante-Sept,** 16 rue Emmanuel Philibert (ℭ 04-92-04-02-81), stocks beautifully unique Art Deco *objets d'art.*

Nightlife

Nice has some of the most active nightlife and cultural offerings along the Riviera. Big evenings out usually begin at a cafe or bar, take in a restaurant, opera, or film, and finish in a club. The website **riviera.angloinfo.com** lists all the week's English-language movies in *version originale*.

The major cultural center on the Riviera is the **Opéra de Nice,** 4 rue St-François-de-Paule (www.opera-nice.org; ℰ **04-92-17-40-00**), built in 1885 by Charles Garnier, fabled architect of the Paris Opéra. It presents a full repertoire, with emphasis on serious, often large-scale operas, such as "Tristan and Isolde" and "La Boheme," as well as a *saison symphonique* dominated by the Orchestre Philharmonique de Nice. The opera hall is also the major venue for concerts and recitals. Tickets are available (to concerts, recitals, and full-blown operas) right up until the day of performance. You can show up at the box office (Mon–Thurs 9am–5:30pm; Fri until 7:45pm; Sat until 4:30pm) or buy tickets in advance online. Tickets run from 10€ to 80€.

A chic gaming spot is the **Casino in the Palais de Méditerranée,** 15 promenade des Anglais (www.casinomediterranee.com; ℰ **04-92-14-68-00**), which offers a similar experience daily from 10am for slot machines, 8pm for gaming tables.

At the hip end of the spectrum is **Smarties,** 10 rue Defly (www.nicesmarties.free.fr; ℰ **04-93-62-30-75**), a cocktail lounge with great DJs. The Old Town's most happening spot is **Villa,** 7 rue Raoul Bosio (ℰ **04-93-87-99-45**), whose house aperitif is the wickedly named Putain de le Palais: crushed strawberries topped with Champagne. Within the cool-kitsch decor of a former garage in the port area, talented staff serve up fruity cocktails and organic local wines at **Rosalina,** 16 rue Lascaris (ℰ **04-93-89-34-96**).

The party spirit is best lapped up in the alfresco bars on the **cours Saleya.** Otherwise, head 1 block inland to **Wayne's Bar,** 15 rue de la Préfecture (www.waynes.fr; ℰ **04-93-13-46-99**), where dancing on the tables to raucous cover bands is the norm. For excellent house tunes, nonstop dancing, and heaps of understated cool, head to **Bliss,** 12 rue de l'Abbaye (ℰ **04-93-16-82-38**).

VILLEFRANCHE-SUR-MER ★★

935km (580 miles) S of Paris; 6.5km (4 miles) E of Nice

Just east of Nice, the coastal Lower Corniche sweeps inland to reveal Villefranche, its medieval Old Town tumbling downhill into the shimmering sea. Paired with a dazzling sheltered bay set against picturesque Cap Ferrat beyond, it's little wonder than countless artists made this beachy getaway their home—or that it's served as the cinematic backdrop for numerous movies.

Essentials

ARRIVING   **Trains** arrive from all the Côte d'Azur's coastal resorts from Cannes to Monaco every 30 minutes or so. For rail schedules, visit www.voyages-sncf.com or call ℰ **36-35. Ligne d'Azur** (www.lignesdazur.com; ℰ **08-10-06-10-06**) maintains a **bus** service at 5- to 15-minute intervals aboard line no. 100 from Nice to Monte Carlo via Villefranche. One-way fares cost 1.50€. Buses deposit passengers just above the Old Town, almost directly opposite the tourist information office. Many visitors **drive** via the Basse Corniche (Lower Corniche).

VISITOR INFORMATION   The **Office de Tourisme** is on Jardin François-Binon (www.villefranche-sur-mer.com; ℰ **04-93-01-73-68**).

[FastFACTS] VILLEFRANCHE

ATMs/Banks   **LCL Banque,** 6 av. du Maréchal Foch (📞 **04-93-76-24-01**).

Internet Access   **Chez Net,** 5 place du Marché (www.cheznet.com; 📞 **04-89-08-19-43**).

Mail & Postage   **La Poste,** 6 av. Albert 1er (📞 **36-31**).

Pharmacies   **Pharmacie Laurent,** 2 av. du Maréchal Foch (📞 **04-93-01-70-10**).

Where to Stay

Hotel Villa Patricia ★   Yes, this petite seaside hotel really does have double rooms for under 50€ in the height of summer. A 5-minute stroll from the water, it also boasts a shared garden sheltered by lemon trees. As one might expect for the price, some rooms are small, while others are oddly shaped, but all are stylish, smart, and exceptionally clean, and share a large lounge area complete with book swap, outdoor sofas, and a piano. It's a gentle 10-minute stroll from Villefranche, Beaulieu, and Cap Ferrat.

310 Avenue de l'Ange Gardien. www.hotel-patricia.riviera.fr. 📞 **04-93-01-06-70.** 12 units. 44€–89€ double; 80€–110€ suite. Free parking. Closed last week Dec, first week Jan. **Amenities:** Free Wi-Fi.

Hôtel Welcome ★   Villefranche's most prestigious hotel, the Welcome sits in the center of town and has been home to Riviera artists since the 1920s, including author and filmmaker Jean Cocteau (in room 22). Every one of the modern hotel's midsize-to-spacious rooms possesses a balcony and sea views. The on-site **wine bar** spills out onto the quay in warm weather. The hotel also rents out *Orphée,* its eight-person private sailboat, for daily cruises; prices from 650€ per half-day with crew.

3 quai Amiral Courbet. www.welcomehotel.com. 📞 **04-93-76-27-62.** 35 units. 135€–345€ double; 212€–810€ suite. Parking 45€. **Amenities:** Bar; babysitting; room service; free Wi-Fi.

Where to Eat

Le Cosmo ★★ MEDITERRANEAN   This friendly sidewalk cafe has been pulling in punters for a decade—and with good reason. Prices are reasonable, the creative menu is perfectly executed, and the setting is sublime: The restaurant's terraced seating overlooks Cocteau's Chapelle St-Pierre and the seafront beyond. Sample sautéed scallops with aubergine caviar, or *salade Cosmo,* topped with avocado, shrimp, grapefruit, and hearts of palm. Dozens of fantastical ice cream creations (think yogurt ice cream piled high with strawberries and raspberry puree, or a tower of praline ice cream, whipped cream, and chocolate sauce) are also on offer.

11 pl. Amélie Pollonais. www.restaurant-lecosmo.fr. 📞 **04-93-01-84-05.** Main courses 14€–25€. Daily 7:45am–2am.

Exploring Villefranche

Villefranche's long arc of golden sands, **plage des Marinières,** is the principal attraction for most visitors. From here, **quai Courbet** runs along the sea to the colorful Old Town past scores of bobbing boats; it's lined with waterside restaurants.

Old-town action revolves around **place Amélie Pollonnais,** a delightful square shaded by palms and spread with the tables of six easygoing restaurants. It's also the site of a Sunday antiques market, where people from across the Riviera come to root through vintage tourism posters, silverware, 1930s jewelry, and ex-hotel linens.

The painter, writer, filmmaker, and well-respected dilettante Jean Cocteau left a fine memorial to the town's inhabitants. He spent a year (1956–57) painting frescoes on the 14th-century walls of the Romanesque **Chapelle St-Pierre,** quai Courbet (© **04-93-76-90-70**). He presented it to "the fishermen of Villefranche in homage to the Prince of Apostles, the patron of fishermen." In the apse is a depiction of the miracle of St. Peter walking on the water, not knowing that an angel supports him. Villefranche's busty local women, in their regional costumes, are honored on the left side of the narthex. Admission is 2.50€, free for children under 15. In spring and summer, it is open Wednesday to Monday 10am to noon and 3 to 7pm; fall and winter hours are Wednesday to Monday 10am to noon and 2 to 6pm. It's closed from mid November to mid December.

A short coastal path leads from the car park below place Amélie Pollonnais to the **16th-century citadelle.** This castle dominates the bay, and its ramparts and small interior museums can be wandered around at leisure.

ST-JEAN-CAP-FERRAT & BEAULIEU-SUR-MER ★★

939km (582 miles) S of Paris; 9.5km (6 miles) E of Nice

Of all the oases along the Côte d'Azur, no other place has the snob appeal of Cap-Ferrat. It's a 15km (9¼-mile) promontory sprinkled with luxurious villas and outlined by sheltered bays, beaches, and sun-kissed coves. In the charming port of St-Jean, the harbor accommodates yachts, fishing boats, and a dozen low-key eateries.

Cradled on the mainland just east of Cap-Ferrat, the Belle Epoque resort of Beaulieu-sur-Mer has long attracted *bonnes vivantes* with its casino and fine restaurants.

Essentials

ARRIVING **Trains** connect Beaulieu with Nice, Monaco, and the rest of the Côte d'Azur every 30 minutes. Many visitors take a **taxi** to St-Jean from Beaulieu's rail station; alternatively, it's a 30-minute walk along Cap-Ferrat's coastal pathway. For **rail** information, visit www.voyages-sncf.com or call © **36-35. Bus** line no. 100 from Nice to Monte Carlo passes through Beaulieu, while the hourly no. 81 connects Nice with St-Jean. One-way fares costs 1.50€. For bus information and schedules, contact **Ligne d'Azur** (www.lignesdazur.com; © **08-10-06-10-06**). By **car** from Nice, take D6098 (the *basse corniche*) east.

VISITOR INFORMATION St-Jean's **Office de Tourisme** is on 59 av. Denis-Séméria (www.saintjeancapferrat.fr; © **04-93-76-08-90**). Beaulieu's **Office de Tourisme** is on place Georges Clémenceau (www.beaulieusurmer.fr; © **04-93-01-02-21**).

[FastFACTS] ST-JEAN & BEAULIEU

ATMs/Banks **Banque Populaire Côte d'Azur,** 5 av. Claude Vignon, St-Jean 06230 (*©* **04-89-81-11-42**).

Mail & Postage **La Poste,** 51 av. Denis Séméria, St-Jean 06230 (*©* **36-31**).

Pharmacies **Pharmacie Pont Saint Jean,** 57 bd. Dominique Durandy, St-Jean 06230 (*©* **04-93-01-62-50**).

Where to Stay

Grand Hôtel du Cap-Ferrat ★★★ Put simply, this grande dame of a hotel is the greatest building on Europe's richest peninsula. It's sumptuous, stylish, and incredibly sexy. Set on 17 acres of tropical trees and manicured lawns, it's been the exclusive retreat of the international elite since 1908. The **Cellu M6** spa spills outside into curtained cabanas, where massages and other treatments can be indulged in. Aside from the modernist guestrooms, the coolest place to hang out is the seaside **Club Dauphin** beach club (nonguests can gain access for 90€ per day). It's reached by a funicular rail pod that descends from the hotel. The children of many visiting celebrities, including the Kennedys and Paul McCartney, have learned to swim in the Olympic-size infinity pool. **Le Cap,** the hotel's acclaimed gourmet restaurant, is overseen by head chef Didier Aniès. His Michelin-starred cuisine is heavy on caviar, oysters, and luxurious French classics, while the wine list runs from rare local Bellet vintages to the esteemed Château d'Yquem.

71 bd. du Général-de-Gaulle. www.grand-hotel-cap-ferrat.com. *©* **04-93-76-50-50.** 73 units. 275€–1,100€ double; 600€–4,200€ suite. Closed Jan and Feb. Amenities: 3 restaurants; bar; babysitting; beach club; bikes; Olympic-size heated outdoor pool; room service; spa; tennis; free Wi-Fi.

Hôtel Brise Marine ★ An Italianate villa constructed in 1878, the Brise Marine is tucked into a quiet residential neighborhood south of St-Jean. Rooms are simply furnished and sunny, with enchanting sea views. Breakfast on the rose-twined terrace, and you can almost imagine you're aboard one of the luxury superyachts bobbing off nearby Paloma Plage.

58 av. Jean-Mermoz. www.hotel-brisemarine.com. *©* **04-93-76-04-36.** 16 units. 155€–197€ double; 185€–227€ triple; 176€–206€ studio. Parking 15€. Closed Nov–Feb. **Amenities:** Bar; room service; free Wi-Fi.

Where to Eat

The African Queen ★ FRENCH/INTERNATIONAL A lively mix of yachties, celebrity patrons, and excellent cuisine makes this portside restaurant perennially popular. Wood-fired pizzas are superb; the finely chopped *salade Niçoise* is dressed at your table; the sole *meunière* a buttery classic. Service can be erratic, but both the menu and the atmosphere are a delight. Celebrity-spotting opportunities abound all summer long.

Port de Plaisance. www.africanqueen.fr. *©* **04-93-01-10-85.** Reservations recommended. Pizzas 12€–28€; main courses 12€–80€. Daily noon–midnight. Closed some holidays.

Capitaine Cook ★ PROVENÇAL/SEAFOOD Perhaps the peninsula's most beloved eatery, Capitaine Cook is run by husband-and-wife team Lionel and Nelly Pelletier. Dine outdoors on the leafy terrace or indoors within the ruggedly maritime dining room. The menu is particularly strong on hearty yet imaginative fish dishes, from stuffed sardines to salmon ravioli.

11 av. Jean-Mermoz. ℰ **04-93-76-02-66.** Reservations recommended. Main courses 18€–30€; fixed-price menu 27€–32€. Fri–Tues 12:30–2pm; Thurs–Tues 7:30–10:30pm. Closed mid-Nov to Dec.

Exploring St-Jean & Beaulieu

One way to enjoy the area's beautiful backdrop is to stroll the public pathway that links Beaulieu and St-Jean. It eventually circles the entire peninsula, winding past deserted coves and alongside the gardens of countless millionaire dwellings. The most scenic section runs from chic **plage de Paloma,** near the Cap-Ferrat's southernmost tip, to **pointe St-Hospice,** where a panoramic view of the Riviera landscape unfolds. Allow around 3 hours to hike from St-Jean to family-friendly **plage Passable,** on the north-western "neck" of the peninsula.

Villa Ephrussi de Rothschild ★★ HISTORIC HOME/MUSEUM The winter residence of Baronne Béatrice Ephrussi de Rothschild, this Italianate villa was completed in 1912 according to the finicky specifications of its ultra-rich owner. Today the pink edifice preserves an eclectic collection, gathered over her lifetime: 18th-century furniture, Tiepolo ceilings, tapestries from Gobelin, a games table gifted from Marie-Antoine (Ephrussi's hero) to a friend, and tiny seats for her beloved poodles. The nine themed gardens, from Florentine to Japanese, are a particular delight. An attractive tea salon overlooks the Bay of Villefranche.

1 av. Ephrussi de Rothschild. www.villa-ephrussi.com. ℰ **04-93-01-33-09.** Admission 13€ adults, 9.50€ students and children 7–17, free for children 6 and under. July–Aug daily 10am–7pm; Feb 15–June and Sept–Oct daily 10am–6pm; Nov–Feb 14 Mon–Fri 2–6pm, Sat–Sun 10am–6pm.

Villa Kérylos ★★ HISTORIC HOME/MUSEUM This replica ancient Greek residence, constructed between 1902 and 1908, was painstakingly designed by archaeologist and devoted Hellenophile Theodore Reinach. Both indoors and out, the villa is a fastidiously flawless copy of a second-century Greek home. All period furniture was re-created using traditional Greek methods, while various rooms incorporated 20th-century conveniences, such as running water in the villa's *balaneion,* or thermal baths. The bucolic waterside gardens are dotted with olive and pomegranate trees and offer sweeping vistas over nearby Cap-Ferrat.

Impasse Gustave Eiffel. www.villa-kerylos.com. ℰ **04-93-01-01-44.** Admission 11€ adults, 8.50€ students and children 7–17, free for children 6 and under. July–Aug daily 10am–7pm; Feb 17–June and Sept–Oct daily 10am–6pm; Nov–Feb 16 Mon–Fri 2–6pm, Sat–Sun 10am–6pm.

EZE & LA TURBIE ★★

942km (584 miles) S of Paris; 11km (6¾ miles) NE of Nice

The hamlets of Eze and La Turbie, 6.5km (4 miles) apart, are picture-perfect hill villages that literally cling to the mountains. Both have fortified medieval cores overlooking the coast, and both were built during the early Middle Ages to stave off raids from Saracen pirates. In Eze's case, it's now tour buses, not coastal raiders, that make daily invasions into town. Impossibly cute streets contain galleries, boutiques, and artisans' shops. La Turbie is much quieter, offering a welcome respite from the coast's summertime heat.

Essentials

ARRIVING **Trains** connect Eze-sur-Mer with Nice, Monaco, and the rest of the Côte d'Azur every 30 minutes. You may take a taxi from here up (1,400 ft.) to Eze; alternatively, bus no. 83 connects the rail station with the hilltop village. For rail information, visit www.voyages-sncf.com or call ℰ 36-35. **Bus** line no. 82 runs between Nice and Eze around every 90 minutes, while five to seven daily buses (no. 116) connect Nice and La Turbie. Both journeys take 40 minutes. One-way fares cost 1.50€. For all bus information and schedules, contact **Ligne d'Azur** (www.lignesdazur.com; ℰ **08-10-06-10-06**). By **car** from Nice, take the spellbindingly pretty D6007 (the *moyenne corniche*) east.

VISITOR INFORMATION Eze's **Office de Tourisme** is on place du Général-de-Gaulle, Eze-Village (www.eze-tourisme.com; ℰ **04-93-41-26-00**). La Turbie's small **tourist information point** is at 2 place Detras, La Turbie (www.ville-la-turbie.fr; ℰ **04-93-41-21-15**).

[FastFACTS] EZE & LA TURBIE

ATMs/Banks **Société Générale,** place de la Colette, Eze 06360 (ℰ **04-92-41-51-10**); **BNP Paribas,** 6 av Général de Gaulle, La Turbie 06360 (ℰ **08-20-82-00-01**).

Mail & Postage **La Poste,** av. du Jardin Exotique, Eze 06360; **La Poste,** place Neuve, La Turbie 06360; both (ℰ **36-31**).

Pharmacies **Pharmacie Lecoq,** place Colette, Eze 06360 (ℰ **04-93-41-06-17**); **Pharmacie de La Turbie,** 6 av Général de Gaulle, La Turbie 06360 (ℰ **04-93-41-16-50**).

Where to Stay

Château de la Chèvre d'Or ★★★ No hotel better sums up the glamour and grace of the French Riviera than La Chèvre d'Or. This resort hotel is built into and around the elegant hilltop town of Eze. Each sumptuously decorated suite is a grand apartment with a panoramic view of the coastline. It's a habitual favorite of royalty and A-listers, and recent makeovers have made it popular with vacationing families and young hipsters as well. The 38 terraced gardens drip down the hill towards the Mediterranean to ensure absolute privacy—indeed there's a ratio of one garden and three staff members to each room or suite. The best thing about La Chèvre d'Or? That would be the eponymous double-Michelin-starred **restaurant** overseen by top chef Ronan Kervaree (set menus 75€–230€). Experimental dishes include a vegan square decorated with an edible garden of herbs and flowers; San Remo shrimp wrapped in oyster-infused gossamer-thin pasta; and baby lamb shot through with parsley and violet.

Rue du Barri. www.chevredor.com. ℰ **04-92-10-66-66.** 37 units. 280€–850€ double; suites from 720€ suite. Parking 15€. Closed Dec–Feb. **Amenities:** 4 restaurants; bar; babysitting; exercise room; outdoor pool; room service; sauna; free Wi-Fi.

Where to Eat

Gascogne Café ★ FRENCH/ITALIAN   On the main road just outside of Eze's fortified Old Town, this bustling eatery is a friendly spot to sample authentic local fare. The menu ranges from traditional flavors (homemade lasagna, sea bass on a bed of ratatouille) to more creative offerings (Asian-style rolls stuffed with snails and garlic cream). Tasty pizzas are also available. Ambience is decidedly casual.

151 av. de Verdun, place de la Collette, Eze 06360. www.gascogne-hotel-restaurant.fr. ℂ **04-93-41-18-50.** Main courses 10€–24€; fixed-price menus 17€–29€. Daily 12:30–3pm and 7:30–10pm.

Exploring Eze & La Turbie

Aside from its pretty lanes, the leading attraction in Eze is the **Jardin d'Eze** ★, 20 rue du Château (ℂ **04-93-41-10-30**). Here exotic plants are interspersed with feminine sculptures by Jean Philippe Richard, all perched atop the town at 1,400 feet. Admission is 6€ adults, 2.50€ students and ages 12 to 25, and free children 11 and under. In July and August, it's open daily 9am to 7:30pm; the rest of the year it opens daily at 9am and closes between 4 and 7pm, depending on the time of sunset.

La Turbie boasts an impressive monument erected by Roman emperor Augustus in 6 B.C., the **Trophée des Alps (Trophy of the Alps)** ★. Still partially intact today, it was created to celebrate the subjugation of the French Alpine tribes by the Roman armies. The nearby **Musée du Trophée d'Auguste,** avenue Albert-1er (ℂ **04-93-41-20-84**), is an interactive mini-museum containing finds from digs nearby, a historical 3D film, and details about the monument's restoration. Both the ruins and the museum are open Tuesday to Sunday mid-May to mid-September 9:30am to 1pm and 2:30 to 6:30pm, and mid-September to mid-May 10am to 1:30pm and 2:30 to 5pm. Admission to both sites is 5.50€ adults, free children 17 and under.

MONACO ★★

939km (582 miles) S of Paris; 18km (11 miles) E of Nice

This sunny stretch of coast became the property of the Grimaldi clan in 1297, when one Francesco Grimaldi tricked his way into the fortress protecting the harbor. The dynasty has maintained something resembling independence ever since. In recent decades the clan has turned Monaco into the world's chicest city-state with its own mini-airport (with direct helicopter links to Nice and St-Tropez, no less).

Hemmed in by France on three sides and the Mediterranean on the fourth, this feudal anomaly harbors the world's greatest number of billionaires per capita. And as almost everybody knows, the Monégasques do not pay taxes. Celebrity exiles—including tennis player Rafael Nadal and racing driver Lewis Hamilton—are attracted by the tax regime too. Nearly all of Monaco's revenue comes from banking, tourism, and gambling. Better still, in an astute feat of cunning, local residents aren't allowed to gamble away their inheritance, so visitors must bring a passport to play on the Principality's famed poker, roulette, and blackjack tables.

Monaco, or, more precisely, its capital of Monte Carlo, has for a century been a symbol of glamour. The 1956 marriage of Prince Rainier III to American actress Grace Kelly enhanced its status. She met the prince when she was in Cannes to promote "To Catch a Thief." Their daughter Caroline was born in 1957; a son, Albert, in 1958; and a second daughter, Stephanie, in 1965.

Prince Rainier was nicknamed the "Builder Prince" as he expanded the territory by building into the Mediterranean. There were once more elaborate plans afoot to construct a Venetian lagoon of canals just off the coast, while as recently as 2008 American architect Daniel Libeskind proposed a 12-hectare "Land Sea" island off the coast. Prince Albert took over from his late father in 2005 and burnishes his "Eco-Prince" credentials with pride. Newer, more environmentally conscious land-reclamation schemes are scheduled to start near the Fairmont Hotel. The Principality also has its own green car manufacturer, Venturi—although this marquee specializes in a typically Monégasque market for all-electric supercars.

Fortunately for the Grimaldi line, Albert married his girlfriend, South African swimmer Charlene Wittstock, in July 2011, now Her Serene Highness The Princess of Monaco. Despite rumors of a pre-wedding fallout, the couple are idolized in the Principality. Following a crash course in both Monégasque dialect and European court protocol, Princess Charlene is now a familiar sight at society events. The royal couple's official portrait has pride of place in every bar, hotel, and bakery in the land.

Essentials

ARRIVING Monaco has rail, bus, highway—and helicopter—connections from other coastal cities, especially Nice. There are no border formalities when entering Monaco from France. The 19km (12 miles) **drive** from Nice takes around 30 minutes and runs along the N7 Moyenne Corniche. The pretty D6098 coast road takes a little longer. **Ligne d'Azur** (www.lignesdazur.com; © 08-10-06-10-06) runs a **bus** service at 15-minute intervals aboard line no. 100 from Nice to Monte Carlo. One-way bus transit from Nice costs 1.50€. **Trains** arrive every 30 minutes from Cannes, Nice, Menton, and Antibes. Monaco's underground railway station *(gare)* is on place St. Devote. A system of pedestrian tunnels, escalators, and elevators riddle the Principality, and such an underground walkway links the train station to Monte Carlo. The scheduled **chopper** service to Nice Airport costs 120€ via **Heli Air Monaco** (www.heliairmonaco.com; © 92-05-00-50). By **bus** it's just 20€ (www.niceairportxpress.com; © 04-97-00-07-00).

VISITOR INFORMATION The **Direction du Tourisme et des Congrés** tourist office is at 2A bd. des Moulins (www.visitmonaco.com; © 92-16-61-16).

CITY LAYOUT The second-smallest state in Europe (Vatican City is the tiniest), Monaco consists of four parts. The Old Town, **Monaco-Ville,** on a rocky promontory 60m (197 ft.) high. It's the seat of the Prince's Palace and the government building, as well as the Oceanographic Museum. To the west, **La Condamine** is at the foot of the Old Town, forming its ritzy harbor and port sector. Up from the port (Monaco is seriously steep) is **Monte Carlo,** the playground of royalty and celebrity, and the setting for the casino, the Tourist Office, and various luxurious hotels. The fourth part, **Fontvieille,** is a neat industrial suburb housing the

---

Earth Calling Monaco

To call Monaco from within France, dial 00 (the access code for all international long-distance calls from France); followed by the **country code, 377;** and then the eight-digit local phone number. (Don't dial 33; that's the country code for France.)

Monaco Football club, which was purchased by Russian billionaire Dmitry Rybolovlev. Thanks to the Russian's financial backing, the club was promoted to the French premier league in 2013.

SPECIAL EVENTS   Two of the most-watched **car-racing events** in the world are in January (Le Rallye) and May (the Grand Prix). The **Monte-Carlo Masters** ATP tennis tournament (www.monte-carlorolexmasters.com) takes place in April. The **Monte-Carlo International Fireworks Festival** lasts all summer long. The skies above the harbor are lit up several times a week as millions of euros go up in smoke, courtesy of those who can assuredly afford it.

8 [FastFACTS] MONACO

ATMs/Banks   Among many others, there are several banks along boulevard Albert 1er behind the Port of Monaco.

Internet Access   **Bilig Café,** 11 rue Princesse Caroline (✆ **97-98-20-43**).

Mail & Postage   **La Poste,** place de la Mairie in Monte-Carlo (✆ **36-31**).

Pharmacies   **Pharmacie Internationale,** 22 rue Grimaldi (✆ **04-93-50-35-99**).

Getting Around

BY FOOT   Aside from two very steep hills, the world's second-smallest country is **pedestrian-friendly.** Hardy local Jean-Marc Ferrie at **Monaco Rando** (www.monaco-rando.com; ✆ **06-30-12-57-03**) organizes **guided hikes** around his hometown from 10€ per person with an interpreter in-tow.

BY TAXI   **Taxis** wait outside Monaco train station, or call ✆ **08-20-20-98-98.**

BY PUBLIC TRANSPORT   CAM (www.cam.mc; ✆ **97-70-22-22**) runs buses inside the Principality. Lines nos. 1 and 2 link Monaco-Ville with the casino area. CAM's **solar-powered shuttle boat** hops between the banks of Monaco's port every 20 minutes. The ride is great for kids and connects the casino area with foot of Monaco-Ville. All CAM tickets cost 2€.

BY OPEN-TOP BUS   **Monaco–Le Grand Tour** (www.monacolegrandtour.com; ✆ **97-70-26-36**) open-top minibuses allows visitors to hop-on and hop-off at the Principality's 12 main sights. Day passes cost 18€ adults; 7€ children between 4 and 11; free children under 4.

Exploring Monaco

Monaco's main sights—including its glamorous port, casino and hotels—are clustered around the pedestrianized Place du Casino Square. Its principal museums, including the Prince's Palace and Oceanographic Museum, are situated on the history-laden rock of Monaco-Ville.

Collection des Voitures Anciennes de S.A.S. le Prince de Monaco ★ MUSEUM   This massive showcase of Prince Rainier's private collection exihibits more than 200 vintage autos, including the 1956 Rolls-Royce Silver Cloud in which the prince and princess were transported on their wedding day. Other cool exhibits include a 2009 Mercedes McLaren SLR and a 1986 Lamborghini Countach. The most recent exhibit is a Toyota Lexus with a bulletproof glass roof, the royal wedding car for the marriage of Prince Albert and Charlene Wittstock in 2011.

Museums are all well and good, but to survey the soul of Monaco you need a credit card, a suntan, and a late-morning wake-up call. Early-evening glamour revolves around the bars that surround the historic port. Here, locally based luxury yacht agencies like **Y.CO** (www.ycoyacht.com; ✆ **93-50-12-12**) charter 50m-long (262 ft.) sailing craft for around $100,000 per week. At sundown the action moves uphill to Casino Square, where **Buddha Bar** (✆ **98-06-19-19**) is bedecked with chinoiserie, Asian statues, and a raised DJ booth. For sheer class, the **Crystal Bar** (✆ **98-06-98-99**) inside the Hôtel Hermitage pulls out all the stops. Elegant dress, vintage Champagne, and the odd feather boa sets the scene until 1am. **Le Bar Américain** (✆ **98-06-38-38**), in the Hôtel de Paris, is far more raucous, with chillingly expensive cocktails and nightly jazz. Across place du Casino the timeless superclub **Jimmy'z** (✆ **98-06-36-**

36), open nightly 11pm to 5am, has attracted stars from Farrah Fawcett to George Clooney. But it's the mythical **Casino de Monte-Carlo** (www.monte-carlocasinos.com; ✆ **98-06-21-21**) that lends the square its name. Since 2012 the casino's marble-floored Atrium has been open—for free—to all comers from 2pm who wish to shoot slots or play blackjack in the hallowed Salle des Amériques or try their luck at roulette in the Salle Europe. For roulette, *trente et quarante*, and Texas Hold'em in the private areas of rococo Salon Touzet and Salon Médecin, gamers must pay a 10€ fee. Entrance to Les Salons Supers Privés is by invitation only (heh, they've got our number!) and requires smart dress and nerves of steel. Another great summer addition is the Casino de Monte-Carlo **alfresco** terrace. Here visitors may play roulette and poker overlooking the moonlit Mediterranean. Now *that's* glamorous.

Les Terrasses de Fontvieille. www.palais.mc. ✆ **92-05-28-56.** Admission 6€ adults, 3€ students and children 8–14, free for children 7 and under. Daily 10am–6pm. Closed Christmas.

Les Grands Appartements du Palais ★ PALACE

The home of Monaco's royal family, the Palais du Prince dominates the Principality from the Rock. A tour of the Grands Appartements—with audio tour recorded by none other than Prince Albert himself—allows visitors to glimpse the Throne Room and artworks by Bruegel and Holbein. The palace was built in the 13th century, and some of it dates from the Renaissance. The ideal time to arrive is 11:55am, so you can watch the 10-minute **Relève de la Garde (Changing of the Guard).** Summer concerts by the **Monte-Carlo Philharmonic Orchestra** are held outside in the courtyard.

Place du Palais. www.palais.mc. ✆ **93-25-18-31.** Admission 8€ adults, 4€ children 8–14, free for children 7 and under. Daily Apr–Oct 10am–6pm. Closed Nov–Mar.

Musée Océanographique de Monaco ★ AQUARIUM

This mammoth oceanfront museum was founded by Albert I, great-grandfather of the present prince, in 1910. It's now a living, breathing science lesson covering the world's oceans by way of a Mediterranean aquarium, tropical tanks, and a shark reserve. A delight for budding marine scientists is the 18m-long (60-ft.) whale skeleton that washed up on a local beach a century ago. As compelling are the scientific specimens brought up from the ocean depths over the past 100 years.

If you insist on the likes of Hermès, Gucci, and Lanvin, you'll find them cheek by jowl near the Hôtel de Paris and the Casino de Monte-Carlo. But the prize for Monaco's hippest store goes to **Lull,** 29 rue de Millo (© **97-77-54-54**), awash in labels like Dries Van Noten and Raf Simons. Almost next door, **Une Femme à Suivre** (© **97-77-10-52**) sells French classics from the likes of Tara Jarman and Mariona Gen. The **Galeries du Métropole** is packed with high-fashion and specialty stores.

As well as Dunhill and Gant, try **McMarket** (© **97-77-12-12**). Serious labels in this fashion emporium include Balenciaga, Louboutin, and Jimmy Choo. **FNAC** (© **08-25-02-00-20**) is recommended for English-language novels, Monaco history books, and the latest electronics. For real-people shopping, stroll **rue Grimaldi,** the Principality's most commercial street, near the fruit, flower, and food market at **place des Armes,** which opens daily at 7:30am until noon.

Av. St-Martin. www.oceano.mc. © **93-15-36-00.** Admission 14€ adults, 7€ children 4–18, free for children 5 and under. Apr–June and Sept daily 10am–7pm; July–Aug daily 10am–8:30pm; Oct–Mar daily 10am–6pm.

Nouveau Musée National de Monaco ★★ ART MUSEUM   Over the past decade Monaco has touted its cultural credentials to bring in a savvier, younger, and more artistically aware crowd. The new Villa Sauber and Villa Paloma museums are two stunning art spaces set in palatial former homes across the city from one another. Both bring in global culture vultures by the score by way of contemporary-art exhibitions and shows covering sculpture, architecture, photography, and the glamorous history of the French Riviera.

Villa Sauber, 17 av. Princess Grace; Villa Paloma, 56 bd. du Jardin Exotique. www.nmnm.mc. © **98-98-16-82.** Admission to both 6€ adults, free entrance for visitors 26 and under. June–Sept daily 11am–7pm. Oct–May daily 10am–6pm.

Opéra de Monte-Carlo ★ OPERA HOUSE   Monaco takes music seriously. In 2013 both Rihanna and Carlo Bruni played live to sell-out crowds. The Principality's lavish Opera House sits next to the casino, where its Salle Garnier hosts rock, pop, classical and opera events—and even hosted the wedding reception of Prince Albert and Charlene Wittstock in 2011. For big-hitting pop and DJ events, try the **Grimaldi Forum,** 10 av. Princesse-Grace (www.grimaldiforum.com; © **99-99-20-00**).

Place du Casino. www.opera.mc. © **98-06-28-28.** Year-round admission prices 20€–120€ adults, reduced entrance for visitors 26 and under.

Outdoor Activities

BEACHES   Just outside the border, on French soil, the **Monte-Carlo Beach Club** adjoins the **Monte-Carlo Beach Hotel,** 22 av. Princesse-Grace (www.monte-carlo-beach.com; © **93-28-66-66**), a five-star sister establishment of the ultra-elegant Hôtel de Paris. Princess Grace used to frolic on the beach here in flowery swimsuits, and today it's an integral part of Monaco social life. It now has an Olympic-sized swimming pool, a La Prairie spa, cabanas, a poolside fine dining restaurant called Le Deck, and a low-key Mediterranean restaurant with lunch buffet called La Vigie. Sea Lounge is an afternoon and late-evening club featuring live DJs and *nargile* hubble-bubble pipes. Beach activities include donuts, jet skis, and parachute rides. As the temperature drops in late October, the beach closes for the winter. The admission charge of 45€ to 140€, depending on the season, grants you access to changing rooms, toilets, restaurants, and bar, along with use of a mattress for sunbathing.

More low-key swimming and sunbathing is also available at **Plage du Larvotto,** off avenue Princesse-Grace. Part of this popular man-made strip of sand is public. The other part contains private beach clubs with bars, snacks, and showers, plus a kid's club. A jogging track runs behind the beach.

SPA TREATMENTS The century-old **Thermes Marins,** 2 av. de Monte-Carlo (www.thermesmarinsmontecarlo.com; ℰ **98-06-69-00**), is wellness at its most chic. Spread over four floors is a pool, Turkish *hammam* (steam bath), healthy restaurant, juice bar, tanning booths, fitness center, beauty center, and private treatment rooms. A day pass, giving access to the sauna, steam rooms, fitness facilities, and pools, is 90€. Therapies include an hourlong Dead Sea salt peel for 150€.

SWIMMING Overlooking the yacht-studded harbor, the **Stade Nautique Rainier-III,** quai Albert-1er, at La Condamine (ℰ **93-30-64-83**), a pool frequented by the Monégasques, was a gift from Prince Rainier to his subjects. It's open May to October daily 9am to 6pm (until 8pm June–Aug). Admission costs 5.30€ per person. Between November and March, it's an ice-skating rink.

TENNIS & SQUASH The **Monte Carlo Country Club,** 155 av. Princesse-Grace, Roquebrune-Cap Martin, France (www.mccc.mc; ℰ **04-93-41-30-15**), has 21 clay and 2 concrete tennis courts. The 43€ fee provides access to a restaurant, health club with Jacuzzi and sauna, putting green, beach, squash courts, and well-maintained tennis courts. Guests of the hotels administered by the Société des Bains de Mer (Hôtel de Paris, Hermitage, Monte Carlo Bay, and Monte Carlo Beach Club) pay half-price. It's open daily 8am to 8 or 9pm, depending on the season.

Where to Eat

Pinch yourself. This postcard-sized Principality boasts a total of seven Michelin stars, and includes the most highly rated eatery on the entire Mediterranean, Le Louis XV.

Bouchon ★ TRADITIONAL FRENCH A refreshing new addition to the Principality's über-hip dining scene, Bouchon purveys classic bistro cuisine at distinctly un-Monaco prices. Art Deco *objets d'art* hand-selected from the flea markets of Paris and Nice set the scene. Breakfast kicks off with eggs and *viennoiseries*. Lunch continues with salade Niçoise and *moules marinières*. Dinner is slightly grander, although dishes like *filet de boeuf* or seared tuna won't break the bank when ordered with a *pichet* of wine.

11 ave Princesse Grace. www.bouchon.mc. ℰ **97-77-08-80.** Main courses 19€–21€; fixed-price lunch 17€. Daily 7:30am–11pm.

Café Llorca ★ MEDITERRANEAN Super-chef Alain Llorca recently opened the very restaurant that Monaco lacked: an affordable contemporary eatery overlooking the shimming sea. Café Llorca is a bargain. Daily lunch mains at press time included crab spring rolls and Niçois beef stew (Mon), red mullet terrine and sautéed kidneys (Wed), and mackerel marinade and Provençal aioli (Fri). Call ahead for dinner—the establishment is often booked up for events.

11 ave Princesse Grace. www.cafellorca.mc, © **99-99-29-29.** Main courses 16€–26€; fixed-price lunch 20€. Daily 11am–11pm.

Le Café de Paris ★ MODERN FRENCH   Pricey, pretentious, and ever-popular, this Parisian-style restaurant-café on place du Casino has a location to die for. The menu has taken on an even more classic edge under head chef Jean-Claude Brugel, who trained alongside several top Riviera chefs including Roger Vergé and Joël Garault. Simple starters like garlic escargot and *croque-monsieur* share the menu with more innovative mains like filet of plaice (a North Sea fish) with pumpkin purée or steak tartare. From October to March, a special seafood stall dispenses Oléron oysters, sea urchins, and platters of chilled crab to passersby.

Place du Casino. © **98-06-76-23.** Reservations recommended. Main courses 14€–49€; fixed-price menu 35€. Daily 8am–2am.

Le Louis XV ★★★ MEDITERRANEAN   In the Hôtel de Paris, the Louis XV offers one of the finest dining experiences on the Riviera, and thus the world. Superstar chef Alain Ducasse oversees the refined but not overly adorned cuisine. The restaurant's head chef, Franck Cerutti, can be seen in Nice's market at dawn buying local cheeses or wandering through the corridors of the Hôtel de Paris carrying white truffles purchased from over the Italian border. Everything is light and attuned to the seasons, with intelligent, modern interpretations of Provençal and northern Italian dishes. You'll find chargrilled breast of baby pigeon with sautéed duck liver, and an ongoing specialty known as Provençal vegetables with crushed truffles. All is served under a magnificent frescoed ceiling, which includes the portraits of Louis XV's six mistresses. The restaurant celebrated 25 years as the Principality's top eatery in 2013.

In the Hôtel de Paris, place du Casino. © **98-06-88-64.** Reservations recommended. Jacket and tie recommended for men. Main courses 75€–125€; fixed-price lunch 145€, dinner 230€–310€. Thurs–Mon 12:15–1:45pm and 8–9:45pm. Closed last 2 weeks Feb.

Where to Stay

Fairmont Monte Carlo ★   The five-star hotel is easily Monaco's most fun. It combines fine-dining restaurants, a spa, and a rooftop pool with an unstuffy attitude; albeit one backed by a legion of ever-smiling, mostly Italian, staff. Of course, this vision of modern opulence is also one most valuable pieces of real estate on the Côte d'Azur. It drips into the Mediterranean from behind the Casino de Monte-Carlo—indeed, a private passageway runs to the casino's rear entrance—and guests may combine the endless breakfast with the best sea views in the Principality. Formula 1 fans should also note that the fastest park of the Monaco Grand Prix zips right beneath the ground floor. Rooms and suites are furnished in contemporary maritime style with lashings of fine Italian marble.

12 av. des Spélugues. www.fairmont.com/montecarlo. © **93-50-65-00.** 602 units. 279€–879€ double; from 889€ suite. Parking 45€. **Amenities:** 2 restaurants; 2 bars; babysitting; concierge; health club; 2 outdoor pools; room service; spa; Wi-Fi (20€/day or free if you enroll in the Fairmont President Club at no charge at check-in).

Hôtel de Paris ★★★   Never has so much history and glamour been suffused into 182 effortlessly chic guest rooms. Two styles dominate these private palaces: contemporary and period. La Prairie products and free access to the **Thermes Marins spa** (p. 239) come as standard in them all. Accommodation culminates in two splendid super-suites, one of which, the "Churchill," overlooks the harbor and features Sir

Winston's furniture. The former British Prime Minister used to sneak along a secret rooftop passageway to **Le Grill,** one of three award-winning restaurants in the hotel (see also the Louis XV; p. 240). If that isn't enough, the Hôtel de Paris boasts several sister hotels, including the five-star family friendly **Monte-Carlo Beach Hotel** (www.monte-carlo-beach.com; ☏ **93-28-66-66**)—whose **Restaurant Elsa** received the region's first 100 percent organic certificate in 2013—and the imposingly elegant **Hôtel Hermitage** (www.hotelhermitagemontecarlo.com; ☏ **98-06-40-00**), just around the corner.

Place du Casino, Monaco 98007. www.montecarloresort.com. ☏ **98-06-30-00.** 182 units. 435€–1,020€ double; from 740€ suite. Valet parking 38€. Amenities: 3 restaurants (see "Where to Eat," below); bar; babysitting; concierge; exercise room; large indoor pool; room service; sauna; Thermes Marins spa offering thalassotherapy; Wi-Fi (free in lobby, or 20€/day).

PLANNING YOUR TRIP TO FRANCE

O f almost any destination in the world, flying into France is one of the most effortless undertakings in global travel. There are no shots to get and no particular safety precautions, and more and more French people now speak English. With your passport, airline or train ticket, and enough money, you just go. In the pages that follow, you'll find everything you need to know to plan your trip: finding the best airfare, deciding when to go, getting around the country, and much, much more.

GETTING THERE

By Plane

The two Paris airports—**Orly** (airport code: ORY) and **Charles de Gaulle** (airport code: CDG)—are about even in terms of convenience to the city's center. Orly, the older of the two, is 13km (8 miles) south of the center; Charles de Gaulle is 22km (14 miles) northeast. Air France serves Charles de Gaulle (Terminal 2C) from North America. U.S. carriers land at both airports. Flight status and transport information for both airports can be found online (www.aeroportsdeparis.fr). If you're heading to the South of France, **Nice Côte d'Azur** (airport code: NCE; www.nice.aeroport.fr) is served by direct flights from New York.

Most airlines charge their lowest fares between November and mid-March. The shoulder season (Oct and mid-Mar to mid-June) is a bit more expensive, but we think it's the ideal time to visit France.

By Train

Paris is one of Europe's busiest rail junctions, with trains departing from its seven major stations every few minutes. If you are in the U.K., Germany, Holland, Italy, or Spain, our recommendation would be to travel to the country by train.

Eurostar (www.eurostar.com; ✆ **800/387-6782** in the U.S.) links London directly with Paris Gare du Nord station from as little as $69 one-way; trip time just over 2 hours. It also runs direct seasonal routes to Disneyland Paris, Avignon, and Aix-en-Provence. Better still, trips from London can be booked online to any major station in France. For the best deals, book as tickets become available exactly 3 months in advance. Highly recommended is train and accommodation specialist **Railbookers** (www.railbookers.com; © **888/829-3040** in the U.S.). Their specialized teams can plan bespoke rail journeys throughout France. Start out from Paris and discover rural France and the Côte d'Azur, or tick off the essential European cities before a European Grand Tour.

By Bus

Paris is a major arrival and departure point for Europe's largest bus operator, **Eurolines** (www.eurolines.fr; © **08-92-89-90-91**). Its rather nasty bus terminal, Gallieni, is a 35-minute Métro ride from central Paris, at the terminus of line no. 3 (Métro: Gallieni). Despite the inconvenience, tickets are cheap, cheap, cheap. Standard singles to London are $29; trip time is around 7 hours.

Long-haul buses are equipped with toilets, and they stop at mealtimes for rest and refreshment. Tickets must be purchased online before you travel.

By Car

The major highways into Paris are A1 from the north (Great Britain and Benelux); A13 from Rouen, Normandy, and northwest France; A11 from Nantes and the Loire valley; and the A6 from Lyon, Provence, the Riviera, and Italy.

By Boat from England

Ferries and hydrofoils operate day and night from the English channel ports to Normandy. The major routes include at least 12 trips a day between Dover or Folkestone and Calais or Boulogne. Ferries often drop passengers off by the rail junction of each port.

There are various operators of ferries across the channel depending on your destination. **P&O Ferries** (www.poferries.com; © **0871/664-5645** in the U.K.) operate car and passenger ferries between Dover, England, and Calais, France (more than 20 sailings a day; 90 min. each way). **Brittany Ferries** (www.brittanyferries.com; © **0825/828-828**) operates ferry services from Portsmouth and Poole, England, to Cherbourg, Caen or Le Havre, France (one or two departures a day; 3–4 hr. each way). **DFDS Seaways** (www.dfds.co.uk; © **0871/574-7235** in the U.K.) operates two sailings per day between Portsmouth and Le Havre (8 hr. each way). It also sails up to 44 times daily between Dover and Calais (1½ hr.) and Dover and Dunkirk (2 hr.).

SPECIAL-INTEREST TRIPS & TOURS

Academic Trips & Language Classes

The **Alliance Française,** 101 bd. Raspail, Paris 75006 (www.alliancefr.org; © **01-42-84-90-00**), is a nonprofit French-language teaching organization with a network of 1,040 establishments in 136 countries. The school in Paris is open all year; month-long courses range from 232€ to 1,196€.

Just outside Nice, the **Institut de Francais,** 23 av. Général-Leclerc, Villefranche-sur-Mer 06230 (www.institutdefrancais.com; © **04-93-01-88-44**), offers highly acclaimed month-long French immersion courses. Each day includes 8 hours of lessons, plus breakfast and lunch taken together with professors. Prices range from 2,800€ to 3,400€.

A clearinghouse for information on French-language schools is **Lingua Service Worldwide** (www.linguaserviceworldwide.com; ✆ **800/394-5327**). Its programs are available in many cities throughout France. Cost ranges from around $200 to close to $6,000 per week, depending on the city, the school, and accommodation.

Adventure Trips

BARGE CRUISES   Before the advent of rail, many crops, building supplies, raw materials, and finished products were barged through France on a series of rivers, canals, and estuaries. Many of these waterways retain their old-fashioned locks and pumps, allowing shallow-draft boats easy access through idyllic countryside.

Go Barging (www.gobarging.com; ✆ **800/394-8630**) operates 6-night river cruises departing from Paris along the River Seine, as well as trips through the Loire Valley and Canal du Midi. Fares range from $3,060 to $5,360 per person (double occupancy) including all meals and drinks.

Viking River Cruises (www.vikingrivercruises.co.uk; ✆ **44/808-252-0708**) leads 1-week tours from Paris through Normandy, with stops in Rouen and at the D-Day beaches, and along the Rhône, taking in Arles and Avignon en route. For double occupancy, prices start at £1,345.

Food & Wine Trips

The famous/infamous Georges Auguste Escoffier (1846–1935) taught the Edwardians how to eat. Today the Hôtel Ritz maintains the **Ecole Ritz Escoffier,** 15 place Vendôme, Paris 75001 (www.ritzescoffier.com; ✆ **01-43-16-30-50**), with culinary, cocktail, and pastry workshops, as well as professional-level courses and lessons for kids. The school reopens in 2014 after 2 years of renovations; further details can be found online.

Established in 1895, **Le Cordon Bleu,** 8 rue Léon Delhomme, 75015 Paris (www.cordonbleu.edu; ✆ **01-53-68-22-50**), is the most famous French cooking school, where Julia Child learned to perfect her *pâté brisée* and *mousse au chocolat.* The best-known courses last 10 weeks and cost 8,950€, after which you are awarded a certificate. Many enthusiasts prefer a less intense immersion, opting for a 4-day workshop (from 940€) or a 1- to 2-hour demonstration class (from 45€).

Less formal but equally enjoyable are the cooking classes offered by **La Cuisine Paris** (www.lacuisineparis.com; ✆ **01-40-51-78-18**), a friendly school set up by a Franco-American team. It offers small classes by professional chefs in both French and English, including the popular French Macaron Class. Prices range from 65€ for 2 hours to 150€ for 4 hours.

At Home with Patricia Wells (www.patriciawells.com) is a Paris- and Provence-based cooking school taught by Patricia Wells, cookbook author and famed former restaurant critic for the "International Herald Tribune." The extremely popular 5-day classes are limited to 12 students and cost $5,000 (accommodations not included).

Les Petits Farcis (www.petitsfarcis.com), run by Cordon Bleu-trained Canadian chef Rosa Jackson, offers tours of Nice's colorful produce market, followed by day-long gourmet cooking sessions. Prices begin at 195€ per person and include a four-course lunch with wine.

Guided Tours

BIKE TOURS   Some of the best cycling tours of France are offered by **VBT** (www. vbt.com; ℭ **800/245-3868**), which offers trips in six of the most scenic parts of France. Rides range from a gentle peddle among the Loire's châteaux to a more challenging exploration of the D-Day beaches. Prices start at $2,545 per person, with airfare packages also available.

Cycling for Softies (www.cycling-for-softies.co.uk; ℭ **44/161-248-8282**) is ideal for easygoing travelers with little cycling experience. Tours cover most of France. Prices vary according to type of tour (both self-guided and small groups are available); buffet breakfasts and gourmet dinners are included.

Fat Tire Bike Tours (www.fattirebiketours.com/paris; (ℭ **01-56-58-10-54**) offers a 4-hour day or night tour of Paris by bike in English; adult tickets cost 30€. It also organizes cycling tours of Versailles and Giverny.

BUS TOURS   Most larger cities in France offer hop-on, hop-off bus tours, ideal for scoping out the lay of the land. See specific chapters for details.

CHAUFFEURED TOURS **4 Roues Sous 1 Parapluie** (www.4roues-sous-1parapluie.com; ℭ **08-00-80-06-31**) offers chauffeur-driven themed rides around Paris in its colorful fleet of Citroën 2CV, the tiny but classic French car described as "4 roues sous 1 parapluie" ("4 wheels under 1 umbrella"). Tours for three start at 10€ per person for 15 minutes and 60€ per person for a 1½-hour tour. The fewer people in the car, the more expensive the tour.

SHOPPING TOURS   Paris is a dream come true for shopaholics. **Chic Shopping Paris** (www.chicshoppingparis.com; ℭ **06-77-65-08-01**) offers tours designed to give visitors a behind-the-scenes shopping experience. Themed tours include Chic and Cheap and Arts and Antiques. All of the standard tours are 4 to 4½ hours and cost 100€ per person.

GETTING AROUND

Within most major cities—including Paris, Marseille, and Nice—public transportation is efficient, comprehensive, and cheap. In smaller towns, such as Rouen, Arles, or Antibes, it's easy to navigate the city center on foot. See each chapter for specific details.

By Plane

Air France (www.airfrance.com; ℭ **800/237-2747**) is the country's primary carrier, serving around 30 cities in France and 30 more destinations throughout Europe. Air travel time from Paris to almost anywhere in France is about 1 hour. **British Airways** (www.ba.com) links London with Paris, Marseille, and Nice. Low-cost airline **Easyjet** (www.easyjet.com) also links London with Paris, Marseille, and Nice. The budget airline offers additional internal French flights between Paris and Nice, and connects both cities to 20 other European destinations.

By Car

The most charming châteaux and country hotels always seem to lie away from the main cities and train stations. Renting a car is a good way to travel around the French countryside, especially along the Normandy beaches, the Loire Valley, and in rural

Provence. Day car hire is inexpensive, so visitors may want to rent a vehicle just for a day en-route if they wish.

Driving schedules in Europe are largely a matter of conjecture, urgency, and how much sightseeing you do along the way. Driving time is 2½ hours from Paris to Rouen, 3½ hours to Nantes, and 7 hours to anywhere in Provence.

RENTALS   To rent a car, you'll need to present a passport, a driver's license, and a credit card. You will also have to meet the company's minimum-age requirement; 21 or above at most rental agents. The biggest agencies have pickup spots all over France, including **Budget** (www.budget.com; ☎ **800/472-3325**) in the U.S. and Canada; **Hertz** (www.hertz.com; ☎ **800/654-3001** in the U.S. and Canada); and **Europcar** (www. europcar.com; ☎ **0825/358358**).

Note: The best deals are always booked online, in advance. Though the rental company won't usually mind if you drive your car into, say, Germany, Switzerland, Italy, or Spain, it's often forbidden to transport your car by ferry, including across the Channel to England.

In France, **collision damage waiver (CDW)** is usually factored into the overall rate quoted, but you should always verify this before taking a car on the road. At most companies, the CDW provision won't protect you against theft, so if this is the case, ask about purchasing extra theft protection. Automatic transmission is a luxury in Europe. If you prefer it to stickshift, you must specifically request it—and you'll pay a little extra for it.

GASOLINE   Known in France as *essence,* gas is expensive for those accustomed to North American prices, although the smaller cars common in Europe use far less gas. Depending on your car, you'll need either leaded *(avec plomb)* or unleaded *(sans plomb).*

Note: Sometimes you can drive for miles in rural France without encountering a gas station; don't let your tank get dangerously low.

DRIVING RULES   Everyone in the car, in both the front and the back seats, must wear seat belts. Children 11 and under must ride in the back seat.

In France, you drive on the right. Drivers are supposed to yield to the car on their right, except where signs indicate otherwise, as at traffic circles.

If you violate the speed limit, expect a big fine. Limits are about 130kmph (81 mph) on expressways, about 110kmph (68 mph) on major national highways, and 90kmph (56 mph) on country roads. In towns, don't exceed 60kmph (37 mph).

Note: It's illegal to use a cellphone while you're driving in France; you will be ticketed if you're stopped.

MAPS   While most Frenchmen are happy with Google Maps, traditional motorists opt for the large **Michelin maps** of the country and regions (www.viamichelin.com) on sale at all gas stations. Big travel-book stores in North America carry these maps as well. GPS navigation devices can be rented at most car-hire stations.

BREAKDOWNS/ASSISTANCE   A breakdown is called *une panne* in France. Call the police at ☎ **17** anywhere in France to be put in touch with the nearest garage. Most local garages offer towing.

By Train

The world's fastest trains—known as *Train à Grande Vitesse,* or TGVs—link some 50 French cities, allowing you to travel from Paris to just about anywhere else in the country within hours. With 32,000km (20,000 miles) of track and 3,000 stations, SNCF (French National Railroads; www.voyages-sncf.com, or call ℂ 36-35 in France) is fabled for its on-time performance and comfy trains. You can travel in first or second class by day and couchette by night. Most trains have light dining facilities.

For information or reservations, go online (www.voyages-sncf.com). You can also visit any local travel agency. If you have a chip credit card and know your PIN, you can use your card to buy your ticket at the easy-to-use *billetteries* (ticket machines with an English-menu option) in every train station.

RAIL PASSES   Rail passes as well as individual rail tickets are available from **Rail Europe** (www.raileurope.com; ℂ **800/622-8600** in the U.S.). Options include a 5-day rail pass usable for a 1-month period for $297. **Eurail** (www.eurail.com) offers regional rail passes throughout Europe, including a France-and-Italy combined pass for $434, allowing 6 days of first-class travel within a 2-month period.

By Bicycle

Over the past few years, most cities and towns throughout France have initiated bike-sharing schemes. You can register online or directly at one of the city's dozens of bike stands; in most cases, you'll need a credit card and a mobile phone. Average fees range from 1€ for 1 day to 7€ for a week and entitle you to use any of the city's hundreds of bikes for up to 30 minutes at a time. When you're finished, just slot the cycle back into any allocated bike stand around town. Among many others, Paris, Rouen, Caen, Avignon, Aix-en-Provence, Marseille, and Nice all offer city-wide bike-sharing. See each chapter for specific details.

[FastFACTS] FRANCE

Business Hours   Business hours in France can be erratic. Most banks are open Monday through Friday from 9:30am to 4:30pm. Many, particularly in small towns, take a long lunch break. Hours are usually posted on the door. Most museums close 1 day a week (often Tues), and they're generally closed on national holidays. Usual hours are from 9:30am to 5pm. In Paris or other big French cities, stores are open from around 10am to 6 or 7pm, with or without a lunch break (up to 2 hr.). Some shops, delis, cafes, and newsstands open at 8am and close at 8 or 9pm.

Disabled Travelers   Facilities for travelers in France, and nearly all new or modern hotels, provide disabled access. The TGVs (high-speed trains) are wheelchair accessible; older trains have compartments for wheelchair boarding. If you visit the Paris tourist office website (www.parisinfo.com) and click on "Practical Paris," the

section "Practical information for Disabled Visitors" includes links to a number of websites dedicated to travelers with disabilities. For disabled-access to Paris public transport, see www.infomobi.com.

Doctors   Doctors are listed in Pages Jaunes (Yellow Pages; www.pagesjaunes.fr) under "Médecins: Médecins généralistes." The minimum fee for a consultation is about 23€—for this rate, look for a doctor who is described as "secteur 1." The higher the "secteur," the higher the fee. **SOS Médecins** (www.sosmedecins.fr; ℂ **36-24**) can make house calls. See also "Emergencies" and "Health" later in this section.

Drinking Laws   As well as bars and restaurants, supermarkets and cafes sell alcoholic beverages. The legal drinking age is 18, but persons under that age can be served alcohol if accompanied by a parent or guardian. Drinking and driving is illegal, and incurs a heavy fine.

Drugstores Spot French *pharmacies* by the green neon cross above the door. If your local pharmacy is closed, there should be a sign on the door indicating the nearest one open. Alternatively, **Pharmacies de Garde** (www.pharmaciesdegarde.com; ☏ **32-37**) can direct you to the nearest open pharmacy.

Electricity Electricity in France runs on 220 volts AC (60 cycles). Adapters or transformers are needed to fit sockets, which you can buy in branches of Darty or FNAC.

Embassies & Consulates If you have a passport, immigration, legal, or other problem, contact your consulate. Many are open Monday to Friday, approximately 10am to 5pm. However, call or check online before you visit to confirm.

Australian Embassy: 4 rue Jean-Rey, 15e (www.france.embassy.gov.au; ☏ **01-40-59-33-00;** Métro: Bir Hakeim).

Canadian Embassy: 35 av. Montaigne, 8e (www.amb-canada.fr; ☏ **01-44-43-29-00;** Métro: Franklin-D-Roosevelt or Alma-Marceau).

Irish Embassy: 4 rue Rude, 16e (www.embassyofireland.fr; ☏ **01-44-17-67-00;** Métro: Etoile).

New Zealand Embassy: 7ter rue Léonard de Vinci, 16e (www.nzembassy.com; ☏ **01-45-01-43-43;** Métro: Victor Hugo).

UK/British Embassy: 35 Rue du Faubourg St-Honoré, 8e (http://ukinfrance.fco.gov.uk; ☏ **01-44-51-31-00;** Métro: Concorde or Madeleine).

United States Embassy: 2 av. Gabriel, 8e (http://france.usembassy.gov; ☏ **01-43-12-22-22;** Métro: Concorde).

Emergencies In an emergency while at a hotel, contact the front desk. If the emergency involves theft, go to the police station in person. Otherwise, call ☏ **112** from a cellphone. The fire brigade can be reached at ☏ **18.** For an ambulance, call ☏ **15.** For the police, call ☏ **17.**

Etiquette & Customs French value pleasantries and take manners seriously: Say "Bonjour, Madame/Monsieur" when entering an establishment and "Au revoir" when you depart. Always say "Pardon" when you accidentally bump into someone. With strangers, people who are older than you and professional contacts use *vous* rather than *tu* (*vous* is the polite form of the pronoun *you*).

Health For travel abroad, Non–E.U. nationals should consider buying medical travel insurance. For U.S. citizens, Medicare and Medicaid do not provide coverage for medical costs incurred abroad; check your health insurance before leaving home. U.K. nationals need a **European Health Insurance Card** (**EHIC;** www.ehic.org.uk) to receive free or reduced-cost medical care during a visit to a France.

If you take regular medication, pack it in its original pharmacy containers, along with a copy of your prescription

Holidays Major holidays are New Year's Day (Jan 1), Easter Sunday and Monday (late Mar/Apr), Labor Day (May 1), VE Day (May 8), Ascension Thursday (40 days after Easter), Pentecost/Whit Sunday and Whit Monday (seventh Sun/Mon after Easter), Bastille Day (July 14), Assumption Day (Aug 15), All Saints Day (Nov 1), Armistice Day (Nov 11), and Christmas Day (Dec 25).

Hospitals Dial ☏ **15** for medical emergencies. In Paris, the **American Hospital,** 63 bd. Victor-Hugo, in the suburb of Neuilly-sur-Seine (www.american-hospital. org; ☏ **01-46-41-25-25;** Métro: Pont-de-Levallois), operates a 24-hour, bilingual emergency service. For hospitals in other major French cities, see individual chapters.

Hotlines SOS Help is a hotline for English-speaking callers in crisis ☏ **01-46-21-46-46** (www.soshelpline.org). Open 3 to 11pm daily.

LGBT Travelers France is one of the world's most tolerant countries toward gays and lesbians. Paris boasts a large gay population, with many clubs, restaurants, organizations, and services. Lesbian or bisexual women can pick up a copy of **"Muse & Out"** (www.muse-out.com), available at Paris's best-stocked gay bookstore, **Les Mots à la Bouche,** 6 rue Ste-Croix-de-la-Bretonnerie, 4e (www.motsbouche.com;

ℭ **01-42-78-88-30;** Métro: Hôtel-de-Ville). Both www.paris-gay.com and www.gayvox. com have updated listings about the gay and lesbian scene.

Mail Most post offices in France are open Monday to Friday from 8am to 5pm and every Saturday from 8am to noon. A 24-hour post office is located in Paris at 52 rue du Louvre 1e (ℭ **36-31**). Allow 5 to 8 days to send or receive mail from home. Stamps are also sold in *tabacs* (tobacconists). For more information, see www. laposte.fr.

Mobile Phones You can use your mobile phone in France, provided it is **GSM** (Global System for Mobile Communications) and triband or quad-band; just confirm with your operator before you leave.

Using your phone abroad can be expensive, so it's a good idea to get it "unlocked" before you leave. This means you can buy a French SIM card from one of the three main French providers, **Bouygues Télécom, Orange,** or **SFR.** Or do like the locals do and use **Skype** for long-distance calls.

Money & Costs Frommer's lists exact prices in the local currency. The currency conversions quoted above were correct at press time. However, rates fluctuate, so before departing, consult a currency exchange website such as www.oanda.com to check current rates.

It's always advisable to bring a mix of cash and credit cards on vacation. Before you leave home, exchange enough petty cash to cover airport incidentals, tipping, and transportation to your hotel. Alternatively, withdraw money upon arrival at an airport ATM. In many international destinations, ATMs offer the best exchange rates. Avoid exchanging money at commercial exchange bureaus and hotels, which often

have the highest transaction fees and terrible exchange rates. ATMs are widely available in France.

Newspapers The most popular French newspapers are **Le Monde** (www.lemonde. fr), **Le Figaro** (www.lefigaro.fr), and left-leaning **Libération** (www.liberation.fr).

The English-language **International Herald-Tribune** (www.iht.com), based in Paris and published Monday to Saturday, is distributed all over France.

Passports Citizens of the U.K., New Zealand, Australia, Canada, and the United States need a valid passport to enter France. The passport is valid for a stay of 90 days.

Police In an emergency, call ℭ **17** or **112** from a mobile or land-line phone anywhere in France.

Safety The most common menace, especially in large cities, is the plague of **pickpockets.** Take precautions and be vigilant at all times: Don't take more money with you than necessary, keep your passport in a concealed pouch or leave it at your hotel, and ensure that your bag is firmly closed at all times. In cafes, bars, and restaurants, it's best not to leave your bag under the table, on the back of your chair, or on an empty chair beside you. Keep it between your legs or on your lap. Never leave valuables or luggage in a car, and never travel with your car unlocked.

In general, Paris is a safe city and it is safe to use the Métro late at night, though it is always best to not drawn attention to the fact you are foreign by speaking loudly in English. Use common sense when taking public transport at night.

Although there is a significant level of discrimination against West and North African immigrants, there has been almost no harassment of African-American tourists to

THE VALUE OF THE EURO VS. OTHER POPULAR CURRENCIES

Euro (€)	US$	C$	UK£	A$	NZ$
1	1.33	1.38	0.86	1.48	1.69

Paris or France itself in recent decades. However. **S.O.S. Racisme,** 51 av. de Flandre, 19e (www.sos-racisme.org; ✆ **01-40-35-36-55**), offers legal advice to victims of prejudice and will even intervene to help with the police.

Female travelers should not expect any more hassle than in other major cities, and the same precautions apply. Avoid walking alone at night and never get into an unmarked taxi. If you are approached in the street or on public transportation, it's best to avoid entering into conversation, and walk into a well-lit, populated area.

Senior Travel   Many discounts are available to men and women over 60. Senior citizens do not get a discount for traveling on public transport in Paris, but national trains hve senior discounts. Check out www.voyages-sncf.com for more information. Frommers.com offers more information and resources on travel for seniors.

Smoking   Smoking is banned in all public places in France, including cafes, restaurants, and nightclubs. It's permitted on outdoor and semi-enclosed terraces.

Student Travel   Student discounts are less common in France than other countries, but simply because young people under 26 are usually offered reduced rates. Be on the lookout for the **Ticket Jeune** when using the Métro in Paris. It can be used on a Saturday, Sunday, or bank holiday, and provides unlimited travel in zones 1 to 3 for 3.65€. SNCF also offer discounts for under-26-year-olds traveling on national trains (www.voyages-sncf.com).

Taxes   As a member of the European Union, France routinely imposes a value-added tax (VAT in English; TVA in French) on most goods. The standard VAT is 19.6 percent, and prices that include it are often marked TTC (*toutes taxes comprises,* "all taxes included"). If you're not an E.U. resident, you can get a VAT refund if you're spending less than 6 months in France, you purchase goods worth at least 175€ at a single shop on the same day, the goods fit into your luggage, and the shop offers *vente en détaxe* (duty-free sales or tax-free

shopping). Give them your passport and ask for a *bordereau de détaxe* (export sales invoice). When you leave the country, you need to get all three pages of this invoice validated by France's Customs officials. They'll keep one sheet, and you must post the pink one back to the shop. Once the shop receives its stamped copy, it will send you a *virement* (fund transfer) using the payment method you requested. It may take several months.

Telephones   Public phones can still be found in France. All require a phone card (known as a *télécarte*), which can be purchased at post offices or *tabacs.*

The country code for France is 33. To make a local or long-distance call within France, dial the person or place's 10-digit number. If you're calling from outside of France, drop the initial 0 (zero).

Mobile numbers begin with 06 or 07. Numbers beginning with 0-800, 0-804, 0-805, and 0-809 are free in France; other numbers beginning with 8 are not. Most four-digit numbers starting with 10, 30, and 31 are free of charge.

Time   France is on Central European Time, which is 1 hour ahead of Greenwich Mean Time. French daylight saving time lasts from the last Sunday in March to the last Sunday in October, when clocks are set 1 hour ahead of the standard time. France uses the 24-hour clock (so 13h is 1pm, 14h15 is 2:15pm, and so on).

Tipping   By law, all bills in **cafes, bars, and restaurants** say *service compris,* which means the service charge is included. However, it is customary to leave 1€ or 2€, depending on the quality of the service; in more upscale restaurants leave 5€ to 10€. **Taxi drivers** usually expect a 5 percent to 10 percent tip, or for the fare to be rounded up to the next euro. The French tip **hairdressers** around 15 percent, and if you go to the theater, you're expected to tip the **usher** about 2€.

Toilets   If you're in dire need, duck into a cafe or brasserie to use the lavatory. It's customary to make a small purchase if you do so. Paris is full of gray-colored automatic street toilets, which are free to use and are washed and disinfected after each use. France still has some hole-in-the-ground squat toilets. Try not to lose your change down the pan!

Visas E.U. nationals don't need a visa to enter France. Nor do U.S., Canadian, Australian, New Zealand, or South African citizens for trips of up to 3 months. Nationals of other countries should make inquiries or look online at the nearest French embassy or consulate.

Visitor Information Before you go, your best source of information is the **French Government Tourist Office** (www. francetourism.com).

Water Drinking water is generally safe. If you ask for water in a restaurant, it'll be served bottled (for which you'll pay), unless you specifically request *une carafe d'eau* or *l'eau du robinet* (tap water). Your waiter may ask if you'd like your water avec gas (carbonated) or sans gas (without bubbles).